Memoirs Of A Griffin
Or,
A Cadet's First Year In India

By

Francis John Bellew

Double 9
BOOKS

Memoirs Of A Griffin
Or,
A Cadet's First Year In India
by Francis John Bellew

ISBN: 978-93-59955-40-7
Published by

DOUBLE 9 BOOKS

2/13-B, Ansari Road
Daryaganj, New Delhi – 110002
info@double9books.com
www.double9books.com
Tel. 011-40042856

ABOUT THE AUTHOR

Francis John Bellew became a remarkable British writer known for his insightful and attractive tour literature. One of his incredible works is "Memoirs of a Griffin." This book gives readers a captivating and certain account of his experiences in India throughout the British colonial technology. Bellew's "Memoirs of a Griffin" sheds mild on the lifestyles of a "griffin," a term used at some point of the colonial duration to explain a young and green individual who arrived in India, regularly as part of the British management. Bellew's narrative is a window into the demanding situations and adventures confronted by way of those beginners as they navigated an overseas and complicated society. The ebook immerses readers in the shiny landscapes, cultures, and customs of India, at some point of Bellew's observant and eloquent prose. His storytelling is marked by using a true interest approximately the people and locations he encounters, as well as an eager sense of humor and an eye for detail. Francis John Bellew's "Memoirs of a Griffin" now not most effective gives ancient insights into the British colonial revel in however also serves as a precious resource for know-how the cultural dynamics of India at some stage in that time.

CONTENTS

PREFACE

Good wine, says the proverb, needs no bush; on the same principle, some will think that a book, if readable, may dispense with a preface. As a general rule this may be true, but there are occasions, and I take leave to deem this one of them, when, from the peculiar nature of the subject, a few preliminary observations, by creating a clear and possibly a pleasant understanding between the author and the gentle reader, may not be unacceptable or out of place. In the following little narrative, in which I have blended fact and fiction—though always endeavouring to keep the *vraisemblable* in view—my object has been to depict some of those scenes, characters, and adventures, which some five-and-twenty or thirty years ago a "jolly cadet"—alias a Griffin—was likely to encounter, during the first year of his military career; men, manners, and things in general have, since that period, undergone considerable changes; still, in its main features, the sketch I have drawn, admitting its original correctness, will doubtless apply as well to Griffins in the present mature age of the century, as when it was in its teens. The Griffin, or Greenhorn, indeed, though subject, like everything else, to the external changes incident to time and fashion, is, perhaps, fundamentally and essentially, one of the "never ending, still beginning" states, or phases of humanity, destined to exist till the "crash of doom."

The characters which I have introduced in my narrative (for the most part as transiently as the fleeting shadows of a magic lantern across a spectrum) are all intended to represent respectively classes having more or less of an Oriental stamp, some still existing unchanged—others on the wane—and a few, I would fain hope, who, like the Trunnions and Westerns (*parva componere magnis*) of the last age have wholly disappeared before the steadily increasing light of knowledge and civilization—influences destructive of those coarse humours, narrow prejudices, and eccentric traits, which, however amusing in the pages of the novelist, are wondrously disagreeable in real life. It is true, the gradual disappearance of these coarser features imposes on the painter of life and manners the necessity of cultivating a nicer perception—of working with a finer pencil, and of seizing and embodying the now less obvious indications of the feelings and passions—the more delicate lights and shades of mind and character—but still in parting in a great measure with the materials for coarse drollery and broad satire, the world perhaps on the whole will be a gainer; higher feelings will be addressed than those which minister to triumph and imply humiliation: for though 'tis well to laugh at folly and expose it—'twere perhaps better to have no folly or error to laugh at and expose.

In the following pages, my wish has been to amuse, and where I could—without detriment to the professedly light and jocular character of the work—to instruct and improve. To hurt or offend has never entered into my contemplation—if such could ever be my object, I should not do it under a mask.

I deem it necessary to make this observation *en passant*, lest, like a young officer I once heard of in India, who, conscience-stricken on hearing some of his besetting sins, as he thought, pointedly denounced, flung out of the church, declaring "there was no standing the chaplain's personalities," some of my readers should think that I have been taking, under cover, a sly shot at themselves or friends. That the characters lightly sketched in these Memoirs have been taken from life—*i.e.*, that the ideas of them have been furnished by real personages—I in some measure candidly allow, though I have avoided making the portraits invidiously exact; as in a dream, busy fancy weaves a tissue of events out of the stored impressions of the brain, so, of course, the writer of a story must in like manner, though with more congruity, arrange and embody his scattered recollections, though not necessarily in the exact shape and order in which the objects, &c., originally presented themselves. Moreover, I believe I may safely add, that the originals of my sketches have, for the most part, long since brought "life's fitful fever" to a close.

To the kind care of the public I now consign the "Griffin," particularly to that portion of it connected with India, a country where my best days have been spent, the scene of some of my happiest hours, as alas! of my severest trials and bereavements; hoping, on account of his "youth," they will take him under their especial protection. To the critics I also commend him, trusting, if they have "any bowels," that they will, for the same reason, deal with him tenderly.

London—queen of cities!—on sympathetic grounds, I hope for your munificent patronage. Griffins[1] are your supporters, then why not support my "Griffin?"

If encouraged by the smiles of a "discriminating public," I may, at some future period, impart the late Brevet Captain Gernon's post-griffinish experiences amongst Burmahs, Pindaries, and "Chimeras dire," with his "impressions of home," as contained in the remaining autobiography of that lamented gentleman, who sunk under a gradual decay of nature and a schirrous liver, some time during the last hot summer.

It is proper I should state that these Memoirs, in a somewhat different form, first saw the light in the pages of the *Asiatic Journal*.

CHAPTER I

Pleasant days of my Griffinhood!—green oasis of life's desert waste!—thoughtless, joyous, happy season, when young Hope told "her flattering tale," and novelty broke sweetly upon a heart unsated by the world, with what fond and regretful emotions do I now look back upon you through the long, dim, dreary vista of five-and-twenty years!

But I think I hear a raw reader exclaim, "Griffins!—are there griffins in the East?" "Assuredly, sir. Did you never hear of the law of Zoroaster quoted in *Zadig*, by which griffins' flesh is prohibited to be eaten? Griffins are so common at the different presidencies of India that nobody looks at them, and most of these animals are very tame." I will not, however, abuse the traveller's privilege.

Griffin, or more familiarly a *Griff*, is an Anglo-Indian cant term applied to all new-comers, whose lot has been cast in the "gorgeous East." Whether the appellation has any connection with the fabulous compound, the gryps or gryphon of armorial blazoning, is a point which I feel myself incompetent to decide.[2] A griffin is the Johnny Newcome of the East, one whose European manners and ideas stand out in ludicrous relief when contrasted with those, so essentially different in most respects, which appertain to the new country of his sojourn. The ordinary period of griffinhood is a year, by which time the *novus homo*, if apt, is supposed to have acquired a sufficient familiarity with the language, habits, customs, and manners of the country, both Anglo-Indian and Native, so as to preclude his making himself supremely ridiculous by blunders, *gaucheries*, and the indiscriminate application of English standards to states of things to which those rules are not always exactly adapted. To illustrate by example:—a good-natured Englishman, who should present a Brahmin who worships the cow with a bottle of beef-steak sauce, would be decidedly "griffinish," particularly if he could be made acquainted with the nature of the gift; nevertheless, beef steak, *per se*, is an excellent thing in an Englishman's estimation, and a better still with the addition of the before-mentioned condiment. But to return to our subject.

At the termination, then, of the above-mentioned period, our griffin, if he has made the most of his time, becomes entitled to associate on pretty equal terms with those sun-dried specimens of the *genus homo*, familiarly called the "old hands:"—subs of fifteen years' standing; grey-headed captains, and superannuated majors, critics profound in the merits of a curry, or the quality of a batch of Hodgson's pale ale. He ceases to be the butt of his regiment, and persecutes in his turn, with the zeal of a convert, all novices not blessed with his modicum of local experience.

Youth is proverbially of a plastic nature, and the juvenile griffin, consequently, in the majority of instances, readily accommodates himself to the altered circumstances in which he is placed; but not so the man of mature years, to whose moral and physical organization forty or fifty winters have imparted their rigid and unmalleable influences. Griffins of this description, which commonly comprises bishops, judges, commanders-in-chief, and gentlemen sent out on special missions, &c., protract their griffinage commonly during the whole period of their stay in the country, and never acquire the peculiar knowledge which entitles them to rank with the initiated. The late most excellent Bishop Heber, for example, who to the virtues of a Christian added all the qualities which could adorn the scholar and gentleman, was nevertheless an egregious griffin, as a perusal of his delightful travels in India, written in all the singleness of his benevolent heart, must convince any one acquainted with the character of the country and the natives of India.

Autobiographers love to begin *ab ovo*, and I see no reason why I should wholly deviate from a custom doubly sanctioned by reason and established usage. It is curious sometimes to trace the gradual development of character in "small" as well as in "great" men; to note the little incidents which often determine the nature of our future career, and describe the shootings of the young idea at that vernal season when they first begin to expand into trees of good or evil. In an old manor-house, not thirty miles from London, on a gloomy November day, I first saw the light. Of the home of my infancy I remember little but my nursery, a long, bare, whitewashed apartment, with a tall, diamond-paned window, half obscured by the funereal branches of a venerable yew-tree. This window looked out, I remember, on the village churchyard, thickly studded with the moss-grown memorials of successive generations. In that window-seat I used to sit for many a weary hour, watching the boys idling on the gravestones, the jackdaws wheeling their airy circles round the spire, or the parson's old one-eyed horse cropping the rank herbage, which sprouted fresh and green above the silent dust of many a "village Hampden." The recollections of infancy, like an old picture, become often dim and obscure, but here and there particular events, like bright lights and rich Rembrandt touches, remain deeply impressed, which seem to defy the effects of time; of this kind is a most vivid recollection I have of a venerable uncle of my mother's, an old Indian, who lived with us, and whose knee I always sought when I could give nurse the slip. My great uncle Frank always welcomed me to his little *sanctum* in the green parlour, and having quite an Arab's notion of the sacred rights of hospitality, invariably refused to give me up when nurse, puffing and foaming, would waddle in to reclaim me. I shall never forget the delight I derived from his pleasant stories and the white sugar-candy, of which he always kept a stock on hand. Good old man! he died full of years, and was the first of a long series of friends whose loss I have had to lament.

My father was, truly, that character emphatically styled "an Irish gentleman," in whom the suavity of the Frenchman was combined with much of the fire and brilliancy of his native land. Though of an ancient family, his fortune, derived from an estate in the sister kingdom, was very limited, the "dirty acres" having somehow or other, from generation to generation, become "small by degrees, and beautifully less." He was of a tender frame, and of that delicate, sensitive, nervous temperament, which, though often the attendant on genius, which he unquestionably possessed, little fits those so constituted to buffet with the world, or long to endure its storms. He died in the prime of manhood, when I was very young, and left my mother to struggle with those difficulties which are always incident to a state of widowhood, with a numerous family and a limited income. The deficiency of fortune was, however, in her case, compensated by the energies of a masculine understanding, combined with an untiring devotion to the interest and welfare of her children.

Trades and professions in England are almost as completely hereditary as among the castes of India. The great Franklin derived his "ponderous strength," physical if not intellectual, from a line of Blacksmiths, and I, Frank Gernon, inherit certain atrabilious humours, maternally, from a long series of very respectable "Qui Hyes."[3] Yes, my mothers family—father, grandfather, uncles, and cousins—had all served with exemplary fidelity that potent merchant-monarch affectionately termed in India the Honourable John (though degraded, I am sorry to say, into an "old woman" by his native subjects); they had all flourished for more than a century under the shade of the "rupee tree," a plant of Hesperidean virtues, whose fructiferous powers, alas! have since their time sadly declined. These, my maternal progenitors, were men both of the sword and pen; some had filled high civil stations with credit, whilst others, under the banners of a Clive, a Lawrence, or a Munro, had led "Ind's dusky chivalry" to war, and participated in many of those glorious, but now time-mellowed exploits, from which the splendid fabric of our Eastern dominions has arisen. This, and other circumstances on which I shall briefly touch, combined to point my destiny to the gorgeous

East. My mother, for the reasons given, and the peculiar facilities which she consequently had for establishing us in that quarter, had from an early period looked fondly to India as the theatre for the future exertions of her sons. But long before the period of my departure arrived—indeed I may say almost from infancy—I had been inoculated by my mother, my great uncle, and sundry parchment-faced gentlemen who frequented our house, with a sort of Indo-mania. I was never tired of hearing of its people, their manners, dress, &c., and was perfectly read on the subject of alligators and Bengal tigers. I used, indeed, regularly and systematically to persecute and bore every Anglo-Indian that came in my way for authentic accounts of their history and mode of destruction, &c. One most benevolent old gentleman, a fine specimen of the Indian of other days, and a particular friend of my family, used to "fool us to the top of our bent" in that way. I say us, for the Indo-mania was not confined to myself.

My mother, too, used to entertain us with her experiences, which served to feed the ardent longing which I felt to visit the East. How often in the winter evenings of pleasant "lang syne," when the urn hissed on the table, and the cat purred on the comfortable rug, has our then happy domestic circle listened with delight to her account of that far-distant land! What respect did the sonorous names of Bangalore and Cuddalore, and Nundy Droog and Severn Droog, and Hookhaburdar and Soontaburdars, and a host of others, excite in our young minds! In what happy accordance with school-boy thoughts were the descriptions she gave us of the fruits of that sunny clime—the luscious mango—the huge jack—the refreshing guava— and, above all, the delicious custard-apple, a production which I never in the least doubted contained the exact counterpart of that pleasant admixture of milk and eggs which daily excited my longing eyes amongst the tempting display of a pastry-cook's window! Sometimes she rose to higher themes, in which the pathetic or adventurous predominated. How my poor cousin Will fell by the dagger of an assassin at the celebrated massacre of Patna; and how another venturous relative shot a tiger on foot, thereby earning the benedictions of a whole community of peaceful Hindoos, whose village had long been the scene of his midnight maraudings: this story, by the way, had a dash of the humorous in it, though relating in the main to a rather serious affair. It never lost its raciness by repetition, and whenever my mother told it, which at our request she frequently did, and approached what we deemed the comic part, our risibles were always on full-cock for a grand and simultaneous explosion of mirth.

Well, time rolled on; I had doubled the Cape of Good Hope, sweet sixteen, and the ocean of life and adventure lay before me. I stood five feet nine inches in my stockings, and possessed all the aspirations common to my age. "Frank, my love," one day said my mother to me, at the conclusion of breakfast, "I have good news for you; that most benevolent of men, Mr. Versanket, has complied with my application, and given me an infantry cadetship for you; here," she continued, "is his letter, read it, and ever retain, as I trust you will, a lively sense of his goodness." I eagerly seized the letter, and read the contents with a kind of ecstasy. It expressed sympathy in my mothers difficulties, and an invitation to me to come to London and take advantage of his offer.

I will not dwell on the parting scenes. Suffice it to say, that I embraced those dear objects of my affection, many of whom I was never destined to embrace again, and bid a sorrowful long adieu to the parental roof. I arrived in the great metropolis, and prepared for my outfit and departure. Having completed the former—sheets, ducks, jeans, and gingerbread, tobacco to bribe old Neptune, brandy to mollify the sailors, and all *et ceteras*, according to the most approved list of Messrs. Welsh and Stalker—nought remained but to pass the India House, an ordeal which I was led to view with an indefinable dread. From whom I received the information I now forget, though it was probably from some one of that mischievous tribe of jokers, who love to sport with the feelings of youth; but I was told that it was absolutely necessary that I should learn by heart, as an indispensable preliminary to passing, the "Articles of War and Mutiny Act," then forming one volume. What was my state of alarm and despondency as I handled that substantial yellow-backed tome, and reflected on the task I had to perform of committing its whole contents to memory in the brief space of one week! It haunted me in my dreams, and the thought of it, sometimes crossing my mind whilst eating, almost suspended the power of swallowing. I carried it about with me whereever I went, applying to it with desperate determination whenever a leisure moment, of which I had very few, would admit; but what I forced into my sensorium one moment, the eternal noise and racket of London drove out of it the next. To cut a long story short, the day arrived, "the all-important day," big with my fate. I found myself waiting in the India House, preparatory to appearing before the directors, and, saving the first two or three clauses, the "Articles of War" were to me as a sealed volume. I was in despair; to be disgraced appeared inevitable. At last came the awful summons, and I entered the apartment, where, at a large table covered with green cloth, sat the "potent, grave, and reverend signiors," who were to decide my fate. One of them, a very benevolent-looking old gentleman, with a powdered head, desired me to advance, and having asked me a few questions touching my name, age, &c., he paused, and, to my inexpressible alarm, took up a volume from the table, which was no other than that accursed piece of military codification of which I have made mention. Now, thought I, it comes, and all is over. After turning over the leaves for some seconds, he said, raising his head, "I suppose you are well acquainted with the contents of this volume?" Heaven forgive me! but the instinct of self-preservation was strong upon me, and I mumbled forth a very suspicious "Yes." Ye generous casuists, who invent excuses for human frailty, plead for my justification. "Well," continued he, closing the book, "conduct yourself circumspectly in the situation in which you are about to enter, and you will acquire the approbation of your superiors; you may now retire." Those who can imagine the feelings of a culprit reprieved, after the fatal knot has been comfortably adjusted by a certain legal functionary; or those of a curate, with £50 per annum, and fifteen small children, on the announcement of a legacy of £10,000; or those of a respectable spinster of forty, on having the question unexpectedly popped; or, in short, any other situation where felicity obtrudes unlooked for, may form some idea of mine; I absolutely walked on air, relieved from this incubus, and gave myself up to the most delightful buoyancy of spirits. A few days more, and Mr. Cadet 9Francis Gernon found himself on board the *Rottenbeam Castle*, steering down Channel, and with tearful eyes casting a lingering gaze on the shores of old England.

CHAPTER II

The first scene of this eventful drama closed with my embarkation on board the *Rottenbeam Castle*, bound for Bengal. Saving an Irish packet, this was the first ship on which I had ever set foot, and it presented a new world to my observation—a variety of sights and sounds which, by giving fresh occupation to my thoughts and feelings, served in some measure to banish the tristful remembrance of home. All, at first, was a chaos to me; but when the confusion incidental to embarkation and departure (the preliminary shake of this living kaleidoscope), a general clearing out of visitors, custom-house officers, bum-boat women, *et hoc genus omne*, had subsided, things speedily fell into that regular order characteristic of vessels of this description—each individual took up his proper position, and entered in an orderly manner on his prescribed and regular routine of duty; and I began to distinguish officers from passengers, and to learn the rank and importance of each respectively.

Before proceeding further with ship-board scenes, a slight sketch of a few of the *dramatis personæ* may not be unacceptable. And first, our commander, the autocrat of this little empire. Captain McGuffin was a raw-boned Caledonian, of some six foot three; a huge, red-headed man of great physical powers, of which, however, his whole demeanour, singularly mild, evinced a pleasing unconsciousness; bating the latter quality, he was just such a man of nerves and sinews as in the olden time, at Falkirk or Bannockburn, one could fancy standing like a tower of strength, amidst the din and clash of arms, "slaughing" off heads and arms, muckle broad-sword in hand, with fearful energy and effect. He had a sombre and fanatical expression of visage; and I never looked at his "rueful countenance" but I thought I saw the genuine descendant of one of those stern covenanters of yore, of whom I had read—one of those "crop-eared whigs" who, on lonely moor and mountain, had struggled for the rights of conscience, and fought with indomitable obstinacy the glorious fight of freedom.

I soon discovered I was not "alone in my glory," and that another cadet was destined to share with me the honours of the "Griffinage." He was a gawky, wide-mouthed fellow, with locks like a pound of candles, and trousers half-way up his calves; one who, from his appearance, it was fair to infer had never before been ten miles from his native village.

It was a standing source of wonder to all on board (and to my knowledge the enigma was never satisfactorily solved), by what strange concurrence of circumstances, what odd twist of Dame Fortune's wheel, this Gaspar Hauserish specimen of rusticity had attained to the distinguished honour of being allowed to sign himself "gentleman cadet," in any "warrant, bill, or quittance;" but so it was. The old adage, however, applied in his case; he turned out eventually to be much less of a fool than he looked.

Our first officer, Mr. Gillans, was a thorough seaman, and a no less thorough John Bull; he had the then common detestation of the French and their imputed vices of insincerity, &c., and in endeavouring to avoid the Scylla of Gallic deceit, went plump into the Charybdis of English rudeness. He was in truth, a blunt, gruff fellow, who evidently thought that civility and poltroonery were convertible terms. The captain was the only person whom his respect for discipline ever allowed him to address without a growl; in short, the vulgar but expressive phrase, as "sulky as a bear with a sore head," seemed made for him expressly, for in no case could it have been more justly applied. The second mate, Grinnerson, was a gentlemanly fellow on the whole, but a most eternal wag and joker. Cadets had plainly, for many a voyage, furnished him with subjects for the exercise of his facetious vein, and "Tom," *i.e.* Mr. Thomas Grundy, and myself, received diurnal roastings at his hands. If I expressed an opinion, "Pardon me, my dear sir," he would say, with mock gravity, "but it strikes me that, being *only a cadet*, you can know nothing about it;" or, "in about ten years hence, when you get your commission, your opinion 'on things in general' may be valuable." If I flew out, or the peaceable Grundy evinced a disposition to "hog his back," he would advise us to keep our temper, to be cool, assuring us, with dry composure, that the "cadets on the last voyage were never permitted to get into a passion." In a word, he so disturbed my self-complacency, that I long gravely debated the question with myself, whether I ought not to summon him to the lists when I got to India, there to answer for his misdeeds. As the voyage drew towards a close, however, he let off the steam of his raillery considerably, and treated us with more deference and respect; thereby showing that he had studied human nature, and knew how to restore the equilibrium of a young man's temper, by adding to the weight in the scale of self-esteem. Our doctor and purser are the only two more connected with the ship whom I shall notice. The first, Cackleton by name, was a delicate, consumptive, superfine person, who often reminded me of the injunction, "physician, heal thyself." He ladled out the soup with infinite grace, and was quite the ladies' man. His manners, indeed, would have been gentlemanly and unexceptionable had they not been for ever pervaded by an obviously smirking consciousness on his part that they were so. As for Cheesepare, the purser, all I shall record of him is, that by a happy fortune he had dropped into the exact place for which nature and his stars appeared to have designed him. He looked like a purser—spoke like a purser—ate and drank like a purser—and locked himself up for three or four hours *per diem* with his hooks and ledgers like a very praiseworthy purser. Moreover, he carved for a table of thirty or forty, with exemplary patience, and possessed the happy knack of disposing of the largest quantity of meat in the smallest given quantity of time of any man I ever met with, in order to be ready for a renewed round at the mutton.

Of passengers we had the usual number and variety: civilians, returning with wholesale stocks of English and continental experiences and recollections of the aristocratic association, &c., for Mofussil consumption; old officers, going back to ensure their "off-reckonings" preparatory to their final "off-reckoning;" junior partners in mercantile houses; sixteenth cousins from Forres and Invernesshire obeying the spell of kindred attraction (would that we had a little more of its influence south of the Tweed!); officers to supply the wear and tear of cholera and dysentery in his (then) Majesty's regiments; matrons returning to expectant husbands, and bright-eyed spinsters to get—a peep at the country—nothing more;—then we had an assistant surgeon or two, more *au fait* at whist than Galenicals, and the two raw, unfledged griffins—to wit, Grundy and myself—completed the list. But of the afore-mentioned variety, I shall only select half a dozen for particular description, and as characteristic of the mass.

First, there was Colonel Kilbaugh, a colonel of cavalry and ex-resident of Paugulabad, who, in spite of his high-heeled Hobys, was a diminutive figure, pompous, as little men generally are, and so anxious, apparently, to convince the world that he had a soul above his inches, that egad, sir, it was dangerous for a man above the common standard of humanity to look at him, or differ in opinion in the slightest degree. His was in truth

A fiery soul, which, working out its way,

Fretted the pigmy body to decay.

He excelled (in his own estimation) in long stories, which he told with an extraordinary minuteness of detail. They generally began with, "Shortly after I was appointed to the residency of Paugulabad," or, "The year before, or two years after, I left the residency of Paugulabad:" in short, that was his chronological starting-point. The colonel's *yarns* principally (though not entirely) related to wonderful sporting exploits, and the greater the bounce the more scrupulously exact was he in the *minutiæ*, magnanimously disregarding the terrors of cross-examination, should a seven-foot mortal venture one. "It was the largest tiger that, sir, I ever killed; he stood 4 feet

4¾ inches to the top of his shoulder—4 feet 4¾ was it, by-the-bye?—no, I'm wrong; 4 feet 4½. I killed him with a double Joe I got from our doctor; I think it was the cold season before I left the residency of Paugulabad." It was one of the most amusing things in the world to see him marching up and down the poop with our Colossus of a skipper—"Ossa to a wart"—one little fin of a hand behind his back, and laying down the law with the other; skipper, with an eye to future recommendation, very deferential of course.

Next, in point of rank, was Mr. Goldmore, an ex-judge of the Sudder Dewanny Adawlut; a man of birth and education, and an excellent sample of the distinguished service to which he belonged. His manners were kind and urbane, though he was a little peppery sometimes, particularly when I beat him at chess. He had come home a martyr to liver; and the yellow cheek, the lacklustre eye, and the feeble step, all told too plainly that he was returning to die. His wife, fifteen years younger than himself, exhibited beside him a striking contrast; she, "buxom, blithe, and *debonnair*"—a vigorous plant in florid pride; he, poor fellow, in the "sear and yellow" leaf. She was a warm-hearted, excellent creature, native goodness beaming in her eye, but had one fault, and that a prominent one. Having in India, as is often the case with the sex, been thrown much at out-stations amongst male society, she had insensibly adopted a "mannish" tone, used terms of Indian conventional slang—bad in a man, but odious from female lips—laughed heartily at stories seasoned with equivoque, and sometimes told such herself with off-hand *naïveté* at the cuddy-table, producing a wink from Mr. Grinnerson to Ensign O'Shaughnessy, and an uncommon devotion to his plate on the part of Mr. Goldmore himself.

Major Rantom, of the Dragoons—soldierly, gentleman-like, and five-and-thirty—commanded the detachment of troops, to which were attached Ensigns Gorman and O'Shaughnessy, two fine "animals," that had recently been caught in the mountains of Kerry; and an ancient centurion, Capt. Marpeet, of the Native Infantry, must conclude these samples of the masculine gender. Marpeet was a character, upon the whole—a great man for short whist and Hodgson's pale ale. The Sporting Magazine, Taplin's Farriery, and Dundas's Nineteen Manœuvres, seemed to have constituted the extent of his reading, though some conversation he one day had about "zubber, zeer, and pesh," and that profound work the Tota Kuhannee, seemed to indicate that he had at least entered on the flowery paths of Oriental literature. Dundas, however, was his strong point—his tower of strength—his one idea. Ye powers! how amazingly convincing and fluent he was when he took that subject in hand! Many a tough discussion would he have with the pompous little colonel, whether the right or left stood fast,

&c., and who, having been a Resident, and knowing, therefore, everything, of course knew something of that also.

But *places aux demoiselles*! make way for the spinsters! Let me introduce to the reader's acquaintance Miss Kitty and Miss Olivia Jenkins, Miss Maria Balgrave, and Miss Anna Maria Sophia Dobbikins. The first two were going to their father, a general officer in the Madras Presidency; the eldest, Kitty, was a prude, haunted by the "demon of propriety," the youngest, dear Olivia, a perfect giggle—with such a pair of eyes!—but "thereby hangs a tale." Miss Maria Balgrave was consigned to a house of business in Calcutta, to be forwarded, by the first safe conveyance, up the country to her dear friend Mrs. Kurrybhat, the lady of Ensign Kurrybhat, who had invited her out; she was very plain, but of course possessed its usual concomitant, great amiability of temper. Miss Dobbikins was a Bath and Clifton belle, hackneyed and *passé*, but exhibiting the remains of a splendid face and figure; it was passing strange that so fine a creature should have attained a certain age without having entered that state which she was so well calculated to adorn, whilst doubtless many a snub-nosed thing had gone off under her own nose. I have seen many such cases; and it is a curious problem for philosophical investigation, why those whom "every one" admires "nobody" marries.

Having given these sketches of a few of my companions, let me now proceed with my voyage. Leaving Deal we had to contend with contrary winds, and when off Portsmouth, they became so adverse, that the captain determined on dropping anchor, and there wait a favourable change. In three days the wind became light, veered to the proper quarter, and our final departure was fixed for the following morning. My last evening off Portsmouth long remained impressed on my memory. Full often, in my subsequent wanderings in the silent forest or the lonely desert, in the hushed camp, or on the moon-lit rampart, where nought save the sentinel's voice broke through the silence of the night, have I pictured this last aspect of my native land. I had been engaged below, inditing letters for home and other occupations, the whole day, when, tired of the confinement, I mounted on the poop: the parting glow of a summer's evening rested on the scene—a tranquillity and repose little, alas! in consonance with the state of my feelings, once more painfully excited at the prospect of the severance from all that was dear to me. Hitherto excitement had sustained me, but now I felt it in its full force.

> Land of my sires, what mortal hand
>
> Can e'er untie the filial band
>
> That knits me to thy rugged strand?

I leant my head upon my hand, and gave myself up to sad and melancholy reflections. On one side stretched the beautiful coast of the Isle of Wight, whilst the fast-gathering shades of evening were slowly blending into one dark mass the groves and villas of Cowes; lights from many a pleasant window streamed across the rippling sea—lights, methought, cheering circles of happy faces, like those I lately gazed upon, but which I might never see more. Many a tall and gallant man-of-war rode ahead of us, fading in the gathering mist; boats, leaving their long, silvery tracks behind them, glided across the harbour; whilst the lights of the town, in rapid succession, broke forth as those of the day declined. The very tranquillity of such a scene as this, to a person in my then state of mind, by mocking, as it were, the inward grief, made it to be more deeply felt. I looked at my native shores, as a lover gazes on his mistress for the last time, till the boom of the evening gun, and the increasing darkness, warned me that it was time to go below.

> Calm were the elements, night's silence deep,
>
> The waves scarce murmuring, and the winds asleep.

In a few days we were in the Bay of Biscay—and now my troubles began.

CHAPTER III

The Bay of Biscay well merits its turbulent character; of this we soon had ample demonstration, for the *Rottenbeam Castle* had scarcely entered within its stormy bounds, when the wind, hitherto moderate, became rough and boisterous, and in a little time freshened almost to a gale; the vessel began to pitch and roll—the shrouds cracked—the few sails set were strained almost to splitting—and mountain seas with wild, foamy crests ever and anon burst over us, clearing the waist and forecastle, and making the "good ship" quiver through every plank and timber. These *sublimities* were quite new to me, and produced their usual effects on the unseasoned—an involuntary tribute to Old Ocean—not a metrical outpouring, but one of a less spiritual quality, on which it would be superfluous to dilate.

Our first day's dinner on board, with things in the state I have described—*i.e.* the *Rottenbeam Castle* reeling and staggering like a drunken man—was a most comical affair, and I should have enjoyed it extremely had my nausea been less. It is true, with some variations, the scene was afterwards frequently repeated (except when sea-pie was the order of the day); but then, though I was no longer qualmish, it in turn had lost the master-charm of novelty. We were summoned to dinner as usual, on the day in question, by the drummers and fifers—or rather, to be more respectful, the "Captains Band;" but, from the difficulty of preserving an equilibrium, these worthies mangled the "Roast Beef of Old England" most unmercifully. The dapper little steward, with his train of subordinates, had some difficulty in traversing the deck with their savoury burthens; unable to march as before, heads erect, like a squad of recruits, the grand purveyor, with his silver tureen in the van, they now emerged theatrically from the culinary regions—advancing with slides and side-steps, like a *corps de ballet*—now a halt, then a simultaneous run—then balancing on one leg—and finally (hitting the moment of an equipoise) a dart into the cuddy, where, with some little difficulty, each contrived to deposit his dish. The passengers, emerging from various doors and openings, tottering and holding on as best they might, now made their way to seats, and amidst the most abominable creaking and groaning that ever saluted my ears the operation of dinner began. In spite of sand-bags, however, and all other appliances, there was no restraining the ambulatory freaks of the dishes, and we were scarcely seated when a tremendous lee-lurch sent a tureen of peasoup souse over the doctor s kerseymere waistcoat and Brummel tie; and a roast pig, as if suddenly resuscitated and endued with a spirit of frenzy, darted from its dish, and, cantering furiously down the whole length of the table, finally effected a lodgment in Miss Dobbikins' lap, to the infinite dismay of that young lady, who uttering a faint shriek, hastily essayed, with Ensign O'Shaughnessy's assistance, to divest herself of the intrusive porker. I, for my part, was nearly overwhelmed by an involuntary embrace from the charming Miss Olivia; whilst, to add to the confusion, at this particular moment, Mr. Cadet Grundy, governed rather by sight than a due consideration of circumstances and the laws of gravitation, made a desperate lunge at one of the swinging tables, which he thought was making a most dangerous approach to the perpendicular, in order to steady it, and the immediate result was, a fearful crash of glasses and decanters, and a plentiful libation of port and sherry.

"Are ye mod, sir, to do that?" exclaimed the captain, with ill-suppressed vexation at the destruction of his glasses, and forgetting his usual urbanity.

"I thought they were slipping off, sir," said Grundy, with great humility.

"Ye ha' slupped them off in gude airnest yeersel, sir," rejoined Captain McGuffin, unable, however, to repress a smile, in which all joined, at the idea of Grundy's extreme simplicity. "Dinna ye ken, sir, that it's the ship, and not the swing-table, that loses its pairpendicular? Here, steward," continued he, "clare away these frogments, and put mair glasses on the table."

The colloquy ended, there was a further lull, when, heave yo ho! away went the ship on the other side; purser jammed up against the bulk-head—rolls—legs and wings—boiled beef, carrots, and potatoes, all racing, as if to see which would first reach the other side of the table. At this instant snap went a chair-lashing, and the ex-resident of Paugulabad was whirled out of the cuddy door, like a thunder-bolt.

"There she goes again!" exclaimed the second mate; "hold on, gentlemen." The caution was well-timed, for down she went on the opposite tack; once more, the recoil brought the colonel back again, with the force of a battering-ram, attended by an awful smash of the butlers plate-basket, and other deafening symptoms of reaction. Oh, 'tis brave sport, a cuddy-dinner in an Indiaman, and your ship rolling gunwales under.

"By the powers, now, but this hates everything entirely," exclaimed Ensign Gorman, who, like myself, was a griff, and had never witnessed anything of the sort before.

"Oh, its nothing at all this—mere child's play, to what you'll have round the Cape," observed the second mate, grinning with malice prepense.

"The deuce take you, now, Grinnerson, for a *Jove's* comforter," rejoined the ensign, laughing; "sure if it's worse than this, it is we'll be sailing bottom upwards, and ateing our males with our heels in the air."

"Oh, I assure you, it's a mere trifle this to the rolling and pitching I myself have experienced," said the little colonel, who having recovered his seat and composure, now put in his oar, unwilling to be silent when anything wonderful was on the *tapis*. "I remember," continued the ex-resident, picking his teeth *nonchalamment* (he generally picked his teeth when delivered of a bouncer), "that was—let me see, about the year 1810—shortly after I resigned the residency of Paugulabad—we were off Cape Lagullas, when our vessel rolled incessantly for a fortnight in the heaviest sea I ever remember to have seen; we were half our time under water—a shark actually swam through the cuddy—everything went by the board—live stock all washed away—couldn't cook the whole time, but lived on biscuit, Bologna sausages, Bombay ducks, and so forth. To give you an idea of it—ladies will excuse me—I actually wore out the seats of two pair of inexpressibles from the constant friction to which they were subjected—a sort of perpetual motion—no preserving the same centre of gravity for a single moment."

This sally of the colonel's had an equally disturbing effect on the gravity of the cuddy party, and all laughed heartily at it.

"You were badly enough off, certainly, colonel," said our wag, the second officer (with a sly wink at one of his confederates); "but I think I can mention a circumstance of the kind still more extraordinary. When I was last in the China seas, in the *John Tomkins*, she rolled so prodigiously after a tuffoon, that she actually wore off all the copper sheathing, and very nearly set the sea on fire by this same friction you speak of. It's strange, but as true as what you have just mentioned, colonel."

"Sir," said the colonel, bristling up, for he did not at all relish the drift of this story, "you are disposed to be pleasant, sir; facetious, sir; but let me beg in future that you will reserve your jokes for some one else, and not exhibit your humour at my expense, or it may be unpleasant to both of us."

All looked grave—the affair was becoming serious—the colonel was a known fire-eater, and Grinnerson, who saw he had overshot the mark, seemed a little disconcerted, but struggled to preserve his composure—it was a juncture well calculated to test all the powers of impudence and tact of that very forward gentleman; but, somehow or other, he did back cleverly out of the scrape, without any additional offence to the colonel's dignity, or a farther compromise of his own, and before the cloth was removed, a magnanimous challenge to Mr. Grinnerson, "to take wine," came from the colonel (who at bottom was a very worthy little man, though addicted, unfortunately, to the Ferdinand Mendez Pinto vein), and convinced us that happily no other sort of challenge was to be apprehended. And so ended my first day's dinner in a high sea in the Bay of Biscay.

Now had the moon, resplendent lamp of night,
O'er heaven's pure azure shed her sacred light.

In plain prose, it was past seven bells, and I (like Mahomet's coffin) was swinging in the steerage, forgetful of all my cares; whether in my dreams I was wandering once more, as in childhood's days, by the flowery margin of the silver Avon, listening to the blackbird's mellow note from the hawthorn dell—lightly footing the Spanish dance in Mangeon's ball-room at Clifton—or comfortably sipping a cup of bohea in the family circle at home—I do not now well remember: but whatever was the nature of those sweet illusions, they were suddenly dispelled, in the dead of the night, by one of the most fearful agglomerations of stunning sounds that ever broke the slumbers of a cadet: groaning timbers—hoarse shouts—smashing crockery—falling knife-boxes—and the loud gurgling bubble of invading waters—all at once, and with terrible discord, burst upon my astonished ear. Thinking the ship was scuttling, or, that some other (to me unknown) marine disaster was befalling her, I sprung up in a state between sleeping and waking, overbalanced my cot, and was pitched out head-foremost on the deck. Here a body of water, ancle-deep, and washing to and fro, lent a startling confirmation to my apprehensions that the ship was actually *in articulo immersionis*. I struggled to gain my feet, knocked my naked shins against a box of saddlery of the major's, slipped and slid about on the wet and slimy deck, and finally, my feet flying from under me, came bump down on the broadest side of my person, with stunning emphasis and effect. Another effort to gain the erect position was successful, and, determined to visit the "glimpses of the moon" once more before I became food for fishes, I hurriedly and instinctively scrambled my way towards the companion ladder. Scarcely was I in its vicinity, and holding on by a staunchion, when the vessel gave another profound roll, so deep that the said ladder, being ill-secured, fell over backwards, saluting the deck with a tremendous bang, followed by a second crash, and bubbling of waters effecting a forcible entry. Paralyzed and confounded by this succession of sounds and disasters, I turned, still groping in the darkness, to seek some information touching this uproar, from some one of the neighbouring sleepers. I soon lighted on a hammock, and tracing the mummy-case affair from the feet upwards my hands rested on a cold nose, then a rough curly pate surmounting it, whose owner, snoring with a ten-pig power, would, I verily believe, have slept on had the crash of doom been around him. "Hollo! here," said I, giving him a shake. A grunt and a mumbled execration were all it elicited. I repeated the experiment, and having produced some symptoms of consciousness, begged earnestly to know if all I had described was an ordinary occurrence, or if we were really going to the bottom. I had now fairly roused the sleeping lion; up he started in a terrible passion; asked me what the deuce made me bother him with my nonsense at that time of night, and then, consigning me to a place whence no visitor is permitted to return, once more addressed himself to his slumbers. This refreshing sample of nautical philosophy, though rather startling, convinced me that I had mistaken the extent of the danger; in fact, there was none at all; so feeling my way back to my cot, I once more, though with becoming caution, got into it, determined, sink or swim, to have my sleep out. On rising, disorder and misery, in various shapes, a wet deck and boxes displaced, met my view; I found my coat and pantaloons pleasantly saturated with sea-water, which it appeared had entered by an open port or scuttle, and that my boots had sailed away to some unknown region on a voyage of discovery. "Oh! why did I 'list?'" I exclaimed, in the bitterness of my discomfort; "why did I ever 'list?'" Ye cadets, attend to the moral which this narrative conveys, and learn, by my unhappy example, always to secure your toggery, high and dry, before you turn in, and to study well the infirmities of that curious pendulum balance, the cot, lest, like me, ye be suddenly decanted therefrom on the any-thing-but-downy surface of an oaken deck!

With what feelings of delight does the youth first enter upon the fairy region of the tropics, a region which Cook and Anson, and the immortal fictions of St. Pierre and De Foe, have invested in his estimation with a sweet and imperishable charm! The very air to him is redolent of a spicy aroma, of a balmy and tranquillizing influence, whilst delicious but indefinable visions of the scenes he is about to visit—of palmy groves, and painted birds, and coral isles "in the deep sea set," float before him in all those roseate hues with which the young and excited fancy loves to paint them. Paul and Virgina—Robinson—Friday—goats—savages and monkeys—ye are all for ever bound to my heart by the golden links of early association and acquaintanceship. Happy Juan Fernandez, too! Atalantis of the wave—Utopia of the roving imagination—how oft have I longed to abide in ye, and envied Robinson his fate—honest man of goatskins and unrivalled resources! But one ingredient, a wife, was wanting to complete your felicity; had you but rescued one of the Miss Fridays from the culinary fate designed for her brother, and made her your companion, you would have been the most comfortable fellow on record.

Griffin as I was I partook strongly of these common but delightful feelings I have attempted to describe, and in the change of climate and objects which every week's sail brought forth, found much to interest and excite me—the shoal of flying-fish, shooting like a silver shower from the ocean, and skimming lightly over the crested waves; the gambols of the porpoise; the capture of a shark; fishing for bonetta off the bowsprit; a waterspout; speculations on a distant sail; her approach; the friendly greeting; the first and last!—were all objects and events pleasing in themselves, but doubly so when viewed in relation to the general monotony of a life at sea. Nothing, I think, delighted me more than contemplating the gorgeous sunsets, as we approached the equator. Here, in England, that luminary is a sickly affair, but particularly so when viewed through our commonly murky atmosphere, and there may be some truth in the Italian's splenetic remark in favour of the superior warmth of the moon of his own country. But in the fervid regions of the tropics it is that we see the glorious emblem of creative power in all his pride and majesty, whether rising in his strength, "robed in flames and amber light," ruling in meridian splendour, or sinking slowly to rest on his ocean couch of gold and crimson, in softened but ineffable refulgence; it is (but particularly in its parting aspect) an object eminently calculated to awaken the most elevated thoughts of the Creator's power, mingled with a boundless admiration for the beauty of His works. Yes, neither language, painting, nor poetry, can adequately portray that most glorious of spectacles—a tropical sunset.

Ensign O'Shaughnessy having sworn "by all the bogs in Kerry," that he would put a brace of pistol-balls through Neptune, or Juno, or any "sa God" of them all, that should dare to lay hands upon him; and a determination to resist the initiatory process of ducking in bilge-water, and shaving with a rusty hoop, having manifested itself in other quarters, Captain McGuffin, glad of a pretext, and really apprehensive of mischief, had it intimated to the son of Saturn and his spouse, that their visit in crossing the line would be dispensed with. In so doing, it appears to me that he exercised a wise discretion; Neptune's tomfooleries, at least when carried to their usual extent, being one of those ridiculous customs "more honoured in the breach than in the observance;" one which may well be allowed to sleep with "Maid Marian," "the Lord of Misrule" and other samples of the "wisdom of our ancestors," who were emphatically but "children of a larger growth," to whom horse play and "tinsel" were most attractive. On crossing the equator, however, the old but more harmless joke of exhibiting the *line* through a telescope was played off on one greenhorn, sufficiently soft to admit of its taking effect.

"Do you make it out, Jones?" said Grinnerson, who had got up the scene, to one of the middys, a youngster intently engaged in reconnoitering through a glass half as long as himself.

"I think I do, sir," said Jones, with a difficultly-suppressed grin.

"What is he looking for?" asked the simple victim.

"The Line, to be sure; didn't I tell you we were to cross it to-day?"

"Oh yes, I remember; I should like amazingly to see it, if you would oblige me with the telescope."

"Oh, certainly; Jones, give Mr. Brown the glass."

The soft man took it, looked, but declared that he saw nought but sky and sea.

"Here, try mine," continued the second mate; "'tis a better one than that you have," handing him one with a hair or wire across the large end of it. "Now do you see it?"

"I think I do; oh, yes, most distinctly. And that really is the line? Bless me, how small it is!"

This was the climax; the middys held their mouths, and sputtering, tumbled in a body down the ladder to have their laugh out, whilst a general side-shaking at the griff's expense took place amongst the remaining group on the poop.

Well, the stormy dangers of the Cape safely passed, the pleasant isles of Johanna, sweet as those which Waller sung, duly visited—Dondra Head— Adam's Peak—the woody shores of Ceylon here skirted and admired, those beautiful shores, where

> Partout on voit mûrir, partout on voit éclore,
>
> Et les fruits de Pomone et les présents de Flore;

and the "spicy gales" from cinnamon groves duly snuffed up and appreciated (*entre nous*, a burnt pastile of Mr. Grinnerson's, and not Ceylon, furnished the "spicy gales" on this occasion), we found ourselves at last off the far-famed coast of Coromandel, and fast approaching our destination.

It is pleasant at certain seasons to glide over the summer seas of these delightful latitudes, whilst the vessel spreads abroad all her snowy canvas to arrest every light and vagrant zephyr, to hang over the side, and whilst the ear is soothed by the lapping ripple of small, crisp waves, idly breaking on the vessel's bows as she moves scarce perceptibly through them, to gaze on the sky and ocean, and indulge in that half-dreamy listlessness when gentle thoughts unbidden come and go. How beautiful is the dark blue main, relieved by the milk-white flash of the seabird's wing! how picturesque the Indian craft, with their striped latteen sails, as they creep along those palm-covered coasts, studded with temples and pagodas! and seaward resting on the far-off horizon, how lovely the fleecy piles of rose-tinted clouds, seeming to the fancy the ethereal abodes of pure and happy spirits! There is in the thoughts to which such scenes give birth a rationality as improving to the heart as it is remote from a forced and mawkish sentimentality. Such were my sensations as we crept along the Indian coast, till in a few days the *Rottenbeam Castle* came to anchor in the roads of Madras, amidst a number of men-of-war, Indiamen, Arab grabs, and country coasters.

The first thing we saw, on dropping anchor, was a man-of-war's boat pulling for us, which created a considerable sensation amongst the crew, to whom the prospect of impressment was anything but agreeable. The boat, manned by a stout crew of slashing young fellows, in straw hats, and with tattooed arms, was soon alongside, and the lieutenant, with the air of a monarch, mounted the deck. He was a tall, strapping man, with a hanger banging against his heels, loose trousers, a tarnished *swab* (epaulette) on his shoulder, and a glazed cocked-hat stuck rakishly fore and aft on his head: in my idea, the very *beau idéal* of a "first leftenant."

CHAPTER IV

In the last chapter I left the *Rottenbeam Castle* just arrived in the roads of Madras, and the frigate's boat alongside. Our commander, with a grave look, advanced to meet the officer, who, saluting him in an easy and off-hand manner, announced himself as lieutenant of H.M. ship *Thunderbolt*, and desired him "to turn up the hands." Captain McGuffin was beginning to remonstrate, declaring that some of his best sailors had been pressed a few days before (which was the fact), and that he had barely sufficient to carry the ship round to Bengal, &c., when the lieutenant cut him short, declaring he had nothing to do with that matter; that his orders were peremptory, and must be obeyed.

"I shall appeal to the admiral," said our skipper, rather ruffled.

"You may appeal to whom you choose, sir," replied the lieutenant, somewhat haughtily, and giving his hanger a kick, to cause it to resume its hindward position; "but now, and in the meantime, if you please, you'll order up your men."

These were "hard nuts" for McGuffin "to crack;" on his own deck too, where he had reigned absolute but a few minutes before—

The monarch of all he survey'd,

Whose right there was none to dispute.

But he felt that the iron heel of a stronger despotism than his own was upon him, and that he had no resource but submission. He consequently gave the necessary orders, and straightway the shrill whistle of the boatswain was soon heard, summoning the sailors to the muster.

"Onward they moved, a melancholy band," slouching and hitching up their trousers, and were soon ranged in rank and file along the deck. The lieutenant stalked up the line (he certainly was a noble-looking fellow, just the man for a cutting-out party, or to head a column of boarders), and turned several of them about, something after the manner in which a butcher in Smithfield selects his fat sheep, and then putting aside those he thought worthy of "honour and hard knocks" in his Majesty's service, he ordered them forthwith to bring up their hammocks and kits, and prepare for departure. Amongst those thus unceremoniously chosen to increase the crew of the *Thunderbolt*, were two or three ruddy, lusty lads, who had come out as swabs, or loblolly boys, and were making their first voyage, to see how the life of a sailor agreed with them, little thinking, a few days before, of the change that awaited them. I think I see them now, blubbering as they descended the side, with their hammocks and small stocks of worldly goods on their shoulders, waving adieu to their comrades, and thinking, doubtless, of "home, sweet home," and what "mother would say when she heard of it." On one old man-of-war's man of the *Rottenbeam Castle*, whom I had often noticed, the lieutenant, keen as a hawk, pounced *instanter*; his experienced eye detecting at once in the long pigtail, corkscrew ringlets, and devil-may-care air of honest Jack, the true outward characteristics of that noble but eccentric biped, a downright British tar, and prime seamen. "You'll do for us," said the lieutenant, taking him by the collar of his jacket, and leading him out. "There's two words to that there bargain, sir," said Jack (who had had *quantum suff.* of the reg'lar sarvice), with the air of one who knew that he stood on unassailable ground. So squirting out a little 'baccy juice, and rummaging his jacket-pocket, he produced therefrom a tin tobacco-box, of more than ordinary dimensions, from which, after considerable fumbling (for Jack was evidently unused to handling literary documents of any kind), he extracted a soiled and tattered "protection," which, deliberately unfolding (a ticklish operation, by the way, the many component parallelograms being connected by the slenderest filaments), he handed it over to the lieutenant. Having so done, he hitched up his waistband, with his dexter fin, tipped his comrades something between a nod and a wink, as much as to say, "I think that'll bring him up with a round turn," and stroking down his hair, awaited the result. The officer cast his eye over the thing of shreds and patches. It contained a "true bill," so he returned it; and Jack, having carefully packed and re-stowed his *"noli me tangere,"* gave another squirt, and rolled off in triumph to the forecastle. The only fellow glad to go "to sarve him Majesty"—I blush whilst I record it—was Massa Sambo, a good-humoured nigger, and a fine specimen of the mere animal man, who, having received more of what is vulgarly termed "monkey's allowance" on board the *Rottenbeam Castle* than suited him, left us in a high glee, grinning, capering, slapping his hands and singing "Rule Britannia" in regular "Possum up a gum-tree" style, to the great amusement of us all.

Madras, from the roads, wore to me a very picturesque and interesting appearance; the long ranges of white verandahed buildings, the noble fort, with England's meteor standard floating from the flag-staff, the beach, the blue sky, the cocoa-nut trees, the white wreaths of breaking surf, the shipping, the Massoolah boats, the native craft, all constituted a novel and striking *coup d'œil*, which fully realized what in imagination I had pictured it. Looking over the side, shortly after we had anchored, I perceived to my astonishment, a naked figure walking apparently on the surface of the sea, and rapidly approaching us. This was a catamaran man, the bearer of a despatch from the shore. His diminutive bark, three or four logs, half submerged, and on which he had ploughed through the surf, was soon alongside, and the brown and dripping savage (for such he looked) scrambling on board. He sprung upon the deck, as a favourite opera-dancer bounds upon the stage, confident of an applauding welcome, and, making a ducking salaam, proceeded, in a very business-like manner, to disengage from his head a conical salt-basket sort of hat, from which, secured under a fold of linen, he produced his letters safe and dry; these with the words, "chit, sahib," spoken in tones as delicate as the frame of the speaker, he immediately delivered to the captain. The arrival of this messenger caused a considerable sensation, and the griffs of all descriptions gathered round him, conning the strange figure with open mouths and wondering eyes. The ladies, too (stimulated by curiosity), rushed to the cuddy door to have a peep at him, but made a rapid retreat on perceiving the paradisiacal costume of our hero. I shall never forget Miss Olivia's involuntary scream, or Miss Dobbikins' expression of countenance, on suddenly confronting this little swarthy Apollo: —

Horror in all his majesty was there,

Mute and magnificent without a tear.

Our admiration of the catamaran man had hardly subsided when a far more extraordinary character made his appearance. "Avast there, my hearties!" sounded the rough voice of a seaman, "and make way for the commodore." As he spoke, the crowd of sailors and recruits opened out, and his Excellency Commodore Cockle, chief of the catamarans, was seen advancing in great state from the gangway. This potent commander, who, by the way, had performed his toilet *in transitu*, after passing through the surf, was attired in an old naval uniform coat, under which appeared his naked neck and swarthy bosom; a huge cocked-hat, "which had seen a little service," a pair of kerseymere dress shorts, without stockings, and a swinging hanger banging at his heels, made up as strange a figure of the genus scarecrow as I ever remember to have seen out of a cornfield.

"By the powers, Pat, and what have we here?" said Mick Nolan, one of the recruits, to his comrade Pat Casey.

"Faith," says Pat, "and myself can't tell ye, unless 'tis one of them *Ingine* rajahs, or ould Neptune himself, that should have been after shaving us off the line."

"Devil a bit," rejoined Mick; "I'm thinking it's something of an *Aistern* Guy Fawkes, that's going to play off some of his fun amongst us."

Thus speculated the jokers, whilst the commodore, fully impressed with a sense of his importance, swaggered about the deck with all the quiet pride of a high official, putting questions, and replying to the queries of old acquaintance. Alas! poor human nature! thou art everywhere essentially the same. Dear to thee is a little power and authority in any shape, and thou exhibitest thy "fantastic tricks" as much in the bells and feathers of the savage, as under the coif of the judge, or the ermine of the monarch! The "Commodore," to whom the English cognomen of "Cockle" had been given, exercised his high functions under a commission furnished him by some wag, but of which he was quite as proud as if it had emanated from royalty itself. It was couched in the proper *lingua technica* of such instruments, and commenced in something like the following manner: "Know all men by these presents, that our trusty and well-beloved Cockle is hereby constituted Commodore and Commander of the Catamaran Squadron, and duly empowered to exercise all the high functions thereunto appertaining. The aforesaid Cockle is authorized to render his services to all parties requiring them, on their paying for the same. All captains and commanders of his Majesty's and the Honourable Company's ships, and of all other ships and vessels whatsoever, are hereby required and directed to take fruit, fish, eggs, &c., from the said Cockle (if they think fit), on their paying him handsomely in the current coin of the realm, &c."

The next day the passengers went ashore; officers full fig; ladies, civilians, and cadets, all in their best attire, crowding the benches of the Massoolah boat, and balancing, and holding on as best they could. Of all sea-going craft, from the canoe of the Greenlander to the line-of-battle-ship, the Massoolah boat is, perhaps, one of the most extraordinary. Imagine a huge affair, something in shape like one of those paper cock-boats which children make for amusement, or an old-fashioned tureen, or the transverse section of a pear or pumpkin, stem and stern alike, composed of light and flexible planks, sewn together with coir, and riding buoyant as a gull on the heaving wave, the sides rising six feet or so above its surface, the huge empty shell crossed by narrow planks or benches, on which, when seated, or rather roosted, your legs dangle in air several feet from the bottom: further, picture in the fore-part a dozen or more spare black creatures, each working an unwieldy pole-like paddle to a dismal and monotonous chant— and you may have some idea of a Massoolah boat and its equipage; the only thing, however, that can live in the tremendous surf that lashes the coast of Coromandel.

"Are you all right there, in the Massoolah boat?" shouted one of the ship's officers.

"Ay, ay, sir," responded a little middy in charge of us.

"Cast her off then," said the voice; and immediately the connecting rope was thrown on board, and off we swung, gently rising and falling on the long undulations, which were soon to assume the more formidable character of bursting surges. As we advance, I honestly confess, though I put a bold face on it, I felt most confoundedly nervous, being under serious apprehensions that one of the many sharks I had just seen would soon have the pleasure of breakfasting on a gentleman cadet, *cote-lettes à la Griffin*, no doubt, if gastronomy ranks as an art amongst that voracious fraternity. On approaching the surf, the boatmen's monotonous chant quickened to a wild *ulluloo*. We were *in medias res*. I looked astern, and there, at some distance, but in full chase, advanced a curling mountain-billow, opening its vast concave jaws, as if to devour us. On, on it came. "*Ullee! ullee! ullee!*" shouted the rowers; smash came the wave; up flew the stern, down went the prow; squall went the ladies, over canted the major, Grundy, and the ex-resident, while those more fortunate in retaining their seats held on with all the energy of alarm with one hand and dashed the brine from their habiliments with the other. The wave passed, and order a little restored, the boatmen pulled again with redoubled energy, to make as much way as they could before the next should overtake us. It soon came, roaring like so many fiends, and with nearly similar results. Another and another followed, till, at last, the unwieldy bark, amidst an awful bobbery, swung high and dry on the shelving beach; and out we all sprung, right glad once more to feel ourselves on *terra firma*, respecting which, be it observed, *en passant*, I hold the opinion of the Persian, that a yard of it is worth a thousand miles of salt-water.

Here then was I at last, in very truth, treading the soil of India—of that wondrous, teaming, and antique land, the fertile subject of my earliest thoughts and imaginations—that land whose "barbaric pearl and gold" has stimulated the cupidity of nations down the long stream of time, from Sabæan, Phœnician, Tyrian, and Venetian, to Mynheer Van Stockenbreech, and honest John Bull himself—whose visionary luxuries have warmed full many a Western poet's imagination, and whose strange vicissitudes have furnished such ample matter to adorn the moralist's and historian's pages.

As I gazed on the turbaned crowds, the flaunting robes, the huge umbrellas, the passing palankeens, the black sentinels, the strange birds, and even (pardon the climax) the little striped squirrels, which gambolled up and down the pillars of the custom-house—sights so new and strange to me,—I almost began to doubt my own identity, and to think I had fallen into some new planet. Assuredly, of all the sunny moments which chequer the path of life's pilgrimage here below, there are few whose brightness can compare with those of our first entrance on a new and untrodden land. What music is there in every sound! What an exhilarating freshness in every object! The peach's bloom, the butterfly's down, or the painted bubble, however, are but types of them. Alas! as of all sublunary enjoyments, they vanish upon contact, or at best, bear not long the grasp of possession.

My feelings were still in a state of tumultuous excitement, when, gazing about, I observed a native, in flowing robes and large gold ear rings, bearing down upon me. With a profound salaam, and the smirking smile of an old acquaintance, he proceeded to address me:

"How d'ye do, Sare?" said he.

"Pretty well, thank you," said I, smiling; "but who are you?"

"I, Ramee Sawmee Dabash, Sare, come to make master proper compliment. Very glad to see master safe on shore; too much surf, I think, and master's coat leetle wet."

"Not a little," said I, "for we have all had a complete sousing."

"Oh, never mind souse, Sare; I take to Navy Tavern there makee changee—eat good dinner. Navy Tavern very good place—plenty gentlemen go there."

"Where you please," said I; "I am at your service."

"Ver well, Sare; but (in a tone of entreaty) you please not forget my name, Ramee Sawmee Dabash—master's dabash—I am *ver* honest man; too much every gentleman know me."

Here Ramee Sawmee unconsciously spoke the truth, as I had afterwards full occasion to discover. I was soon besieged with more of these gentry offering their services; but Ramee Sawmee, having the best right to pluck me, by reason of prior possession, ordered them off indignantly; and not to incur risks by unnecessary delays, he called a palankeen, and requested me to get into it. In I tumbled, wrong side foremost, and off we started for the Navy Tavern. He ran alongside, not wishing to lose sight of me for a moment, pouring his disinterested advice into my ear in one voluble and continuous stream.

"Master, you please take care; dis place," said he, "too much dam rogue, this Madras; plenty bad beebee, and some rascal dabash ver much cheatee gentlemen. I give master best advice. I ver honest man."

I thought myself singularly fortunate, in the simplicity of my griffinish heart, in having fallen in with so valuable a character; but, in the sequel, as has been before hinted, I discovered what, I dare say, many a griff had discovered before, that Ramee Sawmee had a little overestimated himself in the above particular article of honesty.

Sweltering through a broiling sun, and abundance of dust, we reached the Navy Tavern, a building somewhat resembling, if I recollect rightly, one of our own green verandah'd suburban taverns, in which comfortable cits dine and drink heavy wet in sultry summer evenings. Here I found a vast congregation of naval and military officers, red coats and blue; mates, midshipmen, pursers, captains, and cadets; some playing billiards, some smoking, and others drowning care in bowls of sangaree, in which fascinating beverage, by the way, with guavas, pine-apples, &c., I also indulged, till brought up, some time after, by a pleasant little touch of dysentery, which had nearly produced a catastrophe; amongst the dire consequences of which would have been the non-appearance of these valuable Memoirs. From the Navy Tavern, Grundy and I went the next day to the quarters appointed for young Bengal officers detained at Madras. These consisted of some tents pitched in an open sandy spot, within the fort, and presented few attractions; besides some small ones for dormitories, there was a larger one dignified with the appellation of the mess-tent. Here, at certain stated hours, a purveyor, denominated a butler, but as unlike "one of those gentlemanly personages so called at home as can well be imagined, placed breakfast, tiffin, and dinner, on table at so much ahead. For two or three days I revelled in the delights of sour Madeira, tough mutton, and skinny kid, with yams, and other miserable succedanea for European vegetables. An Egyptian plague of flies, and a burning sun beating through the single cloth of the tent, made up the sum of the agreeables to which we were subjected. My faith in the "luxuries of the East" had received a severe shock, and I was fast tending to downright infidelity on that head, when a big-whiskered fellow, with turban, badge, and silver stick, put a billet into my hand, which was the means of soon restoring me to the pale of orthodoxy. It was from an eccentric baronet, to whom I had brought letters and a parcel from his daughter in England, and ran thus:

"Col. Sir Jeremy Skeggs presents his compliments to Mr. Gernon, and thanks him for the care he has taken of the letters, &c., from his daughter. Mrs. Hearty, Sir J. Skeggs sister, will be happy to see Mr. G., and will send a palankeen for him."

I packed up my all (an operation soon effected), got into an elegant palankeen, which made its appearance shortly after the note, and escorted by a body of silver-stick men (for Mr. Hearty was "a man in authority"), I bade adieu to the tents, and leaving Grundy and some other cadets, though with a strong commiserative feeling, to struggle with the discomforts I have mentioned, was conveyed at a slapping pace to my host's garden residence, on the Mount Road. This was a flat roofed building, in the peculiar style of the country, of two stories—a large portico occupying nearly the whole length of the front. It was approached by a long avenue of parkinsonias, and surrounded, and partly obscured, by rich masses of tropical foliage, in which the bright green of the plantain contrasted pleasingly with the darker hues of the mango and the jack. Beyond the house stretched a pleasant domain, slightly undulating, dotted with clumps, and intersected by rows of cocoa-nut trees. Here it constituted one of my chief pleasures to saunter, to chase the little striped squirrels up the trees, or to watch the almost as agile ascent of the toddyman, as he mounted by a most simple contrivance the tall and branchless stems to procure the exhilarating juice; or to pelt the paroquets, as they clung screaming to the pendent leaves. To possess a parrot of my own, in England, had long constituted one of the unattainable objects of my juvenile ambition. I had longed so much for it, that an inordinate idea of the value of parrots had clung to me ever since. To see them, therefore, by dozens, in their wild state, was like in some measure spreading out before me the treasures of Golconda.

Mr. Hearty met me at the entrance, shook me very cordially by the hand, and taking me into the apartment where his wife and several other ladies were sitting, he presented me to the former, by whom I was very graciously received.

"Mr. Gernon, my love," said he, "whom your brother, Sir Jeremy, has been so kind as to introduce to us."

"We are very glad indeed to see you," said the lady, rising and taking my hand, "and hope you will make this house your home whilst the ship remains." I profoundly bowed my thanks.

"Mr. Hearty, my dear, will you shew Mr. Gernon his room—he may wish to arrange his things—and then bring him back to us?"

This was cordial and gratifying. I am apt to generalize from a few striking particulars. So I set the Madrassees down at once as polished and hospitable in the extreme—a perfectly correct inference, I believe, however precipitately formed by me on that occasion. Mr. Hearty was a fine, erect, fresh old gentleman, of aristocratic mien and peculiarly pleasing address. His manners, indeed, were quite of what is termed the old school, dignified and polished, but withal a little formal; far superior, however, to modern *brusquerie*, and that selfishness of purpose which, too often disdaining disguise, sets at nought the "small courtesies" which so greatly sweeten existence. His wife, much his junior, was a handsome woman of eight-and-twenty, gay and lively, and apparently much attached to her lord, in spite of the disparity of their years. He, in fact, was one of those rarely-seen well-preserved old men, of whom a young woman might be both proud and fond. My host lived in the good old style of Indian hospitality, of which absence of unnecessary restraint, abundance of good cheer, and the most unaffected and cordial welcome, constituted the essential elements.

In India, from various causes, perhaps sufficiently obvious, the English heart, naturally generous and kind, has or had full room for expansion; and the "luxury of doing good," in the shape of assembling happy faces around the social board, can be enjoyed, without, as too frequently the case here, the concomitant dread of outrunning the constable, or trenching too deeply on the next day's quantum of hashed mutton. Certainly, our close packing in these densely populated lands may give us polish, but it rubs off much of the natural enamel of our virtues.

Mr. Hearty's house was quite Liberty Hall, in its fullest meaning. Each guest had his bedroom, where he could read, write, or doze; or if he preferred it, he could hunt squirrels, shoot with a rifle, as my friend, the Scotch cadet, and I did; sit with the ladies in the drawing room and play the flute, or enjoy any other equally intellectual amusement, between meals, at which the whole party, from various quarters, were wont to assemble, rubbing their hands, and greeting in that warm manner, which commonly results where people have been well employed in the interim, and not had too much of each other's company. Mr. Hearty's house was full of visitors from all points of the compass.

There was a captain of cavalry and lady, from Bangalore; a very dyspeptic-looking doctor from Vizagapatam; a missionary, bent on making the natives "all samo master's caste," through the medium of his proper vernacular; a strapping Scotch artillery cadet, before alluded to, some six feet two, and who was my particular friend and crony, with several others, birds of passage like myself. Amongst these, to my great delight and astonishment,

I found the lovely Miss Olivia and her sister. Now, then, reader, prepare yourself for one of the most soul-stirring and pathetic passages of these Memoirs. Shade of Petrarch, I invoke thee! spirit of Jean Jacques, impart thy aid, whilst in honest but tender guise I pour forth my "confessions." Yes, as an honest chronicler of events, I am bound to tell it—the candour of a griffin demands that it should out. I fell over head and ears in love—'twas a most violent attack I had, and I think I was full three months getting the better of it. It would be, however, highly derogatory to the dignity of that pleasing passion, were I to trail the account of its manifestations at the fag end of a chapter; I shall, therefore, reserve my confessions of the "soft impeachment," and my voyage to Calcutta, for the next.

CHAPTER V

"Peace be with the soul of that charitable and courteous author, who, for the common benefit of his fellow-authors, introduced the ingenious way of miscellaneous writing!" — so says the great Lord Shaftesbury; and I heartily respond to the sentiment, that mode admitting of those easy transitions from "grave to gay, from lively to severe," which so well agree with my discursive humour. Having thus premised, let me proceed with my story, which now begins to assume a graver aspect.

Love, that passion productive of so many pains and pleasures to mortals, the most easily, perhaps, awakened, and the most difficult to control, begins full early with some of us (idiosyncratically susceptible) to manifest its disturbing effects: the little volcano of the heart (to speak figuratively) throws out its transient and flickering flames long anterior to a grand eruption. Lord Byron's history exhibits a great and touching example of this; his early but unrequited attachment to the beautiful Miss Chaworth served undoubtedly, in after-life, to tinge his character with that sombre cast which has imparted itself to the splendid creations of his immortal genius. Like him (if I may dare include myself in the same category), when but nine or ten summers had passed over my head, I too had my "lady love," who, albeit no Mary Chaworth, was nevertheless a very pretty little blue-eyed girl, the daughter of our village doctor. I think I now behold her, in the eye of my remembrance, with her white muslin frock, long pink sash, and necklace of coral beads, her flaxen curls flying wildly in the breeze, or sporting in all conceivable lines of beauty over her alabaster neck and forehead. Full joyous was I when an invitation came for Master Frank Gernon and his brother Tom to drink tea at Dr. Anodyne's. How motherly and kind was good Mrs. Anodyne on these occasions! how truly liberal of her pound-cake and syllabub!

Dear woman! spite of thy many failings, which all "lean to virtue's side," in the sweet relations of mother, wife, sister, friend, thou art a being to be almost worshipped. 'Tis you who hold man's destinies in your hands. Harden your minds without the limits of blue-stockingism, as a counterpoise to the softness of your hearts; acquire independence of thought and moral courage, and you will yet convert the world into a paradise! The little bard of Twickenham has, on the whole, maligned you: mistaken the factitious for the original; the faults of education for the defects of nature; the belle of 1700 for the woman of all time—but was still right when he said,

> Courage with softness, modesty with pride,
> Fix'd principles—with fancy ever new;
> Shake all together, it produces—you.

Pretty Louisa! my first love, long since perhaps the mother of a tribe of little rustics; or sleeping, perchance, soundly in your own village churchyard! like a fairy vision, you sometimes visit me in my dreams, or, when quitting for a season the stern, hard realities which environ my manhood, I lose myself in the sweet remembrances of boyhood's days! Well, this was my first grand love affair; now for my next, to which I deem it a fitting preliminary. Griffins, look to your hearts, for you will have some tough assaults made upon that susceptible organ on the other side of the Cape, where (owing, I am told, to the high range of the thermometer) it becomes morbidly sensitive. Take care, too, you do not have to sing, with a rather lachrymose twist of the facial muscles, "Dark is my doom!" or, led on by your sensibilities within the toils of a premature matrimonial union, you have not to inscribe over your domicile, "*spes et fortuna valete!*"

The party at Mr. Hearty's, or some of them, rode out every evening in the carriage, and I generally, like a gallant griffin, took up a position by the steps, for the purpose of handing them in—that is, the female portion. The precise amount of pressure which a young lady of sixteen (not stone, but years, be pleased to understand, for it makes a material difference) must impart to a young gentleman's hand, when he tenders his services on occasions of this nature, in order to be in love with him, is a very nice and curious question in "Amorics" (I take credit for the invention of that scientific term). In estimating it, however, so many things may affect the accuracy of a judgment, that it is perhaps undesirable to rely on deductions therefrom, either one way or the other, as a secure basis for ulterior proceedings. Touching the case of the charming Olivia and myself, though there was certainly evidence of the *high-pressure* system, I might long have felt at a loss to decide on the real state of her feelings, had not my hand on these occasions been accepted with a tell-tale blush, and a sweet and encouraging smile, that spoke volumes. Let me not be accused of vanity, if I say, then, that the evidence of my having made an impression on the young and susceptible heart of Olivia Jenkins was too decided to be mistaken. I felt that I was a favourite, and I burned with all the ardour of a griffin to declare that the "*sentiment si doux*" was reciprocal. The wished-for occasion was not long in presenting itself.

One evening, Olivia and some of the party remained at home, the carriage being fully occupied without them. Off drove Mr. and Mrs. Hearty, and a whole posse of friends and visitors, to take their usual round by Chepauk and the Fort; kissing hands to Olivia and one or two others, who stood on the terrace to see them depart. They were no sooner gone than I proceeded to enjoy my accustomed saunter in the coco-nut grove, at the back of the house. There was a delicious tranquillity in the hour which produced a soothing effect on my feelings. The sun had just dipped his broad orb in the ocean, and his parting beams suffused with a ruddy warmth the truly Oriental scene around. Flocks of paroquets, screaming with delight, were wheeling homewards their rapid flight; the creak of the well-wheel, an Indian rural sound, came wafted from distant fields, and the ring-doves were uttering their plaintive cooings from amidst the shady bowers of the neighbouring garden—

The air, a chartered libertine, was still.

I walked and mused, gazing around on the animated scenes of nature, which always delight me, when suddenly one of the most charming of all her works, a beautiful girl, appeared before me. It was Olivia, who met me (undesignedly of course) at a turn of the avenue. She appeared absorbed in a book, which, on hearing my steps, she suddenly closed, and with a blush, which caused the eloquent blood to mount responsive in my cheeks, she exclaimed.

"Oh, Mr. Gernon, is this you? Your servant, sir! (courtesying half-coquettishly); who would have expected to meet you here all alone, and so solemnly musing?"

"Is there any thing more extraordinary in it, Miss Olivia," said I, "than to find you also alone, and enjoying your intellectual repast, 'under the shade of melancholy boughs?' The Chinese, I believe, think that human hearts are united from birth by unseen silken cords, which contracting slowly but surely, bring them together at last. What think you, Olivia?" I continued (we grow familiar generally on the eve of a declaration), "may not some such invisible means of attraction have brought us together at this moment?"

Olivia looked down, her pretty little foot being busily engaged in investigating the character of a pebble, or something of the sort, that lay on the walk, and indistinctly replied, that she had really never much considered such weighty and mysterious subjects, but that it might be even so. Encouraged by this reply, yet trembling at the thought of my own audacity (bullets whizzing past me since have not produced half the trepidation), I placed myself near her, and gently taking the little, soft, white hand which listlessly, but invitingly, hung by her side, I said (I was sorely puzzled what to say),

"I—I—was delighted, dear Olivia, to find you a visitor here on my arrival the other day."

"Were you, Mr. Gernon," said the lively girl, turning upon me her soft blue eyes, in a manner which brought on a fresh attack of *delirium tremens*; "'delighted' is a strong term, but Mr. Gernon, I know, is rather fond of such, little heeding their full import."

"Strong!" I replied, instantly falling into heroics; "it but feebly expresses the pleasure I feel on seeing you. Oh, dearest Olivia," I continued, all the barriers of reserve giving way at once before the high tide of my feelings, "it is in vain longer to dissemble" (here I gently passed my other unoccupied arm round her slender waist); "I love you with the fondest affection. Deign to say that I possess an interest in your heart."

A slight and almost imperceptible increase of pressure from the little hand locked in mine, and a timid look from the generally lively but now subdued and abashed girl, was the silent but expressive answer I received. It was enough, for a griff, at least. I drew her closer to my side—she slowly averted her head; mine followed its movement. The vertebral column had reached its rotary limit—so that there was a sort of surrender at discretion—and I imprinted a long and fervent kiss on the soft and downy cheek of Olivia. Oh, blissful climax of a thousand sweet emotions; too exquisite to endure, too precious for fate to accord more than once in an existence—the first innocent kiss of requited affection—how can I ever forget ye?

> Let raptured fancy on that moment dwell,
>
> When my fond vows in trembling accents fell;
>
> When love acknowledged woke the trembling sigh,
>
> Swelled my fond breast and filled the melting eye.

Yes, surely, "love is heaven, and heaven is love," as has been said and sung any time for the last three thousand years; and Mahomed showed himself deeply read in the human heart, when he made the chief delight of his paradise to consist in it; not, I suspect, as is generally imagined, the passion in its purely gross acceptation, but that elevating and refining sentiment which beautifully attunes all our noblest emotions; which, when it swells the heart, causes it to overflow, like a mantling fountain, to refresh and fertilize all around. No, I shall never forget the thrill of delight with which I committed that daring act of petty larceny.

"Yes," I continued, "dearest Olivia, I have long loved you. I loved you from the first, and would fain indulge a faint hope" (this was hypocritical, for I was quite sure of it) "that I am not wholly indifferent to you."

The deepest blush overspread Olivia's neck and face; she was summoning all her maidenly resolution for an avowal: "Dear Mr. Gernon," she said, "believe me, —"

"Stope him! stope him, Gernon," roared a stentorian voice at this moment; "cut the deevil off fra' the tree!"

It was that confounded Patagonian Scotch cadet, in full cry after a squirrel, which, poor little creature, in an agony of fear, was making for a tree near to which we stood. "As you were," never brought a recruit quicker into his prior position, than did this unseasonable interruption restore me to mine. Olivia hastily resumed her studies and her walk, whilst I, to prevent suspicion, and consequent banter, joined in the chevy to intercept the squirrel, secretly anathematizing Sandy McGrigor, whom I wished, with all my heart, in the bowels of Ben Lomond.

Reader, you may be curious to know whether Olivia Jenkins became in due time Mrs. Gernon. Ah, no! Ours was one of those juvenile passions destined to be nipped in the bud; one of those painted baubles, swelled by the breath of young desire, which float for a brief space on the summer breeze, then burst and disappear: or a perennial plant, whose beautiful maturity passes rapidly to decay.

Our destinies pointed different ways. Too much calculation was fatal to her happiness; too little has been, perhaps, as detrimental to mine. Years on years rolled on, chequered by many strange vicissitudes, when, in other scenes and under widely different circumstances, we met again: the flush of youth had long departed from her cheeks—the once laughing eyes were brilliant no more—and

> The widow's sombre cap concealed
>
> Her once luxuriant hair.

"Do you remember," said I, adverting to old times, "our meeting in the coco-nut grove at Madras?"

"Ah!" she replied, with a sigh, "I do indeed; but say no more of it; a recurrence to the sunshiny days of my youth always makes me sad: let us speak of something else—the recent, the present, the future."

> There was one little thing dey do call de mosquito,
>
> He bitee de blackmans, he no let him sleep-o-
>
> Sing ting ring, ting ting ring ting, ting ring ting taro.

So then runs the negro's song; and unless all is illusion and delusion, as the Berkleyans hold, the "whitemans," as I can vouch from actual experience, are equally entitled to have their misfortunes as pathetically recorded. I believe, however, it would be as difficult to say anything entirely original about musquitoes as to discover a new pleasure, or the long sought desideratum of perpetual motion; nevertheless, my subject being India, it would not be *en régle* to pass them over altogether in silence; suffice it therefore to say, the first nights of my stay at Mr. Hearty's I was by a cruel oversight put into a bed without the usual appendage—a set of gauze curtains. The door of my apartment, which was on the ground floor, opened on the garden, and a well, a pool, and a dense mass of foliage, formed a splendid musquito-preserve, within a few yards of it. A couple of oil-lights, in wall-shades, burnt in the room; the doors were open, the night close and oppressive. It was truly "the genial hour for burning," though not exactly in Moore's sense of the passage; and then such a concerto!—"Quack! quack! quack!" said the *mezzo-soprano* voices of the little frogs—"croak! croak! croak!" responded in deep bass the huge Lablaches of the pool—"click! click!" went the lizards—"ghur! ghur!" the musk-rat, as he ricketed round the room, emitting his offensive odour; whilst

Countless fire-flies, gems of light,

Bright jewels of the tropic night,

spangled the trees in all directions. The idea of Aladdin's garden, to which his *soi-disant* uncle introduced him, was presenting itself to my mind, when the nip of a musquito recalled me from the fanciful to the consideration of painful realities. The sultry heat of an Indian night in the rains is sometimes terrific: not a breath moving; but, to make up for it, a universal stir of reptile and insect life, with a croak, hum, hiss, and buzz, perfectly astounding. What a prize for the musquitoes was I—a fine, fresh, ruddy griffin, full of wholesome blood, the result of sea-breezes and healthy chylification! and, in good sooth, they did fall foul of me with the appetite of gluttons. Sleep! bless your dear, simple heart, the thing was about as possible as for St. Lawrence to have reposed on his gridiron. I tingled from top to toe with an exquisite tingling. In vain I scratched—in vain I tossed— in vain I rolled myself up like a corpse in a winding-sheet. Nought would do; so out I jumped, half phrenzied, and dipping my hand in the oil glasses of the lamps, I rubbed their unctuous contents over my body, to deaden the intolerable itching—an effect which in some degree it produced. Thus I spent the long hours of the sultry night; towards morning, the musquitoes being gorged, tortured into insensibility, and nature fairly worn out, I procured a little rest.

At breakfast I made my appearance on two consecutive mornings a ludicrous figure, the object at once of pity and amusement: eyes bunged up, lips swelled, and cheeks puffed out, like bully *Ajax* in *Homer Travestie*, all of which, to a young man of decent exterior, and who, in those days, rather valued himself on his appearance, was exceedingly annoying. Mrs. Hearty, though with a look in which the comic and the tragic struggled for the mastery, now took compassion on me, expressed great regret for the oversight, and furnished my bed with a set of musquito-curtains. "Whine away, you rascals," said I then to the musquitoes, exultingly; "blow your penny trumpets, you everlasting vagabonds! you have had your last meal on me, rest assured." What glorious sleep I had after that!

After a fortnight's stay at Madras, and a vain search for Ramee Sawmee Dabash, who, having some linen of mine to get washed, and a small balance of money to account for, thought it "too much trouble" to make his appearance, I bid adieu to my hospitable friends, reembarked on board the *Rottenbeam Castle*, and set sail for Bengal. Our society, officers and passengers, met again with renewed pleasure, temporary separation being a great enlivener of the kindly feelings, which, like everything else, require tact and management to keep them in a state of vigour. Each, during his sojourn on shore, appeared to have renovated his stock of ideas, and to have picked up something congenial to his peculiar humour. The colonel had met with several old friends, and matters to be told, "wondrous and strange," and quite out of the common, followed as a natural consequence. Grinnerson had had some "rare larks and sprees" ashore, and been "coming the old soldier" over some young hands at the Navy Tavern. Miss Dobbikins criticised rather severely (as her Bath experiences gave her every right to do) the *tournure* of the Madras belles, whom she had seen at balls and *conversazione*. Capt. Marpeet, who had been at sundry drills and reviews, favoured us with elaborate discussions on the military performances of the *Mulls*,[4] which he considered very inferior to those of the *Qui hyes*, by whom, to borrow his own nervous and expressive phraseology, "they were beaten by chalks." Even the usually taciturn Grundy became eloquent, when he spoke of the *luxuries* of the tents, and his sufferings from the musquitoes; and as for myself, being of an artistical turn, I enlarged principally on the interesting character of Oriental scenery, but omitting, of course, some of the peculiar attractions of the "coco-nut grove."

CHAPTER VI

On leaving the roads of Madras, we bent our course to the eastward. For a day or two we had light winds and agreeable weather, and our gallant vessel glided on, under a cloud of snowy canvas, like some stainless swan before the dimpling breezes of a mountain tarn, little heeding the coming danger, which was to lay all her bravery low. Soon, however, a (by me) never-to-be-forgotten tornado, which I shall attempt to describe, burst in upon us in all its fury.

The first indication we had of the coming storm (being still but a short distance from Madras) was on the morning of the third day, when a few wild clouds began to scatter themselves over the face of the hitherto spotless sky. The breeze freshened, and an occasional squall made the good ship *salaam* deeply to the waves. Captain McGuffin looked to windward, shook his head, and appeared grave. He now (for there was evidently mischief brewing) held a brief consultation with Gillans, the chief mate, and then immediately ordered the small sails to be taken in. At about 8 P.M. of the same day, the fore and main topsails, as I was told, were double-reefed, and the mainsail and maintopsail furled. The next morning, the breeze still continued strong, and the albatrosses and gannets, heralds of the storm, skimmed wildly over the yeasty waves. A heavy and a turbulent sea now got up, which broke over the ship, causing her to roll heavily, and admit much water.

"We're in for it, I'm afraid," said Grinnerson to the first mate, "and no mistake."

"You may say that, when you write home to your friends," growled forth that sententious worthy; "I'd rather be looking at the end than the beginning of it, I can tell you."

Scarcely were the words out of Gillan's mouth, when a screeching blast flew through the shrouds and ratlines; "bang!" went one of the sails, with the report of a six-pounder, and the *Rottenbeam Castle* took a deep and fearful heel to leeward.

"How's her head now?" said Gillans, with energy, starting up, to the man at the wheel.

"North-east, and by east, sir," was the quick reply.

"All hands aloft," roared the mate, "to take in mainsail;" and away went the tars swarming up the rigging, poor little shivering middies and all, and the perilous duty was soon performed, the sail being set to steady her. Towards noon, the wind and sea increased, and the weather wore a still more threatening appearance.

There are few situations which more thoroughly call forth all the noble energies and resources of man's mind, than the working of a vessel in a tempest, or the ordering of troops in the heat of a battle. A cool head, and nerves as steady as a rock, are essentially necessary in both. McGuffin was quite a Wellington in his way; and on the present occasion, I felt a pride in my countrymen, as I marked him, the officers, and men, calmly preparing, as it were, move by move, for the coming onset of the gale.

"Down royal-masts and top gallant yards," shouted the iron-tongued Gillans; and down, spite of the flapping of canvas and banging of blocks and ropes, they came in a trice. This precautionary measure was not taken a whit too soon, for the wind rapidly increased to a gale, and the ship rolled heavily, from the violence and irregularity of the sea. At this moment, Grundy, evidently very uneasy, and in violation of all nautical decorum, began to whistle, less, probably, from want of thought, than with a view to drown it. This brought the first mate upon him immediately.

"Halloa, sir," said he, "haven't we got wind enough, but you must be whistling for more? Drop that music, if you please."

Grundy incontinently held his peace. The dismayed passengers now sought shelter in their cabins, with the exception of a few well-muffled storm amateurs, who clung about the cuddy doors, casting furtive glances aloft at the wild-driving scud, and listening to the manly voices of the officers, and seamen as heard above the roaring of the gale. A rough cradle, and a dismal lullaby, indeed, was this, for myself and the other nautical *infants* on board.

At about 11 o'clock the wind increased; the decks were almost continually submerged, the fore and maintopsails were furled, and soon after the ship was wore, the sea running mountains high, under the fore and maintop-mast stay-sail. The captain, having ordered the foresail to be hauled up, the ship, in nautical language, was hove-to, the gale blowing with uncommon fury. The sky now began to assume a most threatening and lurid aspect. Just such a murky gloom surrounded us as that in which Satan is finely described by Milton; when "aloft incumbent on the dusky air," he hovered over that "ever-burning" region, which his "unblest feet" were about to tread. The barometer fell rapidly, and our courage, that is, of us landsmen, in a proportionate ratio, whilst the vast and angry billows, like wild and maned steeds above prostrate foes, swept in rapid succession over our quivering bark. With what intense longing to be there did I now think of the snug green parlour and blazing sea-coal fire at home! Ah! thought I, with a sigh, how true it is, "we never know the value of a friend till we lose him!"

An attempt to take in, and house, the top gallant masts, failed, owing to the violent rolling of the ship; but every thing practicable was effected by our indefatigable crew, although reduced by the recent impressment, to secure the masts from the evidently increasing hurricane. The hatches were battened down, and all made snug for the approaching "tug of war." All was now breathless suspense and a stern gravity sat on the boldest countenance, when a sudden and tremendous blast threw the ship on her beam-ends, and, with a terrific crash, the mainmast went by the board, carrying with it, in its fall, the mizen-yard, poop, sky-lights, hen-coops, larboard quarter gallery, and three of our seamen. Here was "confusion worse confounded"—passengers and servants making their escape from beneath the wreck—sailors shouting, tugging, and hauling—a chaos of disasters enough to daunt, one would suppose, the stoutest heart; but he little understands the stuff of which English seamen are composed, who thinks there was any quailing or relaxation of energy here. Sudden as the disaster were the efforts made to repair it. The voice of the officer was instantly heard above the storm, giving directions, and the active crew immediately at work, with their axes, cutting the shrouds and ropes, for the purpose of detaching the wreck of the mast from the vessel, which, beating furiously against the bottom and sides, seemed to threaten her with instant destruction.

With infinite difficulty, this operation was at last effected, and the short but delusive "pleasures of hope" once more dawned upon us. On getting clear of the wreck, the vessel partially righted, the hurricane raging with awful violence, the sea running right over her, and sweeping, with resistless force, every opposing article from the deck. Our only remaining sail, the foresail, was now, with much difficulty, taken in, and the vessel scudded under bare poles. Throughout the remainder of the day, the hurricane raged with unabated fury: the ship rolled gunwales under, and the water poured in through the aperture caused by the broken mast. Never can I forget the sounds and scenes below—the groaning of the timbers, the labouring and lurching of the ship, like the throes and struggles of a dying man; the moans and cries of the women—stores, cargo, cabin, bulk-heads, baggage, and a cannon or two, all loose and adrift, and dashing with frightful violence from side to side, as if animated by some maddening spirit of destruction.

"Colonel," said Marpeet rather archly:—who, in or out of season, loved a joke—to the ex-resident, clinging on close to me, his teeth chattering like a pair of castanets; "Colonel, *you*, I take it, have never seen anything to beat this?"

"Eh! why—no! not exactly," said the colonel, who, having the fear of Davy's Locker before his eyes, seemed rather loath to indulge in anything apocryphal.

But the climax was yet to come. About 8 P.M. the wind suddenly shifted to an opposite quarter, and blew, if possible, with greater fury. My feelings, however, exhausted by excitement, now sank into that state of apathetic quiescence which disarms death of all its terrors; when, in fact, we can feel no more, but patiently await the worst. Nature thus wisely, at a certain point, always brings insensibility to our relief—the last sigh of departing hope gives birth to resignation. About one o'clock the next day a tremendous sea broke on board, burst open and destroyed the remainder of the poop-cabins and cuddy, and swept chairs, tables, medicine-chests, and every movable they contained, overboard, filling the lower deck with water; but providentially no more lives were lost. The hurricane still raging, clouds and sea commingled; the foremast snapped short off by the deck, and falling athwart the bows, carried with it the jib-boom, leaving the battered hulk, with one mutilated mast, to contend alone with the fury of the elements. A wave, moreover, at this instant, dashed one of our boats to splinters, and nearly made a wreck of another. Thus were the grounds of hope giving way, like a quicksand, under our feet. To add to the intensity of our distress, a pitchy darkness enveloped us when the foremast fell overboard, and the sea breaking, in one continued mighty volume, over the vessel, none could go forward to cut it away; perilous to our safety as was its continuing attached to the bows. Oh! for the genius of a Falconer, that I might adequately depict the horrors of the scene at this moment! Ye "fat and greasy citizens," ye grumbling John Bulls of every grade, who own the great oracle of retrenchment as your leader, little need ye grudge the soldier or sailor his hard-earned pittance, the price of perils such as these. An inky night, whose gloom was, ever and anon, pierced by a long, blue, zigzag flash of lightning, like one of those wrath-directed bolts of heaven, which Martin, with such fine effect, introduces into his pictures—the roar of elements—the crippled and lumbered vessel, rolling and plunging like a maddened steed, encumbered with the wreck of a shattered vehicle, the few dim lanterns, buttoned up, and hugged to the bosoms of the quarter-masters, the dripping, comfortless, but uncomplaining tars; the captain and his officers, muffled in fear-noughts, and the group, of which I formed one, clinging on here and there, in order to see the worst of what we had to encounter, formed a portion of the picture. Then the stifled sobs, and shrieks and prayers from the women below, filling, like the voices of wailing spirits, the momentary lullings of the gale; the violent beatings of the fallen mast, like a catapult, against the bows, felt through the whole vessel, and filling, even the stout hearts of the captain and his crew with well-founded dismay at each successive thump, formed some of its alarming accompaniments.

"Gillans, we maun get clear of that mast, or 'twill be the ruin of us all," shouted the captain through his trumpet.

Gillans paused a moment: "It must be done, sir," said he; "but how to get to her head through this mountain sea I hardly know."

"I'll try it," said the gallant Grinnerson—the wag now transformed into the hero—"happen what may."

Saying this, he seized an axe, and accompanied by a part of the crew, dashed forward, holding by the shattered bulwarks as they advanced. A few seconds of breathless suspense now elapsed, when a long dazzling flash illumined the vessel; down she lay, deep in the trough of the sea, whilst, by its light, a mountain wave appeared hanging over her, like a spirit of evil, and about to break by its own enormous weight. It broke—down it came, with a stunning smash, on the devoted vessel, taking her on the forecastle and midships, sparkling and fizzing in the lurid glare of the lengthened flash. The ship dived down, as if about to be engulphed. "We're gone!" burst forth from many a voice. Slowly, however, she rose again from the effects of the stunning blow, and another flash exhibited a group of sailors on the forecastle, actively cutting and hacking away at the ropes and shrouds. In a few seconds the vessel seemed eased; the mast had been cut away, and shortly after, the heroic Grinnerson, streaming with sea-water, was amongst us. He had escaped, though two of the gallant fellows who had accompanied him had been swept away to a watery grave.

"The Lord be thankt! ye ha'e done weel, sir," said McGuffin, wringing the second mate's hand in his iron gripe; "ye ha'e saved the ship."

The ship was now relieved, and the wind evidently falling, hope revived. I descended below, and throwing myself into my cot, slept, spite of the uproar, soundly till morning.

On rising, I found the wind had greatly subsided; but a heavy sea still remained, in which our mutilated vessel rolled and tumbled like a porpoise. All danger, however, was past, and the sea was rapidly going down. Damages were partially repaired. The crew and passengers refreshed themselves, and deep and heartfelt congratulations were exchanged. Captain McGuffin, towards evening, the vessel being steadier, assembled the crew on deck, and offered up thanksgivings to Him who "stilleth the raging of the storm," for our happy preservation. It was an impressive sight to behold the weather beaten tars, their hats reverentially doffed, ranged along the deck, their lately excited energies sunk into the calm of a thoughtful and devotional demeanour; the pale and jaded passengers, seated abaft, many an eye gratefully upturned; the wild sea and battered hull; and in the centre, bare-headed and erect, the tall and brawny, yet simple-hearted man, our commander, his prayer-book resting on the capstan, his left hand on the leaves, and his right stretched out, as, with a fervour which nothing but his religious feeling could have excited in him, he read firmly, in his broad but nervous Scotch accents, the form of thanksgiving due to Him who had succoured us in our danger, and "with whom are the issues of life and death."

To prove a particular providence is a hard and baffling task; but we can never err—or if we do it is on the right side—when we pour out our hearts in gratitude to God, for every blessing or deliverance, come to us by what concurrence of causes it may.

By an observation we now found we were off the Tenasserim coast. The ship's head was consequently put to the northward, and on we sailed towards our destination. At length, on a fine blowing day in the S. W. monsoon, the good ship the *Rottenbeam Castle*, after a five months' voyage, entered on the turbid waters of the Sand Heads, renowned for sharks, shipwrecks, and the intricacy of its navigation, dashing on in good style, despite of the battering of the late gale, under all the sail she could carry on the foremast, and two spars rigged out as substitutes for those we had lost. All eyes were, at this time, anxiously on the look-out for the pilot. At length a sail was visible on the horizon, and ere long, a rakish little brig, with the Company's Yankee-looking pilot-colours flying from the peak, came bowling down, and was pronounced *nem. con.* to be (strange misnomer) the pilot schooner. Not a moment elapsed ere a boat, manned by lascars, put off from her, and in a few minutes more, the rattle of oars and the boatswain's whistle announced its arrival alongside. The pilot, accompanied by a bronzed stripling of fifteen, in a seaman's round jacket and large straw hat, and whose business was to cast the lead, now mounted the side, and as he stepped on deck, touched his hat in a consequential sort of manner, which plainly indicated that pilots were no small men, in these latitudes. Mr. Merryweather, for so I believe he was called, was one of a numerous class, variously subdivided, called the pilot-service, whose extreme utility none can question who studies a chart of the Sand Heads, and the embouchure of the Ganges. The seniors, or branch-pilots, are, some of them, excellent old fellows, have their vessels in high order, give capital *feeds* out of silver plate, and have generally some valetudinarian from Calcutta on board, invigorating the springs of existence by copious indraughts of the sea-breeze. Mr. Merryweather had quite the cut of an original, and I cannot, therefore, resist the inclination I feel to present the reader with a sketch of him. He was a sturdy, square-built man, of about forty, of whose jolly countenance it might be truly said, and in the language of the Latin grammar, "*qui color albus erat, nunc est contrarius albo.*" It presented, at one view, one of the most singular compounds of brown, brickdust, and purple I ever beheld; clearly indicating that it had long been the scene of a fierce struggle for the ascendency between the skyey influences of the Sand Heads, on the one hand, from without, and those of aqua vitæ, from within. Sun and wind, on the whole seemed to have had the best of it; but the forces of aqua vitæ had made a most determined stand on that elevated position, the nose, from which there appeared little chance of their being dislodged. Our sturdy Palinurus was attired in a camlet coat, with the uniform lion button, the colour whereof, once blue, now exhibited in its latter days, like a dying dolphin, a variety of interesting shades; a pair of tight nankeens, extending about half-way down the calf, encased his lower extremities, very fully exhibiting their sturdy and unsymmetrical proportions, in which the line of beauty, admitting that to be a curve, had by Dame Nature been most capriciously applied. He would have met with a distinguished reception in Laputa, being built on strictly mathematical principles; for one leg exhibited the segment of a circle, the other something very like an obtuse angle. In a sinewy and weather beaten hand, "spotted like the toad," he grasped a huge telescope, covered with rusty green baize, the length of which was nearly "the standard of a man;" whilst a large white hat, which bore nearly the same proportion to his size that a mushroom does to its stalk, completed a manly, but not very inviting, portrait.

"Mr. Merryweather, ma gude friend, I'm glad to see ye luking sae weel," exclaimed our Scotch commander, who, it appeared, was an old acquaintance of the pilot's. "Why, somebody telt me at Madras, that ye'ed been near deeing sin' we were here last."

"Ay, ay, they told you right, captain; I had a very tightish touch of the *mollera corbus,* or whatever 'tis called, after you left us. Yes, I was within a pint of getting a birth in Padree Shepherd's godown; howsomever, the old 'ooman and Dr. Dusgooly brought my head round to the wind somehow, and now I'm as fresh as a lark, as a man might say in a manner, and ready for a tumbler of your toddy, captain, with as little daylight in it as you please,—ha, ha, ha!"

Thus he ran on for some time, and then in a similar style, gave us the latest news of the presidency, which, to the best of my recollection, consisted of a mutiny, death of a puisne judge, and a talked-of-war with Nundy Row Bickermajeet, a potentate of whom none of us had heard before.

The captain now duly deposed, Mr. Merryweather took charge of the vessel, and marched up and down the deck with all the confidence of a small man invested with "a little brief authority," now peering under the sail, and conning the bearings of the buoys, which here and there rode gallantly in the channel, like the huge floats of some giant "bobbing for whale;" anon asking briskly the man at the wheel how her head was, or thundering out some peremptory order for trimming or shortening the sail. Thus we glided on through the turbid channel, whilst strong ripples or long lines of surf, on either hand, with here and there the slanting masts of a stranded vessel, indicated the perilous nature of the navigation. At last we caught a glimpse of a small island, but recently emerged from the waves, being like many others at the mouths of great rivers, of rapid diluvial formation, and immediately after, the low, marshy and jungle-covered shores of Saugor Island broke in sight.

To those whose Oriental imaginings have led them to expect in the first view of Indian land some lovely scene of groves, temples, and clustering palm-trees, the sight of the long low line of dismal sunderbund and swamp must not be a little disappointing. Saugor, however, Bengal tigers, and the fate of young Munro, are associated subjects, naturally blended with our earliest recollections. Full oft in my boyish days had I gazed on a picture representing the monster springing open-mouthed on his victim, and wondered if it would ever be my lot to visit a country where pic-nics were disturbed by such ferocious intruders. Viewed, then, as the head-quarters of the tigers, and the scene of this memorable exploit of one of their body, and also as the outpost of our destination, I deemed Saugor a sort of classic ground, and gazed upon it with a proportionate interest. Many an eye, too, besides my own, was bent towards the island, which wore a most sombre and miserable aspect.

Thinking Mr. Merryweather a person likely to be well informed on the subject, I ventured to ask him, civilly, if tigers were as numerous on the island as in young Mr. Munro's time. I at the same time solicited the loan of his telescope, thinking, peradventure, I might by its aid descry a royal Bengal tiger, in full regalia, enjoying his evening perambulation on the beach. The pilot stared at me, with as much astonishment as the Brobdingnag did at the Splacknuck, when he heard him talk, or Mr. Bumble, in Dickens' admirable novel, when the unfortunate Oliver asked for more soup; but soon settled it in his mind that I was an arrant griffin, and that it was not worth his while to be particularly civil to me.

"Tigers!" he grunted out; "Ay, ay, there's plenty o' them, I dare say; but I've something else besides tigers to think about, young gentleman; and you mustn't talk to me d'ye see, when I'm engaged with a wessel. As for the glass, it's in hand, and you'd better ask some one else to lend you one."

To borrow the language of the fancy, I was regularly floored by this rebuff, and incontinently held my peace, determining to reserve my zoological inquiries for a fitter occasion and more communicative person; at the same time, lost in astonishment that a man could actually pass his life in sight of Saugor island, and yet feel no interest in royal Bengal tigers. The delusion is a common one, and not confined to griffins, which leads people to imagine that others must be interested in what they are full of themselves.

The wind now suddenly rose, and the sky, which had long been lowering, assumed an inky hue. Mr. Merryweather looked anxious and uneasy, and I heard him observe to the captain, that we were in for a north-wester, and that he feared it would overtake us before we reached the anchorage at Kedgeree. What a north-wester was I did not exactly know, but the precautionary measures taken of diminishing the sail, closing hatches and scuttles, &c., and the appearance of the heavens, left me no room to doubt that it was one of the various denominations of the hurricane family.

Mr. Cadet Francis Gernon, anxious to discover a
Royal Bengal Tiger, falls in with a Bear

The scene at this moment, to one unacquainted with these tropical visitants, though rather alarming, was singularly wild and magnificent. All around, to the verge of the horizon, the sky was of the deepest indigo hue, whilst dark masses of rolling clouds, like hostile squadrons, were slowly marshalling over head to the thunder's deep rumble and the lightning's flash, which shot like the gleaming steel of advancing combatants across the dun fields of death. From the setting sun, a few long rays, like rods of gold, shot through openings of the clouds, streaming brightly over sea and land, bringing forth the lustrous green of the mangroves, and touching, as with a dazzling pencil of light, the distant sail, or milk-white seabird's wing.

At length, the sough of the coming tempest was heard mournfully sweeping through the shrouds, and a few heavy drops fell on the deck. The ladies' scarves and shawls began to flutter, and one two hats were whisked overboard, on a visit to the sharks. This was a sufficient hint for the majority of the idlers, and they forthwith dived below. I lingered awhile, and casting my eyes over the stem at this moment, beheld the storm driving towards us—spray, screaming gulls, and tumbling porpoises heralding its approach. In a moment it was upon us. Sheets and floods of driving rain burst on the ship, as on she hissed through the frying waters. Buoy after buoy, however, was safely passed, though it was once or twice "touch and go" with us; and ere long, to the infinite joy of all on board, we dropped anchor in safety off Kedgeree.

Never did I listen to more pleasant music than the rattle of the chain-cable, as it brought us up safe and sound, or rather unsound, in this harbour of refuge. Here, in the mouth of the Hooghly river, was comparative calm and tranquillity, and as we cast our eyes seaward, and saw the dark brown turbulent sea (for here it is not green) heaving and tossing, with the surrounding tempestuous sky, and night closing in, and contrasted our position with that of several far-off vessels, some of them hull-down, struggling under a press of canvas to reach the safe berth we had gained, before night and the falling tide might leave them "outside," environed by perils, we could not help indulging in very agreeable self-congratulations. 'Tis a sad reflection that our joys should often derive so much of their intensity from the foil of others' misfortunes; but, alas! so it is.

Here a fresh supply of fruit, and vegetables, and fish, from the shore; a batch of Calcutta papers; and sundry other little matters, made things very pleasant. All were "alive" and cheerful, and at ten o'clock I turned in and rose in the morning like "a giant refreshed," full of agreeable anticipations of the scenes on which I was about to enter.

CHAPTER VII

The morning after our arrival at Kedgeree I arose early, and, on coming on deck, found the weather perfectly calm, and presenting a striking contrast to its appearance on the previous day. A burning Bengal sun, however, shone around in all its glory, and was reflected with painful and dazzling brightness from the now unruffled surface of the Hooghly. Boats, to me of singularly novel and picturesque forms—some thatched, others open, and all with long galley-like prows and sterns—were moving here and there, mingled with market-boats, laden with fruit and vegetables, and light and graceful dingies, or fishing-canoes, floating down with their outspread nets and dusky crews on the gentle undulations of the falling tide. Near us, ships of various descriptions were riding at anchor, from the stately Indiaman of those days, with her double tier of ports, and looking like a seventy-four, to the Arab grab and country-coaster.

This was a day of considerable bustle and excitement. The passengers were looking up their baggage, getting out their letters, or despatching special messengers to their friends in Calcutta. Boats from the presidency were continually arriving alongside, freighted principally with baboos or circars, good-looking fellows for the most part, with huge green or yellow curly-toed shoes, and flowing muslin robes, as light as the gossamer, and white as swans'-down. Some came to secure constituents; others were deputed by merchants or parties interested in the ship or passengers; and not a few keen-witted fellows, like my friend Ramee Sawmee Dabash, were on the look-out for "pigeons." With all these arrivals, our deck began to assume a very lively and animated appearance.

I could not help being forcibly struck with the marked dissimilarity between the two races, who, here respectively the subjects of a common power, and from the antipodes, were engaged in objects of mutual interest, or busy in the exchange of friendly greetings. There stood the sturdy Englishman, with his ruddy face, iron muscles, and broad shoulders, strong in his straightforward hyperborean honesty; before him, like some delicate spaniel, or Italian greyhound, coaxing a bluff old Jowler of a mastiff, were the wily Asiatics, chattering and salaaming, fearful to offend, their slender and supple limbs all in motion, and supplying by quickness and address the want of energy and boldness.

The family union, which had now for five months so pleasantly subsisted between our party on board, was about to be dissolved, and already were their thoughts and feelings on the wing, impatient for other scenes and objects. The cup of pleasure is seldom unalloyed, and with mine, at that moment, mingled a drop of bitterness, as I thought that an important scene of my life was about to close for ever, and that many of the actors in it, with whom I had so pleasantly "strutted my hour," I might never see again. To think that we are leaving even an inanimate object for ever is a painful thought, but it acquires almost a solemnity when man, "the mind, the music, breathing from his face," is the being we are now about to quit. Honest McGuffin, methought, have I heard your broad Scotch for the last time? Grinnerson, my merry wag, will you roast me no more? Gillans, bluntest of seamen, will thy hoarse voice, in the midnight watch, never again startle my ear, when through the shrouds (rudest of Æolians) the rough winds pipe their wild accompaniment? And, oh! Jemmy Ducks, thou Pariar of the *Rottenbeam Castle*, thou great conservator of chickens, shall I never again see thee scramble over the hen-coops, or be more enlivened with a pleasant vision of thy tarred and ragged breeks? *Sic transit gloria mundi!*

As a party of us, including the second mate, were chattering and laughing on the deck about noon, our attention was suddenly attracted to a handsome pinnace, with green sides and venetians, and of a light and beautiful rig, gliding down the river, with all sail loosened, which, however, the light winds had barely power to distend. As it approached, we observed an old gentleman, and a numerous group of attendants on the chut or roof. Marpeet immediately observed that we were about to be visited by one of the Calcutta big wigs; and Grinnerson, applying the glass to his eye, exclaimed, after a little reconnoitring and slapping his leg with delight,

"By the piper that played before Moses, if it isn't that old Tartar, General Capsicum; he'll keep us all alive if he comes on board."

The general was seated in an easy chair, smoking a magnificent hooka, the silver chains and other brilliant appendages of which were conspicuous even at a distance. Altogether, with his troop of attendants, he looked not a little like the chief of Loochoo, as depicted in Captain Hall's voyage to that interesting island. Of the liveried and whiskered group about him, one swung a huge crimson silk punkah, or fan, with a silver handle, the end of which rested on the deck; a second held an umbrella of the same colour over his head; two more worked chowries, or whisks, to keep off the flies; and behind his chair stood his pipeman, or hookhaburdar, a black-bearded fellow, with his arms folded, and looking as grave and solemn as a judge. At the back of all these again, and forming a sort of rear-guard, were a body of mace-bearers and silver-stick men, awaiting the slightest order of the chief.

Well, this is something like Eastern magnificence, indeed, thought I—*nil desperandum*—"Frank Gernon, hold up your head; you may be a nabob yet."

Upon the arrival of the pinnace within a very short distance of the ship, the old gentleman, assisted by his obsequious attendants, arose from his chair, and moving to the verge of the roof or poop, with a gait almost as unsteady as the toddle of an infant, gave us a full view of about as odd a figure as can well be imagined. In height, he was below the middle size, and as thin and shrivelled as an old baboon, to the physiognomy of which animal his own bore no inconsiderable resemblance; indeed, till I saw him, I never thought much of Lord Monboddo's theory. He wore a red camlet raggie, or Swiss jacket, with blue collar and facings, which hung in bags about him, and a white waistcoat, wide open, from which a volume of frill protruded. His nether man was encased in a pair of tight nankeens, buttoned at the ancle (a singular perversity common to old gentlemen whose calves have gone to grass), and which exhibited the extraordinary slenderness of his frail supporters in a very striking point of view. A queue (the general being one of the "last of the pigtails"), a round hat of black silk, a good deal battered, with a bullion loop and button, completed the outward appearance of the Bengal veteran, who soon, however, satisfied us that, spite of appearances, he was, as Grinnerson said, a stout-hearted old fellow, with plenty of pluck and mental vigour still about him; one of whom it might be said, that "E'en in his ashes glowed their wonted fires."

When pretty close, the little old man, from whom a squeaky and faltering treble might have been expected, astonished us by shouting out, in a stentorian voice, and with a tone and accent smacking strongly of the "first gem of the sea,"

"Is that the *Rottenbame Castle*, sur?"

Being answered in the affirmative, he continued, "Is Captain McGuffin on board, sur?"

McGuffin, who by this time had come to the side, replied to this question himself. Taking off his hat, and waving it, he said,

"Hoo air ye, general? I'm glad to see you, sir, luking sae weel. Will you come on board, sir?"

"Hah! McGuffin, is that you? How are you, my good sur?" returned the general, raising his hat, too, with all the dignity of the old school, or of the guardsman at Fontenoy. "Sorry to see you in this ugly pickle, though. Have you got my Cordalia on board?" alluding to his daughter, a widow lady, one of our passengers from Madras, and who, at this instant, having heard of her father's arrival, rushed to the side, and kissing one hand with *empressement*, whilst she waved her handkerchief in the other, soon afforded him satisfactory evidence of her existence.

After some little trouble, the pinnace was safely moored alongside, and the old general securely, though with equal difficulty, and a few volleys of abuse to his servants, deposited by instalments on the deck. Here, however, he appeared in some danger of suffocation, from the vigorous embraces of the buxom young widow, who yielding to the impulses of natural feeling, and regardless of standers-by, rushed into his arms, and kissed him with the warmest affection, knocking off his hat by the collision, and exhibiting to our view the generals venerable head, white with the snows of seventy or eighty winters.

Here, then, in the shrivelled old soldier standing before me, I beheld a warrior of the days of Clive, a last representative, probably, of a generation long gone down to the dust, whose thoughts, dress, and manners so essentially differed from our own, and who (all honour to their three-cornered hats and big waistcoats!) had baffled the Indian in the field and the cabinet, and laid the foundation of this proud dominion, on which I was about to set foot. I looked on him with that respect with which we contemplate a grey ruin of other days, with its silent courts, its "banquet-hall deserted," and all its glorious associations, and which long has withstood the tempests of the world.

General Capsicum on Board the "Rottenbeam Castle."

After retiring to the cuddy, and some private conversation with his daughter, the general again came on deck, and had a renewed round of handshaking with the captain, and some other of his acquaintance, whom he expressed himself as devilish glad to see in India again, "the best country in the whole world, by all that's good!" He concluded with a look redolent of gunpowder and hair-triggers, though half jocular, "And where is the man that will say me nay?" It was obvious at a glance the general was what an old Scotch author calls

A fiery Ettercap, a fractious chiel;

As hot as ginger and as true as steel;

with not a little of that *refined savageism* in him, which exalts the *duello* into the first accomplishment of a gentleman.

In Colonel Kilbaugh he recognized an old friend and brother campaigner, and right cordial was the greeting between them. A tremendous refighting of battles would then and there have taken place, it was quite clear, had time allowed of it; unless, upon the principle that two negatives make an affirmative, they should have neutralized their kindred *fortes*. The general, amongst his peculiarities of the old school, swore like a trooper; indeed, so free was his indulgence in that once fashionable, but now, amongst gentlemen, exploded vice, that had he been in England, he would doubtless have been liable to an indictment from the Society for the Suppression of Vice, for profane swearing.

"By G— —, you're looking well, though, Kilbaugh, d— —d well, upon my soul; you've taken a new laise of your existence since you went home."

"Why, eh—yes," said the little colonel, pulling up his collar-gills complacently, and looking extremely large for his size, "we are certainly a new man, general; nothing like a few hogsheads of Cheltenham waters for setting a dyspeptic man on his legs again."

"Indeed, then that's true; but, Kilbaugh, though you and I have had some rale plissant days together in old times—eh?—you didn't trouble the water much then by G— —, and liked your glass as well as any of us, and (with a palpable wink) that same *minus* the g, too—*minus* the g—eh? ha, ha, ha!"

With this, he made a pass at the ex-resident's ribs with his extended finger, which the other dexterously avoided, though with a complacent chuckle which shewed that he was not displeased at this allusion to his youthful frolics.

"Well," continued the general, "you'll put up at my place, and I'll give you a cast in the pinnace. By-the-bye, you liked a good bottle of beer,

Kilbaugh, I remember right well, and just now I can give you one, a rale foamer; got in a splendid batch lately; it is from Bell, and by G—— it bears a bell, too."

So he rattled on; and the ex-resident having signified his acceptance of the general's offer, the trio, after a hearty leave-taking, were soon on board the pinnace, and on their way to Calcutta.

This was the first time I had seen the Mohamedan domestics of this part of India, and I was agreeably struck by their handsome and manly appearance, and the becoming costume of those in the old general's suite. Their turbans, vests, loose *pajammas* or trousers, and *kummerbunds* or girdles, set off by their crimson belts and metal badges, and their massive silver batons, gave them a very striking and picturesque appearance, enhanced by luxuriant beards or mustachios, large eyes, and high features.

There are some strange anomalies attendant on the march of civilization, and none more so, perhaps, than the indifference, or rather want of real taste, which nations in a high state of refinement evince in regard to costume. Whether it is that scientific pursuits, and the busy occupations of the thoughts on matters of high social, moral, political, and commercial interest, leave no time for men to study the graces of attire, or that such a study is really unworthy of, or incompatible with, cultivated minds, or, as the Quakers think, unfavourable to morality, certain it is that the art of decorating the person does not keep pace with other improvements.

Our commander (finding he could not leave Kedgeree till the following morning), Marpeet, Grundy, and I, accepted the obliging invitation of Capt. Grogwell, of the *Rohomany* barque, country trader, a friend of the captain, to accompany him in his vessel, then under weigh for Calcutta.

"I can give you a glass of grog, gentlemen, and a bit of curry, and there's my cabin for you to turn into if you should stay with me overnight," said the frank and good-humoured sailor; "but," added he, "there's no time to be lost for those that go, as the tide's already on the turn."

A few bags and boxes were soon stowed in Captain Grogwell's boat, and after many warm adieus from our friends on board, and the expression of mutual hopes that we should meet again in Calcutta, off we pushed for the *Rohomany* barque.

As we approached her, two or three bronzed faces, surmounted by straw hats, rose above the side, and were directed expectantly towards us, whilst the whistling pipe of the serang, or native boatswain, announced the skipper's approach alongside. We mounted through a bevy of the sable crew, and soon stood on the deck of the country ship, just arrived from a voyage to the Eastern Islands.

"Welcome on board the *Rohomany*, gentlemen, where I hope you will make yourselves at home and comfortable," said Captain Grogwell. "My first officer, Mr. Dobbs, gentlemen," he continued, presenting a tall, brawny, and fine-countenanced man. Mr. Dobbs made his best leg; was glad to see us on board.

The lascars now began to weigh the anchor to a wild and not unmusical chant, with an agreeable chorus of *Ya Ullahs!* All was soon bustle, the anchor a-peak, and the mates shouting forth their commands in the most extraordinary lingo that ever grated "harsh music" on my ears.

"Trinkum Garvey de man," said one; "Garvey brass trinkum de man," roared another; whilst Mr. Dobbs, in a tremendous fury (why I knew not), and stamping like a madman, sung out "Chop and string your goosey, and be d——d to you all."

These are a few specimens. On hearing the last, I certainly was inclined to think that the death-warrant of one of those *capitol* birds who feed on our commons, and on whom our commons feed (excuse the double pun), had been pronounced. I wish some Oriental philologist would give us a history of this nautical jargon, which, I take it, is a sort of *olla podrida* of Portuguese, Bengalee, and heaven knows what dialects besides—the *lingua franca* of the Indian seas. On we glided; passed the "silver tree," a singular vegetable production, composed of brick and mortar; "Diamond Harbour," another misnomer, but very Golcondahish in the sound; and finally, a stiff wind setting in dead ahead, found it impossible to get round a certain peninsula, sometimes called "Hooghly Point," but amongst sailors, rejoicing in the less euphonious appellation of "Point Luff and be d——d." There was no help for it, so down went the anchor, and there seemed every prospect of our having to conjugate the verb *ennuyer* till a fresh flow of tide and shift of wind should enable us to pass this most troublesome part of the river, and the dangerous shoal of the James and Mary. The reader must understand that all this was before the days of steam.

Leaving the white tavern of Fultah, where the Calcutta *bon vivant* eats mango-fish—the whitebait of India,—we soon passed Budge Budge, the scene of the sailor's unique exploit—a story too well known, I fancy, to need repetition here—and in a short time after, on turning "Hangman's Point" (where once stood an outpost of civilization), found ourselves opposite

"Garden Reach," the sylvan vestibule of Calcutta. I have seen few sights in my wanderings more beautiful and imposing than the approach to this Petersburgh of the East, this magnificent capital of our Eastern empire. On the left was the Botanical Garden, with its screen of tall dark cypress trees; on the right, a long succession of beautiful villas, situated amidst verdant lawns and park-like pleasure-grounds, sloping gently down to the water's edge. Here the eye was caught by some pretty kiosk or summer-house, like the *lust-haus* of a Dutch retreat, or such as we sometimes see in the stately gardens attached to some mansion of the olden time here at home. There it rested on a ghaut, or flight of steps leading to the water, with urns or balustrades, before which, in the mellow *chiar-oscuro* of some overhanging banyan-tree, lay moored the elegant covered pleasure-boat of the owner—hurrying through the grounds, a palankeen would appear, with its scampering bevy of attendant bearers and running peons, the huge red chattah or umbrella to shield the master from the sun, when making his *exits* and *entrées*, bobbing up and down—standing before many a porticoed mansion, gigs, or other equipages would appear in waiting, to take the Sahibs to town, or on their rounds of morning visits, and mingling in pleasing contrast with the Europeanized character of these beautiful domains, the lofty palm or kujjoor would here and there raise its head, the perch of a knot of solemn vultures; or parting the grounds one from another, lofty fences of the graceful and pensile bamboo, might be seen drooping in rich clusters, like plumes of ostrich feathers. Numerous boats glided up and down the river, with here and there a vessel like our own, obeying the whirling impulses of the tide, and rapidly approaching its destination—all, in fact, bespoke the close vicinity of a great capital.

The reach nearly past, the proud citadel of Fort William broke in view, its grinning batteries opening upon us, one after the other, and affording a lively idea of the sort of gauntlet which an enemy might reasonably expect, should one sufficiently hardy ever dare to confront them. Here and there on the long-extended rampart, the sentry "walked his lonely round," his musket and bayonet gleaming brightly in the noontide rays, whilst crowds of natives, passing palankeens, and stately adjutant birds stalking "in grey attire" on the banks, gave life and animation to the scene—a few minutes more, and a long forest of shipping, with masses and lines of stately mansions reposing under the still calm sky, like some Grecian capital of old, bespoke the City of Palaces, the proud metropolis of British India.

Here was a sight at which a Briton might honestly exult, and, young as I was, I gazed with pride on this magnificent creation of my country's civilization and power—the point from which she governs the countless millions of the dependent Empire which Providence, for the wisest of purposes, has submitted to her benignant sway. Old England! mighty heart! long may thy vigorous pulsations be thus felt to the utmost bounds of our earth! Nations, like individuals, have their stages of existence—their infancy, their manhood, and their decline; some fall into premature decrepitude and dissolution, and leave but the memory of evil deeds behind them; whilst others sink in glorious maturity, under the weight of years and honours, leaving the fruits of a well-spent life behind them, to be embalmed for ever in the hearts of a grateful posterity. May such be thy lot, O my country!

CHAPTER VIII

We dropped anchor off the city, amongst a crowd of shipping and a swarm of boats, with which the river seemed actually alive; some of them home along by the headlong "freshes," and athwart the bows of the vessel, with fearful and dangerous velocity. I was all anxiety to get on shore; so, without waiting for Marpeet and Grundy, who had some small toilet-matters, &c., to arrange, I put my boxes and bags into a *paunchway*—a native boat of a particular description, several of which lay alongside—and, after shaking Captain Grogwell and his mate by the hand, thanking them cordially for their hospitality, and expressing a hope that I should see them again before I left Calcutta, I descended the side, and was soon on my way to the shore.

"Take care of the land-sharks, sir," said Grogwell, as I pushed off.

"Have your eyes about you, Gernon, my boy, and take care of yourself," cried Marpeet, "and I'll beat up your quarters in a day or two."

At the Ghaut, or landing-place, to which my rowers forced their way through a thick phalanx of boats of all sorts and dimensions—cutters, dingies, and jolly-boats; paunchways, budgerows, and bowlias, the two last with painted venetians and goggle-eyed figure-heads—I landed amidst a crowd and bobbery to which even the Tower-stairs, or the piers of Boulogne and Calais, with all their motley and voluble groups, can hardly furnish a parallel. Men, women, and children, sipping, dipping, and dabbling, like ducklings in a shower; females bearing pots or jars on their heads, and children, resembling little black monkeys, astride on their hips; bhisties, or water-carriers, filling their bags from the turbid tide, well seasoned with cocoa-nut husks, defunct brahmins, dead dogs, &c.; puckalls, or bullocks, bearing huge skins of the same *pure* element; palankeen-bearers, gabbling (to me) unintelligible abuse, in eager competition, pushing into the very river, and banging their portable boxes one against the other in their struggle to secure fares amongst the frequent arrivals from the shipping; baboos, parroquet-venders, chattah-bearers, sailors, lascars, and adjutant-birds—Europe and Asia commingled in heterogeneous but pleasant confusion.

I had scarcely attained the top of the Ghaut, or flight of steps, where I waited till my baggage was brought up and coolies were obtained to transport it, than I found myself besieged by a bevy of fellows, mentioned before as baboos, or sircars, and who, though of a distinct species, I saw at once belonged to the same genus as my friend Ramee Sawmee Dabash.

"Good marning, Sar," said one (it was near sunset), ostentatiously displaying his first *chop* English, approaching with an easy bend, and pressing his right palm somewhat gracefully to his forehead: "Master, I perceive, is recintly arrive at Bengal pris'dency?"

"That's pretty clear," said I; "but can you direct me to the Custom-house, and after that to some good hotel or tavern?"

"Oh, sartainly, Sar; every thing master require than I can do; meditly box come up, I disperse off with coolie."

"Gentilman," said another, in a milder key, "you require 'spectable sircar; I got highest tistimonial of character; you please read this, Sar; this from Gin'nel Wilkisseen Sahib, this Wakeel Ishtivil Sahib;" and so he ran on, murdering several other English names and titles in succession.

A third, a wizened old fellow, with a pair of spectacles perched at the end of his nose, proffered his services somewhat in the same way; but I told them not to trouble themselves or me, as I had determined on honouring with my commands the first who had presented himself to my notice. My new *employé*, who rejoiced in the pleasant cognomen of Chattermohun Ghose, now again put in his oar:

Griffin on Landing besieged by Baboos.

"Masters name, I think, will be Mr. Gernon"—the rascal had read it on my box,—"same gentleman as was expect by *Rottenbeam-i-castle*?"

"Yes, it is indeed," said I, astonished to find myself known; "but how the devil came you acquainted with it?"

"Oh," he replied, "we always ver well know whin military gentilmen are expected at pris'dency from ship; beside—I not know, but I think, master will have some relation this country—face all same—one gentleman I know, only more young—leetle more handsome."

I interposed with "Stuff! none of your blarney; but, perhaps, you mean, my uncle, Colonel Gernon," rather pleased to meet so soon after landing with one even amongst the natives who had probably known a relative: young people hear so much of their uncles and grandfathers, &c., at home, that they enter life with an idea that all the world must know something about them.

"What!" exclaimed Chattermohun—who was a thorough Don Raphael in his way,—and with well-dissembled pleasure, "What Connel Gernon Sahib master uncle? I think that all same time. Connel very good gentilman, my bist of frind—always he impeloy me when he come Calcutta. Connel command Europan rig'ment, I think, at Danapoor?"

"Oh, no," I rejoined; "you mistake; my uncle has been some time dead, and I think was never in a European regiment."

"That I know, Sar, ver well," continued Chattermohun briskly, and not at all disconcerted; "but when live, I mean, belong native rig'ment (I make small obliteration before) that some time was that place."

"Yes, yes; he was in the native infantry, certainly," said I; "but where stationed is more than I can tell. And so you really knew my uncle, did you, eh? And think me like him? Perhaps, too, you have heard of another relation of mine here in India—Mr. Duggins?"

"What Mr. Duggin, what was civil sarvice?"

"No, no," I answered; "here in the law, in Calcutta."

"Oh! what master mean Mr. Duggin 'sliciter? Yes, sar, I know him ver well; he greatly respect-i-me—that time he was live."

"Why, I trust he's not dead?" I exclaimed, in astonishment: "he was well at Bombay the last accounts we had of him."

"No, Sar, not dead; master not underistand; I mean that time was live here, Chowrunghee."

Though rather green and guileless in those days, as maybe inferred from the foregoing example, and unwilling, unless on something stronger than mere *primâ facie* evidence, to imagine deception; yet I began to suspect that the rascal was humbugging me for a purpose, and was about to let him know as much, in rather strong terms, when he adroitly changed the key.

"Master will be in 'tillery, I think?"

"No," said I impatiently; "infantry, infantry; but don't bother, and us be off."

"All same," he continued, determined to have his talk out; "master will require plenty thing, all which I can supply—bist of quality—if require too good-i-sarvant: will you take this man?—plenty character he got."

So saying, he presented to my notice a queer, raffish-looking fellow, with a bush of hair and a black beard, and dressed in quite a different style of costume to that of the others. This worthy—a Mussulman khidmutgar or footman—made his salaam, and thrust into my hand two or three well-soiled certificates, which stated that Ramjahn Khan (*ang.* Rumjohnny,) had served the writers (captain this and lieutenant that) with zeal and fidelity, and to their perfect satisfaction. Of these "characters," by the way, all domestics have a stock, or, if not, they borrow or hire them (being as accommodating one to another in that way, as was the Irish priest who, as related by the pleasant author of *Wild Sports of the West*, on a pinch, and to save appearances, gave his friend, the Protestant curate of Connemara, the loan of his congregation), with sufficient information touching the subscribers to allow of some slight questioning, though by no means of an adroit cross-examination—a thing at this time, however, in the native language, quite beyond my powers, albeit I had puzzled my brains a little on ship-board with a certain celebrated philologist's orthoepigraphico-pseudolatitudio-logical works, and could patter a few sentences of Hindostanee in the "*Myn nuheen kitai hoon*" style, in a way really to "astonish the natives."

To cut the matter short, however, I hired Rumjohnny on the strength of his testimonials; and having now got my baggage all up, moved off with him and Chattermohun Ghose to the Custom-house. Having arranged matters there, I proceeded through the thronged streets of Calcutta to a tavern or punch-house, somewhere in the aristocratic region of Ranamoody Gully; a sort of place of entertainment which, in those days (though, from their improved character the case is now, I understand, different), it was considered quite *infra dig.* in a gentleman to visit. However, being a griff, I knew nothing of this, and if the case had been otherwise, I should have been without an alternative. Dirty tablecloths, well spotted with kail and mustard; prawn curries, capital beef-steaks, domestics of the cut of

Rumjohnny, a rickety, rusty, torn billiard-table, on which, day and night, the balls were going, lots of *shippies*, and a dingy bed, were the leading features of this establishment, not forgetting clouds of voracious and well-fleshed musquitoes, to which those of Madras were a mere joke.

I shall not inflict on the reader a dry detail of the occurrences of the next three days; let it suffice to state, that at the end of that period, having duly reported my arrival, &c., I found myself in possession of an advance of 150 sicca rupees, sterling money of Bengal, four bare walls and a puckah floor in the south barracks of Fort William, and about to fit up the same in the first style of griffinish fashion, under the able direction of Chattermohun Ghose.

The south barracks is one of several ranges within the Fort, and allotted principally to the accommodation of unmarried subs. Like the Burlington Arcade, it has a long passage down the centre, into which the doors of the several quarters open; but here the resemblance ceases. Here I had a practical illustration of the ill-working of the social system, the living in a species of community under the present discordant and defective state of our feelings and habits. The passage was sounding and reverberating, and each occupant of a quarter had much of the benefit of his neighbour's flute, fiddle, or French horn, whether "i' the vein" for harmony or not; shoe brushings, occasional yells of servants undergoing the discipline of fist or cane, jolly ensigns and cadets clattering up and down, cracking horsewhips, whistling the "*Flaxen-headed Cow-boy*" or "*Begone Dull Care*," the arrival of files of coolies laden with purchases from the China Bazaar or Tulloch's Auction Room, pleasantly varied by interminable wranglings on the part of master's sirdar or bursar, touching payments and *dustoorie*, or custom; payees urging pleas in deprecation of abatement, sirdar overruling the same—constituted a few of the *désagrémens* of a south-barrack life. The optical department was not less varied and novel; but it could be shut out at pleasure, an advantage not predicable of the former.

The aspect of the passage varied with the hour; he who strolled down it, about the hour of dawn, or a little after, might catch glimpses, through half-opened doors, of all stages of the toilet, from soap-suds and dressing-gowns, to what painters term the "*ultima basia*" or finishing touches; possibly, too, he might have a peep at the ensign's lady, "the soldier's bride," divested of all the romance with which song-composers and novelists are wont to invest her; hair *en papillottes*, sleeves tucked up, and washing Augustus or Tommy. At ten, the scene was changed; without the doors, on the ground, might be seen a goodly display of trays, with egg-shells, fish-bones, rice, muffin, and other wrecks of breakfast; sweepers—certain degraded menials, "all same caste as master,"—squatting near and waiting for the said remnants; hookhas or kulians in course of preparation for those who indulged in the luxury of smoking; and here and there, perhaps, a sergeant, havildar, or strapping grenadier sepoy, waiting for the summons from within to give this morning's report:—noon and evening, tiffin and dinner, each brought its appropriate proceedings, and varied the aspect of the common passage, which will long, with the force of a first impression, remain strongly engraven on my memory.

Of late years, with the view of protecting young officers on their arrival, from those impositions, scrapes, and embarrassments, to which, owing to their youth and inexperience, they were formerly exposed, the Government has considerately created an appointment, called the "superintendent of cadets,"—a measure well calculated to mitigate the evil.

The system of sending youths to India at the early ages of fifteen or sixteen, appears to me to be one fraught with evil, against which its advantages weigh but as dust in the balance. At that early age, the character and principles are generally quite unformed, and, intoxicated on becoming uncontrolled master of himself, emancipated from the thraldom of home or school, the cadet launches or did launch (unless, in this "go-ahead" age, things have greatly altered) into idleness, dissipation, and frivolity, feeling through life (if not cut off in his prime) the effects of habits and follies which, under all circumstances, and knowing youth's plastic nature, it was not probable he would avoid.

Often the finest natures are the first to fall victims to the absence of salutary restraint, or they plough their way to wisdom through bitter experience, finding that "gem above price" when it is probably too late to be of use to them. The wildnesses and consequent *escapades* of such boys have tended to lower the European character very considerably in the estimation of the natives; and the sepoys, and above all, the veteran native officers, must, and I am convinced do, feel strongly their being subjected to the control and caprice of such striplings. It is, perhaps, an unavoidable consequence of our anomalous rule in India, that the native should in no case be allowed to command the European; but, wherever possible, we should at least avoid placing hoary age and madcap inexperience in such a degrading juxtaposition. I have known such youths (truth obliges me to include myself amongst the number) order about, and not unfrequently use harsh and unbecoming language to venerable native officers, whose silver beards, and breasts covered with medals, spoke of many a campaign, and services rendered to the state, before probably even the stripling's sire was in existence. As the empire of opinion—the awe which our superior energy and science have inspired—dies away, and even now it is on the wane—it will be well to have a store of affection on which to fall back—an anchorage in the hearts of the people of India, when our power over their prejudices has relaxed its hold.

Chattermohun Ghose, having, as a preliminary proceeding, given me a list of things which I *must have*—Bengal indispensables—and having been duly authorized to procure the same, he very soon made his appearance with about a dozen and a half of coolies or porters, bearing, amongst other articles, a camp-table, a cane-bottom sleeping-cot, a *setringie*, or cotton carpet, about one-third the size of my room, two chairs, some Chinese chinaware, and copper cooking-utensils, and a huge basin, something of the shape of Mambrino's helmet, on an iron tripod stand, which it puzzled me sorely to guess the use of.

"What do you call this, Chattermohun?" said I; "is it a chafing-dish, or what?"

"Chafey-dish! no, Sar; that call *chillumchee*, for wash hand, with ablution—all gentilmen have chillumchee."

The appendages of the toilet, by the way, and the manner in which it is performed, in India, amongst Europeans, differ so essentially from those of home, that they excite considerable surprise in the new comer.

"Master, I think, will want mil'tary coat," said my grand purveyor!

"Faith! that's true," said I; "and it reminds me that I have some red cloth, furnished by Messrs. Welsh and Stalker, for the express purpose."

"Ver well, Sar; then I bring dhirgee (tailor), make up in room; same time, I bring small piece yellow-cloth for facing; also one *ishilki* sash, and reg'lation sword, all complit."

"Bring a tailor!" said I; "what, do your tailors here go out to work?"

"Yes, Sar; this custom this contree; not all same Calcutta as Europe."

"So I perceive," I replied.

The tailor shortly after made his appearance, squatted himself cross-legged in the apartment, and was soon hard at work at my red jacket. He was a little old fragile fellow, who sat and plied his needle, the only instrument he seemed fitted to wield, with an air of apathetic quietude and resignation, which it seemed as if no conceivable movement of the outside world could for a moment disturb, and which, to one of my then mercurial temperament, was utterly astounding. This little fractional portion of humanity, who was bent from age or infirmity, took my measure with exceeding gentleness, and I think I now see him with the few scanty hairs of his grey moustache, and his thin horny nose, pinched by a pair of spectacles secured by a thread pinned to the front of his turban, as he moved silently about me, in the calm exercise of this incipient act of his vocation. Poor little old Kalipha! Long since, doubtless, hast thou closed the "even tenor of thy way;" thy quiet, inglorious, though useful occupation; and added thy handful of soda and potash to the ever-changing bosom of old mother-earth!

After having established myself pretty comfortably in the south barracks, I despatched my letters of introduction to the several parties to whom they were addressed; amongst the number was one to General Capsicum. A few were from weighty and influential persons at home, and all had thumping big seals, and "favoured by Mr. Cadet Gernon" written in the corners. I used to reckon them up about once a week on ship-board, as a miser counts his treasures; speculating on their contents, and building *chateaux en Espagne* touching the pleasant results which would, I imagined, doubtless follow their delivery. This, thought I, constructing my airy fabric after the manner of Alnaschar, and gazing complacently on my *cheval de bataille*, my "great gun," furnished by a certain member of the peerage, this will inevitably bring an aide-de-camp, post-haste, to invite me to the Government-house. I shall be placed on the staff, wear a cocked-hat and aiguilettes, carve the hams and turkeys, laugh at the Governor-general's jokes, carry the Governor-general's lady's prayer-book—live in clover, loved and respected, the pet and confidential friend of the family: a capital appointment will follow in due course; wealth, honour, will pour upon me; and, to crown my felicity, some high-born damsel will eventually become Mrs. Gernon! Ye gods! what a career of prosperity did I picture, as I contemplated that massive letter with its coronetted seal and crest (an ominous griffin) all *proper*. Heigho! Four dinners, three breakfasts, and a tiffin, were all I gained by the whole batch of introductions; and as for the Governor-general, I grieve to say, that I found him lamentably deficient in that penetration and power of just appreciation of character for which I had given him credit.

I was sitting in my barrack-rooms next morning after breakfast, amusing myself by pitching bones and crusts out of the window to a bevy of adjutant-birds below, opening their jaws expectingly, or clattering their huge beaks whilst contending for a bone, with the sound of marrow-bones and cleavers, when the door opened, and, to my agreeable surprise, in walked Captain Marpeet, his face radiant with smiles. A cordial greeting followed for, though coarse and illiterate for a man in his station, Marpeet was a warm-hearted, blunt, and generous fellow, and I had a sincere regard for him. Being an "old hand," he assumed the Mentor towards Grundy and me, to which office, as it was not often offensively obtruded, I quietly submitted, with proper griffinish humility.

"Well!" said he, looking up and down and round about, "so here you are, all snug and tight, regularly boxed up in this noisy hole?"

"Any thing by way of exchange," I replied, "after five months on shipboard; but to tell you the truth, it has its merits, and I rather like it on other grounds. Here, you see, I am, with all my comforts about me," pointing rather ostentatiously to my two chairs, cot, and camp-table, and to my brazen chillumchee, in radiant brightness standing in the corner, "and from these, my head-quarters, I mean to sally out ever and anon, to mingle a little in the gay world of Calcutta, before I start for the Upper Provinces."

"Well," said Marpeet, laughing; "I see, 'for a griff,' that you have a pretty good notion of things in general, and I don't care if I join you in a spree or two before I leave. You griffs require an 'old hand' to look after you, or you will be always doing some soft thing or another. But have you been playing a knife and fork anywhere yet? been to any grand 'feed' since you arrived?"

"Dinners and parties, eh? No, not as yet; but there is abundance of time for that, for it was only yesterday that I fired off a grand salvo of letters, which will doubtless, in due time, bring invitations 'as thick as leaves on Vallombrosa.'"

"Leaves on! pshaw! can't you say 'black-berries' at once? I wish, Gernon, you were not so confoundedly poetical; I hate poetry mortally; it is griffinish; give me matters of fact, something I can understand. Dundas, or a number of the *Sporting Magazine*, or the like."

"There's no help for it," said I; "it's my nature, and nature we may modify, but cannot radically change."

"Philosophizing; that's worse still. But, joking apart, don't be too sure of the invitations, or you may reckon without your host. I'm an 'old hand' (Marpeet's everlasting boast), and have seen a little of Calcutta in my time, and I know, whatever the folks once were, they are now becoming most infernally *pucka* (stingy), and will soon, I verily believe, be as bad as they are in England, where a leg o'mutton goes through the nineteen manœuvres before it is dismissed, and a man thinks he confers an everlasting obligation if he asks you to dinner."

"Ha, ha, ha! you old splenetic *Qui Hye*," I exclaimed, "you are too hard on us 'Englishers;' you don't consider the difference of circumstances, and that, where mouths are many and legs o'mutton few, we must resort to expedients to square supply and demand."

"But," resumed the rough-spun captain, "now let me fulfil the principal object of my visit, which is to congratulate you."

"For what?" I asked.

"What? why are you so ignorant, so out of the world, as not to know that you are promoted?"

"Promoted!" exclaimed I; "why Grinnerson said I should be in luck if I got my commission in five years."

The captain put a *Gazette* into my hand, doubled it up in a compact form, and, striking a particular portion *con spirito* with his forefinger, "Read that," said he.

I took it in a sort of ecstacy, caught a glimpse of my own name. Yes— there I was, actually in print: "Mr. Gernon, appointed by the Honourable Court of Directors a cadet on this establishment, having reported his arrival at Fort William, is admitted to the service accordingly, and promoted to the rank of ensign."

"Yoics! full ensign!" shouted I, springing up, snapping my fingers, and capering round the room arms a-kimbo, hip and toe, like a sailor dancing a hornpipe, to the infinite astonishment of Marpeet, who thought I had been bitten by a scorpion or snake.

"Hey! hey! what's the matter Gernon? are you mad, you Griff, are you mad?"

"I am mad, old square-toes; come along," said I, hauling him out of his chair; "come and rejoice with me. Promoted already! Yoics! Tally-ho!"

In the midst of our uproar and saraband, Grundy entered, and gazed with open mouth, like one moonstruck, at our mad dervish dance. His appearance, however, calmed any ebullition, and pushing Marpeet into his seat, I sunk into mine.

"What's the matter?" said he.

"Why, I'm promoted, my honest young ploughshare," said I, "that's all; we were footing a jig on the strength of it. I dare say you will find your name there too."

"Oh, yes," observed Marpeet; "the whole batch of the last griffs are in the general orders. There," added he, tossing the paper to Grundy, "you'll find yourself there, farmer, at full length."

Grundy took the paper, and beheld his own mellifluous name; but his pleasure manifested itself in a different manner from mine; he "grinned horribly a ghastly smile."

"As you are so fond of dancing," said Marpeet, "what say you to joining a hop to-morrow evening?"

"With all my heart," said I; "always ready for a 'trip on the fantastic toe;' but who is your friend?"

"Why," rejoined the captain, "I have a 'provoke' here from the mistress of the Kidderpore establishment for the orphan daughters of officers (where, by the way, I expect my young Mogulanee will figure some of these days), to attend a dance to-morrow; they have a ball there once a fortnight (I believe), to show off the girls, and give them an opportunity of getting spliced."

"That's a new feature of schools; in England, if I remember rightly, the efforts of the mistresses tend all the other way—to keep the girls from getting married."

"That," said Marpeet, "would never do in India, where women are thinking of getting buried about the age at which they talk of being married in lat. 50° N. Yes, this is the place for the man who wants a wife, and wishes to be met half-way, detesting, like me, the toil of wooing. There he can go, and if he sees a girl he likes, good fore-hand, clean about the fetlock-joints, free in her paces, sound and quiet, and not too long in the tooth, if not bespoke, he'll not find much difficulty in getting her. But if you and Grundy will go, I'll get you smuggled in somehow or other, and will call for you in proper time to-morrow."

"Thank you," said I; "never fear for me, for I'm all anxiety to see these young ladies of the equestrian order, whom you so pleasantly describe. Besides, old Stultz, here in the corner, has just finished my red coat, and I am all anxiety to sport it for the first time."

"Well, good-bye, lads," said the captain; "I'm off to Tulloh's auction, to see if I can't pick up a cheap buggy, and a few other things I want."

So saying, he disappeared, leaving Grundy and me to ruminate on the foregoing matters.

"Grundy," said I, after a pause, "you must really get a red coat, sword, and sash, and make yourself look like a Christian, if you go to this ball to-morrow night; excuse my giving you a hint."

"I'm afraid there's not time for it," said Grundy, "and I have nothing of the sort as yet."

"Well, leave it to me; Chattermohun is a sharp fellow, at a pinch; and I'll engage, with his assistance, to rig you out for the evening."

CHAPTER IX

Captain Marpeet made his appearance at the hour appointed on the following evening, and off we started for the Kidderpore school, which, by the way, is, or was, a rather large and imposing structure, at some distance from Calcutta; mussalchees, or link boys, with blazing flambeaux, scampering ahead in good, tip-top style.

Having passed the bazaar, we turned sharply from the main road, into a pretty extensive compound or domain, and soon found ourselves before the portico of the school, amongst buggies, palankeens, and other conveyances appertaining to visitors who had preceded us. Leaving our palankeens, we entered the house, passed through several rooms, one of them devoted to refreshments, and partly filled with gay Lotharios, some few military, the rest belonging to the orders "shippy" and "cranny,"[5] and finally entered the ball-room. This we found thronged with dancers, in a blaze of light, and resounding to the merry notes of a band, which, though not exactly equal to Weippert's, seemed, nevertheless, as a locomotive stimulus, to be quite as effective. The country-dance then flourished in its green old age, and the couples at the Kidderpore hop were flying about in great style—poussette, hands across, down the middle, and back again—evincing, in spite of the temperature, all that laudable perseverance so essential to the accomplishment of such laborious undertakings.

Marpeet, at my particular request, and to keep us in countenance, wore his uniform, though he had previously declared (considering the season) that it was a most griffinish proceeding to sport broadcloth, and decidedly against his conscience. "You griffs, however," said he "will have your way, and we must humour you sometimes." As for myself, in my scarlet raggie, brimstone facings, black waist-belt, and regulation sword, in my own opinion I looked quite the god of war, and was fully armed for execution.

What an era in the life of a soldier is his first appearance in regimentals, "his blushing honours thick about him!" how he then pants for love and glory; the tented field and the clash of arms! At forty or fifty, possibly, if of a thoughtful vein, his sword converted to a hoe or pen, a mighty change comes o'er him, and he thinks, perhaps, that he might have done better had he stuck to a black or a blue one. Sometimes, it is true, when warmed with a flicker of his youthful fire, like Job's war-horse, he loves to "snuff the battle from afar," and "saith to the trumpets, 'ha! ha!'" But, mainly, war delights him no more, for he sees the wide-spread evils which lurk under its exciting pomp and meretricious glitter, and his heart and mind yearn towards those more ennobling pursuits and occupations, which tend to elevate his species, to give to the intellectual and moral their due ascendency, and which speak of "peace and good-will to man."

The dancers being in motion, we did not advance, but contented ourselves with occupying a position by the door, and leisurely surveying the scene. At one end of the apartment, on chairs and benches, sat certain elderly matrons, amongst whom were the superiors of the establishment, looking complacently at the young folks, and calculating in all probability the amount of execution likely to result from the evening's amusements.

The young ladies, however, whose sylph-like forms were gliding through the mazes of the dance, were the "orient pearls at random strung," which principally attracted my attention. As the flush of a summer's noon fades by insensible degrees into the ebon shades of night, so did the complexions of these charming damsels graduate from white to black. Youth, however, smiling, buxom youth, like the mantle of charity, covers a multitude of defects, or, if I may help myself to another and apter simile, possesses an alchymic power, which converts all it touches to gold. There were eyes, teeth, sportive ringlets, and graceful forms enough, in the Kidderpore ball-room, stamped with all its freshness, to atone for the darker shadings of the picture.

For the first time, indeed, though previously imbued with the common and illiberal European prejudice against black, I began to experience a wavering, and to think that dark languishing eyes and a dash of bronze imparted what is often wanted in English beauties, somewhat of soul and character to the countenance. Music, lights, the excitement of the ball-room, are, however, it must be confessed, sad deceivers, producing illusions full oft, which painfully vanish with the morning's light. For young ladies of thirty or thereabouts (an age, though now-a-days, I am credibly informed, never attained by spinsters), the ball-room and its factitious glare have some decided advantages. By day, Cupid, the sly urchin, can only make his attacks from smiles and dimples; but by night, at a pinch, he may launch a shaft with effect even from a wrinkle.

The dance at length ceased; beaux bowed, ladies courtesied, and the throng broke into couples, and promenaded the apartment. Exhausted belles sunk into seats, whilst attentive youths fanned and *persiflaged*, laughed at nothing, and studied "the agreeable." Such was the posture of affairs, when the head of the establishment, a lady of about five-and-forty, of pleasing appearance and address, seeing we were strangers, approached, and kindly bade us welcome. There was an amiability, and at the same time a firmness and decision in her manner, a happy admixture of the *suaviter* and *fortiter*, which showed that she was peculiarly well qualified for the arduous task she had to perform of presiding over this establishment—a sort of nunnery travestied, in which perpetual celibacy formed no part of the vows, and the vigils differed widely from those which "pale-eyed virgins keep" in the gloomy seclusion of the convent.

"Would you like to dance, sir?" said the lady, addressing herself to Captain Marpeet.

"No, I thank you, ma'am," said my blunt companion; "I am a little too stiff in the joints, and my dancing days are all over."

The fact was, that Marpeet had passed five consecutive years of his life in the jungles, where, as it frequently happens in India, he had acquired what, for want of a better term, I will call a *gynophobia*, or woman-horror, which the occasional appearance of a spinster in those deserts wild rather tended to confirm than allay. A short residence in England had, it is true, in some degree, moderated this dread of the respectable portion of the softer sex; but still much of it remained, and he shunned with morbid aversion all situations imposing the painful necessity of whispering soft nothings and "doing the agreeable" with the ladies. The good dame of the school smiled expressively on receiving Captain Marpeet's answer; it was a smile which said, as plain as smile could speak, "You are an odd fish, I see, and one on whom pressing would be quite thrown away."

"Perhaps," said she, turning to me, "you will allow me to introduce you to a partner, and if so, I shall have great pleasure in presenting you to one of our young ladies?"

I had none of Marpeet's scruples, expressed my acknowledgments, accepted her offer, and was led full clank across the ball-room, and presented in due form to Miss Rosa Mussaleh, as an aspirant for her fair hand in the ensuing dance. Miss Rosa Mussaleh was a fine bouncing girl of eighteen, still in high blow from the effects of her recent exertions. Form unexceptionable: complexion rather tending to a delicate saffron, bespeaking plainly her Asiatic maternity.

"If not engaged, Miss Rosa," said the school-mistress, presenting me, "Ensign Gernon" (I had previously communicated my name and *rank*, though there was not much danger of mistaking me for a major-general) "will be happy to dance with you."

"I shall be ver happie; I am not engaged," said Miss Rosa, in a singular variety of the Anglo-Saxon tongue called the *Cheechee* language (Hindustanee idiom Englished), then new to me—a dialect which constitutes a distinguishing mark of those born and bred in India, and the leading peculiarity of which consists in laying a false emphasis, particularly on such small words as *to, me, and,* &c. The lady of the establishment having performed her *devoir,* as mistress of the ceremonies, made a courteous inclination, and withdrew, leaving us to ourselves.

As a rather precocious juvenile, I had danced with some of the fair and well-born damsels of my own land at Bath, Clifton, and elsewhere, and was, therefore, not to be daunted with the mahogany charms of Miss R. M.; so, *sans cérémonie,* I dashed into conversation.

"You have a great many charming young ladies here," said I.

"Oh, yes," said my partner, "great manie; but they are not all here; *the* little girls are gone *to* bed. Do you then admire our young ladie?"

This was rather a pointed question; but I replied without hesitation, "Oh, excessively; there appear to be some lovely creatures amongst them, and (giving a flourish) with charms enough to move the soul of an anchorite."

"Oh," said Miss Rosa, with a smile and downward look, wishing to be complimentary, "I think dey are more fond of the military."

I was on the point of emitting that expressive note of astonishment—*whew!* but checked myself.

"I think," said I, "you rather mistook me, though I can hardly regret that which has been the cause of so flattering an admission, but I alluded to an ascetic."

"Asiatic!" said the young lady, with some hauteur, and a toss of the head, "no native come to these ball, I assure you."

I could not suppress an emphatic "humph!"

The fiddles now began again; I presented my arm, divested myself, though with reluctance, of my trusty Solingen blade, and took my place in the set. A tremendous long set it was, and after slaving for half an hour, I found myself at the head of it. Grundy, with a face like that of the Marquess of Granby on a sign-post, standing next to me, and streaming like the apotheosis of a river god.

"Well, how do you get on, Grundy?" said I.

"Oh, it's cruel hot work," said he, with a sigh, which was perfectly heart-rending.

"Hot, indeed," I rejoined, giving sigh for sigh; "they don't catch me dancing again in a red coat."

If working up the dance was fatiguing, the going down it was still more so. My partner, a practised hand, skipped about without the smallest signs of fatigue, whilst I, reeking from every pore, was dragged up and down and whirled round and about till my head spun, and I thought I should have verily gone into a fit, or sunk from sheer exhaustion on the floor. I did, however, contrive to hold out till we finished the dance, five-and-twenty couples at least, when, with a staggering bow, I tendered my arm and led my partner to her seat.

"Are you fond of dancing?" said she, with the coolest assurance.

"A little of it," said I, with a sigh, "when in practice, the set not too long, and the weather not too hot."

A gentleman, chained, ringed, and be-broached, stout and bronzed, now came up, and engaged my partner for the next dance, chatted for some time with the air of an old acquaintance, gave a "bye-bye" sort of a nod, and passed on.

"Do you know Captain Trinkum?"

"No," said I; "what does he belong to?"

"To the *Rustomjee Bomanjee*," said she.

"The *Rustomjee Bomanjee*," I rejoined; "pray what regiment is that? some irregular corps, I suppose."

This remark of mine set her off in a violent fit of laughter, of which (rather confused) I begged to know the cause.

"It's a country ship," screamed she, "not a regiment." Going off again at a tangent, "Oh, now I see you are a griffin."

Thus she balanced the anchorite account, and turned the tables. I can't say I was sorry when he of the *Rustomjee Bomanjee* came smirking up, and relieved me from the raillery of Miss Rosa, who, though herself guilty of corrupting the kings English, was an arrant quiz, and not disposed to spare my griffinish blunders.

Marpeet now joined me, and after a little banter touching the style in which Miss Rosa had trotted me about, proposed an adjournment to the refreshment-room. To this I joyfully acceded, suggesting that it would be a charity to take poor Grundy with us, if his dissolution had not already taken place.

"Come, Grundy," said Marpeet; "come along with us; we're going to victual and refit, and would recommend the same to you, for you seem in need of it."

Grundy assented with pleasure, and, linked arm-in-arm we entered the refreshment-room.

Here was a scene of considerable bustle; some were preparing acidulous compounds for the ladies in the ball-room; others doing the like for themselves. As we entered, a staid and exemplary young man, with his cargo of negus and cake, balancing the same with the nicety of a juggler, was making his way out, when in banged a six-foot ensign to do the bidding of his fair inamorata, and charged with her fan and gloves, and going full butt against the exemplary beau, upset both negus and cake. The ensign, a flighty fellow in every respect, made a hasty apology, and off, leaving the beau to wipe his waistcoat and repair the damages as best he might. Knots of young fellows were there, laughing, eating sandwiches or brewing negus, lounging, and clanking their swords. Native servants belonging to the visitors or the establishment were bustling about, and making themselves useful; whilst here and there, in a corner, and availing herself of the solitude of a crowd, a young lady might be seen, her back against the wall, listlessly sipping her negus, or balancing a spoon over a jelly-glass, and listening, with downward look and in mute entrancement, to some handsome *militaire*, whilst he was pouring into her attentive ear the "leprous distilment" of honied words.

Recruited and refreshed, we returned to the ball-room, and in spite of my recent resolution, I again joined the dance, which was kept up till a late hour, when my friends and I returned to my room in the fort, where, fairly *done* up, I betook myself to rest, the fiddles still sounding in my head, to dream of Miss Rosa, and all I had seen and heard; and so terminated my first ball in the East.

The Kidderpore hops, I hear, are now no more; from which I conclude that some other matrimonial plan has been devised for disposing of the young ladies, more in consonance with the refined delicacy of the age, which, though recognizing the necessity of matrimony, seems to discountenance any expedient which smacks of the slave-market.

On the following evening, Captain Marpeet, according to engagement, called in a hired buggy, to take me a drive on the Course. The Course, as is well known, is the grand resort of the *beau monde* of Calcutta, which, like a colony of owls or bats from a ruin, emerge at sundown from all parts of that extensive city, to see and to be seen, and to enjoy the coolness of the evening breeze.

Seated in his gig, Marpeet drew up before the barrack in all his glory, handling the ribbons with the peculiar and finished grace of a man who had made it his study. Great, indeed, were his pretensions in that way, and I am confident he would rather have been the leader of the four-in-hand club, than have written the *Principia* of Newton.

In I jumped; Marpeet cracked his whip to mettle up his ticca[6] tit—an animal deficient in flesh and blood, certainly, but exhibiting an amazing deal of bone. Away we went. The evening gun had just boomed; the myriad crows of the Fort cawed querulously responsive from the trees; the bugles sounded; the drums beat; the guards at the gates, European and native, were turned out; captains and lieutenants, flushed with tiffin or a nap, swords under their arms, sauntered along to join them. The firefly here and there twinkled in the trees, and the far-off yell of the jackall proclaimed the approach of night, when away we whirled through covered ways and over thundering drawbridges, past scarp, counter-scarp, and glacis, and in a few minutes found ourselves amidst the throng of carriages and equestrians on the Course, the mass of the Government-house, with its capacious dome and lion-crowned gates, rising in front, and the vast semicircle of Chowringhee, with its aggregation of snow-white structures, stretching away far to the right.

What a singular scene here presented itself to my admiring sight! What an admixture of nations, and their several modes and peculiarities—of English turn outs and Indian piebald imitations—with strange equipages, combining European finish with the native original! Carriages and equestrians, walking, trotting, or galloping, passing and repassing!

This is the Hyde Park of the East, where, though less of splendour than in its great prototype, there was far more variety to be seen. There came the Governor-General, the viceroy of British India, open barouche and four (all dignity and gracious bows); cocked hats and feathers flying; black body-guard before and behind, in a long trot; sabres flashing, and scabbards rattling. Near, by way of antithesis, might be seen a palankeen carriage "creepy crawley," drawn by two enormous bullocks, with monstrous dewlaps, bearing some fat old Portuguese lady, black as Erebus or Nox, to take the air, driver working hard to rouse them to a transient hobble. There, four or five abreast, rode sundry dashing young officers, displaying themselves and their uniforms to the best advantage, "pride in their port, defiance in their eyes;" whilst near, in some open landau or barouche, the "cynosure of neighbouring eyes," would appear the newly-arrived beauty, the belle of the season, her English roses contrasting with the reigning *pallor* around, wearing a look of conscious power, and exhibiting herself to the admiring gaze of the gossiping world. Happy creature! all is *couleur de rose* with you! No thoughts of the future disturb the self-satisfied emotions of thy exulting bosom! And who is he beside her—the handsome young aide-de-camp? With easy bend he leans gracefully towards the carriage, and checks his fiery Arab. Mark how he rattles, and says his agreeable things, with all the airs of a conscious "eligible," whilst the gratified vanity of the woman sparkles in her eyes and glows in her animated countenance. Here comes an intruder, bound for a distant bazaar—jingle, jingle, jingle! What a contrast! a native ruth or bylie, bullocks in a long trot, a pretty black damsel,

> With rings on her fingers,
>
> And bells on her toes—

she of childhood's song to a nicety—peeping from behind the blinds. "Ah! turn not away those sweet eyes!" Egad, she's off—driver twisting the tails and goading the quarters of his cattle to "keep up the steam." There whirl past in tilbury or tandem a brace of recently-arrived writers, regular Meltonians, doing the thing *secundum artem,* and determined to astonish the crowd. How knowingly, his person obliqued-quarter front, does the driver sit! With what gentlemanly *abandon* does the drivee loll back in the vehicle! These are high-spirited fellows, who drink their claret, and have never known a care, and "d——n every thing that is low!"

See, with *andante* movement now advances the ponderous chariot of the great Baboo Maha Raja Spooney Persaud Mullik, the great milch-cow of the lawyers, and who gives his lac at a time from the genuine impulses of a *native* benevolence; turbaned coachman; Baboo within, wrapped in cashmeres, fat, yellow, and bolt upright as the effigy on a tombstone.

Halloo, there! what's this? A race—clear the way! There they come, hired for the evening, "two blind uns and a bolter;" heads down, ears viciously inclined. "Go it, my middies!" Look at the reefer in advance—all aback, toes in his horse's nose, head on the crupper, tugging for bare life to make his craft steer or wear. I thought so—snap go the tiller-ropes—a man overboard—the blue-jacket rolls in the dust: he's up again, hat rammed over his eyes—but the bolter's off—catch him who can!

There goes, at a gee-up hobble, a shandry-dan, with two Armenians in it—highly respectable men, with queer velvet caps, and very episcopal-looking aprons—strange mixture of European and Asiatic, neither flesh nor fowl—Topee Wala or Puckree Bund.[7] They nod to two gentlemen passing in a gig, of the gimcrack order—gentlemen in white jackets and ditto hats; highly *polished* men, *i.e.* in the face, which seems, indeed, to have had the benefit of a bottle of Day and Martin's real japan blacking—who are they?

Valiant Lusitanians, illustrious descendants of Albuquerque and Vasco de Gama—Messrs. Joachim de Reberero and Gomez de Souza, writers in the office of the salt and opium department. Who is this in cords, top boots, and white jacket—a dapper, well-fed little man, on a tall English horse, to which he bears about the same relative proportions that Falstaffs bread did to his sherris sack?—Ay, who?

Come, tell it, and burn ye—

He is—can he help it?—a special attorney—

an *attaché* of the Supreme Court.

Such, then, is the Course of Calcutta; and such a little melodramatic sketch may give some idea of the varied objects which there meet the eye.

We drove up and down several times, and recognized not a few of our ship companions; amongst others, the little colonel, in a barouche with some ladies, whom he was evidently entertaining with a "yarn." Darkness now came on apace. The mussalchees, or link boys, with their flaring mussauls, met their masters at turns of the roads, to light them to their several homes, and we thought it time to depart. Marpeet drove to his quarters, where he invited me to pass the evening, to which I assented. Sitting over our wine, Marpeet discussed the Course, and gave me a few bits of scandal, touching sundry ladies and gentlemen we had seen, over which I yawned, for I have ever abominated what are called private histories.

"Well," said Marpeet, "I think I shall start for the Upper Provinces, and leave you sooner than I thought. The lads there in the old corps are very anxious to have me amongst them once more. I have a letter to-day from Tippleton—an old friend of mine, who is a real good fellow, with no nonsense about him (I hope to bring you acquainted some day)—urging my going up without delay. Let me see," said he, feeling his pocket, "I think I have it somewhere about me. Oh, yes, here it is, and you may read it, if you like. He is rather fond, you will perceive, of the Hindoostanee zuban, and so forth, but he does not set up for a great scribe, but is what is better, a devilish honest fellow. Come governor, toss off your heel-taps, and take some more wine."

Every language has, probably, terms which, from their superior terseness or euphony, express more fully the meanings they are intended to convey than corresponding words in another tongue; and this certainly justifies their adoption. But there is also a practice of using foreign phrases indiscriminately, when the native ones would do quite as well. Shortly after the last peace, novel-writers could express nothing with point and effect but in French and Italian; so in India there are a class of men, generally small wits, who interlard their conversation with Hindoostanee words and phrases; these they often sport in England, where of course they are unintelligible and out of place. Ye guardian genii! who watch over the "well of English undefiled," whilst you admit what will purify and sweeten, prevent its unhallowed pollution from garbage thrown into it by every idle and thoughtless hand! And now for Captain Tippleton's letter, which though rather more fully charged with Hindoostanee terms than any the writer ever met with, yet presents some likeness of a certain species of Indian epistolary style (of the slip-slop and slang-wanging order):—

Grillumabad, Aug. 18—

My dear Marpeet,

Just now taking a *dekh* (look) at the Calcutta *Khubber* (News), I saw your name amongst those of a batch of griffs and *Tazu wulaits* (fresh Europeans), having arrived by the *Rottenbeam Castle*. Welcome back, my dear fellow, to *John Kumpany ka raj*. I hope you will cut Calcutta, and lose no time in *puhonchowing* (conveying) yourself up by *dawk* to join the old *pultun* (battalion), in which, I am sorry to say, things have been quite *oolta poolta* (topsy-turvy) since you left us. Tims has quitted the corps, as you probably know. He was a d——d *puckha* (stingy) hand, and a *muggra* (sulky) beast into the bargain. However, I don't think we have gained much by his *budlee* (successor), our new *kummadan* (commandant)—a regular *bahadur* (great person), who *dicks* our lives out with *kuddum ootou* (drill), *dumcows* (bullies) the native officers, and *gallees* (abuses) the Jacks (sepoys). Tomkins and I still chum together; he, as *gureeb* and *soost* (quiet and lazy) as ever, and as fond of the *brandy pawney*, sends his *bhote bhote salaam* to Marpeet Sahib. Station dull—no *tumasha* (fun), as in the old times, when we were first here. The other day, however, old Dickdar, our brigadier, gave a *burra khanna* (dinner); his *loll* (claret) was bang-up and you may be sure we did not spare the *simpkin* (champagne); *burra beebee* (great lady) very gracious, and a great show-off of the *bal butchos* (children). We had the old *bajja* (band), your creation and hobby, in attendance, and got up a *nautch*. Smirks, our adjutant, quite a *burra admee* (great man) since he mounted the *kantas* (spurs), bucking up to and devilish sweet on the spinster; but it won't *hoga* (do); nothing under the revenue or judicial department will go down there—Samjah Sahib?—You understand me. Tip us a *chit*, my dear fellow, by return of *dawk*, and believe me,

My dear Marpeet, ever yours very truly,

Jonas Tippleton.

"Well," said I, "as far as I can understand, it seems a very friendly sort of a letter; but I should be better able to judge if you would give me the English of it."

Marpeet laughed, called me a critical dog, and put the letter in his pocket.

"Come," added I, "since you have shown me your letter, I will read you mine; one I have received from my factotum, Chattermohun Ghose, accounting for his temporary absence, which, for the choiceness of its language, is quite a *bijou* in its way. Chattermohun tells me he was for some time a writer in an adjutant's office, as also in a merchant's counting-house here in Calcutta, which doubtless accounts for the phraseology smacking not a little of the technical language of both those schools. Here it is:—

"'Most respectful and honoured Sir,

"'Greatly labouring for fearful apprehension that sudden non-appearance should dictate condemnation from the sensible benignity of your excellency's reverence, and feeling in concatenation that explanation was indispensable, I have herewith the honour to inform you, that one of my family (now consisting of six children effective of various denominations) was recently solemnized in holy matrimony and adoptedly conducted according to prescribed rite and custom of native religion. This solemnization was carried into production my house in country by Boitacoolah T'hannah, wither in my patriarchal duty have repair for a few day.

"'According to last order of your reverence, have instruct to Gopee Nauth, of China Bazaar, to disperse to your quarter goods as per margin,[8] for which he expect the favour of early remittance. I have also passed to credit of master account 16 rupees 8 annas, leaving balance my favour 256 rupees 5 annas 3 pice, as per account enclosed. Trusting from this statement of explanation your honour not think me absent without leave, I have honour to be, with deep respect and consideration,

"'Your most obedient humble servant,

"'Chattermohun Ghose, *Sircar*.

"'To his Exc. Ensign Gernon, South Bks.'"

"Well," said Marpeet, "that beats cock-fighting."

CHAPTER X

Two great sources of attraction to young men existed in Calcutta at the time of which I am now writing (upwards of twenty-five years ago), and do still exist, for anything I know to the contrary, Tulloh's and other auction-rooms, and the China bazaar. At the former almost daily sales took place of every kind of property from a ship to a penknife, a rabbit to an elephant; in the latter, all the heterogeneous commodities of an American store were to be seen mingled pell-mell—raspberry jam, Milroy's saddles, best pickles, regulation-swords, wall-shades, China dishes, hog-spears, Harvey's sauce, &c.—of which, however, more anon. Catalogues of the various articles to be disposed of at the day's sale at Tulloh's are (or were) left daily at the houses in or near Calcutta, and made their appearance, regularly with the newspapers at the break-table, tempting to extravagance, by stimulating latent desires or creating fictitious wants.

In our commercial country and its dependencies, where Plutus is the deity chiefly adored, it seems proper and strictly in character that the pulpits connected with his worship, however remotely, should be ably and efficiently filled. Here, in England, we know this to be generally the case, and what lustre the eloquence of some of our leading auctioneers has shed on the profession; how truly, indeed, more than one of them merit the praise which Johnson, happily quoting from Horace, bestowed on the genius of Goldsmith:—"*Nihil quod tetigit non ornavit.*"

There was no lack of this shining talent, oratorical power, and technical tact, amongst the auctioneers of Calcutta, seasoned with humour, pathos, or persuasion, according to the occasion. How often have I heard the merits of a venerable steed proclaimed; his infirmities and defects (with a delicate regard to his presence) lightly touched upon, or at most so disposed, like the shades in a picture, as to heighten and improve the general effect! How frequently have I been pleasantly reminded of the good old maxim "*de mortuis nil nisi bonum,*" when listening to the commendations of a batch of dead and ullaged beer! And how often tempted to make an investment in a cheap "gross of green spectacles," "a lot of damaged huckaback," or the like, from a strong impression, fostered by the auctioneers persuasive eloquence, "that they might some day come into use," a contingent probability largely insisted upon!

What a Herculean task it is to conjure money out of some people's pockets! Consummate tact is requisite to effect this end. What a world of machinery must be put in motion before the movable crank, the owner's hand, finds its way into that pecuniary receptacle! A bungler may fumble for a month and not find the motive spring, whilst an adept will touch it in a moment. Yes, I see no reason on earth why the auctioneers should not rank with the liberal professions. Does not the craft combine, in an eminent degree, many of the leading features of those professions, which (always considering the predominant turn of the national mind) unaccountably rank higher in public estimation—the special pleading of the lawyer, the eloquence of the senator, and the business-like airs of the merchant? Does not the auctioneer, like another Charles Martel—ay, and with the same weapon, too—knock down his lots with as much effect as the soldier does his? Does he not pronounce orations over the dead, as has been already shown, and display a beautiful morality in covering, as with the mantle of charity, a multitude of defects? Is not his "going, going, gone," too, a brief and pithy sermon, touchingly calculated to remind us of our common mortality?

And in all these, are not the functions of a higher pulpit strikingly exercised? Ought he not to be a poet, painter, critic—in short, a man of taste and general information, or how is he to descant with effect on the merits of his multifarious wares? Should he not be a phrenologist, that he may suit his arguments to the several developments of his bidders; a physiognomist, that he may judge of the effect by the unerring index of the countenance, whether rallying, bantering, bullying, or wheedling, is the cue; and a casuist, that he may reconcile his mind to the various tricks of the trade? and, finally, should he not have a deep insight into human nature in general, and know well its various assailable points? "Shall I say, 1,000 rupees for you, sir, for that Arab? no animal can look better, well mounted, I assure you; he will suit your weight and figure to a nicety—was ridden by the Hon. Capt. Dangle, just gone home, a gentleman very much of your appearance, sir, and who lately, to borrow the language of our immortal bard, was wont on our course here 'to witch the world with noble horsemanship,' upon that very Arab. Sir—shall I take your bid?" A complaisant nod—the business is done. "Thank you, sir—1,000 rupees for the Arab—going, going, gone!"

One morning, Grundy and I breakfasted together in my room, which was within a few doors of his own, when one of the afore-mentioned catalogues found its way into our possession.

"Grundy," said I, "whilst I despatch this fish and rice, as you appear to have done, do just read what there is for sale to-day at the auction. I have a feeling that I want something, though, hang me if I can exactly tell what it is."

Grundy commenced, and read as follows:—"Lot 1st. Three fine alderney cows."

"Deuce take the cows," said I; "push on."

"Three calves belonging to ditto."

"Fire away."

"Three Cape sheep, of the Doombah breed."

"Doombah breed! that sounds well; egad, I think I must have a bid for the sheep—what comes next?"

"A noble French mastiff, two bull-dogs, two wire-haired Scotch terriers, and a greyhound bitch with pup, just imported by the *Founderwell*."

"That's the ticket," I exclaimed, with eagerness; "I'll have some of the dogs, if they go reasonably—that's a settled point—for there's rare hunting to be had, I hear, on the way up."

Grundy ran down several columns more of live and dead stock; and there were many things, without which I found I could not comfortably exist for twenty-four hours longer, though, I must confess, I had not thought of them before.

"By-the-bye," drawled Grundy, "talking of dogs, there was a black fellow at my door just now with one for sale."

"Was there?" I eagerly asked; "what sort of an animal, and what did the fellow want for it?"

"Why," said my friend, "I think it was a sort of a terrier; but if you choose, I'll get my servant to call the man; he can't be very far off."

"Do," said I, "send for him."

In a few moments, the arrival of the dog and man was duly announced, and both were admitted to my apartment. The vendor was one of those black, dirty, low-caste natives, generally attached to European corps, and denominated "cookboys." Dress—a soldier's old castoff coat, a dirty cloth round his loins, and a skull-cap on his head. As for the dog, he is not, perhaps, so easily described; he was reddish, stood high on the legs, and had a wild look; his tail and ears, however, were clipped in a very *varment* sort of manner, evincing decided science in the operator; and his owner assured me, in broken English, that he was "berry high caste dog," a thoroughbred terrier; his name Teazer, and a capital fellow to worry a cat or a jackal.

The creature did not certainly look altogether like the terriers I had been in the habit of seeing in England; but still, the state of the ears and tail, the name, and above all, the qualifications, were strong *primâ facie* proofs that he was one. As for the points of difference, they might, I thought, have resulted from the influence of climate, which, as it alters the appearance of the European biped very considerably, might, I very logically inferred, have a similar effect on the quadrupeds imported, or their descendants, in the first or second generation at least. In short, I bought him for Rs. 10, and a great bargain I thought I had; tied him up to the leg of my cot, intending that he should form the *nucleus* of a future pack. I was, however, destined very shortly after to be put a good deal out of conceit of him.

A few days after I had made my purchase, Captain Marpeet dropped in, and took a seat on my cot as he was wont. Hearing the rattling of a chain underneath, he said,

"What the deuce have you got here, Gernon?"

"A dog," said I; "a terrier I lately bought."

"A terrier! eh? Let's have a look at him."

Teazer, on being summoned, came out from under the bed, gave himself a shake, and, on seeing Marpeet, who was strange to him, and rather an odd-looking fellow to boot, incontinently cocked up his nose and emitted a most lugubrious howl, one with which the Pariars[9] in India are wont to serenade "our chaste mistress, the moon."

"Halloo," said Marpeet, with a look of surprise, "where on earth did you get this beast? Why, he's a regular terrier *bunnow*."[10]

"A terrier *bunnow*," said I, "what's that?"

"Why," rejoined the captain, "he's a thorough Pariar docked and cropped to make him look like a terrier; it's a common trick played upon griffs, and you've been taken in, that's all. What did you give for him?"

"Why, ten rupees," I replied; "and I thought I had him remarkably cheap."

"Cheap!" said the captain, with infinite contempt; "he's not worth five pice; kick him out! hang him!"

"Thank you," said I; "but as I've bought him, I'll keep him; he'll help to make up a pack, and I don't see why he should not act up to his assumed character, and hunt very well; you see he knows how to give tongue, at all events."

"Ha! ha!" said Marpeet; "come, that's not so bad; but he's a brute, upon my life—a useless brute, kick him to the d—l."

"No," I rejoined, a little nettled to hear my dog abused after that fashion; "I tell you I'll keep him; besides, I have no acquaintance in the quarter you mention, and should be sorry to send him where he would be likely to annoy you again."

Here were symptoms of downright insubordination. The captain stared at me in astonishment, and emitted a long and elaborate "whew!"

"'Pon my honour, regular disrespect to your superior officer. Well, after that, I must have a glass of brandy-pawny."

"So you shall," said I, "with all my heart; but you really were a little too hard, and forgot the saying, 'Love me, love my dog.'"

To return, however, from this little episode. Grundy and I, in pursuance of our determination to visit the auction, got into our palankeens, and soon found ourselves amidst the dust, noise, and motion of Tank Square, near which the auction, or outcry (as it is more usually termed in India) is held. A long covered place, something like a repository, filled with palankeens, carriages, horses, &c., for sale, had to be passed through before we reached the auction-room, where goods of all kinds were disposed of. This we found crammed with natives, low Europeans, black Portuguese, and others of the motley population of Calcutta, mingled with a few civilians, and a "pretty considerable" sprinkling of redcoats from Barrackpore or the fort, all more or less intent upon the bidding.

The auctioneer, a good-looking man and remarkably fluent, was mounted on his rostrum, and holding forth upon the merits of certain goods, which a native assistant, on a platform a little lower than the pulpit, was handing round for inspection. Grundy and I forced our way in, watching anxiously to see if any thing "in our way" was exhibiting. At last, the auctioneer took up a goodly-sized knife, with some dozen blades, &c. These he opened daintily and deliberately, and then, holding up the knife and turning it about, he said,

"Now here's a pretty thing—a highly-finished article—a perfect *multum in parvo*. Don't all of you bid for this at once, gentlemen, if you please. Here's a large blade, you see, to cut bread and cheese with, a small one to mend your pens, a corkscrew to open a bottle of Hodgson's pale ale when you are out shooting, tweezers to pull the thorns out of your toes, pincers, file, gimlet—all complete. A most useful article that, and (with marked emphasis, and an eye towards Grundy and me, which made us exchange looks significant of purchase), one which no young sportsman should be without."

That was sufficient; I was determined to have it, and after an eager bid or two, it was knocked down to me. I found afterwards, however, to my extreme surprise and dismay, I had unconsciously purchased a lot of three dozen of them, enough to set up a cutler's stall in a small way. There was no help for it, however; I was obliged to take them all, though I determined in future to study well the catalogue before I ventured on a bid.

The dogs, I found, had attracted the particular notice of more sportsmen than myself. A young ensign from Barrackpore carried off the greyhound hitch for Rs. 200, a little more than a month's pay. A writer in the buildings bought the French mastiff and the terrier, which went high, and I was obliged to content myself with one of the bull-dogs, a sinister-looking old fellow, with one eye, who went cheap, and would have been cheaper still, had not Grundy, whom I requested to secure it, bidden silently against me in the crowd several times before I had providentially discovered my opponent. Poor beast! he died three months after, on my way up, of *nostalgia*, I rather think, and I gave him decent sepulture on a spit of sand in the Ganges.

From the auction we proceeded to the China bazaar.

"Grundy," said I, as we went along, rather *nonchalamment*, "you need not say anything to Captain Marpeet, about my buying those knives."

"What knives?" he asked.

"I have my reasons for it," said I, "that's enough."

Grundy promised to be mum.

The China bazaar! What Bengalee, military man in particular, who does not know that attractive resort—that repository of temptations! What a host of pleasant recollections it is calculated to revive!

This place is situated at the back of Tank Square, and is enclosed by walls, and entered by gates, at several points. The shops are in long flat-roofed ranges, generally of (I believe) two stories, intersecting each other at right angles; a margin of terrace, a foot or two from the ground, runs along the front of the several shops or stores. Sheltered here and there by an eave or thatched projection, seated in chairs, cross-legged, and in other un-English attitudes, quite at their ease, and smoking their pipes, the baboos, or shopkeepers, may be seen, each opposite his emporium, into which they invite the numerous visitors to the bazaar to enter, assuring them they will find everything they may want "chip," and of the first quality.

As Grundy and I sauntered down one of the streets, we were struck by the appearance of one of the native shopkeepers, who, with an air of courtier-like urbanity, invited us to enter his store. In stature, he was about six feet three or four, stout in proportion; a muslin chudder or toga was thrown over his shoulders, and a piece more round his waist, but slightly concealing his brawny form; altogether he was the finest-looking Bengalee I ever beheld; indeed, I thought it a pity such thews and sinews, so well calculated for the tug of war, should be lost in the inglorious inaction of the China bazaar. This worthy I afterwards learnt was that celebrated character "Jawing Jack," well known amongst cadets for his *copia verborum* and dignified address. Nature and destiny had evidently been at cross-purposes in the management of Jack; the former had clearly intended him morally for what he was physically, a great man, but his stars had thwarted the design.

Jack rose from his chair as we drew near, overshadowing us striplings with his Patagonian bulk. I, for my part (being then what is vulgarly called a "lathy chap"), felt myself disagreeably *small* beside him, doubly so he being a "black fellow," and thought I was under the necessity of speaking pretty big, in order to make up for the deficiency, and to place myself more on a level with him. "Jawing Jack" had had large experience of griffs, and, though he treated us in a kind of patronising manner, he cautiously avoided anything that might lead to offence, and a consequent lowering of his own dignity.

There is a sly satire sometimes in the calm and imperturbable deportment of the Asiatic, when dealing with the rattling, blustering, overbearing European, which conveys a tacit censure well calculated to shame our boasted civilization. "Lately arrived from Europe, gentlemen, I suppose? Hope you are quite well? Will you please do me the honour to walk into my shop—shall be happy to supply anything re-qui-red, at very reasonable price. I have honour to be well known to all military gentlemen at Barrackpore, and sell best of European articles, and no 'Niverpool[11] goods.'" Having rummaged "Jawing Jack's" shop, and bought a few articles, we took our departure, promising at parting to honour him with our future custom.

The Bengalese have a wonderful deal of versatility and acuteness, certainly not naturally the mental power and energy of the European; but as they live temperately, and do not clog the intellectual wheels with beef and malt liquor, the mental machinery is generally in capital working order.

On returning to my quarters, I found a chuprassy, or messenger, with a note from General Capsicum, acknowledging the receipt of a letter I had sent him from his friend Sir Toby Tickle, and requesting my company to tiffin and dinner on the following day, at his house at Garden Reach.

A little before the appointed hour, I ordered a palankeen, and proceeded to the general's residence, situated in a pleasant domain, some two or three miles from Calcutta. On arriving, I was shown up-stairs into the drawing room, which commanded a pleasant view of the Hoogly, with its moving scene of boats and shipping, and a distant peep of Fort William.

I was standing gazing on the prospect, admiring the boats under sail gliding from side to side, walking as it were the minuet of the waters, the shadows skimming over the river, and the milk-white villas on the opposite bank starting out from amidst the bright green of surrounding groves, when the rustle of a gown and a slight touch on the shoulder aroused me from my state of abstraction. It was the young widow of whom I have already made mention, "the softened image" of the rough old general, my Hibernian host.

"How do you do, Mr. Gernon?" said she, extending her hand with exceeding frankness and smiling cordiality; "I am so glad to see you again and not looking in any way the worse for your sojourn in Calcutta." (Oh! that our English pride and sensitiveness, those adamantine trammels of caste, which strangle so many of our virtues, would let us have a little more of that single-hearted openness "which thinketh no evil"—it is so comfortable!) "Have you seen my father yet?" asked Mrs. Delaval, for that was her name.

I answered in the negative.

"Oh, then," she continued, "he will be here immediately when he knows of your arrival, for he is anxious, I know, to see you; he is somewhere in the house, amusing himself with his violin. But pray, Mr. Gernon, be seated," she continued, "and tell me how you like India, now that you have seen a little more of it."

"I like it much," I replied, "and never was happier in my life. I have got my commission, and as soon as posted to a regiment, am off to the Upper Provinces by water. I have some idea of applying for a particular corps, but have not yet decided on that point: they say you should not interfere with the operations of the Fates, but leave yourself to their direction. What, madam," continued I, "would you advise me to do?"

"Oh! really," said Mrs. Delaval, smiling at the idea of my asking her advice on such a point, "I fear I am incompetent to advise you, not knowing all the circumstances of your position; you ought, of course, to consider well before you act, and having so done, leave the result to Providence. I am, however," said she, somewhat seriously, "a decided predestinarian, and believe that

'There is a providence that shapes our ends,

Rough-hew them how we will.'"

"It is a puzzling subject," said I, "and one that is rather beyond me; one if I remember rightly, that even bewildered the devils in Pandemonium. However, I think the safest maxim to hold by is, that 'conduct is fate.'"

This was rather a philosophical opinion for a griffin, but one which I have always held, though young blood at that time and since has often capsized the philosopher.

"Well, Mr. Gernon," continued she, "you have my best wishes for your happiness and success in life; all is *couleur de rose* with you now; may it ever so continue! Already," said she, and the tear glistened, "the clouds of life are beginning to pass over me."

As she said this, she crossed her fair white hands on her lap, and the widow's eyes sadly dropped on her wedding ring, the little golden circlet type of eternal fidelity. I understood it, and was silent. Silence is preferable on such occasions, perhaps, to the commonplaces of condolence. We both continued mute for some moments; she looking at her ring, I out of the window.

At length, I ventured to say,

"Dear madam, do not deem me impertinent, I pray; but cheer up; remember, as my Irish half-countryman beautifully expresses it, 'every dark cloud has a silver lining,' and there are doubtless many, many happy days yet in store for you."

I should have premised, that Mrs. Delaval had lately lost her husband, a fine young fellow, who fell in the storm of a small Polygar fort on the coast, and Time had not yet brought that balm with which in due course he heals the wounds of the heart, unless the very deepest. I was certainly waxing tender, when the idea of Olivia, my poor abandoned Olivia, crossed my mind. "What would Mrs. Grundy say," thought I, "if she knew of it?"

The widow gave her auburn locks a toss, made an effort at self-possession, smiled through her tears, and was herself again.

"By-the-bye, Mr. Gernon," said she, "though but a recent acquaintance, I will assume the privilege of an old friend, and give you some little information whilst we are alone, which may be of some advantage to you in your intercourse with this family."

I looked alarmed, not knowing what was forthcoming. She perceived what was passing in my mind.

"You need not think, Mr. Gernon," and she smiled, "that you have come amongst giants or ogres, who are likely to form designs against your life and liberty. Nothing quite so bad as that—no. What I wished to say is, that my father is a man of warm and generous impulses, but violently passionate and eccentric; and I entreat you to be cautious in what you say before him, and do not press any subject if you find him evincing impatience. If he likes he may serve you; but if he takes a prejudice, he is exceedingly persecuting and bitter: a warm friend but an inexorable foe. Mrs. Capsicum, to much vulgarity adds all my father's violence and irritability, with none of his redeeming qualities. You must be submissive, and prove yourself a 'good listener,' or you will have little chance of standing well with her."

This was said with some little asperity of manner, plainly indicating that the step-mother was not more popular than step-mothers generally are.

"As for the others you will see here, you may safely be left to the guidance of your own judgment and discretion in your conduct towards them."

I thanked Mrs. Delaval for her information, which, I saw, emanated from the purest feeling of womanly kindness, and promised to be on my guard, and endeavour to profit by it.

CHAPTER XI

I must here interrupt the thread of my narrative, in order to give a few particulars respecting my host and his family, which may serve as samples of the olden time of India.

The general was the youngest of the ten sons of Sir Gerald Capsicum, a fire-eating baronet of a "rare ould ancient Irish family," and was sent to India about anno 1750, with little more than his sword, his brogue, and the family love of fighting wherewith to assist him on in the world. The general's career had been varied, and he had gone through all the adventures, public and domestic, which usually happened to those whose lot, in respect to time and place, had been similarly cast.

I have said the general was an Irishman; it follows as a natural consequence, that he was extremely susceptible of the tenderest of passions; and as in his early days there were few white dames in the land, like many others he e'en put up with a black one—attached himself to Sung Sittara Begum (the "Queen of Stars"), one of the gazelle-eyed daughters of Hind.

This union, though not cemented by the forms of marriage, was, on the whole, more harmonious and enduring than many that are. I say on the whole; for if tradition may be depended on, the Queen of Stars was wont, now and then, to exhibit traits of vivacity, which were rather of a *striking* than of a pleasing nature. With these trifling breaks, the union long harmoniously subsisted, and was not finally dissolved till the angel of death, one fine day, summoned the Begum to the seventh heaven.

By the Begum, the general had Major John Capsicum, an officer in the service, and commanding the forces of his highness Ram Row Bhow Punt, the Jam of Ghurrumnugger, a Mahratta potentate of small note, whose territories it might be difficult to discover in the map; secondly, Augustus, an indigo planter in the district of Jessore, commonly called by the general's native servants (who, like all the rest of the fraternity, were not *au fait* at European names) "Disgustus Sahib;" and Mrs. Colonel Yellowly, a lady of high and indomitable spirit, who died some years before the period to which I am referring, and of whom I could learn little more from record or tradition than that she was rather celebrated for the manufacture of Chutnee and Dopiajah curry, talked a good deal of a certain *terra incognita* called "home," and ultimately went off rather suddenly,—as some affirm, from chagrin in consequence of having a point of precedence decided against her, arising out of a dispute with Lady Jiggs at a presidency party as to who *de jure* should first come in or go out.

The stickling for precedency, by the way, is a disorder very prevalent in colonial dependencies; and like gravitation, which increases with the squares of the distance, its intensity seems to be governed by a somewhat similar law, and to exist in an inverse ratio to the apparent cause for it.

Long after the general had passed his fiftieth year, he married the mother of the amiable widow (a nonpareil grafted on a crab), by all accounts a charming person, who, yielding to importunity, took old Capsicum to gratify the ambition of worldly parents, in whose opinion wealth and rank are all that are essential to connubial happiness.

Poor thing! she gave her hand, but her heart was another's. The worm-i'-the-bud was there, and soon did the business. Opportunity offered— nature was too powerful for the colder suggestions of duty—she eloped with the man she loved; but even love cannot flourish in an atmosphere of scorn. Mankind are intensely gregarious. Shunned—deserted by her own sex, who, like birds (though from more obvious cause), peck their wounded fellows to death—she died in a lone outpost, and the winds of the jungles pipe over her solitary grave.

"C'est bien difficile d'être fidèle

A de certains maris, faits d'an certain modelle,

Et qui donne à sa fille un homme qu'elle haït.

Est responsable au Ciel pour le mal qu'elle fait."

Admirable Molière! you never penned a more striking truth. Parents, ponder it well.

The general, after the lapse of some years, with the characteristic valour of the Capsicums, boldly ventured, a short time before I knew him, on a second marriage; but here he caught a Tartar. Mrs. Capsicum the second was an Irish lady (woman I should perhaps say), who came out to India avowedly on spec., with the full determination of marrying a good establishment, with comfortable reversionary prospects, however they might happen to be encumbered. She made play at the general, sang "Erin mavourneen" and "Cathleen O'More," talked of the Callaghans and Brallaghans, revived the general's boyish reminiscences of the green hills of Sligo, and ultimately led him, or rather had him carried, to the hymeneal altar! Of love—the proper cement of the marriage-union—there was none, on her side at least.

But to return to my narrative.

The widow and I had not been long engaged in conversation (which, as I before hinted, was becoming rather interesting), when we heard the scrape of a violin outside in the passage.

"Oh, here is my father," said Mrs. Delaval, "coming from his room. Now remember my caution."

I was about to reply, but she laid her finger on her lip expressively, as much as to say, "Another time; he's here."

The old general now entered, with a black velvet sort of nightcap stuck rakishly on his head, and playing rather jauntily "St. Patrick's Day in the Morning," to which he hummed an accompaniment—his voice displaying, as usual, all that vigour in its tones which, as I have before remarked, afforded so striking a contrast to his dried-up and time-worn frame: as he entered with his spindle shanks, huge frill, voluminous upper works, pigtail, and velvet cap, I thought I never saw a droller figure. Still the gallant bearing and nonchalance of the little old Irishman, who evidently was unconscious of anything at all out of the way in himself, rather neutralized any feeling of disrespect which his figure was at first calculated to excite.

On seeing me, he finished off the saint with a few galloping flourishes, pushed the fiddle on the table; transferred the stick to his left hand, and made a rapid advance, or rather toddle, towards me, with his right extended.

"Hah, sur, I'm glad to see you," said he; "Mr. Gernon, I believe? Very happy indeed to have your company, sur; shall be glad to show you ivery attintion in ivery sense of the word, sur, for the sake of my old friend Sir Toby; and I doubt not," he continued, with a low bow of the old school and a smile, "that I shall be able also to add, on your own."

As he made this courteous speech and inclination, his eye lighted on a letter lying on the table, which quickly threw the irritable old fellow off his balance, and put the courtier to flight.

"Why,——mee heart, Cordalia," he thundered out in a voice that startled me; "by all that's good, that egragious ass, Ramdial, has gone without the letter. A man naid have the timper of an angel to dale with these fellows."

Mrs. Delaval, to cut the affair short, rose immediately from her seat, and taking the letter, called a servant to the head of the stairs, and quickly rectified the omission.

"Thank ye, Cordalia, mee love," said the old general as she returned; "thank ye, mee darling;" and taking her hand and drawing the graceful creature towards him, he imprinted a kiss on her cheek.

There's no use mincing matters—I certainly envied him the privilege.

This little interruption over, I returned to a speech which, having previously worded and fashioned in rather a superior style, I thought it a pity should be lost.

I said, after a hem or two, that I felt deeply obliged for his cordial reception of me, that I should study to deserve his good opinion, and to realize the gratifying anticipations he had so obligingly expressed, &c. &c.

"Ye will, sur; ye will, sur," said the general; "I've not the laste doubt of it; and, plase God, we'll some day see you as accomplished a soldier as was your poor uncle, the colonel."

"What! sir," said I, pleased with the discovery, and with no fear that *he* was about to come Chattermohun over me; "did you then know my uncle, Colonel Gernon?"

"Know him!" said the general, with energy and warmth—"I did, and right well too; we were in Goddard's march together and the Rohilla campaign, and in many places besides. Yes," he continued, warming as he went on, "poor Pat Gernon and I have broiled under the same tint and fought under the same banner, ay, by G——, and mounted the same brache together; yes," added he, clutching his fiddlestick, and looking as fierce as if he was bursting through the fire and carnage of an assault, "I think I now hear the shouts of the inimy, and see your brave uncle lading on his gallant Sapoys through fire and smoke, his beaver in one hand and his sword in the other. Ah," he went on, touched and overcome, whilst his eye moistened, "them were the days: the thought of them—it is now long, long back—and of all my old companions gone, comes over me sometimes like a faint air or a summer's drame. Know your uncle! Ay did I, and a braver soldier or a better man (though he had his faults, and who the divil has not?) never broke the bread of life."

I felt a sensation of choking, whilst all the ancient blood of the Gernons mantled in my cheeks, as I listened to the veteran's animated laudation of my deceased relative.

"Well, sur," continued the general, suddenly changing the subject, and as if a little ashamed of the weakness and enthusiasm into which he had been betrayed, "and how did you lave my old friend, Sir Toby? Is he as fond of his bottle and his rubber as he used to be? I think he played the best hand at whist of any man I ever knew."

"I believe, sir," said I, "that Sir Toby's habits are unchanged in those respects; though I am unable to speak much of him from personal knowledge, having obtained the letter of introduction which I have had the honour to deliver to you through the kindness of a mutual friend."

"Well, never mind how ye got it, so that ye did get it. I am extramely happy that it has been the manes of introducing to my acquaintance the nephew of my old companion in arms, to whom, by the way, you bear a strong resemblance: so now," he continued, "talk to my daughter, or amuse yourself in any way ye plase till tiffin, and I'll do the same; this is liberty hall, where every man does as he plases. Cordalia, my love, where is your mother?"

"I have not seen Mrs. Capsicum, sir, this morning since breakfast," replied Mrs. Delaval; "but I believe she has gone out to pay some visits."

"Has she?" said the general dryly; "well, now, I thought I noticed a remarkable stillness over the house."

This was said in a manner, I thought, which smacked of what may be termed a bitter mirth.

This conversation had scarcely terminated, when we heard a loud and angry voice on the stairs or landing; and next moment, in sailed Mrs. Capsicum Secunda, with a face that would have made a fine study for a Hecate, a Gorgon, a Fury, or any other of those celebrated characters, in whose countenances the ancients were wont to depict all the wildest play of the passions. Mrs. Delaval turned pale, the old general looked dismayed, and I, for my part, groped for my hat, thinking I might doubtless be *de trop* and better out of the way before the family breeze sprung up, and of which there were such alarming indications.

Mrs. Capsicum seated herself majestically—her lip quivered with rage, and an unhappy poodle, who came to be caressed, and received a sweeping blow from her foot, which caused him to throw a ludicrous somerset. Now, thought I, "look out for squalls."

General Capsicum knew, probably from experience, that his spouse would generally have the last word, but on the present occasion he was determined (or deemed it politic) to have the first.

"Mrs. Capsicum, mee dear," said he, in a deprecating tone, "you don't appear to persave our young friend here, Mr. Gernon" (wishing clearly to throw me out as a tub to the whale). The lady measured me with a momentary glance, and made the stiffest conceivable inclination, accompanied by a look of the concentrated essence of vinegar and brimstone; it was positively annihilating.

After certain premonitory symptoms of Mrs. Capsicum's passion, out it came:—

"Ginrel Capsicum," said she, "aither I lave your house, or that rascal Khoda Buccas, coachmaun, laves your service."

She then proceeded to detail some neglect of which the unfortunate Jehu had been guilty. The general tried to mollify her, but without success, and Khoda Buccas was summoned to the "presence" to answer for his misdeeds: in he came, with a low salaam, and trembling from head to foot.

The general was about to open the charges when Khoda Buccas, who knew all about it beforehand, broke in upon him, and, with the full energy of alarm and great volubility, entered clamorously on his defence.

"*Mera kooch kussor nuheen Kodabund* (No fault of mine, servant of the Lord, and protector of the poor), but *Bijlee Goorah* (the horse Lightning), was sick (*sick maun Hogeya*),[12] and then the roan had lost her hind shoes, *Gureebpurwar*. Here and there, all over the bazaar, your slave hunted for the blacksmith, and could not find him. At last your slave found him, and said, 'Come quick and shoe *Summon Goorah* (the roan horse), for the lady will want the carriage, and her disposition is a little warm (*misaj tora gurrum*), and your slave will be beat and get into trouble;' and so he said to me 'Brother,' said he, &c., &c., and so I was late."

This and a good deal more, as explained to me by Mrs. Delaval, was the rambling defence of Khoda Buccas, coachmaun. The old gentleman seemed disposed to admit its sufficiency; but madame peremptorily ordered off the unhappy charioteer, with the comfortable assurance that he should be flogged and dismissed.

Oh, tyranny, thou propensity of ungenerous souls! like Othello's love, thou growest with indulgence; till, like to every other evil, thou at last evokest the spirit that lays thee low!

Well, the storm at last having fairly subsided, the general hobbled to the couch, and took up a paper, as if glad for a season to retreat within himself. Mrs. Delaval and I carried on a conversation in an under-tone, whilst Mrs. Capsicum in silence digested her choler.

The silence was interrupted by the entrance of a native servant, who, with closed hands, and in a manner profoundly respectful, said something in an under-tone to the beebee sahib.

"Ginrel Capsicum," said Mrs. C., as the servant withdrew, "here is your son Augustus arrived."

"Is he?" said the old general, jumping up and throwing down the paper; "faith, then, I'm glad of it, and ye haven't told me a pleasanter thing for a long time, my deer."

These words were scarcely uttered, when a dark black-whiskered man, of a frank and ingenuous countenance, with a hunting-cap on his head, and a whip in his hand, entered the room, and running up to the old general and seizing his extended hand in both his own, in a manner which bespoke genuine warmth and affection, exclaimed:

"How are you, sir? quite recovered, I hope, from your last attack?"

"Well, my boy, well!" said the general, his eyes sparkling with pleasure as he measured his stalwart dark offspring from head to foot, as if in some doubt as to whether he could really be the sire of such a brawny chiel. "Well! and right glad to see you here; how did you come?"

"Why, I left the factory early this morning, sir," said "Disgustus;" "came on as far as the Budlampore ghaut in the pinnace; from that I drove the buggy down to the Thannah, and there I found Golaub in waiting; I rode him in here at a rattling pace—confounded hot work it was, though; and I expect I've rather taken the shine out of the Arab."

"That's well," said the general, "and now be sated. Augustus, my young friend, Mr. Gernon; Mr. Gernon, my son, Mr. Augustus Capsicum."

I bowed with English formality, but the hearty man of blue did not appear to understand that sort of thing, but came up and shook me by the hand; asked me if I was lately arrived, and said he was glad to see me. This was a pleasing trait, and showed me the frankness of his disposition.

After some little conversation with his mother-in-law, with whom it was easy to perceive he was no particular favourite, and a lively chat with his lovely and generous-minded sister, who it was equally obvious loved her dark brother, in spite of the bend sinister in his escutcheon,[13] General Capsicum again addressed his son:

"Well, Augustus," said he, "what are the prospects of indigo this year? how does the blue look?"

"Oh! fair, sir, very fair. If we have no further rise of the river, and get a few light showers, and the rain does not fall too long to wash the colour out of the plant, and this wind continues, we shall do very well this year. The price is well up, Rs. 300 a maund for the best, and I think we shall make 600. The plant looks beautiful on the Chuckergolly churs—at least it did till the Bobberygunge Talookdar's cows and buffaloes got into it. However, after all, I think we shall, on the whole, have a capital season."

"That's well," said the general. "Egad, I think we'll see you go home with your plum, Augustus, yet."

"Home, sir!" said Augustus; "I know of no home but India. Here I was born, and here, please God, I will die, however singular the determination."

Tiffin was now announced, and we descended to the dining-room. Tiffin, or lunch, is in Bengal a delightful meal, suitable in its character to the climate, which renders the supererogatory one of dinner, particularly in the hot season, with its hecatombs of smoking meat and general superfluity of viands, often very much the reverse.

The tiffin on the whole passed off very agreeably. Mrs. Delaval described society as it exists in the Madras presidency, and much she had seen and heard there. Augustus told us of a recent battle-royal, a sort of Bengalee Chevy Chase, which had been fought between his followers and those of a neighbouring Zumeendar, by way of settling the right to some disputed beegahs of indigo; in which many crowns were cracked, and astonishing feats of chivalry displayed on both sides.

But the parts of his conversation which most delighted me, were the accounts he gave of sundry wild hog and buffalo hunts, which after deducting about 50 per cent. on account of embellishments—for sportsmen, like poets, must be allowed some considerable latitude in that way—were really very exciting. In fact, I told him I was dying to have a touch at the hogs and buffaloes myself, and that I hoped it would not be long before I fleshed my maiden spear on a few of the former.

This looked rather like a fish for an invitation to the Junglesoor Factory, and I won't swear that I was wholly without design on the worthy indigo planter's hospitality in making the remark; whether he, viewed it in this light, or not, I cannot say, but he promptly said he should be happy to gratify my longing in that line, if I would go and spend a fortnight with him at his factory.

I replied, "I should be delighted to accompany him, if I could obtain leave."

"Oh!" said he, "that difficulty can easily be overcome; my father, I dare say, will give you a note to a friend of his in the adjutant-general's office, who'll procure you leave at once."

"I shall have a grate dale of pleasure in so doing," said the general; "but Augustus, now, I entrate you, lade the young man into no scrapes: and don't let us hear of his being gored by a buffalo, or ate up by a tiger, or killed by some of them brutes of horses of yours."

"Oh! no," said Augustus, laughing and winking at me; "well take care of all that, sir."

CHAPTER XII

My last chapter left us seated around the social board at Tiffin. A little incident occurred during this meal, which for a moment disturbed the harmony of the party, and, whilst strongly elucidating the character given by Mrs. Delaval of her father, showed that her caution to me, to be on my guard with the atrabilious old hero, was not bestowed without reason. The general's temper truly was like a pistol with a hair-trigger (as I had afterwards further occasion to observe), going off at the slightest touch, and requiring infinite caution in the handling.

Like many old Indians of that day, and I may add, most old gentlemen, the general piqued himself on the quality of his wines. He had a history for every batch; generally ramifying into almost interminable anecdotes of the Dicks and Bobs, defunct *bon vivans* of other days, who in the course of half a century had partaken of his hospitality.

"What do you think of that claret, Mr. Gernon?" asked the old general, after I had duly engulphed a *bonum magnum* of it. "I'll engage you find that good."

Now I must confess that, up to that period (sundry glasses of ginger and gooseberry inclusive), the aggregate quantity of vinous fluid consumed by me, and constituting the basis of my experience, could not have exceeded two or three dozen at the most. But I was flattered by the general's appeal, and, as a military man, I felt that I ought not to appear ignorant and inexperienced on such a matter.

Many young Oxonians and Cantabs, whom I had known at home, little my seniors, had talked flingingly in my presence of "their wine," and the quantity consumed by the "men" of their respective colleges; and why should not I, methought, assume the air of the "*savoir vivre*," and appear at home in these things, who have already figured in print and buckled cold steel on my thigh? I had heard much, too, of light wines, and dry wines, wines that were full and strong-bodied, &c., and, though I attached no very clear and definite ideas to these terms, I had still a hazy conception of their meaning, and was determined, at all events, to sport one or two of them on the present occasion.

In reply to the general's question, I filled a glass, and after taking an observation of the sun through it (just then darting his evening rays through the venetians) with my right eye, accompanied by a scientific screw of the facial muscles, pronounced it, with a smack, to be a fine full-bodied wine, adding, unhappily, that "I should have almost taken it for port."

The general laid down his knife and fork. "Port! Why, sir, sure ye never drank a drop of good claret in your life, if you say so."

"I beg pardon, sir!" said I (I saw I was getting into a scrape), "but I may perhaps be wrong in saying it resembles port. I meant to say—to imply—that is—that it is very strong claret."

"Pooh, nonsense," said the general pettishly, on whom my explanation was far from producing the desired effect. "Ye can know nothing about claret" (he was not very wide of the mark there). "Strong! like port, indeed!!"

"My dear father," said Mrs. Delaval (the women are ever our good geniuses on these occasions), who marked, I have no doubt, the clouds gathering on my brow, "never mind; what does it signify? You know," said she, laying her hand on the general's shoulder, and looking at him with a sweet and beseeching expression, "you know, Mr. Gernon is quite young, and cannot have had much experience in wines."

"Then let him take my advice, Cordalia, and not talk about what he does not understand. Strong! ha! ha! Port, indeed!"

I was thunderstruck, and thought verily I should have launched the bottle at the head of the testy old veteran, so deep a wound had my pride received. I could hardly believe it possible that one of evidently so fine a character in the main, could give way to such unbecoming conduct on so trifling a matter.

The fact is, the general had had his crosses and trials, and such often shatter the temper irretrievably, though the heart and principles may remain sound—much charity and discrimination are requisite to enable us to form a just judgment of others, to decide on the predominant hue of that mingled skein which constitutes individual character.

Augustus, worthy fellow that he was, saw my distress and redoubled his civility, whilst Mrs. Delaval, by that tact and kindness which women best know how to exhibit on such occasions, endeavoured to soften my sense of the indignity; even Mrs. Capsicum took up the cudgels in my behalf, and told the general roundly that he made himself quite ridiculous about his wine. But all would not do; the affront was too recent, and I was moody and glum, pondering within myself as to whether there were any well-established precedents on record, of ensigns of seventeen calling out and shooting generals of eighty.

General Capsicum's irritability, however, soon subsided, and compunctious visitings arose; I could see this by his eye and the softened expression of his countenance, and that he was moreover anxious to make the *amende honorable*; at last he reached the bottle and filled himself a bumper and me another.

"Come," said he, good-humouredly, "let us try another glass, and d——n the port. Here's your very good health, and success to your first day's hog-hunting with Augustus."

I returned the salutation rather stiffly, for, though of a placable nature, I had not digested the affront; however, the tide of my anger was turned, and by dinnertime the general and I were as good friends as if nothing had happened.

We lingered for an hour or two at the tiffin table, Augustus Sahib entertaining me with some details of snipe-shooting, and arranging a programme of our future sporting operations, the general drowsily smoking his hookah and nodding in his chair, with an occasional start and muttered commentary on our conversation, indicative, I once or twice thought, of some fresh explosion.

At length, on the approach of evening, the servants, as is usual in India, unbolted and threw open the long venetian doors, to admit the cool air, and out we sauntered on the lawn, to join the ladies (to whose number some addition had been made), and who had preceded us, and were admiring the moving scene on the river.

The sun had just gone down, and all nature seemed to be with one accord putting forth a rejoicing shout, an excess of that luminary producing all the torpid effects which arise from a deficiency of his beams elsewhere. The kite whistled querulously from the house-top, the maynas and squirrels chattered joyfully in the trees, ring-doves cooed, and the bright yellow mango birds and the dark coel (loved of Indian maids) shot through the cool groves and glades of cocoa-nut and bananas (plantains), uttering their clear and shrilly notes.

Mr. Augustus joined the stately Mrs. Capsicum and the newly-arrived spinster, whilst I paired off with the widow, towards whom I felt myself drawn by an irresistible power of attraction. I felt great delight certainly in the society and conversation of this lady; though then too young to analyze the sources of my admiration, reflection has since shown me what they were, having passed them through the prism of my mind, and separated those pencils of moral light which, united, produced the sum of her excellence. I cannot here resist drawing a little portrait of her.

To a full, yet graceful, person Mrs. Delaval united a countenance, which, if not regularly beautiful, still beamed with goodness and intelligence—sensible, lively, yet modest and discreet, she was all that man should desire, and woman wish to be. Above the common littlenesses of the world, her heart was deeply fraught with feeling and sensibility—though, unlike her sex in general, she could direct and restrain them both by the powers of a clear and masculine understanding. Her Irish paternity had given her impulses; her Saxon blood had furnished their regulating power. She played, sang, drew, and, in a word, was mistress of all those lighter accomplishments which serve to attract lovers, but which alone rarely suffice to keep them; to these she added a mind of an original turn, improved by reading and reflection. Much good advice did she impart, the nature of which the reader may readily imagine, and which it will therefore be unnecessary to repeat. It is from the lips of such Mentors, that "truth" indeed "prevails with double sway"—one smile from them goes further towards convincing than a dozen syllogisms.

Many years have now passed since I took that stroll on the banks of the "dark rolling Hooghly;" many a hand I then clasped has since become cold; and many a voice I loved to listen to, mute for ever; but the scene remains pictured in my mind in strong and ineffaceable colours.

I think I now behold the group we formed, the white dresses of the ladies, making them to look like spirits walking in a garden, and honest Augustus, with his *solah topee*,[14] looking down on his shoes, and saying agreeable things, the shadows of evening closing around us; the huge fox bats sailing heavily overhead; the river spreading its broad surface before us, suffused with the crimson flush of departing day; the boats moving across it afar, their oars dabbling as it were in quicksilver; the mists rising slowly from neighbouring groves stealing over the scene, and then the stilly, tranquil hour, broken only by the plash of passing oars, the sound of a distant gong, or the far-off music of a marriage ceremony, or the hum and drumming of the bazaar—those drowsy sounds of an Indian eve. It was a bit of still life to be ever remembered.

The guests for the *burra khana* now began to arrive. Gigs, carriages, and palankeens, flambeaux, dancing lights, and the musical groans of the *cahars*, or bearers, as they hurried along the winding road, made the general's domain, a few moments before buried in repose, a scene of life and animation.

We returned to the mansion. The reception room was fast filling. Generals, colonels, judges, barristers of the Supreme Court, merchants, agents, writers, with their ladies, the *élite* of Calcutta fashionable society, was, now, for the first time, submitted to my observation. White jackets, and still whiter faces, were the predominating features of the group (except where relieved by English blood and up-country brickdust), whose manners on the whole struck me as being more frank and open than those of people in England, although that freedom occasionally bordered, I thought in many, on a rough, familiar, horse-play sort of manner, which then, at least, was too common in India, where the causes which predispose to a disregard of courtesy are unfortunately too rife.

Some of the party discussed politics, horse-racing, the latest news from up the country, the promotions and appointments, and so forth, in groups; whilst others, four or five abreast, stumped up and down the broad verandah, talking and laughing energetically; their spirits evidently enlivened by the rapid locomotion in which they were indulging.

General Capsicum was very pleasant with the *burra beebee*, a fine stately old dame, with a turban of bird of paradise plumes, and with whom, I afterwards learned he had actually walked a minuet in the year of grace 1770. Mrs. Capsicum, surrounded by a group of military men and young writers, was endeavouring to reduce her large mouth to the smallest possible dimensions—mincing the kings English, and "talking conversation" "mighty illigant" to the whole ring, in whose countenances a certain mock gravity indicated pretty evidently what they thought of her.

At last, the *khansaman-jee*, or chief butler, a very important and respectable personage, with an aldermanic expansion of the abdominal region, a huge black beard, and a napkin hanging from his *kummerbund*, or girdle, with hands respectfully closed, head on one side, and an air most profoundly deferential, announced to the general that the dinner was served *"Tiar hyn?"*

"Dinner ready, did ye say?" said the general, who was a little deaf, and turning up his best ear to catch the reply.

"*Han khodabund*" ("yes, slave of the Lord)," repeated the *khansaman-jee*.

"Come, gintlemen; come, leedies—those who have any mind to ate may follow me."

Thus saying, the general, with great *gaité de cœur*, presented his arm to the old lady of the bird of paradise plume, and hobbled off with her, chattering and laughing, and followed by the whole company. I, the *lanky* griffin, brought up the rear, looking, on the whole rather "small."

The *coup d'œil* of a grand dinner party in Calcutta, given by a rich merchant or high official, is a very splendid affair, and perhaps eclipses anything to be seen in the mansions of persons of the same rank in England.

The generals presented a brilliant sample of oriental style: a long and lofty room in a blaze of lustre, from a row of wall lights; a table, covered with a profusion of plate and glass, occupied nearly the whole length of the apartment; the huge *punkahs*, suspended from the ceiling, with their long fringes, waved to and fro, gently agitating the air in the room, which would otherwise have been hardly endurable from the crowd it contained.

There was much lively conversation, taking wine, and clashing of knives and plates; altogether far less quiet, I thought, than at a dinner in England. The peculiar feature, however, of the scene, and that which marked most strongly its eastern character, was the multitude of servants in attendance on the guests; behind each chair, on an average, stood two *khidmut-gars*, or footmen, with black beards and mustachios, and attired in the various gay liveries of their masters, adapted to the turban and Indian costume; most of them were the domestics of great people, and exhibited in their looks a good deal of that pampered, self-satisfied importance, so often observable in our metropolitan servants here at home—the vulgar reflection of their masters' consequence. Many stood, their arms folded, with Roman dignity, gazing consequentially about them, and mentally making their observations on their fellow-servants and the guests. Dinner over and the ladies withdrawn, the gentlemen closed up, and the conversation became more general.

The Calcutta dinner parties are not usually scenes of uproarious conviviality; yet, as this was the anniversary of some great event in the history of the general, he seemed determined on its being celebrated with something approaching to a "jollification." "Fill your glasses, gintlemen," said he, as we closed up after the usual loyal toasts, "and I'll give ye a sentiment that I remember was a favourite of my father's."

There was a profound silence—the little veteran arose, and valorously grasping his glass, and stretching out his arm, delivered the following, with a rich brogue and a most determined emphasis:—

"May hemp bind the man that honour can't, and the devil ride rough-shod over the rascally part of the community."

The sentiment was drunk with much glee, and many a hearty response, followed by songs and speeches.

It was late when, taking leave of the general's family, I returned to my room in the barracks.

CHAPTER XIII

Having, by General Capsicum's promised interest, obtained a fortnight's leave of absence, I took an affectionate leave of Grundy and Marpeet, and sent on my two or three servants to Mr. Augustus's boat, accompanied by Teazer and the one-eyed bull-dog. The next day, in the early grey of morning, I proceeded with him to Tolly's Nullah, a creek near Calcutta, communicating with the Balliaghāt Passage, where the boat was lying. It was a cool and pleasant morning, the air delightfully fresh. On our way, we met several ladies and gentlemen of Calcutta on horseback.

In India, bathing and early rising principally contribute to create the amount of health generally enjoyed there, which would be far greater and less precarious than it is, were it not for an immoderate indulgence in the pleasures of the table, which inflames the blood, disorders the liver, and renders the whole system peculiarly susceptible of disease; then steps in mercury—the remedy—which is a fearful shatterer of the constitution, and in the end proves worse than the disease.

I would earnestly advise all my brother-griffins, if they value their happiness, to live moderately and simply though generously, and to guard against the insidious habit of drinking *brandy pawney*, to which a hot climate offers strong and peculiar temptations. These precautions observed, and the mid-day sun avoided, a fair average amount of health may be enjoyed for years.

My friend's boat rowed ten or twelve oars, and was of a kind a good deal in use in Calcutta. The front part was decked, and behind it had a cabin, with Venetian windows, occupying about half the length, and rising several feet above the gunwale; inside there was a small table, and on each side lockers, which served for seats; to the back of these again were some cots or dormitories. It differed from the up-country going craft in being keeled, and having on the whole far more of the European long-boat build.

As we shot along the creek for a few miles, each turn gave us peeps of the rich and luxuriant scenery of this part of Bengal. Gardens of plantain, mango, and jack-trees lined the banks, intermixed with clumps of the tapering bamboo; clusters of neat huts, with arched roofs, appeared half-buried beneath their umbrageous foliage, through openings of which, in the dim, chequered light, village girls, with water-pots on their heads, might be seen gliding along, and imparting to the whole scene an air of primeval and truly Eastern simplicity.

Here and there, in front of a hut, mantled with its creeping gourd, would appear the milk-white cow or petted calf, picketed by the nose, and munching his *boosa* [15] under the cool shade of the tamarind or plantain, whilst kids and goats, in various picturesque attitudes, sunned themselves on the ruined wall or prostrate tree. Sometimes we came on fishermen, in their *dingies*, or canoes, with outspread nets catching the much-prized *hilsa*;[16] or we looked on the dark peasantry in the green rice-fields, engaged beneath a fervid sun in their various rural occupations.

Occasionally we came suddenly upon a market, with its congregated fleet of boats, and its busy, squabbling assemblage of villagers, fish, grain, and vegetable venders, &c.; or a thannah, or police station, would break into view, known by its picturesque burkundazes lounging about in front, armed with spears or tulwars, and the portly, bearded thannahdar, *en déshabille*, smoking his *kulian* under the projecting thatch of the entrance. The novelty of the scene, so truly un-English and Oriental, delighted me, and my heart bounded with joy from a feeling of vitality and freedom.

At length we began to approach those vast forests, called the Sunderbunds,[17] stretching for two or three hundred miles across the delta of the Ganges, and through a considerable part of which our route lay. The vicinity of this wild tract was indicated by the gradual termination of the cultivated country, and the commencement of the half-reclaimed lands on the borders, presenting to the view stumps of trees, patches of jungle, and some paddy fields, occasionally a few scattered huts, with their sickly inhabitants huddled around them.

The boatmen being somewhat exhausted, and the tide on the turn, Mr. Capsicum ordered them to drop anchor in the stream not far from the shore, that they might refresh themselves. It was a curve in the river where we brought to, deep and broad, and remote from the habitations of men. The lazy dark tide rolled slowly on, its movement barely indicated by a slight set in the current, with here and there a few tiny curling whirlpools, which seemed to my imagination to tell of the fearful depths and frightful monsters below. An open spot of green sward approached the bank on one side, whilst beyond this, on both banks, the huge trees of the sombre forest hung darkling over the Stygian stream—here emerging into light, as from a realm of dolorous shade which might have daunted Rinaldo himself.

How my thoughts now flew back, awakened by the contrast, to the flowery meads and crystal streams of merry England! My companion now ordered chairs and his hooka to be taken to the roof of the boat, and there, with a teapoy and tumblers between us, we seated ourselves at our ease, a hearer with a large chattah, or umbrella, shielding us from the noontide rays of a powerful sun. A few faint airs, wafting the chirp and pipe of unknown birds, came fanning from the woods, which, with the monotonous bubble of Mr. Augustus's hooka, produced a tranquil and soporific effect upon me.

In the little patch of grass meadow I have mentioned, which lay nearly opposite to us, two or three miserable stunted white cattle were feeding, one of them considerably nearer the margin than the others. Whilst looking towards them, I thought I discerned something dark slowly emerging from the water where the muddy shelving shore dipped into it. I kept my eye steadily fixed upon the object, which evidently moved and presented to my view the resemblance of two large foot-balls, at the end of a rough log of wood. I directed my companion's attention to it, at the same time asking him what it was.

"There, yonder," said I, "just beyond the tuft of reeds. See! see! it moves."

"Oh, I perceive the rascal," said he; "it's a huge alligator, making a point at that poor beast of a cow; but I'll spoil his sport. *Bearah Bundook laou juldee!* bring up the rifle quickly."

Ere gun, however, could be brought, the monster, as if anticipating our intentions, suddenly rushed from his concealment, with a rapid and wriggling motion, and in an instant had the unsuspecting cow by the nose.

The poor brute struggled, her tail crooked with agony, her two fore-feet stuck out, and bellowing most lustily, whilst the alligator hacked rapidly towards the water, dragging the cow along with him.

"Quick! quick!" shouted Augustus, as the servant blundered along, capsizing a bucket or two in his hurry, and handed up the gun.

"Click," went the lock—the rifle was pointed, but it was too late: the scaly monster sunk with his prey, as the bullet cracked sharply over the eddy; a few bubbles and a slight curl of the deep waters alone marking the spot where the poor cow had disappeared in a doleful tragedy—her last appearance in public.

"What a ferocious monster!" I exclaimed; "do they often carry away animals in this way?"

"Oh, yes," replied Augustus, vexed that he had been foiled. "Alligators in the salt and brackish waters of the lower parts of Bengal are dangerous and ferocious; but as you recede from the sea, for some reason or another, they become comparatively harmless, and seldom molest man or beast, confining their depredations to the finny tribe. Near my factory they are continually carrying off the villagers from the ghauts, and I have heard and believe, though I have never witnessed a case, that they sometimes adroitly knock the fishermen from off their dingies by a blow of the tail, and then snap them up in a moment."

"Why do not the people hunt and destroy the brutes?" I asked.

"They require more salt to be put upon their tails than your sparrows at home," said Augustus with a roguish smile, which made me think that he had been cognizant of an early attempt of mine in that way. "However," he continued, "after a good many poor devils have been carried off, blacky's apathy is a little disturbed, and he does sometimes catch them in the following manner. A party row slowly up the stream, dragging a number of hooked lines after them; when these are arrested by the horny hide of the alligator, as he lies in the mud at the bottom, they slowly raise the torpid brute (who seldom makes any resistance) till he appears above the surface; they then simultaneously dart a number of small barbed harpoons into him, to the heads of which (whence the shafts are made to detach easily) stout cords are fastened, and thus they secure his body; to prevent his doing mischief with his jaws, they present a stick, and when he seizes it with a snap, they belay a cord round those formidable instrument of destruction."

After the crew had refreshed, we pursued our voyage, plunging into the dreary solitude, intersected by a labyrinth of creeks and rivers; on each side arose a wall of forest, with a thick undergrowth of the most luxuriant vegetation, springing from the fat alluvial soil.

The silence of death was around, broken only at intervals by the distant crow of the jungle fowl, the cry of the deer, or the blowing of a porpoise, and the measured dash of our oars, as we swept along, sometimes on the surface of a broad river, with bright green trees on each side, and black-faced monkeys chattering in the branches; at others, in some lateral creek, where the boughs almost brushed our deck.

There is something solemnly impressive in such a scene, which seems truly to speak in majestic tones of the power and greatness of the Creator. Such a scene in the howling wilderness carries the imagination back to that primeval period when man was not on this earth, when shipless seas broke on voiceless shores, and the mammoth and the mastodon roamed undisturbed amongst its silent forests and lonely retreats.

Occasionally a Mugh or Arracanese boat, of peculiar construction, with its broad-faced crew and banks of oars, laden with bees' wax, ivory, &c., glided by, or a raft, heavily laden with piles of wood or charcoal for the Calcutta market, swept past us, a momentary relief to the death-like loneliness of the place: the wood they carry is cut and collected by a particular class of men, who pursue their perilous trade in these jungles.

Sometimes, too, the continuity of the forest was broken by a cleared patch, and piles of timber ready for lading; or the hut of one those religious devotees or fakeers, whose austerity acquires for them the respect of the ignorant and superstitious boatmen, whom, by their charms and incantations, they profess to insure from assaults of the alligator and the tiger. Boatmen, however, and even fakeers, are continually carried off; but as superstition always counts the hits, and never reckons the misses, a few favourable predictions sets all to rights again.

At one of these fakeer stations, we made a halt, and a more wretched locality for a man to take up his abode in imagination can scarcely picture. A small spot of about half a quarter of an acre, was cleared from the forest, and in the centre of it was a fragile hut of thatch and bamboo, which a puff of wind might have blown away; a tapering bamboo, with a small red pennon, rose above it, and a little clay durgah for prayer adjoined, to indicate the sacred calling of the lonely occupant.

As we brought to, the fakeer came down to the boat, and was most respectfully received by the crew. He was an aged man, withered up like a potsherd, and smeared with dust and ashes; his long, grizzled, and matted beard swept his breast, and a tiger skin was thrown over his shoulders; he held a long stick in one hand, on which he supported his bent, decrepid form, whilst in the other he carried a dried gourd-shell, or calibash, to receive the contributions of the boatmen.

Here was a Trappist of the East, submitting to every danger and privation from motives somewhat similar to those which actuate the ascetic order all the world over—motives which we cannot but respect, however mistaken we may deem them.

Bidding adieu to this recluse of the woods, we once more pursued our course to the eastward, and after nearly a day's rowing, changed it to the north, following the line of one of the many rivers which, spreading out as they approach the sea in various lateral directions in the Sunderbunds, form that intricate maze.

In a little time, the forest became less dense, and a few miles more brought us again into the cleared and cultivated country. Our eyes once more rested with pleasure upon the green rice-fields, the patch of sugar-cane, the cluster of coco-nuts, and the busy haunts of men.

"Well, Mr. Gernon," said Augustus, "I suppose you are not sorry to be nearly at the end of your voyage."

"No," I replied; "though I have been greatly interested by the wild scene through which we passed. But how far are we now from the Junglesoor factory?"

"Not far," said my friend; "please God we'll sup at my house to-night. There, look!" said he; "do you see yonder white building, and the thick cluster of trees, overhanging it at the turn of the river?"

"I do."

"Well, that's one of my out-factories; there I've ordered some of my people to be in waiting with horses, or an elephant, to take us on to my shop, which is about six miles inland."

"An elephant!" I ejaculated, as I mentally rubbed my hands.

The boatman plied their oars with redoubled vigour, their cheerful songs and shouts bespeaking that buoyancy of hearts which an approach to "home" ever inspires amongst all mankind.

We now neared the white building, which proved to be a small temple, crowning a little ghaut or flight of steps, running down to the water's edge, backed by something like an old ruined fort or factory, overshaded by masses of foliage of the banyan and peepul trees, growing out of fissures of the walls.

On the crest of the ghaut stood an elephant caparisoned with his bright red *jhoul* and *howdah* [18] fanning himself with the branch of a tree; hard by him were a couple of horses, saddled, and held by their *syces* or grooms, each of whom bore a hog-spear; whilst near and around, groups of villagers, factory servants, and followers of Mr. Augustus, in various picturesque costumes and attitudes, some squatting in masses, some standing, others reclining on the steps or abutments of the ghaut, were all impatiently awaiting the arrival of the boat.

These groups, backed by the ruined walls, the massive banyan with its twining roots, and a little sort of bungalow, or summer-house, on the projecting bastion, which stood out in strong relief against the evening sky, all constituted, when viewed in the mellow sunlight of the rich Claude-like repose of the hour, a scene well worthy of the pencil of a Daniell.

The boat moored, a lively meeting and embracing took place between those on board and their friends at the factory, for the Indians, I have observed, though in some thing apathetic, are remarkably affectionate to their relatives.

Augustus himself now stepped ashore with all the dignity of a monarch returning from exile to his dominions, amidst the bows and prostrations of his rejoicing subjects. Great were the salaamings, and manifold the signs of life, which his arrival caused in the group. The syces tightened the girths of the horses; two stately greyhounds rose from a recumbent posture, whilst a couple of little pepper and mustard terriers ran yelping and wagging their tails to greet their master; the *mahout* dug his *ankous*, or goad, into the elephant's head, to rouse him from his drowsy state of abstraction, exciting a loud trumpeting scream, as he drove down towards the boat. The gomastah, or manager, a Bengalee, in flowing muslin robes, now advanced with dignified salaam, and made a report of how things had gone on in his absence, whilst a Portuguese, of the complexion of charcoal, with a battered hat and white jacket, named Alfonso da Silva, also had a great deal to say touching the recent operations connected with the manufacture of his master's indigo.

"Now, Mr. Gernon," said Augustus, "these matters settled, which are you for, a gallop, or a ride on the elephant? take your choice."

"Oh! the elephant," said I, "by all means. I have never ridden on one, and long to be on that noble fellow, who looks like a moving mountain."

"Then," said my kind-hearted host, "let us mount. I see they have put the guns in the howdah, and we may have a shot at something as we go along. I must give you a lesson in shooting off an elephant, which is no easy matter to a young hand. Here, *hauthee laou* ('bring the elephant')."

Another dig and another startling blast, and the leviathan was alongside of us.

"*Buth! buth?*" said the driver, and down knelt the docile beast to receive us.

The coolie, or attendant, now applied the ladder, to his side; Augustus ascended, and I followed him. Here, then, was one of my Oriental day-dreams realized, and I fairly boxed up on "the elephant and castle."

'Tis a fine thing to be mounted on a gallant charger, to spurn the sod, and, catching all his fire, to feel yourself "every inch" a hero; or to dash away in a brave ship over the blue billows with a spanking breeze, as free as the winds that propel you; but I doubt if even they can impart such sensations as you experience when towering aloft on the back of an elephant, nine feet high, moving, with majestic and stately stride, through palmy scenes of orient beauty, you find yourself raised far above the humble pedestrian, and taking in the whole country as with an eagle glance.

We now started at a good, swinging pace, followed by the horses, whilst sundry burkundazes and peons, with spears and staves, trotted on nimbly before, clearing the way of the boys, cows, village pariar dogs, and idlers.

Thus we wound through the village, and soon entered on the open country, which for the most part was perfectly flat, and bounded by villages and topes of mango trees. Here and there the land rose a little, forming a sort of rough pastures, on which herds of the black slouching buffaloes were feeding, mingled with small white Bengalee cows and bullocks, their bells tinkling, and tended by herdsmen enveloped in blanket sort of hoods, with long sticks over their shoulders.

We had not proceeded far on the plain, when a horseman appeared in the distance, approaching us at a hand gallop.

"Halloo!" said Augustus, "here comes my neighbour and brother planter, Mons. De la Chasse, as funny, but as good a fellow as ever breathed. I hope you have a tolerable command of countenance, for you'll require it when you hear our friend's English."

By this time Mons. De la Chasse was sufficiently near for me to distinguish the Gaul in every lineament. He was a long and gaunt man, with the face of a *vieux mousquetaire*, wore a white solah hat, with a vast amplitude of brim, a white jacket, and long military boots. His horse was a large hatchet-faced animal, of a cream colour, with a swish tail, which, however, bore him along over bush and jungle in capital style. As he approached brandishing a hog-spear, he rather brought to my mind the picture of a Spanish bull fighter.

"Velcome! velcome! goot friend; glad to see you back," said he, riding up, and waving his hand as he wheeled his horse about "You look ver well by Jhobs."

"Thankyee, thankyee, Monsieur; all's right with me, but what have you been doing in this part of the world?"

"Oh, de old vay. Ve have had de jodge down, and one of his amis, abote some cochery affairs; had him out for a day after de hogue; killed two, tree—one old boar give fine sport—ver fine; near kill us though, by Jhobs; ha! ha!—but who that wid you, Capsicome?"

"Oh! a young friend of my father's come to see how we carry on the war down here. Let me introduce him to you—Gernon, Mons. De la Chasse, &c."

"Appi see you amongst us, Sare.—By de vay, I not tell a-you I have had 'noder kick ope with dat Bobberygunge talookdar: d—m fellow, his bulloke spoil twenty beegah my plant. I shall him have ope to de jodge, by Jhobs—he is a—a—a (casting about for a suitable expression, and setting his teeth) a frightful shackass."

This moved my risibles, in spite of a gentle poke from Augustus's elbow, and a reproving look compounded of gravity and laughter. Fortunately, at this juncture, a dismal yell broke on our ears, and we perceived ahead of us, slinking across the plain, two animals somewhat larger than foxes.

"What are they?" I asked.

"Oh! a couple of jackals," said my companion. "Would you like to see a run?"

I eagerly expressed my assent.

"De la Chasse," said Mr. Augustus, "take a gallop after those jackals; our friend here wants to see a hunt."

"Oh! ay, ve'll stir dem ope," said the light-hearted Frenchman, who, like his countrymen in general, seemed ready for any thing that promised excitement. "*Choorda khoota choorda!*" ("let loose the dogs, let loose") he shouted, and in a moment the greyhounds were slipped.

"Hark away!" shouted Augustus; the Gaul gave the View halloo, and after the jackals darted the beautiful animals; their bodies undulating like serpents as they emulously strove to pass each other. The small dogs followed in full cry, and my *matur*, or master of the hounds, not to be outdone, and justly anxious for the reputation of his charges, drew the cords of the bull-dog and Teazer, lustily cheering them on.

After killing the jackals, which was soon effected, we regained the road, and in half an hour reached the Junglesoor factory. The residence was a square building of one story, surrounded by a terrace and covered verandah; on one side was a large garden, filled with orange and other trees. Further back were groves of bamboo, mango, &c., intermingled with buildings, vats, stables, &c.

We dismounted, and Augustus invited the Frenchman to come in and sup; but he declined, pleading a necessity for returning home; but he added, "Ven vil you come take your *luck-pote* vid me?"

"Ha! ha! ha! *pot-luck*, I suppose you mean, Monsieur?"

"Yais, to be sure," said the good-natured Frenchman; "but I put de horse before de cart only. What you mean, you dam Capsicome, by laugh at me?" said he, poking at him with the butt-end of his hog-spear.

After other good-humoured passes between them, it was arranged that La Chasse was to come over the day after the ensuing, to breakfast, make a day of it, and "hunt ope de hogue," and he was to bring a friend.

I now entered with my companion, and proceeded to the dining-room. We found the candles lighted and every preparation for a comfortable meal. We had a roast goose, curry-fish, prawns, &c., to which we did ample justice; a cool bottle of claret was then produced; Augustus changed his boots for slippers, cocked his legs on the table, ordered his hookha, and another for the purpose of initiating me, and we were soon in that blissful state, compounded of overflowing health, light hearts, moderate fatigue, and a delightful sense of repletion, when the heart expands, and all the better feelings of our nature predominate. I have always thought, though an inversion of the orthodox rule, that the first and most effectual step towards making men good is to make them happy.

The following day was devoted by Augustus to repose and domestic arrangements—things having fallen a little into arrear during his absence. In the course of the morning, however, he took me round his estate, showed me his garden, his stables, and his farm-yard; also his indigo vats, his drying-houses, &c.; whilst exhibiting the latter, he explained to me the process of manufacturing the dye.

The morrow at length arrived, the sun rose in splendour, the weather for the season (the beginning of October) was breezy and cool, and all things seemed to wear a propitious aspect, and to promise a delightful day's sport. In a short time, De la Chasse arrived, accompanied by a square, tight-built little man, named Tupper, who had recently (as is not unfrequent in India) changed his berth of mate of a country ship for that of an Indigo planter's assistant.

An abundant breakfast duly despatched, there was a buckling of spurs, a slinging of brandy-bottles, an examination of hog-spears, and other preliminary movements for the foray. Outside, too, was a great muster of Augustus's retainers, coolies or factory men, real "blue demons," in almost Paradisaic costume, with long sticks, or *latees*, over their shoulders, wherewith to beat the jungles.

Augustus now vaulted on his Arab, a beautiful creature, with a high reputation, as I was told, as a hog-hunter (horses in India enjoy the sport as much as their masters), and with his spear in hand gave the signal for departure. Out marched the whole cavalcade, I mounted on a sturdy little hill pony, called a tangan, as hard-mouthed and headstrong a little devil, as I afterwards discovered to my cost, as ever tumbled a griffin.

Each of us hunters was armed with a spear, whilst spare ones were carried by the syces. The spear used in this sport, by the way, is a very formidable weapon. The shaft is about seven feet long, the head an elongated heart, or rather leaf-shape, as keen as a razor, and to aid its murderous effect, the butt-end is loaded with about a half-pound of lead.

We now wound along, bending our course for the banks of a river, where wild hogs and other game were said to abound. Having crossed the plain, we found, ourselves amongst mango groves and woodland, interspersed with scattered huts and small villages, and I became, by some accident, separated a good distance from my companions.

In passing the edge of a tope, or mango grove, an adventure happened, which, though somewhat derogatory to my dignity in its results, my integrity as a historian obliges me to relate. A pause in the narrative may, however, be expedient, in order to give me the requisite degree of composure.

CHAPTER XIV

In passing the grove mentioned in the last chapter, by the edge of a fosse, or ditch, overgrown with bushes, and not far from some miserable huts, I thought I heard a rustling, and reining up my tangan and listening, I could distinguish the deep bass of a grunter, with the running treble of sundry little pigs. My heart went pit-a-pat; here, thought I, is a glorious discovery! I shall be the first to rouse the grizzly monster from his lair, and launch a spear at him. I wished, however, to be sure, and listened again — 'twas a palpable grunt.

"Yoicks! tally-ho!" shouted I, waving my hat, as a signal for my friends to come up and share in the anticipated sport.

Roused by my voice, and a stone cast into the ditch by my syce, an unclean beast of large dimensions, black and mangy, issued therefrom, and, rather leisurely, I thought, for a wild boar, jogged across the open space, followed by a tribe of young ones. Now then, Frank Gernon, I mentally exclaimed, gird up the loins of thy resolution, and prepare for desperate deeds.

Thus internally soliloquizing, I slacked my rein, put spurs to my tangan, and, spear in hand, rode furiously at him. La Mancha's knight did not charge his windmill more valiantly. I pushed him hard, but he kept ahead, dodging, joltering, and grunting, and for the life of me I could not place myself in a position to give him the *coup de grace*. At length, by vigorously urging my beast, I found myself alongside; my arm was raised; the glittering javelin poised with as direful a presage as that of one of Homer's heroes; already in imagination my burnished point had searched out the seat of life, and I saw the crimson tide distilling from the wound; I rose to deal the mighty stroke, when snap went the stirrup-leather, away flew my spear, and I, and not the hog, incontinently bit the dust. Yes, down I came, a thundering thump.

Painful was the revulsion of feeling — I never felt more foolish in my life. Away went pig and tangan — and so they might, for aught I cared — whilst I, like a dying gladiator, lay prone on the earth, applying vigorous friction to my shoulder. In a few seconds, my companions rode up, to my confusion, convulsed with laughter, which they vainly strove to repress.

"You're not hurt, I hope, Gernon?" said my host, endeavouring to compose his features into a look of commiseration (a dead failure, by-the-bye).

"No, not much," said I, writhing with pain; "nothing to speak of. It was that confounded rotten stirrup; but I should not have cared, had I speared the hog."

Upon this, there was another volcano of laughter. I felt annoyed, and begged to know, fiercely, what they found so amusing in a friend's nearly breaking his neck.

"Oh, my good ami," exclaimed the Frenchman, "you most pardonnez— but ha! ha! ha! you ave hunt the village pig, ha! ha! ha! and not the vild hogue. Oh, mon Dieu, je vais mourir—oh! oh!"

"Yes," added Augustus, "oh! oh! oh! you really must excuse us, Gernon, he! he! he! for laughing a little at your griffinish mistake; indeed, you have been chasing a villager; but you are not the first that has made such a blunder. Come," he continued, "here's your steed; mount once more, and we'll show you some real sport. I see you are game to the backbone, and will prove a staunch hog-hunter."

I was mortified at my blunder, but this piece of flattery acted as a cataplasm to my wounded spirit; so I thought it best to join in the laugh against myself, and remounting my tangan, and re-adjusting the stirrup, we once more continued our route.

After crossing a bare plain, we found ourselves on the banks of the river, covered for miles with a belt of grass and long reeds. The beaters were now put in, and dismal yelling and shouting commenced. In a few minutes the cry of *sewer, sewer!* ("hog, hog!") arose from many voices; the reeds ahead waved and rustled, and in a moment a tremendous boar burst from the cover, and bore right away across the hard plain, towards the cultivation.

Away went Augustus in gallant style, with a yell or war-whoop that made the welkin ring. The second mate joined chase right before the wind; my little hard-mouthed Punch stuck down his head, laid back his ears, and, unbidden, followed next, keenly alive to the sport, though I had a hard matter to manage him and my long spear to boot; and in a moment more the Frenchman thundered past, with brandished spear and horse tight in hand.

"Ha! ha!" said he, as he passed me, "now you vill see de death of de veritable vild hogue."

Augustus gained on the boar, who, with his milk-white tusks, bristly back, and sidelong look, presented a most formidable aspect, and was evidently an ugly customer. The planter pushed him closely, and, in passing, delivered his spear with such effect, that it stuck bolt upright in the back of the boar, who nevertheless continued his onward course, as if spitted for the feast.

It was now the turn of De la Chasse; up he came, and in capital style delivered his spear with a *coup de théâtre* just behind the shoulder, wheeled round his horse with a "ha! ha!" and the monster rolled over and over. He was a magnificent boar, with a hock like a bullock's, terrific tusks, and such a neck of brawn! e'en such a brute as one sees Madame Diana flying after, barelegged, in an old tapestry, or playing pitch and toss with a score of dogs in one of Snyder's noble pictures. But 'twas all up with him now; his little blood-shot eyes were half-closed, his tongue was out, and all his sinews and muscles were stiffened in death.

"'Tis ver fine hogue," said the Frenchman, looking up, after contemplating, him for some minutes in mute delight, and pulling out his gory spear, buried two feet deep in the shoulder; "but I give him dat last poke ver well, eh! by Jhobs?"

"Yes, you certainly finished him in very sportsmanlike style, Monsieur," replied Augustus; "I thought he would have charged me as I delivered my spear, and am glad he did not, for with those tusks of his, gentlemen, he would have been an ugly customer, and have left his mark on my gallant Rustum and me. But come, we will try up the river again."

The legs of the boar were now tied, a pole was thrust through them, the huge animal was hoisted on the shoulders of four of the coolies, and home along with us.

The beaters now once more advanced, latees waved, the shouts were renewed, and in a few minutes there was a cry of some animal, when a creature of the deer kind, of a slate colour and clumsy shape, bolted from the reeds, and with an awkward up and down sort of movement, made across the plain.

"A hog-deer," shouted Mr. Tupper; and with arms and legs working like a mannikins, spurred after him, the rest of party following.

The hog-deer have little speed or bottom, so he was soon overtaken and killed—casting up a piteous look, as Augustus, who on this occasion gave the Frenchman the go-by, drove his keen spear into him.

After the death of the deer, we all by acclamation voted an adjournment to a neighbouring shady tree; there dismounting, and throwing ourselves on the ground, we commenced a vigorous attack on the cold meat and pale ale, chatting, joking, laughing, and masticating, at one and the same time.

The game was laid out before us, in order that we might feast our eyes on that, at the same time that we gratified our palates.

Returning Home from the Hog Hunt.

The lunch fairly discussed, I was surprised to see a servant hand a small hookha, or *kulian*, covered with silver chains, and emitting a delicious odour, to Augustus. Upon my honour, I mentally exclaimed, you indigo gentlemen seem to have a good notion of comfort. Mr. Augustus wiped the mouth-piece with his thumb and finger, put it between his lips, and emitting an elaborate whiff of a yard and a half long, slowly leaned his back against the trunk of the tree, half-closed his eyes, and exhibited the most perfect appearance of unalloyed sublunary bliss I have ever beheld. After half an hour's rest, and partaking of the *kulian*, which was generously passed round by our friend, we arose, and prepared for a renewal of the campaign.

In this we were as successful as in the commencement of the day. Three more small hogs were killed; on one of which, after sundry abortive attempts, and one or two imminent risks of unshipment, I fleshed my maiden spear—a feat marked by such uncommon skill and unique adroitness on my part, that I made it the leading subject of conversation for a month afterwards.

Our sport over, and man and beast fairly exhausted, we now bent our course towards home, wending our way over the plain we had crossed in the morning. We four cavaliers, our spears over our shoulders, mounted on our steeds of various statures, led the way; then came straggling attendants, lagging heavily along; and lastly, the goodly show of game, slung on poles, and borne on the shoulders of coolies, brought up the rear.

The cavalcade, the game, the wild track of reeds, the distant masses of wood topped with the coco-nut and betel-palm, all seen in the streaming light of the setting sun struggling through the evening's haze, would have made a fine subject for that prince of animal painters, Landseer.

A pleasant meal at my friend's house closed this my first day's hog-hunting in India. I had become a mighty hunter at once, and stood two inches higher whenever the feats I had witnessed crossed my mind; the feeling of exultation would have been unalloyed indeed, but for the adventure of that cursed village pig.

The supper was capital, and, ye powers that preside over gastronomy, how we did eat! It is a fortunate dispensation of Providence that all men are not hog-hunters, or frequent famine would be the inevitable result. Augustus was pleasant, the Frenchman loquacious, Mr. Tupper had much to say, and the hogs were, at a moderate computation, slain over again half a dozen times at least before supper was ended.

Amongst other subjects incidentally discussed, was that of several dacoities, or gang-robberies, lately committed in the neighbourhood, attended with great atrocities.

This part of Bengal had long been famous, or rather infamous, for these plunderers, who, led on by their chiefs, the Robin Hoods of India, were a terror to the country. The bands move about, at times levying contributions from the inhabitants, in numbers often sufficiently great to enable them to defy the police, which is, or was, very inefficient—their leaders are great desperadoes.

"I hear," said Augustus, "that Ramsunker has been plundering in this neighbourhood, and swears he will pay me a visit one of these days; but let him come, and we'll endeavour to give him a warm reception."

De la Chasse and Tupper said they should like nothing better than a skirmish with the banditti, and begged that Augustus would send off an express for them if the aforesaid Ramsunker should ever make his appearance at the Junglesoor Factory.

Augustus promised to do so, saying that he should be equally ready to attend their summons if they were first selected for plunder; in short, a treaty of alliance, offensive and defensive, was then and there struck; after which the high contracting parties, becoming full of Bacchus, sung several songs, disputed, quarrelled, became maudlin, wept, swore everlasting friendship, and retired to rest.

Besides that one to which the permanent residence was attached, Mr. Augustus had several out-laying factories, which he visited from time to time, to superintend the manufacture of his indigo; at all of these he had little bungalows, or temporary abodes, where we tiffed and passed the heat of the day.

We were one morning at the factory on the river, where I have stated that we first landed, quietly smoking in the little turret, or summer-house, when a great hubbub below, and the noise of people running, saluted our ears. Mr. Augustus rose hastily, and ran out to see what was the matter, I following him, at the same time despatching a servant to ascertain the cause of the uproar. He soon returned, and stated that a youth had just been carried off from the ghaut by an alligator, which had snapped him up whilst in the act of washing his cloth or *dhotee*.

Excited by this account, we posted off to the ghaut, where a clamorous crowd was collected, many of them looking and pointing towards the centre of the river. On inquiry, we learnt that the alligator was there, playing with his victim; and, casting our eyes to the middle of the stream, there, sure enough, in the centre of the rapid current, his long jagged tail rising above and occasionally lashing the surface, was the monster, tossing and shaking the lifeless body of the poor black boy, and amusing himself as a cat does with a mouse before she makes a meal of it.

Mr. Augustus sent immediately to the bungalow for his rifle, which soon made its appearance: it was a piece of the kind called commonly in India a "bone-breaker," and carrying a weighty ball, eight or ten to the pound. Having loaded it, he took a deliberate aim at the alligator.

I waited in breathless suspense for the result—bang went the rifle, and the ball dashed up the spray within a foot of the creature's head, and then went ricochetting over the expanse of water.

"A close shave," said Augustus; "but come, we'll try him again."

Once more the rifle was loaded and fired, but on this occasion with more success, a dull, lumpish sound telling that the ball had taken effect. It requires, however, ordinarily, many balls to kill an alligator; but down sunk the head of the monster, his long serrated tail waving in air as he descended to the depths of the river, like a sinking warrior flourishing his broken brand.

This fellow, it appeared, had long been carrying on his depredations in this part of the river, and the boatmen and fishermen determined at last to make an attempt to capture him; this they next day effected in the usual way by dragging the bottom with hooks.

We slept at the out-factory of Gurrialpore that night, and were agreeably surprised the next morning, shortly after breakfast, by a man running in to inform us that the alligator had been captured, and that the muchwas, or fishermen, were then in the act of towing him on shore. We immediately proceeded to the river's brink, and there, sure enough, we observed two dingies, or canoes, fast approaching, and lashed closely side by side.

As they came near, we perceived that the alligator was between them, well secured, his head above the water and projecting in front between the prows, and his long tail laving in the wake behind; in his huge jaws was a stout stick, well belayed with a cord above and below; in short, bridled and bitted for any gentleman who, like the adventurous Mr. Waterton, might have felt disposed to take a ride upon him, which, not being particular, and preferring a horse myself, I certainly felt no inclination to do.

On the boats touching the shore, we stepped on board, and looking between them, found the space, a breadth of a foot or two, occupied by the horny and rugged back of their prize, into which were wedged the barbed heads of some half a dozen small iron harpoons, with cords attached in the manner I have mentioned in a former chapter.

By dint of ropes and bamboo poles, the natives, who showed themselves wonderfully adroit at the business, soon had him on the shelving bank, when my host proceeded very deliberately to put ball after ball through his head, to the number of four or five.

This, for any description of landsman, would have been more than enough; but, as I before observed, an alligator is an inordinate glutton in the way of punishment, and requires much to give him his quietus. However, he was considerably damaged, no doubt—sufficiently so to admit of his being easily thrown on his back, care being still taken to prevent his doing mischief, by the pressure of long bamboo poles on his body and tail.

One of the muchwas now, with a sharp axe, or some such instrument, proceeded to cut him open, and having done so, he removed the intestines as completely as the cook does those of a fish preparatory to consigning it to the frying-pan.

Mr. Augustus now gave the order to remove the "pressure from without," which was accordingly done, when, strange to relate, but nevertheless perfectly true, the *unkillable* monster sprang bodily up, recovered his natural position, and lashing his tremendous tail right and left, made both the dust and the crowd to fly, the latter skipping off nimbly, and giving him what sailors term a wide berth. Thus he continued to lash his tail and move his liberated jaws for some time after, though unable to stir from the spot.

This extraordinary tenacity of life is common to all reptiles and cold-blooded creatures, though not in all to an equal degree; it is very remarkable in the turtle of the Indian rivers, which I have known to scuttle off to the water *minus* their heads, when cut off by the enraged *piscator*, as the shortest way of getting the hooks out of their mouths.

As I watched the dying throes of the alligator, after so long resisting all attempts to extinguish his vital spark, under every circumstance of advantage to his assailants, I could not help feeling in all its length and breadth the utter state of impotency to which the lord of the creation—man—would be reduced, however well supplied with weapons, offensive and defensive, when once fairly grappled by him in his native element. Humiliating thought!

A *post mortem* examination of the alligator showed us Mr. Augustus's ball firmly wedged into the thick part of the tail; and an analysis of the contents of the stomach brought to light two legs, half an arm, and sundry rings and silver bangles, which had once adorned the slender limbs of some hapless village maiden.

Having now gratified our curiosity, and performed our duty to the public, the inquest broke up—verdict, of course, "justifiable *alligatricide*"—and we returned home.

One morning, a few days after this—the most eventful, as will be seen in the sequel, which had occurred to me since I had trodden Indian ground—we were seated at table after breakfast, my host drowsily smoking his hookha and conning the Calcutta paper, I concocting a despatch for home, when suddenly a confused and distant noise was heard, including the rapid beat of a *doog-doogie*, or small native drum.

My host laid down his paper and listened; for a moment it died away, then again rose on the wind; there was a hubbub of voices—of flying footsteps—and lastly, of one or two dropping shots.

"By heavens! there's something wrong," said Augustus, half-rising from his chair, and still intently listening. "*Quon hye?*" ('who waits?')

The words were scarcely uttered, when, wild with alarm, a servant rushed in followed by one or two others, exclaiming, in almost frantic tones, "Sahib! sahib! *dacka! dacka!*"

My host turned pale, started from his chair, and rapidly interrogated the affrighted men, who answered him all clamorously at once, and with the most animated gesticulations.

"In the name of all that's good," said I, thunderstruck at the scene, "what on earth is the matter?"

"Matter! my dear fellow, the dacoits—that's all; the robbers are upon us; we must defend our lives; there is not a moment to be lost."

The plot now began to thicken: three burkundauzes rushed in, with a confirmation of the intelligence that Ramsunker and his gang were close at hand, bent on fulfilling their recent threats, and that they had already plundered two or three neighbouring hamlets.

Not an instant was wasted; the doors were banged to and bolted in a trice, bars laid across, and some heavy boxes piled up against them. Guns, pistols, and hog-spears were put in requisition; the burkundauzes loaded their matchlocks and blew their matches, and the whole of us immediately ascended to the flat roof, determined to defend the fortress.

Having gained this position, the next point was to reconnoitre the force of the enemy, and the posture of affairs outside.

A low parapet wall, some three feet high, encompassed the flat roof of the planter's mansion; and over this last, sheltering as much of our persons as possible, we cast our eyes in the direction of the mass of bamboo and other foliage, amongst which the indigo vats and other out-buildings were principally situated.

All there was ominously still, except that, every now and then, a factory coolie, like a startled hare, would burst forth from his concealment, and with looks of terror, fly across the opposite rice-fields.

The vat-houses, &c., had now, it was clear, been abandoned by all the planters followers, and were in possession of the dacoits, who were probably rifling them. Of this we had speedy confirmation, by perceiving three or four dark, undersized figures, almost naked, and armed with swords and spears, creep cautiously out and cast furtive glances towards the house.

"There they are," said Augustus: "those are some of the rascals preparing, no doubt, to make an assault upon us. Well, we must give them a warm reception. I wish with all my heart we had De la Chasse with us; but how to communicate with him and the distant police station, surrounded as we are, I know not. However," he added, "he cannot fail sooner or later, to learn our situation from some of the runaways. Here, Gernon," said he, handing me a double gun, "here is something for you; now do your best, like a valiant knight, and win your spurs."

Here, thought I, is a pretty adventure! I shall inevitably be figuring in a return of killed and wounded, without ever having joined a regiment. Call you this a party of pleasure, i'faith? I had soliloquized to this extent, when a little white cloud of smoke puffed itself forth from the brightly verdant screen formed by the drooping bamboo hedge, followed by the whistling of a matchlock ball within a few feet of my pericranium.

To tell the truth, this music had no particular charms for me; though, when "honour pricked me on," I could listen to it awhile, buoyed up by visions of glory, promotion, prize-money, and so forth, as well as another.

On hearing the whine of this ragged missile, I instinctively bobbed my head a shade lower than the parapet wall: this little involuntary working of the conservative principle, however, was speedily succeeded by an energetic display of its opposite, as by an active rebound up I started, presented my gun, and dropped shots—one, two—quick as thought, into the spot from which the cloud of smoke had yet hardly disappeared;—how many I killed, I can't say.

Augustus also fired; and immediately, as if roused by our daring, a numerous band of some 200 or 300 dacoits, as ill-looking a set of fellows as I ever beheld, armed with swords, spears, and a rusty matchlock or two swarmed forth from their places of concealment, rushed down upon the house with a frightful yelling, sprung upon the terrace, and endeavoured to force the doors. These, however, though rather fragile, as Indian doors generally are, were sufficient for the moment to resist their efforts.

Our garrison replied by loud shouts of defiance, which, with a volley from the guns and matchlocks, sent them, to our astonishment, to the right-about, and they again sought shelter amongst the trees, carrying off two or three wounded.

I congratulated Mr. Augustus on their unexpected retreat, expressing a hope that we had seen the last of them, for the disparity of force went far towards diminishing the liveliness of the joke.

"Ah!" said my friend, "I would not have you halloo before you're out of the wood, or draw precipitate conclusions; I know the villains too well; they have plenty of pluck, and are now, depend on it, going to make sure of us in some way attended with less risk to themselves."

We now listened, and soon heard the sound of axes in the wood, followed by the crash of falling bamboos.

"What can they now be at?" said I.

"I suspect," replied Augustus, "that they intend to scale the house, and are making ladders of bamboo for the purpose."

Some conversation with the native garrison tended fully to confirm this view of the matter, and 200 or 300 to eight or ten are overwhelming odds.

"I fear," said the planter, "we must beat a parley, unless immediately relieved by De la Chasse or the thannah folks, and make the best terms we can for ourselves, or they will scale the roof, massacre us all in a trice, and then plunder the place. What is your idea of the matter, Gernon?"

"Oh," said I, "I'm for fighting as long as there's a fair chance; but if there's none, as I've no wish to 'adorn a tale' by figuring in a massacre, I vote with you that we give in, provided they grant us an honourable capitulation."

As we were thus speaking, a servant exclaimed that a man was advancing from the wood where the dacoits were carrying on their operations: he was unarmed, and made a sign that he had something to communicate. One of our intelligent burkundauzes hailed and asked him what he wanted.

The reply, as explained to me, was, that he had a message from his sirdar, or chief, the redoubtable Ramsunker, to deliver to the sahib.

He was told to advance with confidence, that he would he admitted to deliver his message, and that no harm would be done to him. On the promise of safe-conduct, the herald came forward, nowise distrustful, and was forthwith admitted.

He was a middle-sized but wiry and athletic fellow, intensely black, half-naked, with matted hair, small, loosely-twisted turban, and a broad untanned leathern belt over his shoulder.

Being asked by Mr. Augustus what he had to say or propose, he replied, that he was sent by his sirdar to state that he was now making ladders, with which he would in a few minutes scale the house at all points, and put every soul to death, unless his terms were at once complied with: these were the immediate payment of Rs. 300, upon which he would at once draw off his band, and give no further molestation to any one.

The indigo planter, finding further resistance would be useless, and knowing that these dacoits, on the principle of honour amongst rogues, were men of their word, fulfilling every engagement, whether to rob and murder, or abstain, with scrupulous fidelity, determined on acceding to their terms; this he intimated to the little plenipo, who thereat made a salaam, grinned horribly a ghastly smile, and returned to report to his superior the success of his mission.

To be brief, there was an immediate stir in the grove, and presently the chief, as sinister-looking a villain as I ever beheld, came forward to about the middle of the open space fronting the house, accompanied by a body of some ten or twelve of his followers.

Mr. Augustus gave him a bag containing the Rs. 300, for which he made an obeisance, and then wheeling about, he rejoined his band, who, after several loud shouts, moved off with their plunder, and without offering us any further annoyance.

"Well," said Mr. Augustus, shaking me by the hand, "how do you find yourself, after being stormed and besieged?—a pretty piece of business this, eh? You little thought of witnessing such an adventure, I'll be sworn, when you came down to sport at the Junglesoor Factory. This was not the shooting you expected."

"I did not, indeed," said I; "however, I think we have saved our honour, and our bodies are certainly intact, albeit you have lost your rupees."

"That's true," said my friend; "but I should still like to give the rascals a trouncing and recover the *spolia opima*, and will try it, if De la Chasse and the police make their appearance before they have got a long start of us."

This was scarcely said when we heard the sound of horses' hoofs, and in a moment De la Chasse and Tupper, in breathless haste, came spurring up to the house. The former threw himself from the saddle, and in a moment had us by the hands.

"My goot Capsicome! my dear young friend! are you all a—live? all well? Dat's goot; thank God—thank God! I hear you vas beseiged by dis raskal dacoit; so Tupper and me, ve mount our 'orse, ride off to the tannah for de police—dey vill be here directly, tannahdar and all, little and pig. But come, tell me *vraiment* all vat was happen—vere are dey?—who have dey kill?—vat have dey rob?—vere are dey gone?—Come tell it all, for I am dam *impashant* to know all."

"It is soon told, Monsieur," said Augustus. "Ramsunker and 300 of his men attacked us; we stood one assault, capitulated, and paid Rs. 300, black-mail, to get out of the scrape."

"Black male! vat de devil's black male?—you mean, I suppose, you pay Rs. 300 to de black males—I not suppose you pay to de black females."

Augustus laughed, and explained.

"Vell, vell, you did your best; de grand Napoleon himself vas obleege to yield to numbers; 300 to ten is too moch. But," added he, "I do hope ve may yet catch dis dacoit, get de money back, and give dem goot trashing beside; dere is 100 of de police, and twenty or thirty more of us—vat say you?"

"Just what I was proposing to our young friend here, as you came up; undoubtedly, let us try; but there's no time to be lost, if we would wish to succeed, for they have already a considerable start of us."

The proposal, indeed, was generally relished; the horses were ordered to be saddled; each of us armed himself in some way or other, and in a few minutes more, the portly thannahdar, or head of the police, as burly a fellow as Shakspeare's fat knight, mounted on a rat of a pony, made his appearance at the head of a numerous body, some 80 or 100, of the neighbouring police, drawn from several stations.

Mr. Augustus intimated to the thannahdar his determination to pursue the dacoits, so soon as his followers had slightly refreshed themselves, of which, after the distance they had come, they evidently stood in need. This the thannahdar intimated to his men; some of whom began to smoke in little knots or groups, squatting on their hams; others drank water, which they drew in their brazen lotas from a neighbouring well; whilst others unfolded little stores of rice, or parched gram, tied up in corners of their vestments, and set to daintily picking and eating the same. Poor prog to fight upon, thought I, holding as I do that the stomach, and not the heart, is the seat of valour.

All the above was mingled with an incessant gabble touching the recent event, with a plentiful outpouring of abuse on the female relations of the aforesaid dacoits.

The police refreshed, off started our little army in pursuit of the enemy, who we calculated could not be many miles off, the four Europeans, (if

Augustus may be included under that denomination) and the thannahdar—the cavalry of the division—taking the lead, whilst the police peons—the infantry—principally armed with spears and tulwars, brought up the rear.

As we advanced, we learnt from the villagers that the body of the dacoits (too large to move unobserved) had proceeded in the direction of a certain ferry on the river. Thither we bent our course, and learnt from the ferry people that they had recently crossed and were close at hand. The remainder of the adventure I shall sum up in a few words.

The dacoits were soon overtaken; like Cæsar, we came, and saw—would I could add, we conquered! but in that, the most essential point, the parallel with the great Roman's despatch unhappily fails.

On approaching the dingy array of the dacoits, they halted and showed a bold front. Augustus and De la Chasse marshalled their men, and addressed what were intended for some spirit-stirring exhortations to them. Tupper and I took the flanks, and doubtless felt (I can speak for myself) rather queer.

We advanced; the dacoits, sword and spear in hand, came forward doggedly to meet us—our line wavered—in vain we screamed and exhorted; the dacoits dashed in—cut down three or four; *sauve qui peut* was the word, and away flew our men over the plain. After a little irregular cutting and slashing, we followed, and with difficulty saved ourselves by the speed of our cattle.

I will leave the reader to imagine the rage of Mr. Augustus, the vehement *pestes* and *sacres* of the Gaul, and the downright straightforward abuse of the stiff little mate, elicited by this shameful misbehaviour of our troops; the censures, reports, &c., arising out of it; and the uneasiness felt, after we had got back to the factory, of another visit from the exasperated Ramsunker. Fortunately, however, he came not; and from fugitives and others we learn that, satisfied with putting us to the rout, he had made off with his gang and booty to a distant part of the country.

All this, of course, formed matter for animated discussion and commentary amongst us four at the factory, De la Chasse and his friend remaining for a couple of days to afford us their countenance and protection. We had a very merry time of it—shooting and boating in the day, and a rubber of whist or a song at night.[19]

CHAPTER XV

I had now been about twelve days a visitor with my hospitable friend, the indigo planter—a period, as the reader has seen, fertile in events—when I began to think of returning, and a letter or two which I received served to hasten my departure. One was from an old friend and schoolfellow, Tom Rattleton, a good deal my senior, and whom I had not seen or heard of for four or five years. It ran thus:—

My dear Frank,

It was by the merest chance that I heard from a Captain Marpeet, who has been staying here, in his way up, of your arrival in India. How I missed seeing your "well-known" name in the papers or General Orders I really cannot imagine. Marpeet says, you only want a little more of his tuition to become a *ne plus ultra*—in short, I must not tell half the handsome things he has said of you; but in all I could not fail to recognize, clearly and distinctly, my old class-mate and companion of the third form.

How I long, my dear fellow, to have a good dish of chat with you about school-days, and all the fun and frolic we have had together in times past! Do you recollect lame Tomkins, the pieman, and your unsuccessful attempt to prove to him, synthetically and dialectically, that long credit and great gains were preferable, as a mercantile principle, to small profits and quick returns, to which logic many an empty pocket sent forth, doubtless, a confirmatory echo? But oh, that stony-hearted man! Orpheus himself could not have moved him—no eloquence, no wiles—nought but the *ipsa pecunia*, the money's chink.

My regiment has lately arrived here from Berhampore. I have been for some time out of my griffinage, and though but a "jolly ensign," like yourself, and not very deep in the mysteries of the *Hindee Bolee*, have lately obtained the command of a company—we being rather deficient in old hands. This works me a good deal, but I like my new powers, and if I could but understand the fellows, I should get on famously.

I have a small bungalow near the river, and am comfortable enough, all things considered, so you must come and spend a month with me at least. Why not get to do duty with our regiment at once? it can be easily managed. I hope you enjoy life amongst the "True Blues" in the Mofussil. I have had some experience of them myself, and a kinder-hearted and more hospitable set of fellows, taking them in a body, does not exist.

Give me a few lines to say on what day I may expect you here, and I will ride out and meet you (if you dawk it) and have breakfast ready. So for the present adieu—*au revoir*.

Your friend and schoolfellow,

T. Rattleton.

P.S.—By-the-bye, do you recollect your changing old Thwackem's digestive pill, daily deposited at the corner of his desk, for a pea rolled in flour (or a bolus of your own manufacture), and how unsuspectingly the old boy would gulp it down, preparatory to locking up his cane and descending from his awful elevation? Many a good laugh I've had at this piece of *friponnerie* of yours.

This letter delighted me, and Mr. Capsicum, to whom I read it, seemed also a good deal amused. I felt an intense longing to see my friend Tom again, and in fact fell into such a fidgety and excited state, that I could take an interest in nothing. Old Time, instead of flying, seemed to me all of a sudden to have lost the power of locomotion altogether. Battleton and I were the Castor and Pollux of the school, sworn brothers—backers and abettors of each other in all fights, scrapes, and difficulties, of which we generally had *quantum suff.* on hand.

School was truly a black passage in my life, in which the happiness was to the misery in about the proportion of honest Jack Falstaff's bread to his quantum of Sherris sack.

"Ah, chien de livre, tu ne me fera plus répandre de pleurs!" exclaimed the enraged Scipio of Le Sage, as he wreaked his vengeance on the *"maudite grammaire,"* the passive instrument of all his sufferings.

I can too well understand the feelings which actuated, on this occasion, the little son of the honest usher of St. Hermandad, for never to this day do I enter a school-room, or my eye light on a grammar, dictionary, or other buff-coloured associate of the long-past days of my pupilage, but a host of painful and degrading recollections rush on my mind, of the hundred thwackings, confinings, mortifications, of which they were the proximate cause, as nauseous to the feelings as the remembrance of a black dose, or James's powder, "grating harsh music" through its envelopment of black-currant jelly. And as I look at a pedagogue, I have such a lively idea of a caning, that I am glad to get out of his way.

The young mind may, in truth, be likened to the notes of an instrument, from which a harmonious result can only be extracted by the hand of a master, acquainted with their respective powers; whilst a bungler may thump away at them to the end of the chapter, and nothing but discord, or the instrument irretrievably put out of tune, will be the consequence. In fact, the art of developing, governing and improving "the young idea," the most important of all, is yet in its infancy, particularly as regards the moral training.

But to curb my erratic vein, and proceed with my narrative.

A period having been fixed for my departure, Mr. Augustus asked me in what manner I proposed to return. I told him, that was a matter I had not considered, but that I should be entirely guided by him.

"Well," said he, "there's the boat you came in at your service; but the Sunderbunds are roundabout, and I'd strongly recommend your going by dawk; you'll find it pleasanter, as you're alone, and you'll reach your destination much sooner."

"Very well," I replied, "let it be so; but may I ask what mode of transport this said dawk is of which I have heard such frequent mention made—'tisn't any sort of animal, is it?"

"Animal!" exclaimed my friend in astonishment, and laughing heartily, "why you are a greater griffin than I took you for: this beats your spearing the village pig. A dawk is a relay of bearers at stages of ten or twelve miles apart, to carry you, at the rate of four or five miles an hour, to your journey's end."

"Thank you," said I, "for the information; but not possessing intuitive knowledge, you see, one can't be expected to know all things until told of them."

Augustus admitted that there was reason in the observation.

Well, it was decided that I was to proceed to Barrackpore on the second night after the day on which this conversation took place; so I wrote at once to my friend Tom, to tell him that he might expect me immediately.

The last day of my stay, De la Chasse and his *fidus Achates* dined with us, and we all appeared depressed at the prospect of separation, for our short acquaintance had already ripened into a friendly feeling.

Like towns in an ill-governed country, where, owing to the absence of sound laws and honest administrators of them, every one is afraid of his neighbour, hearts, in artificial England, are too often petty fortresses, in which pride, caution, and suspicion are incessantly on the watch to guard against surprise, and to break down these barriers and effect a lodgment is frequently the work of years; but in India, amongst Anglo-Indians, the case is reversed; the gates are thrown wide open, and intimacies and cordial (though, perhaps, not always lasting) feelings are generally the result of a few day's acquaintance.

Both extremes are bad, as all extremes are; but it is indubitably far pleasanter to live amongst those, the approaches to whose confidence and kindness are supinely, rather than too rigorously guarded; the one system, 'tis my belief, shuts out more good than the other admits of evil.

"*Sahib, ka daktiar hyr,*" said a servant entering the apartment some time after dark, on the day of which I am speaking.

"Gernon," observed Mr. Augustus, "the best of friends must part: your palankeen is ready outside, and only waits your orders."

I arose, walked to the terrace, and there was my equipage. The sentimental St. Pierre, with all the *accuracy* of a Frenchman, thus describes the equipage of his truth-seeking doctor, who, if as subject to blundering as himself, might have been a long time in discovering that valuable treasure.

"The Company's superintendent of Calcutta furnished the doctor with everything necessary for his journey to Juggernauth, consisting of a palankeen, the curtains of which were of crimson silk, wrought with gold; two relays, of four each, of stout coolies or bearers; two common porters; a water-bearer; a juglet-bearer, for his refreshment; a pipe-bearer; an umbrella-bearer, to shade him from the sun; a nuslogee (!) or torch-bearer, for the night; a wood-cutter; two cooks; two camels and their leaders, to carry his provisions and luggage; two pioneers, to announce his approach; four sepoys, mounted upon Persian horses, to escort him; and a standard-bearer, bearing the arms of England!"

I, being no philosopher, and bound on a less important mission, could pretend to none of this splendour; my turn-out consisted of a palankeen, eight or ten cahars or bearers (for in my time, whatever may have been the case in the doctor's, it was not usual to carry the palankeens upon coolies); a bangby, or two baskets, containing my immediate necessaries, slung on an elastic bamboo; and a mussaulchee, or link-bearer; the torch carried by the latter being formed of rags rolled about an iron spindle, and looking something like a bandaged stump.

I thought there would have been no end to the handshaking and last "adieus," with the repeated injunctions not to forget that I should always find a knife and fork and a hearty welcome at the Junglesoor Factory.

At last, however, I "broke away," as the fox-hunters say, I believe, and threw myself into the palankeen; the bearers, with a groan, lifted their burthen on their shoulders; the mussaulchee poured oil on his link from its long-spouted receptacle, which, flaring up, brought out the whole scene, house, trees, and congregated group on the terrace, with a wild and spectral glare. I waved my hand, half-closed the doors of my palankeen, threw myself back:—the curtain had dropped on act the second of my griffinage, and I was soon on my journey to Barrackpore.

On we went, through the murky gloom of night, dispelled for fifty yards around by the glare of the mussaul; sometimes on a fair and beaten track, at others, splashing through wet rice-fields, or traversing with infinite caution some causeway or embankment, as perilous as the bridge of Al Sirat.

The monotonous *Urree-hy-he-haw* chant of the bearers soon sent me off into a doze, from which I was only aroused occasionally by blundering attempts to put me and my palankeen on board a boat, in crossing some lazy river, on which occasions, the torch-light, the red glare on the water, and the dark figures on board, would bring old Charon and his Stygian ferry to my imagination; or the disturbance arose when they set me down, not over gently, on the skirts of some village or thannah, preparatory to a change of bearers.

At the end of the first stage, one of my active bipeds opened the doors of my palankeen, popped in his greasy frontispiece, reeking with oil and perspiration, and, with a grin, said something I did not understand, but in which the word *buckshish* (presents) was remarkably distinct.

"Go to the d— —l," exclaimed I; "boxes, no *sumjha* [20] boxes."

My friend now tried it on another tack, and, placing the finger of one hand in the palm of the other, with a knowing look, repeated the word "rupee."

Oh, thought I, are you there? I see your drift; but, knowing they had already been paid, I abruptly closed the doors and the conversation at once, with thundering "*Jow-jehanum!*"[21] a phrase I had picked up (without knowing the precise meaning of it) from Capt. Marpeet, who, in his intercourse with the natives, made frequent use of it, as a sort of receipt in full.

I passed the greater part of the following day with a planter on the road, a friend of Mr. Capsicum's, and started again in the evening.

The fresh air of the morn aroused me after my second nocturnal journey, and I looked out. We were in a rich, flat, and luxuriant country; all nature seemed smiling; the ryot was moving out to his work, and ruddy streaks appeared through the tall, tufted stems of coco-nut and taree-palms, blushing Aurora truly looking out of the barred casements of the East.

I calculated that I must now be nearly at the end of my journey; and this supposition was, in a few minutes, most agreeably confirmed by a young officer, in a red raggie and hunting-cap, riding up on a pony, and addressing a few words to my bearers in Hindostanee.

I looked hard at him, and in an instant recognized the well-known features of my schoolfellow, Tom Rattleton. The recognition was mutual, and electrical the effect; out I rolled, *sans chapeau*; off he tumbled from his tattoo, and we were soon locked in a close embrace—aye, I say in a close embrace; true affection, like true courage, is a desperate grappling affair, and a mere handshaking would have been high treason to the feelings which at that moment swelled our bosoms.

"My dear Frank!"

"My dear Tom!"

"How glad I am to see you!"

"How you are grown! but I should have known you anywhere, old fellow."

"So should I you, old boy."

"Well—eh—and how goes it?"

Thus we exploded a volley of queries and interjections, which escaped by fitful jerks, like water from bottles suddenly inverted. There was no acting here, but a hearty burst of honest nature—fresh as the morning air we were breathing.

The warmth of our greeting a little subsided, I resumed my recumbent position in the palankeen, and on went the bearers, jolting along at a rattling pace, having apparently caught all our animation, with revived hopes of "*buckshish.*" Rattleton trotted alongside, talking incessantly, and in a short time the military cantonment of Barrackpore broke in view.

We crossed the parade, where all was life and animation; soldiers drilling, recruits on one leg doing the goose-step, drums beating, drill-sergeants shouting, and bugles sounding.

We passed through the lines, thronged with sepoys in their graceful undress, and were soon at my friend's bungalow, in which, after dismissing my bearers, I entered to take up my quarters. Rattleton gave me another shake, as if he had been working a pump handle and cordially bidding me welcome.

A certain writer, who laid the scene of a romance in India, when not quite so well known as at present, describes our hero, I have been told, as sailing in a bungalow on the broad and placid surface of the Ganges, which, by a slight geographical error, is made to traverse the vale of Kashmere. Now, though I give my reader credit for knowing something more of the matter than this, a slight description of a bungalow may not be unacceptable, nevertheless.

The houses occupied by Europeans in India are of two descriptions; the *pucka* house—*havilee*, or *kottee*—and the bungalow. The former of brick or stone, is flat roofed, and, excepting in Calcutta, almost always of one story; *i.e.* the rooms are all on the ground floor, though considerably raised from the ground; they have green Venetian windows, and are encompassed, wholly or partially, by a terrace, covered with cement, shaded by a verandah or awning.

The bungalow partakes more of the cottage, or, I should perhaps rather say, the barn, being, in nineteen cases out of twenty, covered with a ponderous thatch, requiring frequent renewal, the operations of the white ants and periodical rains soon converting it into a cake of mud, through which pactolean rills frequently find their way to the interior, meandering down the walls.

The bungalow is invariably of one story, and constructed on the principle of a single or double-poled tent, or routie, according to the size; the resemblance to tents occupied by officers is indeed striking, though which is the original and which the copy I cannot say. It has usually double walls, though in some cases that which answers to the outer is little more than a range of pillars.

The space between, called the verandah, is occupied by master's palankeen, camp equipage, &c.; there, too, the bearers, or *cahars*, lie and snore during the sultry hours, till roused from their slumbers by a kick from master's foot; there, too, the patient *dirgee*, or snip, sits cross-legged, hard at work on the beebee sahib's ball-dress, or the sahib's nether garments, which he holds on with his great toe and the next one to it with all the skill of the Order *Quadrumana*, to the astonishment of the griffinish beholder.

Talk of our "light fantastic toes," indeed; what are they to a black fellow's,—adorned, too, with a fine silver great-toe-ring to boot! *Mais revenons.* The ceilings, instead of lath and plaster, are composed of coarse cotton cloth, whitewashed, and tied with numerous tags or strings to a framework of bamboo running round the apartment, and concealed from view by the projecting cornice; between this and the rafters is a dark void, the airy hall of the rats and bandicoots, who sometimes hold their *soirées dansantes* and *conversazione* in it, careering over the cloth with lively and varied squeakings. *Purdahs*, *chicks* (blinds), and *jhamps* (frames of straw and bamboo), and sometimes glass doors, serve to close the entrances; the latter are, indeed, pretty common, except at very uncivilized and out-of-the-way stations.

Furniture harbours reptiles and is expensive to carry about; officers' bungalows are, consequently, but slenderly supplied with moveables. A couch, one or two tables, half a dozen chairs, a book-shelf, a *settrinjie* (or cotton carpet, with blue and white stripes, and which also serves for the tent when marching), and a few wall-shades &c., generally constitute the adornments of an Indian officer's residence.

In the abodes of civilians, whose lots are cast in pleasanter places, and who lead less erratic lives than the military, and have far longer purses, things approximate more nearly to the English standard of luxury and comfort.

At military stations, puckha flat-roofed houses are rare, and generally occupied by the general commanding, or some other exalted functionary in the receipt of large allowances.

My friend's bungalow was a regular Indian sub's abode, and fell wofully below my standard of comfort, though in his opinion, formed on more experienced views of Indian life, it was quite as it should be.

In the first place, the grand *salon*, or *salle à manger*, contained one square camp-table, two chairs and a half, a footstool of basket work, in the shape of a devil (the thing played with two sticks, I mean); his hog-spear and gun occupied one corner, and hard by hung suspended his library; not quite so large as the Bodleian, to be sure, but containing, nevertheless, some very good cut-and-come-again sort of books.

First, there was a family Gibbon, properly docked and curtailed, a present from his grandmother; Gilchrist's Grammar; Williamson's *Vade Mecum*, and Taplin's Farriery; the *Tota Kuhanee*,[22] Mother Glass's Cookery, and a ponderous *tome*, which I at first took for a Family Bible with explanatory notes, but which turned out to be an abridgment of the rules and regulations of the Bengal army, monuments of the legislative skill of all the commanders-in-chief and governors-general from the time of Clive downwards.

Tom's dormitory was still more scantily furnished: it contained a small camp-cot, on which, much at its ease, reposed a terrier bunnow—own brother to Teazer, I could have sworn—a chair, a washhand stand, or chillumchee, a cracked looking-glass, two camel trunks, and as many *pataras*; whilst on a peg hung what he sometimes jocularly termed his badges of slavery—to wit, a sword, a sash, and shoulder-belt.

The third apartment in the bungalow, small and bare, was assigned to me, and Rattleton good-naturedly sent a servant off to the fort to bring up the things I had left there in a *paunchway*.

After showing me the interior, we proceeded to the shady side of the bungalow, where, on a terrace, stood a chair, a teapoy, a small carpet, and other preparations for my friend's second toilet. After parade or the morning's ride, it is the invariable custom to dress again, an operation which, in the hot seasons, is repeated sometimes two or three times in the course of the day.

We should be rather surprised to see gentlemen in England sitting *al fresco* on the lawns, barring a short pair of drawers, as naked as gladiators; but, as I said before, the sun makes a very considerable difference in our perceptions of things in general.

Prior to dressing, it is usual to take a bath, which is effected by the *bhistee's* (water-carrier's) sluicing over you the frigid contents of a *mussack*, or tanned sheepskin bag. This braces the whole system, and adds a fresh edge to the appetite, already sharpened by the ride in the morning air. Breakfast is, consequently, attacked with a degree of vigour and determination not often seen even in our hyperborean clime.

After a comfortable meal, and disposing of a vast quantity of fish, rice, and muffins, Rattleton cocked his legs on the table, bade me do the same, and make myself quite at home. The pipeman brought the hookha, and the bearer pulled the punka, and we proceeded to discuss a plan of proceeding for the morning.

"In the first place, we must call on the colonel this morning," said Rattleton; "he is a very good sort of man, takes matters easily, and patronizes me especially, but is rather tenacious of having proper respect paid to him; then, after that, I'll introduce you to the general, and some of the other officers of the corps and station, and in the evening we'll drive you out in the park, where you'll see all the beauty and fashion of Barrackpore. By the way, Frank, there are some devilish nice spins just now here, which, perhaps, you'll not be sorry to hear."

"Certainly not," I replied; "but I hope, Tom, you're not thinking of committing matrimony just yet, are you?"

"Why, I don't exactly know," said Tom; "there's a very sweet little girl here, who has made a sad hole in my heart; such a pair of eyes as she has— oh! Frank—but you'll see. I have made a hundred resolutions against being spliced, but one glance of those death-dealing orbs sends them all to shivers in a minute. I am like a moth flitting about a candle, and shall go plump into the mischief at last, I see that very plainly. Perhaps, though, Frank, as you are not a bad-looking fellow, you may keep down or divert a little of the fire of that terrible artillery."

"Why, I don't know," said I, laughing; "it is not so easy to create a diversion in these cases, and not over safe; besides, who knows, if successful, but that the fire of your love may be changed into that of jealousy, and that you may be opening another sort of battery on me! But seriously, I can feel for you, Tom, for already my poor heart has been amazingly riddled by a charming young lady we left at Madras, and more recently by a widow. 'Pon my life, I begin to think the Orientals do wisely in locking up their women."

"I begin to think so too," said Tom, with a sigh: "they do a confounded deal of mischief; at all events, those radiant and Mokannah-visaged dames should be closely veiled with good opaque stuff, as you muzzle dangerous dogs."

"What a simile, Tom! But your plan would be of no avail; a mere masking of the battery, which, upon fit occasions, would open upon us with more deadly effect."

Whilst we were thus chatting, the blind of the room was drawn aside, and Cherby Khan and Loll Sing (which translated mean "the fat lord" and "the red lion"), the subadar and lance-naick or corporal of my friend's company, marched in to make their morning's report.

A native of Hindostan, well off in the world, and with a mind at ease, fattens as regularly and surely as a pig or a stall-fed ox. The subadar was consequently a punchy, adipose little fellow, something of the cut and build of "*Mon oncle Gil Perez.*" The naick, on the contrary, was tall and spare, and a very proper and handsome man of his inches.

On entering (stiff as a ramrod), the little subadar, who showed a good civic rotundity in front, threw out his right arm horizontally, with a jerk, which might have almost dislocated it from the shoulder-joint, and then bringing up his hand to his cap, saluted in a most military style, and reported that "all was well," "*sub ucha*" in the company of the "*Gurreeb Purwar*," or "protector of the poor," for so he designated my friend Tom.

This was the statement in the gross, with which, however, it appeared there was little correspondence in the items; these proved, I afterwards understood from Tom, to be—two men dead, five gone to hospital, three deserted, a musket lost, and sundry other mishaps.

The "red lion" now stepped briskly forward, as if going to knock Tom down; recovered his arms with a crack, which made me almost jump out of my chair, and proceeded at once to "unfold a tale" of considerable length, to which my friend replied, "*Ucha*,"[23] and "*Bhote khoob*,"[24] though it was pretty clear, from his perplexed look and embarrassed air, that he did not understand one-third of it. In point of fact, the aforesaid statement was evidently one which involved some knotty point for "the protector of the poor's" decision, and requiring something more tangible in the way of comment than the aforesaid "*Bhote khoob*."

My friend, however, dismissed him with a "*Peechee hookum*," "orders deferred," a sort of "call again to-morrow" phrase, much used in India, when time is sought to be gained. Another salute from the subadar, another formidable crack of the fusee from Loll Sing, and both wheeled on their heels, and *exeunt*. "*Buggy lou juldee*" ("bring quick the gig"), "*Jal kreech do*" (and "give me my sash and sword"), shouted Rattleton.

A sort of whiskey, which my friend sported on his ensign's pay, was soon at the door. He was duly equipped, and in we both stepped, and drove off to the bungalow of Colonel Lollsaug, the commandant of my friend's regiment, which I shall call the 95th N.I., or "*Zubberdust Bullumteers*."

We were ushered in, and found the colonel smoking his hookha, with a sneaker of cold tea before him, a sort of prolongation of the breakfast almost universal in India. He rose as we entered, and shook hands with Tom, who presented me as his friend recently arrived.

The colonel was a gaunt figure of six feet two, or thereabouts, with sallow sunken cheeks, and two little tufts of grizzled whisker near the corner of his mouth; he was dressed in a not uncommon morning dishabille, consisting simply of a shirt and red camlet jacket, a pair of immense *pajammas*, or native trousers, tied with a silken string at the waist, whilst an immense pair of spangled Indian slippers, with curly toes as long as rams' horns, adorned his feet; an embroidered velvet scull-cap was perched on the top of his head: and altogether he was as striking a specimen of the epicene gender of the Orientalized European as I had as yet seen.

The colonel asked me if I had recently arrived? how I liked India? what the folks were doing at home? if St. Paul's stood where it used to do? and sundry other questions of a like nature, to all of which I gave suitable replies.

Rattleton told him we were old schoolfellows, and that I had a strong desire to do duty with his corps for a month, if it could be so arranged. The colonel kindly undertook to manage the matter, and told Tom to introduce me to the adjutant, who would have me instructed in the drill, and manual and platoon, with some other young men then with the regiment.

The colonel now asked my friend if he had been at the grand ball an evening or two before, and how it went off?

Tom said he had, and they had a very pleasant evening, second supper, lots of dancing, and some good songs, and that there were strong suspicions that the general was a little "*fou.*"

"Well," said the colonel; "that's all right, but was *she* there?"

"Who, sir?" asked my friend, very innocently.

"Come, come, that won't do, Mr. Slyboots," said the colonel; "I know all about it; ha! ha! ha!"

"'Pon my honour, sir," said Rattleton, blushing, "you are too enigmatical for me."

"Capital," said the colonel, who was in a bantering humour; "why, Prattle tells me it's all settled, license written for, and that you are going to cart her[25] immediately—ha! ha! ha!"

I saw, of course, that all this had reference to the spinster with the fine eyes. Though my friend affected ignorance of the matter, he was evidently flattered by being made the subject of such an agreeable *on dit.*

Whilst this was going on, I was startled and surprised by seeing the head of a very pretty Indian lady, with jet black locks, large gazelle eyes, and a huge gold ring in her nose, pop from behind the *purdah*, or curtain, and the owner of which exclaimed, at the top of a very shrill voice, "*Urree Dhyya Paundaunneelou.*"[26]

The colonel said something rather sharply.

"*To vau,*" pettishly exclaimed the apparition, and the head and a pretty be-ringed hand were withdrawn, and immediately from an opposite door an elderly black duenna, with a pair of wrinkled trousers, or *pajammas*, and half-concealed by a cowl-like sort of muslin robe, marched in a stately manner, *sans cérémonie,* her anklet bells jingling, right across the apartment, with a huge metal box under her arm, which I afterwards learnt was a betel-box, and which it seems was the article which the colonel's sultana stood in need of.

Egad, thinks I to myself, they order things in the East rather differently from what they do in the West.

After a little more conversation we took our leave, having previously received an invitation to dine the next evening with the quaint commandant.

CHAPTER XVI

The space to which I have limited myself in these Memoirs will not admit a minute account of all I saw, heard, said, and did, during my months sojourn at Barrackpore; it will, therefore, suffice if I touch lightly on a few prominent characters and occurrences illustrative of Indian life, during this period of my griffinage.

"Tom," said I, as we left the colonel's bungalow, "do tell me who that fine dark damsel was, with the ring in her nose, of whom we had a glimpse from behind the curtain."

"Why, that's the native commandant," said Tom.

"Nonsense," said I; "what do you mean?"

"Why, I mean that the colonel commands the regiment, and she commands the colonel."

"Ha! ha! well, that's made out logically enough, certainly; but in that way I suspect you'd have no difficulty in proving a peticoatocracy all the world over: man, good easy soul, fancies himself a free agent, puffs and struts, and is but a puppet after all, of which woman pulls the strings, and yet these provoking creatures are always complaining of want of power and due influence."

"Well done, Frank; ably put, my boy. I see you're as great an inductive philosopher as ever; it's a true bill though; the strongest fortress, too, has its weak points. There's the colonel, for example, a deeply-read man, understands everything, from metaphysics to a red herring; will touch you off a page of Xenophon, or a chapter of Sanscrit, with perfect ease; a man who has thought and read, and read and thought, in that Fortunatus' cap and those curly-toed slippers of his, for the last thirty years, in all the leisure of camp and out-station, fort and jungle; brave as a lion, generous as a prince, and in most matters firm as a rock; and yet that little Delilah can wheedle and wind him round her finger as she pleases. She makes half the promotions in the regiment, I am told; and no one better than blacky understands the value of back-stairs influence, and the mode of working it successfully. But by all accounts these are the men who square best with Jack Sepoy's notions of a proper commander; these are the men whom they would go to the devil to serve; who know how to treat them in their own way, and not your pipe-clay, rigid disciplinarians, who would utterly extinguish the native in the soldier, who make fine troops for a parade, but bad ones for the tug of war, or when their loyalty is assailed. It's splendid to hear the colonel talk to the Jacks; he understands them thoroughly; can make them roar with laughter, or shake in their shoes, as he pleases; true it is, if you would govern men effectually, it must be through the medium of their peculiar feelings and prejudices, and not by taking the bull by the horns."

As he said this, we drove into a pretty extensive compound, and drew up before a large puckha-house, with a bevy of servants and orderlies in the verandah; this was the residence of the general commanding, to whom I was presented in due form.

Tom next took me to the adjutant's, and the rest of his brother-officers, of whom he promised to give me some account on a future occasion, and then we went home to tiffin.

In the evening we had a delightful ride in the Governor-General's park, and as we wheeled along through its mazy rounds, saw all the beau monde of Barrackpore, as also my friend's innamorata, with whom we had some very lively conversation, as we drove slowly alongside the barouche in which, with a party, she was taking the air.

Having visited the menagerie in the park, stirred up the tigers, and plagued the monkeys a little, we drove to Colonel Lollsaug's.

The colonel gave us an excellent dinner, wine admirably cooled, foaming pale ale—India's prime luxury—and some capital home-fed mutton. There were five or six officers present, and the conversation, which was unrestrained and agreeable, turned upon old recollections of former stations; on the prospect of promotion and war or rather war and promotion, for such is their natural order; and gave me a greater insight into what was passing in the Indian military world than I had yet enjoyed.

Being young, and a griffin, I thought it was better for me to listen than to be prominently loquacious; and it was fortunate that I adopted this conclusion, for, amongst other topics, the extreme forwardness and assurance of the youth of the present—*i.e.* of that day—was discussed with much animation.

"It's too true, I fear," said the colonel; "they don't conduct themselves as the young lads did in my juvenile days. I remember," said he, with the regretful air of the *laudator temporis acti*, "when I was a young man and first came out, we thought it necessary and proper to exhibit some little deference and respect to our seniors in age and rank—some reserve and diffidence in our opinions, not, however, inconsistent with a due degree of firmness and self-respect; but now, forsooth, your beardless younker, fresh from school, claps you on the shoulder, and is hail-fellow-well-met with you in an instant, exhibiting all the confidence of a man of fifty—quite destitute of that master-charm of modesty, which, in man or woman, takes so powerful a hold on the affections and good-will."

These observations, though perhaps true in themselves, I thought a little ill-timed, and not wholly consistent with his own proceedings. However, they were cordially assented to by some of the "old hands" present, particularly by one ill-dressed, caustic, and slovenly old captain, named Langneb.

"You're right, colonel, quite right, sir; they're all major-generals now, sir, at starting; know everything and care for nobody. There's young Snapper, who joined us the other day—an idle, dissipated young scamp; keeps four horses, gives champagne tiffins, and is spending three times the amount of his pay—hailed me only last night in the park by my surname, sir—no prefix, by George! no handle, though I haven't spoken to him five times— told me I had got a pretty beast there (meaning my horse), and asked me for the loan of my buggy to-morrow! What do you think of that, sir? Never met such a forward, self-sufficient young fellow in all my life; but he's going to the dogs as fast as he can."

"I am afraid he is," said another; "but there's some allowance to be made for him. Thompson, who knows his family at home, tells me he was brought up by a doating grandmother, who spoilt him, indulged him to the top of his bent, never contradicted—money *ad libitum*—things all his own way: hence pride, selfishness, and an inordinate love of pleasure, the natural results. Never send your children to be brought up by grandmothers; owing to their unbounded affection, which passes through the parent as through a lens, they're sure to spoil them."

A rubber of whist and a game of chess concluded the evening very pleasantly at the colonel's. At parting, he told me with great kindness that he hoped soon to see me on parade, and that he had desired the adjutant to take me in hand, and give me a little preliminary instruction.

The next day Rattleton took me another round of visits to some of the married men of his acquaintance, many of whom seemed agreeable people, but possessed of various degrees of refinement; also to the houses of two or three widow ladies residing at the station, all of whom had pretty daughters or nieces seeking that which it was natural and proper they should seek, eligible partners, youthful "John Andersons," with whom to jog up the hill of life together.

It was abundantly clear, and I soon discovered, that Rattleton's little affair of the heart had got wind pretty extensively, for wherever we went he had to run the gauntlet of banter and sly innuendo in one shape or another. Like Mr. Dangle, however, with his "volunteer fatigue" and "solicited solicitations," he bore it all very philosophically.

Tom was a handsome fellow, and it was well known that he was to have the first vacant regimental staff appointment, his aunt being married to a first cousin of the Governor-General's military secretary's second wife's first husband. Under these circumstances, my friend ranked as an "eligible," and the old ladies could not forgive him altogether for passing over the more valid claims of their daughters and nieces; and the daughters and nieces, though they endeavoured to conceal their chagrin under the guise of a very transparent indifference, were evidently not a whit more satisfied with Mr. Rattleton's presumed election in favour of Miss Julia Heartwell.

The first widow to whom we paid our respects was Mrs. Brownstout; the relict of a field officer who had fallen a victim to jungle fever several years before, and who was residing in great respectability on her pension at Barrackpore, as many other widows did and do. She had lived for some time in England after her husband's death, but quitted it after a time in disgust, finding both climate and people too cold to suit the warmth of an Indian temperament; her frankness startled folks, and her unreserved expression of opinion was looked upon, amongst the worldly-wise, as the evidence of a doubtful sanity.

Of this lady, as one of a class, I must present the reader with a slight memoir.

Mrs. Brownstout, after the loss of her husband, "her poor dear Browny," as she always called him, had nobly set her shoulder to the wheel, and, with all that admirable perseverance quickened by a lively sense of duty and parental affection, which the sex (and none more so than Indian widows) thus circumstanced so often exhibit, had fought a stout battle for her children; for two sons she had obtained military appointments in India, having (armed with those potent weapons, the prayers of the widow and the orphan) laid siege to a good-hearted director, and carried him by storm, after a feeble show of resistance on his part; and for a third she had obtained the management of an indigo factory.

Of three daughters, one had married a doctor within hail of the Medical Board, and Lucinda and Maria were still unmarried, though it was shrewdly suspected they had no intention to die vestal virgins, if it could be decently avoided.

Mrs. Major Brownstout was rather dark, and in Abyssinia, where bulk and beauty are synonymous, would have been considered a remarkably fine woman; but as it was, she exceeded the English standard of beauty by some five or six stone.

Fatness and good-humour are almost invariably found united, but which is the cause and which the effect—whether fat breeds good-nature or good-nature fat—is one of those profound mysteries of nature which old Burton might decide, but for which I have in vain sought a satisfactory solution.

Mrs. Brownstout was quick, penetrating, and possessed a large fund of that frankness and kindliness of heart which I have, in the course of my Eastern experience, almost invariably found to characterize the ladies of mixed blood in India.

Society full oft, by its folly, oppression, and prejudice, begets the faults which it affects to hate and despise; and the fact of any classes being looked down upon, which is more or less the case as regards the half-caste or Eurasian throughout India (though less so in Bengal than in the sister presidencies), has a depressing tendency, which naturally places individuals of that description in a highly disadvantageous position, deadening the energies, and preventing that free and natural play and expansion of the mind and feelings which are ever the results of knowing that we stand well with the world.

In spite, however, of these sinister influences (having the same origin with those which actuate our American brethren in their conduct to their coloured countrymen, and which we so loudly condemn), I must bear my humble testimony in favour of our Eurasian fellow-subjects, who, far from combining the vices and defects of both races, as has often been cruelly and flippantly declared, seem, on the contrary, as far as my experience goes, from griffinage upwards, to unite with the gentleness, placability, and fidelity of the native many of the sterling virtues of the European character, though certainly lacking its strength and energy.

But iron nerves, in which consists the secret of English superiority, require regulation as well as the weak and more delicate organizations of the East; for if the one tends to effeminacy, the other, under the fancied character of manliness, too often tends to ferocity, and that one-sided freedom called tyranny. "Call this a land of freedom where a man mayn't shoot his own nigger!" said Matthews' Yankee; and a volume could not better express that Irish reciprocity of rights which John and Jonathan are so prone to patronize.—But to return.

This engraftment will probably produce those permanent social, moral, and political fruits, which there from neither European nor native singly could be expected.

The English greyhound, taken to India, dies, or loses in time most of his energy and valuable qualities, and the produce decidedly degenerates; but the cross with the native dog of that species produces an animal in which is united the Indianized constitution of the one with much of the speed and courage of the other.

I am sorry to seek an illustration of my position amongst the lower order of creation, but it perhaps holds good.

We found Mrs. Brownstout in the act of explaining some mystery of dress to a *dirgee* (tailor), a little slender ungirdled shrimp, standing, scissors in hand, amidst a vast accumulation of muslin and ribbon. One of the young ladies was penning a billet, the other painting flowers.

"How d'ye do, Rattleton, how d'ye do?" said the old lady, as we entered, addressing my friend bluntly, who was evidently one of her "boys." "I can't get up to you, you see, so talk to the girls."

The young ladies, however, arose, and Tom introduced me to them.

On taking my seat they asked me a few common-place questions, such as how long I had been in India? how I liked it? if I had lately arrived at Barrackpore? and so forth; to all of which I made suitable replies.

This piece of formality over, the old lady and her daughters, evidently impatient to unburthen themselves, opened upon Tom *instanter.*

"Well, Rattleton," said Mrs. B., drily, "what have you been doing with yourself lately? you have become a perfect stranger. Have you brought us any news? what is doing in cantonments? who is dead and who is wed?"

"I know nothing of buryings or weddings," said Tom; "they're grave and melancholy subjects, about which I do not trouble myself."

"Well, indeed!" retorted Mrs. Brownstout; "I admire that amazingly; we all consider you one of the greatest gossips of the station."

"Perhaps, mamma," said Miss Lucinda, archly, "Mr. Rattleton is too much engaged with his own approaching nuptials to think much about those of other people."

"Oh, that's true," said Mrs. B., with mock gravity; "they say you are going to get married; is it true, Rattleton?"

"Oh, nonsense! mere Barrackpore *gup* and scandal; who could have told you that?"

"Oh, we have had it from the very best authority."

Tom laughed.

"Well, Mr. Rattleton, when is it to take place?" asked Miss Lucinda, dipping her brush in her pallet, and touching up her drawing with all the *nonchalance* imaginable. "I do so long to know; and who are to be the bridesmaids? I hope Maria or I shall be admitted to that honour."

"Oh, yes, when I *am* married, you shall be the bridesmaid, certainly, the lady consenting; but that event, I take it, is rather remote. What on earth should a sub like me do with a wife, who can hardly take care of himself?"

Many a true word spoken in jest, Mr. Tom, thought I.

"You'll wait for the vacant interpretership, eh?" said the mamma.

"Well, that's right, and like a prudent young man."

"That is an appointment admirably suited for you, Mr. Rattleton; you speak the language with such fluency and purity," observed Miss Lucinda.

"Upon my life," said Tom, "you're a great quiz; how long, Miss Maria, is it since your sister became so satirical? but as for the language," added Tom, a little piqued, "I don't think I speak that badly, after all. Now I appeal to you, Mrs. Brownstout—you're a judge, and will do me justice."

"Why," said Mrs. B., "pretty well—pretty well, considering you're almost a griffin."

"Oh, yes, you speak it like a native—of England," added Lucinda, laughing.

Tom stood this and a good deal more pretty well, being evidently accustomed to this badinage with the Brownstouts. However, three at once were too much, and I, being a stranger, was inefficient and dummy.

Tom exhausted his stock of repartee; was "beat to a dead stand-still," to borrow the language of the Ring and began, I thought, to look a little grave and cross. The ladies, consequently, changed the theme, and the conversation flowed on in a more equable and rational stream.

At length we arose and took our leave, Mrs. Brownstout begging me to come with Tom and pass the evening with them whenever I felt so disposed.

The following day, at eleven, Rattleton and I walked over to the adjutant's bungalow. I had had two or three days' law and liberty, and it was intimated to me by Tom that I must now attend to duty, or expose myself to be considered one of what are cantly denominated "John Company's hard bargains."

The adjutant was a good-looking young man, of five-and-twenty, somewhat of an exquisite in dress, with large Cossack trousers (then the fashion), and long brass spurs, which I thought he clanked rather ostentatiously.

With all this, however (for the exquisite and the soldier are not incompatible), Adjutant Wigwell was evidently a zealous officer, proud of his regiment, and devoted to drill and duty; this I had learnt, indeed, from recent observation and common report.

We found him amidst a bevy of khote havildars (*i.e.* pay-sergeants), with the sergeant-major, havildar-major—deeply engaged in the very important matter of regulating the length of a pouch-strap, the number of holes it should have, and the precise position of the buckle, and trying the fit of the same on a stalwart grenadier of some six feet two.

The sergeant-major, a thick-set Englishman, little more than half the length and twice the breadth of the gigantic sepoy, was in the act of adjusting it, with the assistance of the havildar-major, the adjutant's native right hand in a sepoy regiment.

Adjutant Wigwell received us kindly, shook me by the hand, and begged us to be seated and amuse ourselves till he had dismissed the business he was then attending to, which would not detain him a moment. This being over, he asked me if I had ever been drilled, and knew any thing of the manual and platoon, &c.; to which questions I was constrained to reply in the negative.

"Well," said he, smiling, "we must take you in hand a little, and make a soldier of you. Sergeant-major," said he, addressing that sturdy little functionary, standing in the verandah.

"Sir," said the sergeant, touching his hat, and slipping in.

"Sergeant Giblett," continued he, "this young gentleman, Mr. Gernon, is doing duty with us; he will soon have to attend all drills and parades; but, in the meantime, you must give him a little instruction in marching, and the manual and platoon, with the other young officers recently arrived to do duty."

The sergeant again saluted, and said it should be attended to.

"Rattleton," said the adjutant, "your men fired badly yesterday; how was that?"

"Why, I believe it was my fault," said Tom; "I was nervous, and that confounded gunpowder, the grains as big as swan-shot, blowing in my face from the men's pans, made me more so; however, I must summon my force next time."

"Do, my dear fellow," said the adjutant; "the colonel noticed it, I assure you, and desired me in a friendly way just to give you a hint."

"He's a noble fellow," said Tom, with warmth, "and I love him; I had rather have my cheeks excoriated, and my eyes damaged in future, than give him cause of complaint."

"Well, that's all as it should be," said Wigwell. "Rattleton, your friend Mr. Gernon had better fall in with your company at parade; it may be pleasant for him, and you, you know," added he with a smile, "can give him the benefit of your experience."

The next day Tom took me to an unoccupied bungalow, near the lines, used for various purposes, in order that I might have my first lesson in the manual and platoon.

We found Sergeant Giblett already there, and talking to several cadets or ensigns, who seemed much amused, and listening to him attentively. "And that, as near as I can kal-ki-late, was when I first jined the army under his Excellency Lifttennant Gineral Lord Lake"—was, however, all we caught of the yarn.

Rattleton now introduced me to my brother-aspirants for military glory—beardless tyros, wild as unbroken colts, and all agog for fun and frolic, in whatever shape it might present itself.

"You've never had no instruction in the man'il and plytoon, I think you said, Sir?" said the sergeant to me, touching his hat.

"You're quite right; I did say so."

"Well then, sir, if you please, as it's the first day, it'll be jist as well for you to look on."

"Now, gin'lemen," said Sergeant-Major Giblett, dismissing at once his countenance of colloquial familiarity, and assuming the "wrinkled front" of stem duty; "now, gin'lemen, if you please—we're a-losing of time, and had better begin. I think you're all here, with the hexception of Mr. Wildman, and he, I am given to onderstand, is ill-disposed this morning."

At this speech one of the young hands in the squad winked to his neighbour, as much as to say, "Twig the sergeant"—he exploded with laughter; his next file gave him a jerk or dig with his elbow—he lost his balance, tumbled against his neighbour, and a general derangement of the ranks followed.

"Come, gin'lemen, gin'lemen," said the sergeant, half angry, "this won't do—this won't never do; if I am to teach you your man'l and plytoon, you must be steady—you must upon my life. Come, tention," said he, briskly squaring up, and throwing open his shoulders, as if determined to proceed to business. "Shoulder! up! Order! up! Onfix bagganets! That's all right. Shoulder! up! That won't do, Mr. Cobbold; you must catch her up sharper than that. Now, please to look at me, sir," taking the musket in hand, and doing the thing *secundum artem*.

Another half-smothered laugh again disturbed the little sergeant's self-complacency.

"Oh! this can't be allowed, gin'lemen. I'll give it up—I'll give it up, I will indeed. I'll report you all to the adjutant, if this here larking goes on, I will."

This threat had a sedative effect on the disorderly rank and file, who now looked wonderfully demure, though with that mock and constrained gravity which threatened a fresh outbreak on the next elocutionary attempt of the self-important sergeant.

"Now, gin'lemen, you'll please to observe that, when I says 'Shoulder!'—will you look this way, Mr. Wildgoose, if you please?—when I says 'Shoulder!' you must each take a firm 'grist' (grasp) of his piece (a titter)—just here, about the middle; and when I gives the word 'Up!' you must chuck her up sharp. Now, then. 'Shoulder!' 'Grist' her higher, Mr. Cobbold. 'Up!' That's it."

"D——n it, Cobbold, take care what you're at, man," exclaimed Cobbold's left-hand man, on getting a crack on the head from the said Cobbold's awkward shouldering.

"Order! as you were!—What are you doing, sir? That's not right. When I says 'As you were,' I means 'As you was;' that is, as you was afore—rewerting to your former pisishion. Right about face! That's it. Now, gin'lemen, when I says 'Left about face,' you'll please to do jist the same thing, only directly the *contrary*. Steady, gin'lemen, if you please—steady! Now march in file—quick march—lock-up step!"

"Brown, mind where you're treading, man."

"D——n it, I can't help it; *don't* be so savage."

"Mark time! that is, keep moving without advancing. Halt front! left back'ards wheel! Now, gin'lemen, you'll be pleased to remember that when I gives the words 'Quick march!' you'll fall back'ards on the pivot man—that is to say, on the wheeling pint—all one as a gate on its 'inges. Quick march! that's it, gin'lemen—that's it."

In this style the good-humoured but consequential little sergeant was wont to instruct us in the rudimental part of the glorious art of war.

On breaking off and dismissing the awkward squad the young men composing it assembled round Sergeant Giblett, who appeared to be a prime favourite amongst them, and he on his part was evidently so much pleased with them, that it was obviously with difficulty that his good-nature allowed him to maintain that dignity which he evidently felt, and which ought to be the inseparable concomitant of command.

"Well, sergeant, how did I do to-day?"

"Why, sir," said Giblett, "it's not my wish to flatter no gin'leman, but you have sartainly improved in your marchings."

"And me, sergeant," said another, "how do I get on?"

"Why, sir, you'll soon be all right, if you pays a little more attention."

"I say, sergeant, what makes you call the musket 'she?'"

"Why, you know, sir, the firelock among 'Ropeyarn[27] sogers (it's different, of coorse, among the Seapies[28]) alw's goes by the denomy-nation of Brown Bess, and so we calls it 'she.'"

"Oh, that's it, is it, sergeant?"

"Take a glass of grog, Giblett, after your fatigues?"

"Thankye, sir, I don't care if I do."

"Here, you bearer, black fellow," said the donor, "*brandy, shrub, pawney, sergeant, ko do*" (*i.e.*, give the sergeant some brandy-and-water).

Sergeant Giblett took the empty glass, extended his arm in one direction to have it filled, whilst he turned his head in another; bearer applies his teeth to the brandy-bottle to get the cork out.

"You were a-axing of me, sir, I think, about the cellybrated battle of Laswarrie, in which we—that is, the ridg'ment I then belonged to—was present, under Lifttennant Gineral Lord Lake; yes, that was pretty near the stiffest business we had. There was the battalions of the French gineral, Munseer Donothing (Duderneg): and very good troops they was, though not so good as our Seapies. Hulloa!" he exclaimed, breaking off in his story, and looking towards the tumbler, which the bearer was busy in filling, "what's this here man about?—he's a-givin me all the bottle of brandy; here come, you must put some of this back."

"No, no—nonsense, sergeant," said the liberal donor, "drink it all—it won't hurt you."

This was just what Sergeant Giblett wanted.

"Well, thankye, sir; but I'm afraid its over strong. Gin'lemen, here's towards your very good healths."

So saying, Giblett drained off the dark potation—a regular "north-wester"—set down the empty glass, and took his leave, reserving his "yarn" for another time.

CHAPTER XVII

Under the able tuition of Sergeant Giblett I became, in a few days, sufficiently a proficient in the mysteries of marching, &c., to allow of my falling in with Lieut. Rattleton's company, the left grenadiers,[29] and it was consequently arranged, with the concurrence of the adjutant, that I should make my *début* on parade when next the battalion was out for exercise.

On the day previous to that event taking place, after tiffin, a sepoy orderly brought in the regimental and station orders; and Tom, after reading them, directed my attention particularly to a paragraph in the former, which ran thus:

"The regiment will parade for exercise to-morrow morning, at a quarter after gun-fire, furnished with ten rounds of blank cartridge per man."

"There! my sub," said Rattleton; "to-morrow you will see a little service, and smell gunpowder for the first time in your life."

"You're wrong there," said I; "you seem to have forgotten my recent engagement with the Dacoits; why sir," said I, affecting to bristle up, "though you do command a company I have seen far more active service than you have. A siege—a pursuit—a rout—and a retreat, are pretty well, I take it, for an ensign of two months' standing."

"Ha! ha! Well, that's true, to be sure," rejoined my friend, laughing; "you have, indeed, seen balls fired with intent to do grievous bodily harm, and against the peace of our sovereign lord the king—but I would sink the *bolt*, Frank, when I talked of my Junglesoor exploits. But, seriously, you must get all your military trappings ready overnight, and I'll see that you are called in good time in the morning."

I retired to bed rather earlier than usual, oppressed with a most unpleasantly alarmed state of feelings, something akin, probably, to that which a man experiences the night before he is hanged—or has to fight a duel—or to encounter any other disagreeable novelty. I wished the initiatory process fairly over, having somehow or other allowed my anxiety to work on my imagination till I pictured it as something very formidable.

I was aroused, next morning, by Rattleton's singing, with reference to my dormant state, I suppose, "Arise, arise! Britannia's sons, arise," and by a rough shake of the shoulder.

"Eh! what?—what's the matter?" said I, starting up, rubbing my eyes, and yawning.

"Come, my sub, jump up, jump up! parade! parade! the gun has fired."

"Why, it's pitch dark, Tom," said I, still stretching; "you surely don't go to parade in the middle of the night?"

Tom assured me it was the proper hour, and that it would soon be light; his bearer ran in at the same moment, open-mouthed, to say the colonel was on horseback and had just ridden past.

This announcement quickened my movements; so I reluctantly jumped out of my warm nest, and, after a miserable cold dabble, dressed myself by the light of a candle, "in the lantern dimly burning," buckled on my Andrea Ferrara, brushed up my hair, took a peep in the glass, to see how I looked on an average, and then, *grande tenue*, and arm-in-arm, marched off to parade with my friend.

"The day, you see, is beginning to break," said he.

"I wish, with all my heart, it would make haste about it," I returned ("and I think I do see a few ruddy streaks in the east), for this is a heathenish hour, a most Cimmerian gloom to manœuvre in. For my part, I am sure I could not distinguish a rank of soldiers from a brick wall."

"You will soon become accustomed to it," answered my commandant, "and find the reasonableness of this and other Indian customs, which now appear singular to you; better to be comfortable in darkness than to grill in broad day."

"Tom," said I, "you must tell me where I am to stand, and what I am to do, for I know no more than the man in the moon."

"You'll have merely to march in the rear of the company," said my commander; "keep step, and salute in passing in review; all that, I think you understand."

As we passed through the sepoy lines, and approached the parade, the men were just in the act of falling in, and my ears were saluted by a strange and confused hubbub, loud shouts, and words of command in odd voices.

There was the "*Hall dreez*" (halt dress), "*Lupt buccas wheel*" (left backwards wheel), and "*Qeeck marruch*" (quick march), of the native officers (by whom one-half of the platoons, at least, were commanded), and the same, though in more intelligible English, in the sharper tones of the Europeans.

Then there was a rattling of muskets, and a ringing of ramrods; the loud voice of the commandant; the clattering of the adjutant's steel scabbard, and the ringing of his horse's hoofs, as he thundered down the ranks in a prodigious fuss—why, I could not tell—unless to create a sensation. Our adjutant, however, of the Zubberdust Bullumteers, was a prodigiously smart officer, and always galloped three times as fast as was necessary.

It was all exciting and strange to me, to find myself thus, for the first time, about to participate in real military proceedings; the actual game of soldiers, which I had hitherto only viewed, with becoming awe, à la distance, or mimicked, as a younker, with penny drum and falchion of tin. I was now about to realize one of my dreams of boyhood.

Time's misty veil has long rested on those days, but still I can recal the stirring interest I used to experience when the recruiting-sergeant, on a fair-day, marched through our village. I think I now behold him, with his drawn sword and flying ribbons, proud as a turkey-cock, with all the tag-rag and bobtail at his heels.

What a glorious thing I thought it was to be a soldier—a real, downright, actual soldier—to wear a red coat, and fight the French! How I longed to be the fifer, or even the little duck-legged drummer, as he strode valiantly through the mud, with his long gaiters—very little older than myself, too, and yet privileged to wear a *real* sword! Even the gawky smock-frock clowns, won by the sergeant's eloquence, touching the joys of a soldier's life, and forming a part of the tail of this flaming meteor, came in for a share of my envy.

"Ah!" I used mentally to exclaim, "I'll certainly be a soldier when I am a man!" Here, then, was the realization; a downright *bonâ fide* regiment, real guns, real colonel, and all, and I a constituent portion of it—in a word, an officer! Thus, my gratification, in a great measure, overcame my uneasiness.

"The battalion will pass in review—march!" roared the colonel; and away we went, as solemn as mutes at a funeral, I behind my sepoys,— sword drawn, stiff as the little man in the Lord Mayor's carriage, right leg foremost. It was an agitating moment, and I in a nervous tremour, lest I should commit some blunder. We turned the angle of the square,—the band struck up,—and we approached the saluting flag.

"Rear rank, take open order!"

The native officers made a long leg; I did the same, and found myself in front of the company, exposed to general notice. To use a coarse, but expressive phrase, I was in a "devil of a stew."

I kept a close eye on my captain, however, thinking, if I did as he did I could not be wrong.

We approached the colonel; I saw he had his eye upon me. Ye powers, if such there be, who preside over steps short and long, and all others the deep mysteries of drill and parade, how much did I then need your aid! What mighty effort did I make to keep step.

Within saluting distance, Tom brought up his sword; I did the same; but, looking forward, omitted to bring it down again, till a cough from Tom, and an "*Isee, Sahib!*" (thus, sir,) from the half-laughing old subadar, caused me quickly to rectify the little omission.

Well, we formed close and open column, solid squares, and squares to receive cavalry, and I know not what on earth besides: there was a fearful drumming, firing, and charging, and I was half-stupefied with the noise and rapid ravelling and unravelling, embodyings and dispersings of this animated Chinese puzzle. However, I stuck close to the rear of my sepoys, and bore up through it wonderfully well upon the whole.

How astonished our descendants, some three or four centuries hence, will be, methinks, when man shall have become one consolidated mass of intellect and morality, as they ponder over our ingenious modes of effecting wholesale extermination! "Thus," they will exclaim, perhaps, as they sigh over the aberrations and follies of their barbarous ancestors, "'twas thus they shot, slashed, and impaled one another; in this way they attacked and defended; and thus they invested the machinery of destruction with all the pomp of music, the glitter of ornament, and the splendour of decoration."

Some, however (distinguished historians and pious Christians too), strangely enough, take a very different view of the matter—maintaining that war is an inherent adjunct of the social state—that without it we should become utterly enervated—sink into stagnation, and that, in short, there can be no healthy action without mutual destruction! that it exists at all is puzzling—but that, it must ever be is both mortifying and astounding. Between, however, man viewed as a mere animal, and man considered as an intellectual and moral being, those who hope for perfection and those who despair of it,—Quaker endurance, that bears to be spat upon, and morbid honour, that fires at a look;—between, I say, all these conflicting views and practices—these cross lights and opposite principles—many honest thinkers are sorely puzzled to make up their minds on the subject—as to whether combativeness is, or is not, an inherent element of our nature, which must as necessarily break out into a conflict occasionally, as the atmosphere brews the tempest—or whether war be not destined to swell the category of past follies, witchcraft, persecutions, astrology, and the like; and to this view I for one honestly incline.

The press and steam, right mental culture—proper social organization and international co-operation, may do wonders; so long, however, as war continues to be the "*ultima ratio regum,*" the arbiter, for want of a better, of national differences, let all honour be shown to those who, in wielding its powers, display, as British soldiers do, some of the noblest qualities of our nature, and who, though yielding to the necessity of shedding blood, still love to temper courage with humanity, and to mitigate its inherent evils.

At length, as all things must, our exercise came to an end. The parade was dismissed. The officers, European and native, fell out on dismissing their companies and advanced towards the commandant, who, as is customary, waited in front to receive them.

Having saluted, and returned their swords to their scabbards, there was a general unbending, and the laugh and the joke and the news went round.

"Well, Rantipole, how does the grey carry you? What did you give for him?"

"Two hundred and fifty dibs" (*i.e.,* rupees); "wouldn't take four hundred for him at this moment."

"Isn't he a little puffed in that off fore-leg?" said Captain Syphax, drily.

"No, not that I know of."

"Who was at Mrs. Roundabout's hop last night? they say that old Crosslight, the brigade major, was more than ordinarily attentive to the widow."

"Oh! I didn't hear that—by the way, Tom, when does your affair come on?"

"Nonsense! how do I know?"

"Hear him; hear him! hear the Benedict!"

"Rantipole, I'll bet you five gold mohurs," said one of the subs, "that my old Toorkie beats your new purchase once round the course, P. P."

"Done! but I don't sport gold mohurs; say five chicks,[30] and it's a bet; or I don't mind if I make it ten."

"Chicks, Tom," said I, aside; "isn't it rather an odd thing to bet fowls on a horse race? this is another of your Indian customs, I suppose, the reasonableness of which is not apparent at a glance."

Tom stamped and laughed at my query, like a madman, to the astonishment of all present.

"Here," said he, in a whisper, and pulling me aside "you great griff you! chicks are sequins, or chequins abbreviated to chicks;—not fowls, as you imagine: have you never heard that before?"

"Never," said I.

"What's the joke, Rattleton, what's the joke?" said the colonel, good-humouredly; "come, let's have it, and don't keep it all to yourself."

"Oh, nothing, sir, nothing particular, sir," said Tom; "nothing, but rather a griffinish query of my friend Gernon's, which tickled me a little."

"I am afraid you are rather too hard upon him," said, the colonel; "remember, Rattleton, I could tell a few stories of griffins if I chose."

Tom felt the rebuke, and had the laugh turned against him.

The colonel now addressed me, and, in a very kind and encouraging manner, eulogized the way in which I had acquitted myself on my first appearance in public, adding, "I hope we shall send you to your regiment up the country quite a proficient, and calculated to reflect credit on your instructors in the Zubberdust Bullumteers."

As our worthy commandant was anxious that I should have an insight into the various branches of military duty, the adjutant was desired to make me attend regimental courts-martial, invaliding committees, guard mountings, &c., that I might see how these duties were carried on.

The first court-martial I attended was a regimental one for the trial of a black drummer for theft.

Tom took me to the bungalow of the superintending officer, who is always an European, and whose duty it is to conduct the proceedings which he records, assisted by the regimental interpreter, who is also the quarter-master of the regiment.

Shortly after our arrival, the native officers composing the court made their appearance; they were all large, portly men, singular compounds of those moral antipodes, the European and the Asiatic.

Instead of the black military stock of the English officer, they wore, over white cotton collars, necklaces of gold, formed of massive embossed beads, each almost as large as a small bean or nutmeg; the overalls of the majority had been pulled up over the *Dotee*, or waistcloth, a Hindoo article of dress, containing almost cloth enough to serve for the envelopment of a mummy.

This swathing of the loins, gathered into a bunch behind and before, renders a considerable amplitude of waistband indispensably necessary, and causes, moreover, very often an unseemly protuberance under the jacket flaps on the hinder regions, ornamental, no doubt, in a dromedary or Hottentot Venus, though any thing but improving to the appearance of a military man.

In spite, however, of these little drawbacks, or, perhaps, I should say humpbacks, there was much in the general appearance of these Indian veterans which to me, as a novice, and not altogether an unobservant one, was exceedingly striking and interesting, not having yet had an opportunity of observing them so leisurely; to those, however, accustomed to see them daily, these feelings doubtless had long since died away.

Two or three were aged men, whose snowy whiskers and mustachios contrasted strikingly with the swarthy hue of their well-chiselled and manly countenances; gold and silver medals hung on their breasts, mementoes of past services under a Wellesley, a Coote, a Baird, a Harris, a Lake, or some other of the many commanders who have led the brave and faithful sepoy, where'er in this hemisphere Britain has had a cause to maintain, and whose deeds are chronicled in some of the brightest pages of Indian military history.

"How is it, Tom," said I, "that the European officers, who have shared in the same dangers, and who have fought in the same fields, exiles from home and kindred, and grilling under your fiery sun here, are not also honoured with medals for remarkable services?"[31]

"Upon my life, Frank, I can't tell you; it is one of those profound mysteries which it does not become unassisted reason to probe too closely: there must be some latent policy in it, though it is far beyond the ken of ordinary mortals. My old native officer, Subadar Davy Persaud, one day, in my presence, asked your friend Captain Marpeet, when lounging at my bungalow, what was the reason of it? 'We are puzzled, Sahib,' said he, 'to make it out; they are either of no value, and given to us, as baubles are to the *Baba Logue* (children), or else you gentlemen, who led us on, and shared in our dangers and hardships, are very ill-treated by the Kumpany Ungruis Bahadour, in not being allowed to share in the distinction, which we should prize much more if our officers did share it.'"

"That seems like a poser," said I.

"It does," replied Tom; "'tis plausible; but it just shows into what errors mere unassisted reason may lead us."

"But what said Marpeet to it? he is a right loyal man, and always sticks up for the 'Honourable John.'"

"Why," said Tom, "Captain Marpeet, being a bit of a logician, proved syllogistically to old Davy Persaud that all was as it should be, thus: 'It was well known,' said he, 'and an established fact, that the Honourable Company are liberal, generous and considerate masters; that they don't do illiberal, impolitic, and inconsiderate things—*ergo*,' and there Marpeet brought his conclusions to bear in high style, and regularly demolished David Persaud's position; '*ergo*, this must be all right, though appearances are the other way.' Your friend, however, confessed to me afterwards, that when at home he should have been glad could he have sported a bit of ribbon at his button hole, or something of the sort, just to show that he had frozen patriotically on the mountains of Nepaul, and struck a blow for old England at Laswarrie and Putpergunge."

I was much surprised, and not a little amused, to observe that each native officer was accompanied by an attendant, generally some simple looking Coolie youth, carrying his chair, and odd three-cornered pieces of furniture some of them were.

"Tom," said I, *sotto voce*, "there seems to be no want of chairmen at your meeting; but, seriously, tell me, is it usual for the native officers to carry about their chairs in this sort of way?"

My friend answered that it generally was, and that not only native, but European officers did the like, subalterns' bungalows not being usually overstocked with furniture.

"The possession of a chair, by the way, and the right to sit in it in the presence of his European officer," added he, "are prerogatives on which the subadur or jemadar sets a high value."

"Enlighten my griffinism a little, Tom," said I, "and expound the cause thereof."

"Why, the reason," rejoined my friend, "is, I believe, this. No inferior in India ever sits in the presence of a superior, unless squatting on his heels on the ground may be so considered; and you must have perceived that a chair is never offered to a sepoy or non-commissioned native officer, under any circumstance of long detention or the like, which it would perhaps be to Europeans of the same rank in those cases; in fact, if it were, it would be stoutly refused, and the man would think you were bantering him. But when promoted, when he gets his commission, he acquires a *status* in society, is an '*uppiser*' (an officer), one of the *sirdar logue*, and in some respects on a par with his European superior. He now sports a gold necklace or *kanta*; and sets up a chair and a tatoo (pony), as indispensable concomitants of his newly-acquired rank—riding on the one, and in all probability sitting on the other, for the first time in his life. I have been a good deal amused," continued Tom, "to see them sometimes, when seated opposite their houses, or rather huts, in the lines, enjoying their *otium cum dignitate* in these same chairs, illustrating amusingly enough the invincible force of habit—legs partly doubled up under them, feet slantingly projecting under the arms thereof, instead of depending before, according to the usages of Christendom. Blacky does not readily adopt new habits and European improvements; or if he does, he often mars their object by engrafting on them something of his own."

"I dare say," said I, "from what I have seen, that this is true enough."

"A gentleman up the country, for example," continued Tom, "some time ago, wished to introduce the use of the wheelbarrow into his garden, with other English improvements; when next he went there, he found the coolie, or gardener's assistant, to his astonishment, carrying the wheelbarrow on his head, with a load of gravel. Why, a week ago, I gave my vagabond *bawurchee* (cook), whom, you know, I sent to the right about yesterday, a tin flour dredger, that I might be spared the mortification of having my food unnecessarily manipulated. The very next time I went to the *bawurchee khana* (cook house), I caught the villain taking the flour in pinches out of the perforated head of my dredger (as one would take a pinch out of a snuff-box) and sprinkling it over the cutlet. Ah! I fear that nature designed natives and jackasses to be managed by the cudgel!"

"Why, that is Captain Marpeet's principle to a T," said I. "Sound thrashings, according to him, with some races, are meant to answer the purpose of sound reasonings with others; it requires caution, however, in applying that principle. For example, it would be far from safe to try it on some of those big-calved fellows one sees behind the coaches at home,—eh, Tom?"

"You're right, Frank—you're right; I see the drift of your remark. It does seem unmanly to thrash those who cannot and will not retaliate. But they're confoundly stupid and provoking; and your crouching spaniel always invites a kick."

By the time we had terminated our "aside," the native officers had saluted, and after some little fuss and rattling of their huge sabres, had settled down into a quiescent state, each man in his own proper chair, and wearing his hat *cum privilegio* as bravely as my Lord Kinsale himself.

The superintending officer, a smart young Light Bob, was in readiness with his recording apparatus—his foolscap, and his pen and ink. The interpreter opened his book, containing the forms of oath to be administered to the assembled Christians, Mahomedans, and Hindoos, all cordially united to administer the common right of every creed and colour—justice.

The black-bearded Moolah stood by with the *Koran*, wrapped in many a fold of linen, to guard it from the polluting touch or look of the infidel, whilst the regimental brahmin, his forehead marked with bars of ochre and pigment, indicative of his sanctity, was also in attendance, holding in his hands a brazen vessel, filled with the *Gunja jhull*, or Ganges water, in which was immersed a sprig of (as I was told) the sacred *toolsie*. On these two symbols, or foundations of their respective faiths, the Mussulmans and Hindoos are sworn.

The superintending officer now directed the prisoner to be brought in, and an orderly sepoy immediately called out *"Aundo Bridgemaum!"*

"What does he mean by that?" I inquired.

"He means," said Tom, "'bring in the prisoner,' *bridgemaum* being the native way invariably of pronouncing the English word 'prisoner.'"

The first native sworn was Rustum Khan, an old Mahomedan subadar.

After saluting with deep respect the volume of his faith, he received it from the Moolah on the palms of his hands, holding it thus, with a look of profound veneration, whilst the regimental interpreter recited the form of the oath, which he repeated after him.

The Hindoos, received the vessel containing the Ganges water in their hands, and were sworn to judge impartially in like manner.

The trial now began.

The prisoner, a poor little black devil of a drummer, was asked by the interpreter if he was guilty, or not guilty; to which he replied *"Jo up ka kooshee"* as interpreted by Tom, "whichever my lord pleases."

This *naïve* reply made the superintending officer relax his judicial gravity. The interpreter also smiled.

The stolid old subadars, however, could perceive nought but stupidity in it, evidently, and one of them angrily said to the prisoner, "*Guddah* (ass), say one or the other."

Being, with the exception of a few words, wholly ignorant of the language, I could not, of course, follow the examination. The reader may, however, rest assured that he has not, in consequence, lost any information which it would be of much consequence for him to obtain.

The superintending officer and interpreter seemed to have it all their own way, rebuking crude judgments and irrelevent questions, &c. (just as a judge bothers a stupid jury); laying down the law to the subadars and jemadars, who nodded like Chinese mandarins, in deep acquiescence to their superior wisdom, saying *"such bhat* and *bhote khoob."*[32]

The native officer, before coming into the Court, has generally (*i.e.*, in five cases out of six) made up his mind after a long *bhat cheet* (chat, or discussion, as to the guilt or innocence of the party), touching both the act and its criminality; but is guided in his verdict or decision, nevertheless, pretty much by what the European officers may say to him: his own peculiar notions of justice and good evidence are, perhaps, clear enough; but, confused by European refinements, the sublimity of which his untutored mind cannot reach, he yields himself passively to be guided by the *dicta* of the *Sahib Logue.*

Upon the whole, when the Court was cleared, and Tom and I repaired to his bungalow, I felt that I had added something to my little stock of experience, in having witnessed this mode of administering *justice* in a sepoy corps.

The next thing of the kind I attended was an invaliding committee, a body assembled periodically for the purpose of examining those soldiers whose age or infirmities rendered them unfit for further active service, which I need not describe.

The system of granting pensions to old and worn-out veterans is an admirable one; it binds the native soldier to us more strongly than anything else, and is one of the firmest foundations of our power in India. Frequently, at a more advanced period of my Indian career, have I had occasion to observe its admirable workings. I have listened to the old veteran, in his native village, with pleasure, surrounded by his children, and children's children, as he has recounted his deeds, showed his medals and his scars, and spoken with, I believe, sincerely grateful feelings of the generosity of the "Kumpany Angraiz Bahadour."

CHAPTER XVIII

A day or two after this, my bearer gave me a little rose-coloured billet, which had been left for me, of which missives (though not always *couleur de rose*) there is a vast circulation in India—almost all communications from house to house, and family to family, being carried on in this way.

The note was from Miss Lucinda; it was written in a delicate crow-quill hand, and sealed with a dainty device (*"qui me néglige, me perd"*), or something of that sort, and contained an invitation, in her mamma's name, to a *soirée musicale*, on the following evening.

"Here is an invitation (a provoke), Tom" said I, "from your friend, the stout gentlewoman; shall we go?"

"Oh, certainly," was the reply. "I have a similar one. Mrs. Brownstout's parties are amongst the most agreeable at Barrackpore; her guests are always well selected and well assorted—the grand *desiderata* of all social meetings. I like her and her daughters amazingly, having uniformly received the most unaffected kindness from both. The old lady, indeed, looks upon me as her son, and, if there were not insuperable obstacles in the way, Frank,— *entendez-vous?*—I might become so in reality."

"Perhaps, Tom," said I, "that's what she is manœuvering to effect."

"No," replied he; "she is above-board, and incapable of such a proceeding; she is no schemer—would be glad, no doubt, to marry her girls to worthy men, in an open, honest way; but would scorn to effect it by little crooked arts: never, Frank, if you please, say a word to the prejudice of Mrs. Brownstout in my presence."

"Why, Tom," said I, astonished, "what's the matter with you? You're warm, my dear fellow; I meant no offence to you, and as for—"

"Say no more, say no more," said Tom, stopping my mouth; "you were jesting, and I was hasty; but I cannot bear the shadow of an imputation on those I regard. If any one said a word against you, Frank, I'd floor him."

I was touched by my friend's generous warmth. "You're a worthy fellow, Tom," said I, squeezing his hand; "but pray heaven we may be spared the necessity of showing our love for one another in that way, though we have battled pretty often in each other's defence in times past. Do you remember, by-the-bye, the joint-stock pummelling we gave Jack Grice, the cobbler, when at old Thwackum's?"

"Ha! ha! I do, indeed, Frank; the fellow thought he had us out of school, and in a *cul de sac*; but he caught a brace of Tartars."

At the appointed hour, the next evening, we found ourselves at Mrs. Brownstout's bungalow. From the number of palankeens and return buggies we met, on our entering the domain, or compound, we were led to infer that the party was pretty numerous, which proved to be the case.

Having deposited our hats in the hall or verandah, which, by the way, was full of hookhas of various degrees of splendour—a luxury then more indulged in than at present—we entered the well-lighted saloon, or reception room; and I confess I was agreeably surprised at the elegance and propriety of the *tout ensemble*.

It is a pleasant sight, in a distant land, thus to meet a social assembly of your countrymen and women, young and old, enjoying music and conversation, and the pleasing refinements of the Western world.

A group of Barrackpore belles occupied one portion of the apartment—a gay parterre—in which, however, the sun flower and the lily greatly predominated over the rose.

In front of them, and standing in groups here and there, were numerous officers of the different regiments at the station, fine, handsome young fellows, for the most part, in the bloom of life, on whom the sword, and time, and care, and the airs of the death-concocting jungles, had yet to do their work. There they were, laughing the light laugh of the careless heart, and doing and saying all those things, the exact counterpart of which, perhaps, had been said and done in that very bungalow by many a set as jocund as they, who had gone before them, had run their brief Indian career, died, and been forgotten.

Then, as a sort of counterpoise to the youth of the party, were certain portly colonels and majors, button-holding in corners over grave discussions of off-reckonings, changes of stations, &c., their goodly and well-matured persons contrasting with those of the slender youths around—as do the gnarled and bulky oaks of many a winter, with the tall and slender saplings of the forest.

Then there was a jovial old surgeon from the north of the Tweed, who took snuff out of a mull, and cracked the driest of jokes in the crabbedest of tongues; and two or three *distingué*-looking civilians, temporary visitants to Barrackpore, exhibiting, in the studied simplicity of their attire and well-tied cravats, a striking contrast to the gay uniforms of the military—who, poor fellows, too often illustrate the proverb, that "all is not gold that glitters;" and hence, indeed, the civilian consoles himself for wanting it on his coat, by the comfortable consideration that he has *quantum suff.* of it in his pocket.

Particularly conspicuous amongst the company assembled at Mrs. Brownstout's, was a jocose old collector, the life and soul of the party, who, being remarkably ill-favoured, and very good-natured, seemed to feel himself privileged, without danger of misconstruction, to be wondrously facetious with the young ladies, whom he roundly declared were all in love with him, and gave him no rest or peace with their incessant attentions.

"There now you see, there it is," said he, starting pettishly away, and looking piteously and appealingly to the company, as Miss Maria touched his elbow, and asked him to take some tea; "there it is again; you see she won't let me alone."

I learnt afterwards that he had been an old friend of the deceased major, with whom he had hunted and shot, and drank pale ale, on and off, for five-and-twenty years; that he was, moreover, Maria's godfather, and the true friend of the family, by whom he was consulted on all weighty and important matters. Though a systematic drole or humourist, he was at bottom a man of sound judgment and extensive knowledge, and the most benevolent of human kind.

Shortly after we had entered, Mrs. Brownstout met us with a greeting which amply made up in cordiality for whatever it might want in refinement, and from Maria and Lucinda we received kind nods of recognition, though too busy to do more. There they were in all their bravery, doing the honours of the tea-table, exhibiting the albums and the caricatures, and endeavouring to make every one at home and happy—cheerful within the limits of propriety and good sense, attentive to all, with kindness and the most obliging tact.

"You're right, Tom," said I, "in your estimate of this family; the mother is, though a little blunt, a worthy woman, and the girls are dear, sweet creatures; I declare I've a good mind to marry them both."

"Both! Are you quite sure that either of them would have you?"

"But Tom, by the way," I continued, "to change the subject from my loves to yours, is not that Miss Julia Heartwell?" directing, at the same time, his attention towards that young lady, who hitherto, from her position, had escaped our observation: "how lovely she looks this evening, with her tiara of white roses!"

Tom coloured: "So it is," he replied; "I did not expect to meet her here."

So saying, and after a pause to muster courage, Ensign Rattleton moved across the room; a fine, well-made, broad-shouldered young fellow he was too, and in his tight, well-fitting raggie, or Swiss jacket (one of the neatest turnouts of Messrs. Gibson and Pawling), his small and gracefully-tied sash, his white Cossack trousers, and grenadier wings (of which he was especially proud), it would have been difficult to conceive a more elegant figure, or one in which youth, strength, and symmetry were more happily blended.

Tom evidently did not wish to appear marked and particular, or to excite more observation than could be well avoided; he consequently made his approaches very gradually, speaking to some other young ladies of his acquaintance in the group before he addressed the *objet aimée.*

I marked the pretty Julia, who, though doubtless aware of the motive, bit her lip, and seemed ill to bear even this assumed indifference. True love is a brittle affair, and, like a box of china, must be managed "with caution."

Tom, however, at length approached; many a curious eye was upon them, and now, "rebel nature" unfurled her crimson flag, and the little god of love beat his rat-tat-too; in other words, the conscious blush overspread the lovely Julia's countenance, and the palpitations of her bosom told full plainly all that was passing in the little heart beneath.

Ensign Rattleton, with an attempt at unconcern, presented his hand, and a seat being unoccupied by her side, he rather awkwardly (for he was not himself) slid into it.

Poor Tom! his efforts at composure, marred by the consciousness that he was the object of observation—his blushes and her tell-tale looks of mingled tenderness and admiration, were all too palpable to escape notice.

"Its all up with him," said the caustic old bachelor captain whom I had met at the colonel's, giving me a slight touch with his elbow; "as dead a case of splice as I ever saw in my life—well, humph!—better let it alone, and remain as he is. He'll think so too when the *butchas* (children) and the bills come tumbling in together by-and-by."

Lucinda now, at the desire of some of the company, gave us some charming airs to the accompaniment of the guitar, which she touched with peculiar grace; Maria afterwards warbled to the piano, and finally, by particular desire, sung a lively native song, the burthen of which was "*Hilly milly puniya,*" the great delight of the old collector, who stood over her, shaking his head, beating time with his hands, as if quite at home in the matter, and occasionally footing it in a mincing burlesque way, which I was afterwards told was a jocular imitation of the Indian nautch girls, with whom this song is a favourite; it constituting one of that mellifluous variety, with which I have often since heard them "startle the dull ear of night."

A good deal of merriment was caused by the collector's animated earnestness, and the young hands cried *"encore!"* One of his friends, an old colonel, present, exclaimed,

"Why, you nautch superbly, Dilkhoob (for that was his name); I did not expect such activity at your time of life."

"Ah! don't I—don't I?" said the merry old gentleman. "But what do you mean, sir, by my time of life? five-and-twenty only last birthday! We young fellows must be always in action—always in action."

"You both play and sing, do you not, Miss Heartwell?" said Maria, addressing herself to Julia.

Julia, of course, said "very little," that she hardly ever played, "excepting at home;" and that, moreover, she was just then haunted by the vocalist's malific genius, a cold.

The facetious collector now seated himself near a very lovely young woman, who, I learnt from Tom, was the adjutant's lady; a pleasant *tête-à-tête* followed; the lady seemed highly amused; the adjutant himself, who was a friend of Dilkhoob, soon joined them.

"Well, sir, here you find me," said the old gentleman, "flirting with your wife. Sir, I love your wife." The adjutant smiled (it was almost a *mauvaise plaisanterie*). "Yes, I've a right to love her, sir; I'm not forbidden to love her as long as I don't covet her; and so I will love her, sir."

The gentlemen laughed—the ladies looked into their fans—but it was only honest Dilkhoob, the privileged man.

Miss Heartwell now sat down to sing, Tom, in the most exemplary and obsequious manner, selecting her book and turning over the leaves.

Julia then drew off, deliberately, first from one hand and then from the other, her silk gloves, of a texture almost as light and delicate as gossamer or a spider's web (which she placed on the piano), displaying two of the whitest, softest, and most beautifully turned little hands that I think I ever beheld; I doubt if Sir Roger de Coverley's widow's could have equalled them.

Having run these delicate fingers—like a bevy of white mice—rapidly over the keys, as if to ascertain the force and tone of the instrument, she paused, looked up, and, with a sort of girlish waywardness, said,—

"Well, now, what am I to sing?"

Tom, with infinite obsequiousness, pointed with his finger to an air he had selected—it was Moore's exquisite song, "Those Evening Bells," a song which will endure as long as man retains a right perception of the touching and the beautiful, and which expresses, in the happiest language, what thousands have felt, when that inexplicably sad and sadly pleasing music, the chime of distant bells floating softly over hill and dale, falls on the listening ear.

Sweet bard of Erin! embodier of our tenderest thoughts—translator of our dumb emotions—fixer of those painted bubbles of the soul which before thee burst at the touch of words—how many exiles have thy glorious songs made glad! how many solitudes have they cheered! how many pensive spirits have they soothed and delighted! how oft have thy soul-breathed words, sung to the strains of old, and falling on the finest chords of the heart, awakened all its noblest responses, to liberty, patriotism, love and glory! Immortal is thy fame, for it is deeply rooted in human hearts and human sympathies, and long after thou hast joined the choir above, may thy melodious strains float down the stream of time to delight the latest posterity!

Julia sung this sweet air, and several others, with a feeling and pathos which convinced me she was not the soulless belle I had at first imagined; indeed, as she sung, every noble and generous emotion beamed from her lovely face.

No wonder poor Tom was far gone *à la Chatelar* though things with him had a somewhat happier termination; as it was, he hung enamoured over her, delighted evidently with the sensation her singing had produced, and, "music being the food of love," as we have it on the best authority, banqueting evidently on this very exciting *pabulum.*

Miss Heartwell having resigned her seat, overwhelmed with praises and acknowledgments, another young lady was prevailed upon to occupy it.

Several other songs followed, when there was a pause.

The silence was at length broken by the old collector, Mr. Dilkhoob, marching up to our hostess, and addressing her, arms, a-kimbo, with well-simulated sternness and severity, in the following manner:—

"Mrs. Major Brownstout," said he, "I've a very serious cause of complaint against you, madam, in which your daughters are in some degree implicated, and in which I will venture to affirm I am joined by all the rest of the young people in this party."

A general smile and interchange of looks between those present was the result of this speech, deemed evidently the precursor of something merry.

"Well, Mr. Dilkhoob," responded the old lady, who seemed perfectly to understand him, "what is my transgression?"

"Why, madam," said he, "I consider that you have acted in a most unusual, a most inconsiderate, and a most extraordinary manner, in inviting so many young folks to your house, myself among the number, without giving them a dance;" the young men here rubbed their hands; "but, madam, as it is never too late to amend our faults, and correct our backslidings, I propose that we do now have a dance, and that my friend here, Lieutenant and Adjutant Wigwell, be solicited to send immediately for a part of his banditti—I beg pardon—band, I meant, in order that we may 'trip it as we go, on the light fantastic toe' this way," said he, seizing the hands of the laughing dame, and cutting one or two most ponderous capers.

"Bravo!" was repeated by many voices.

The motion was carried by acclamation, and Lieut. and Adjt. Wigwell posted off an orderly for some of the musicians.

They soon made their appearance, and a fine swarthy set of fellows they were, with their chimney-pot caps. There was a little preliminary clatter in the verandah, and pitching of instruments, when suddenly clarionet, cymbal, and trombone broke forth in a glorious and soul-inspiring lilt.

Tables were removed, chairs thrust out, partners engaged, and the younger portion of Mrs. Brownstout's party—as if suddenly bitten by tarantulas—were whirling and bobbing through the mazes of the merry dance; I footing it away, with Maria for my partner, as well as the best of them.

A neat supper, with songs, serious and comic, *à la mode Indienne*, and the collector quite uproarious, terminated one of the pleasantest evenings I had yet spent in Bengal.

Miss Julia went home in her palkee; Tom and I escorted her to her bungalow on foot; the former making seven-league strides, in order to converse a little by the way; I pelting away after him as vigorously as the man with the steam leg, though not having an equal interest in such violent locomotion.

The period was now approaching when I was to bid adieu to Barrackpore for the Upper Provinces, and exchange the life of mingled drill and gaiety, of which the foregoing little *tableaux* may serve to give some idea, for one of constant change from scene to scene, and more in consonance with a roving disposition.

I was appointed to a regiment at Agra, but about to move to Delhi, the capital of India, and which is, or was, associated in our minds with all, or much, that is glorious and striking in Eastern history.

A Captain Belfield, of infantry, from Java, one of the Indian army of occupation there, going up the country to a staff appointment, kindly offered to take me under his wing, and afford me the benefit of his experience.

Though a totally different man in every respect, he was a friend of Marpeet, who sent me a letter of introduction to him; the conclusion of it, which I afterwards saw, was rather characteristic of the captain:

"Gernon is a real good-hearted lad, but a devil of a griff; so you must keep a sharp eye upon him as you go up together, that he does not shoot, drown, or hang you or himself."

A week before my departure, I got leave to go down to Calcutta, for a couple of days, for the purpose of hiring a boat to take me up to the great military station of Cawnpore, from whence I was recommended to march. I had also a few necessaries to procure, as well as to take leave of General Capsicum and the widow, of whom I had occasionally accounts through the roundabout channel of my friend the indigo planter.

Battleton having matters of deep moment to attend to in Calcutta, one of which I discovered was to order a splendid set of turquoises, bracelets, brooch, ear rings, all complete, with other *bijouterie*, for the bride elect (for Mrs. Brownstout's hop had fairly brought on the matrimonial crisis), he offered to accompany me.

One day, after breakfast, consequently, we proceeded to the ghaut, where we hired a paunchway to take us to the City of Palaces, for the sum of one rupee; and the tide being in our favour, we struck out into the noble stream, and were soon on our way to our destination.

The scenery between Calcutta and Barrackpore, a distance of sixteen or eighteen miles, I thought then, and have always since considered, extremely rich and picturesque; its characteristics are bold sweeps of the broad Hoogly—banks agreeably diversified, with rich foliage of various forms and tint—clumps of cocoa-nut and bamboo—groves of mango, tamarind, and plantain. Here a ghaut, with crowds of bathers—there a temple, or the white huwailie or kotee house of some European residing on the banks.

We soon passed the Governor-General's country residence, and the extensive and beautifully wooded park adjoining, which has a fine effect from the river; also, riding at anchor among other boats, and at some little distance from the shore, we had a view of the state pinnace, or *Soonamooky*, in which that high functionary makes his progresses to the Upper Provinces. It was an elegant square-rigged vessel, with tapering masts, painted a light green, if my memory is correct, and profusely, though tastefully, gilded; hence, in fact, the name.

On we rowed with the rapid tide, and after coursing along two or three hold sweeps of the river, Calcutta once more broke on my sight—the native town—Howrah—the splendid white buildings of the European quarter—its forest of shipping—swarming ghauts—multitudinous boats—and all the ant-hill scene of commerce, hustle, and animation, opening upon us in rapid succession, like the scenes of a diorama.

This approach to the City of Palaces, however, is by no means equal, in my opinion, to that from the seaward side. Widely different were my emotions when I next visited this spot.

After many years' residence in the Upper Provinces, amongst rajahs, hill forts and Hindoo temples, holy shrines and sacred prayagas, groves resounding with the cry of the peacock, and Mahomedan ruins of departed grandeur, exploring the haunts of the savage Bheel, and pursuing the plundering Pindarry through the scenes of his maraudings, familiarized with scenes, manners, and customs wearing the impress of a hoary antiquity, and as far removed from the go-ahead things of European civilization as it is possible to imagine, I once more found myself off Calcutta.

With my mind thus saturated with new ideas—a sort of "sleepy hollow" state having come over me, and the recollections of "father-land" fast escaping from my still fondly tenacious grasp, the first sight of the tall masts of the shipping, as they burst on my view, on rounding a point, produced sensations of pleasure as hard to describe, as difficult to be forgotten; nor were these feelings diminished, when, gliding past the vessels themselves, I read "London," "Liverpool," and so forth, on their sterns, and beheld the rough red-shirted tars, my ruddy stalwart countrymen, as they gazed at us over the sides, or lounged in groups on the forecastle, and thought that in very truth but a brief period had elapsed since those fortunate fellows had been lying in some crowded bustling port of my own dear native land, with "all her faults," still beloved and dear to me.

A visit subsequently to one of them served, by exhibiting once familiar things, to awaken still more forcibly the recollections of Old England, and to rekindle that love of country, which, next to that of God and kindred, is, perhaps, the noblest feeling that can swell the bosom.

I will venture to say there are many of my Anglo-Indian brethren who have experienced that which I have here feebly attempted to describe.

We landed at Chundpaul ghaut, a spot memorable in my eyes as that of my disembarkation in Calcutta some two or three months before, and of my incipient acquaintance with my grandiloquent factotum Chattermohun Ghose.

From the ghaut we proceeded, in ticca palankeens, to the fort, where Rattleton and I had been invited to take up our quarters with Lieut. Rantipole, of the Zubberdust Bullumteers, then on duty there with his company.

A wonderful place is Fort William, and a hard nut it will be for the enemies of Old England to crack, if they should ever be induced to attempt it, whether it be the wily Russian, the gallant Frenchman, or Brother Jonathan himself.

It is exceedingly wrong to be proud—very wrong indeed—I know it; but, nevertheless, I have always carried my chin at an angle of forty-five degrees with the plane of the horizon, whenever I marched into that bristling *place d'armes*. To other pens, less sketchy and discursive than mine, I must leave its minute description.

Suffice it for my purpose here to observe, that its extent is vast, its defences admirable, and though making little exterior show, its green slopes once passed, a battery on the broad grin meets you at every turn, as much as to say, "A-ha! I've caught you, eh!—*on ne peut pas passer ici;*" in short, its guards, griffs, adjutants, and arsenals, crows, causeways, cookboys and counterscarps, its mountains of balls and acres of cannon, are all wonderful and astonishing.

CHAPTER XIX

The day after my arrival at Calcutta I hastened to pay my respects to the Capsicums. On reaching the portico of the house, I threw myself out of my palankeen.

"Is the general at home?"

"He is, *khodabund*," said the servant, and ascended to announce me. Upon my entering, and making my bow,

"Ha! how are ye, sir; how are ye, sir?" said the old veteran, extending his hand to me at full length, as he reclined in his easy chair; "glad to see you again. Well, sir, and how did you lave my son? But I've heerd of all your prosadings."

Mrs. Capsicum congratulated me on my continued healthy appearance, and condescended to present me with the "tip of her honourable little finger."

I looked around for the dear widow, but she was not there. My pulse sunk below zero with painful misgivings; ideas of death, matrimony, or some other misfortune, flashed on my mind: it is the nature of some men always to fancy things fifty times better or worse than they are, to which category I belong. I ventured to ask the general after the health of his daughter, and was greatly relieved by his reply:

"Oh, she's well, sure—she's well; but you'll see her here immediately to spake for herself."

Some time before dinner was announced, a carriage drove up to the house; it contained Mrs. Delaval, who had been absent the whole day in Calcutta. She soon entered the apartment; it was late in the evening, the light dim and uncertain, and I seated in a recess near the window.

"Well, Cordalia, my dear, have you seen all your friends and executed all your commissions?"

Mrs. Delaval kissed her father, and answered in the affirmative, adding, "the Coppletons have taken their passage home in the *Derbyshire*; young Scapegrace, of the civil service, is to be married to Letitia Flirtwell to-morrow, and Colonel Oddfish sends his *bhote bhote salaam* to you, and hopes to see you soon in town."

After some more gossip of this nature, the general directed the attention of his charming daughter to me, as "a particular friend of hers," and I had the satisfaction of seeing a blush of pleasure and surprise upon her features at recognizing me.

The reader may readily conceive all that passed immediately after this and at dinner, and that I had to recount the adventures of the last six weeks, to fight over again the battle of Junglesoor, and to rekill all the hogs.

As the night wore away, and long after tea, the old general, who had been for some time in a ruminating mood—indeed, we had sunk into that thoughtful state which usually precedes the separation of friends—lit his taper, and rising, though with considerable effort, from his easy chair, beckoned me to follow him.

We entered his dressing room; he desired me to shut the door, and, sitting down, bade me be seated likewise.

"My young friend," said the old man, taking my hand with more feeling than I had ever yet seen him display, "I wished to say a few words to you in private before we part, most probably for ever. I loved your brave uncle, as I have already told you, and I think I should not be showing a proper respect to his memory, or doing my duty towards his nephew, did I not offer ye a few words of counsel, the result of long experience.

"I'm not the hypocrite to preach to you that I have always acted as I would have you to act; no, 'tis not so; I'd be glad, by G——, if it had been otherwise; but my exparience, like that of most men, has been dearly bought. You are young, all the world before ye, and about, probably, to enter on a long and varied career. Life is a game, and a few false moves at the outset, it may never be in your power fully to retrave; it therefore behoves you to be cautious, and to weigh well every step before you take it.

"When you join your regiment, beware of your associates, for on the character of these your future prospects will mainly depend. Be slow in forming intimacies, but at the same time courteous and kind to all. Observe, but do not appear to do so, for people do not love to have spies over them. Take your cheerful glass with your friends, but shun intemperance, the root of gaming and all evil.

"Strive to live within your manes, and let no man laugh you out of your resolution to be 'just before you are generous;' for the time will come, take my word for it, when you will rape the reward of your self-denial. Make yourself master of your profession, and acquire a taste for rading and study; if over wild, 'twill beget a new mind in ye, and is the best manes ye can adopt to save ye from frivolity and dissipation, of which ye'll find plenty here, by G— —.

"Indulge moderately in faild sports, for no man in India ever took his full swing of them that, sooner or later, had not to lament a broken constitution; the strength of Hercules will not enable Europeans to brave exposure to an Aistern sun with impunity.

"Lay down fixed principles for yourself, and let nothing induce ye to swerve from them; they are, if I may so say, the helm of our moral nature; and though the gusts of passion and caprice, or the shoals of unavoidable difficulties, may sometimes drive us out of our course, if we have but these we shall regain it; but without them, we become the sport of every impulse, we drift away to destruction. God knows I've rason to say all this. Acquire courage to say 'no' when ye feel ye ought, and thereby shun that rock of over-aisiness on which so many a youth has made shipwreck of his fortunes.

"As for religion, I lave ye to judge for yourself; make no joke of any man's; whatever has God's glory and man's good as its professed object, however mistaken, desarves a sort of respect even from an opponent. There's good enough in most of them, if we would but stick to the practical part; perhaps, as my old moonshee, Golaum Hyder, used to say, it may be God's pleasure to be approached in more ways than one, so that we do it with honesty of purpose and in singleness of heart.

"Strive to make friends, but of this rest assured, that no friendship can be lasting that is not based on respect for some one sterling quality, at laist, to redaim the many waiknesses which we all, more or less, inherit; when all looks smiling you may think otherwise, and overlook this essential, but you will find eventually that in resting on such summer friends, you lean on a broken reed.

"'Till society finds us other manes of obtaining redress for injuries, and for stopping the tongues of the brawler, the slanderer, and the bully, than by the d— —d tadious and expinsive process by law established; which, I suppose, if a man spit in your face, would require you to prove how much soap it would take to wash it off, and give damages accordingly: I say, till this is done, fight we must sometimes—but avoid quarrels; 'tis aisier and more honourable to keep out of them than to back out of them, and 'tis a dreadful thing for a thrifle (here his voice faltered and he became much agitated) to have the blood of a comrade on your conscience.

"'Tis a hard matter, I know, to put an old head on young shoulders; but maybe, nevertheless, you'll sometimes think of what I've now said to ye.

And now," he added with a smile, "I believe I've finished my sermon, and have nothing more to add, than may God Almighty bless and prosper ye!"

On saying this, the warm-hearted old Irishman, who was evidently affected, applied a key with trembling hand to a little escritoire, from which he took an old-fashioned silver snuff-box. This he rubbed with his sleeve, looking at it wistfully, and then presented it to me, whilst a tear trembled in his eye—the thoughts of other days rushed upon him.

"There," said he; "that belonged to your poor departed uncle; forty-five years ago he gave it to me as a mark of his regard; I now here present it to you as a proof of mine, and in memento of him, the only man on earth I'd give it to before I died. I don't recommend you to snuff yourself generally," added he, "but you'll find a pinch in that," and he smiled, "that'll do you good sometimes, if used with discretion and sparingly, if you're ever in want of a further supply, let me know; and now, if ye plase, we'll rejoin the ladies."

I was deeply touched by the general's kindness, and mentally promised that I would treasure up his counsel, and make it my future guide. I fear, however, his estimate, touching that extremely difficult operation of putting an old head on young shoulders, found little in my subsequent career at all calculated to invalidate its correctness.

Well, I bade a long farewell to the general. Mrs. Capsicum softened as she bid me adieu, and the charming widow could scarcely conceal her emotion.

How dreary—how blank are the first few moments which succeed the parting with friends! their voices still sounding in your ears, their persons still vividly before your eyes—sounds and pictures to be impressed on the sensorium, and carried with you through life, long long, perhaps, after the originals are departed!—undying echoes! and abiding shadows!

I reached my room at about twelve o'clock, and prepared for rest. My first act, however, was to take a survey of my uncle's snuff-box.

It was a singular piece of antiquity, such as might have been handed round in its time at a meeting of wits at Button's or Will's, or tapped by some ruffled exquisite of the glorious reign of Queen Anne. The well-known arms of my family were engraven on the back, but almost obliterated by time and use.

Now, thought I, for a peep at the inside, and a pinch of the general's wonderful snuff. I opened the box, but instead of snuff, I found it to contain, to my great pleasure and astonishment, the following brief, but highly satisfactory document:—

Gentlemen,—

Please to pay to Ens. Gernon, or order, the sum of Rs. 500, on account of,

Gentlemen, your obedient Servant,

Dominick Capsicum,

Lieut.-General.

To Messrs. Princely & Co., *Agents.*

"Generous old man!" I exclaimed, "such snuff as this is indeed useful at a pinch, though, unlike most snuff, by no means to be sneezed at!"

The next day I devoted to hiring a *bolio*, and some other matters.

A bolio, it may be necessary to inform the reader, is a boat constructed on a somewhat similar plan to the budgerow, but longer and narrower, and more confined in its accommodation.

I was to pay Rs. 100, or about £10, for a journey of 700 miles. Tom also ordered his jewellery, visited his agents, and made sundry arrangements connected with the coming event.

I sought out some of my old ship acquaintances, and having transacted all necessary business, and ordered my bolio to Barrackpore, Tom and I returned in a hired gig by land.

We drove through the native town, alive with its heterogeneous population—paroquets, fakeers, baboos, palkees, &c., and through almost an unbroken avenue of trees, to Barrackpore, sixteen miles distant.

The next day I called on Capt. Belfield, with whom I arranged to depart in two or three days. He proposed that I should take my meals with them on my way up as far as Dinapore, to which I consented; this, besides promising to be agreeable in other respects, saved me the expense of a cook-boat.

The captain introduced me to his sister, who had resided with him for some time in Java.

Miss Belfield was "a lady of a certain age," once more briefly expressed by the term "old maid;" but she was neither an envious old maid, nor a spiteful old maid, nor an intensely blue old maid, nor a canting old maid; but she was a cheerful, bland, and intellectual woman of thirty-five, with a mind deeply imbued with religious feeling, and not without a dash of sentiment.

Celibacy, which so often in women turns the milk of human kindness to gall, seemed in her, as sometimes happens, to have had the opposite effect, and to have given it additional sweetness; in fact, all the world was her lover, and she had never given her heart to one, from a feeling, perhaps, that "'twas meant for mankind."

Having lost her last surviving parent, a clergyman, whose income, though large, arose almost solely from his preferment, she had been obliged to change the home of her infancy for a state of galling half-dependence on distant relatives, who made her *feel* their kindness in the least pleasing manner. From this state she was relieved by an invitation from her only and bachelor brother, Capt. Belfield, to come out and superintend his establishment in India; and, certainly, a happier or more amiable pair were never seen together.

Capt. Belfield told me at what ghaut his budgerow, horse, and cook-boat were lying, and recommended me to send my bolio to the same place, as it was his intention to quit Barrackpore in a couple of days.

The next two days were busily occupied in paying farewell visits, packing up my valuables, as also in hiring one or two additional servants, which swelled my establishment to six.

I here recount the names, occupations, and salaries of the individuals.

First in the list was Ramdial, sirdar-bearer, my *valet de chambre*, an old Hindoo, with wondrous frail supporters and a grizzled moustache; he served me for Rs. 6 per mensem; was a truly honest native, and would never allow anybody to cheat me,—but himself.

Next came Rumjan Khan, khitmutgar, or footman; salary, Rs. 7 per mensem. Rumjan served me with fidelity till we got about fifty miles above Calcutta, when, not finding the air of the river to agree with him, he left me rather suddenly, with the contents of my plate-chest,—to wit, six silver spoons and a brace of muffineers.

The third in point of rank in my establishment was Nannoo, dhobee, or washerman; salary, Rs. 6: a hardworking, harmless creature, who pegged away at his wash-board daily. A pretty wife, a large brazen iron (the Hibernianism is unavoidable), and three fat naked piccaninies, always on the crawl at the top of my bolio, seemed to constitute the amount of his earthly treasures.

Fourthly came Bahadoor Khan, mussalchee, or link-boy; the province of this servant is to carry the torch, or lantern, and to scour out the saucepans and tea-kettle, clean knives, fetch milk, &c.; but as I had not much for him to do in that way, I made him my head chasseur; salary, Rs. 4 per mensem, or eight shillings, not too much, one would suppose, for the decent clothing and maintenance of a man and his family.

Next (hired for his special utility on a river journey) came Hyder Bux, bhistie, or water-carrier, a terrible thick-set fellow; a devout Mahomedan, with a beard so bushy and luxuriant, that, with his hooked nose and large eyes, he always reminded me of an owl looking out of an ivy-bush.

Last on the list, but not least in importance, at least to me, was Nuncoo, matar, my master of the buckhounds.

I shall draw a veil over some of the peculiar duties of Nuncoo, but others I shall particularize; they were, the care of Hector the bull-dog, and Teazer the—I was going to say *soi-disant*—terrier, in preparing daily for them a very large mess of rice and turmeric, with a few small bits of meat interspersed.

Poor Bull, this Gentoo fare, I suspect, but ill agreed with your Whitechapel constitution, and seemed to hasten your end.

The prospect of a change was highly agreeable to me, though mingled with a regret at the necessity it involved of a separation from my friend Tom, for whom I had a very warm affection.

Rattleton was equally sorry to part with me, particularly as he wished me to be present at his marriage, in the capacity of bridegroom's man, and which event was to take place in ten days.

"Frank, we must pass the last evening cosily together," said he; "I must be with Julia till half-past seven, but for the remainder of the evening I am yours."

It is needless to trouble the reader with any account of what passed between Tom and me, in this the last evening of our sojourn together; past hours were revived and future pleasures anticipated. Tom spoke in rapture of his approaching happiness, and of the liberality of the young lady's uncle, who had already presented them with a new bungalow.

"She's an angel, Frank," said he, "if ever there was one on earth; may you find just such another! and if you do, and can, by exchange or otherwise, find your way back to the Zubberdust Bullumteers, we shall make the happiest quartet in the country. 'Twill be so pleasant to pass our evenings together, won't it? a little music, and chess, and so forth."

Battleton accompanied me to Captain Belfield's budgerow, where we took an affectionate farewell of each other, he promising to write to me a full, true, and particular account of the wedding.

Poor Tom! the next time we met was some years after; he ascending the Ganges, I going down. It was by mere accident we discovered each other, not having for some time communicated, and cordial was our greeting.

There was still a dash of sadness in it, like a gleam of wintry sunlight. The joyous anticipations of the lover had long since subsided into the cares, the anxieties, and the troubles of the husband and father.

The predictions of the caustic captain had been in some sort realized. The quarter-mastership had, it is true, in due time, become vacant; but, in the interim, "another king had arisen, who knew not Joseph," and Tom had in consequence failed to obtain it.

Thought and moody care sat on the brow of the once joyous Rattleton, for debts were accumulating, children coming fast, and the fair Julia's health was beginning to fail: to send her "home," at the expense of some thousand rupees, or see her die before his eyes, were the painful alternatives between which he would shortly have to choose.

Even Tom himself complained of hepatic derangement—*vulyò*, the liver—and could not take his quantum of beer-shrob as of yore; a springtide of crosses and difficulties, in fact, had set in upon him.

Just before we met, he had sustained a not uncommon river disaster; his horse-boat had been upset by a whirlwind, by which he had lost his buggy, two horses, and other property, to the value of Rs. 1,500, for which he could claim no compensation. Three of his servants went down with the boat, as if to verify the old adage.

He had barely recovered from the shock occasioned by this misfortune, when he had to sustain another, though of a different kind. He had discovered that his child's *dhye*, or native nurse, was in the habit of dosing his infant with opium, that it might not disturb her slumbers. Tom threatened; madam took huff, and marched off; the delicate Julia was in despair. The only succedaneum that might have been rendered available, a goat, had accompanied the horses to the shades below.

Ye who send sons and daughters to India, imagine not that they are always reposing on beds of roses.

Alas! poor Tom, thou hadst a gallant spirit, but heavy was the sigh which ever and anon escaped thee, as thou didst detail thy difficulties to me during the brief hour we then spent together!

Much hadst thou to tell of the trials of a married sub, on small means, and kept much on the move; but I must reserve it for some other occasion, "with the rest of Tom's story," as Corporal Trim would say, "for it forms a part of it."

In Julia—the shawled, be-capped, and languid invalid—I could scarcely think that I was indeed looking on the belle of Barrackpore, truly the "light of the ball-room."

I had nearly omitted to mention a circumstance which occurred on the previous day, with which it is of importance that the reader should be made acquainted—to wit, an unexpected visit I had from my friend Chattermohun Ghose.

On going into Tom's verandah, to order the despatch of some chattels to my bolio, I observed a Bengalee at one extremity of it, his head going like that of a Chinese mandarin.

I discovered that these profound salaams were intended for me. I advanced towards the automaton, and immediately recognized the patriarchal proprietor of "five effective children of various denominations," Chattermohun Ghose.

"Hah! Chattermohun, my fine fellow, is that you?" said I. "What brought you to Barrackpore?"

"I came, sair, for argent private affair; two, three gentilman owe me little bill here, and accidentally I have learn by chance that master was ishtaying here; therefore I think my duty to pay respect; master make me great obligation; master is my father, to whom my everlasting gratitude will be due."

"As for being your father, Chattermohun," said I, laughing, "no one would suspect that, for if I am not mistaken, you are old enough to be mine; and why you should be so grateful towards me, I cannot imagine."

Some writer has well observed, that "gratitude is too often but a lively sense of favours to come;" to Asiatics, or natives of India, at all events, this remark applies with more force than to Europeans in general. That my friend Chattermohun's gratitude partook largely of this prospective character, soon became abundantly apparent.

"Master I understand will shortly go ope contree?"

"Yes, Chattermohun, I'm off to-morrow—please the pigs; have you any commands?"

"No, sair, command not got; but——"

Here was a pause; after which, Chattermohun resumed his plan of operations in the usual wily style of the Bengalee; any one of whom I'll pit against any Jew in the Minories.

"Does master know," said he, with an air of perfect unpremeditation, "one gintleman name Captain Belfil, who was shortly go Danapore?"

"Oh, yes," said I, falling into the trap; "to be sure I do; we're going up together."

"Master go up contree with Captain Belfil? I not know that" (the vagabond had come up on purpose to make his approaches through me); "then that will be good bis'ness for master; master very clever gintleman, but little too much young to go up river by ownself. I think Master Belfil will be in paymaster bis'ness—got good 'pointment up contree?"

"Yes," I replied, "I believe he has—paymaster of invalids, somewhere or other. But now, Chattermohun, my good fellow, make yourself scarce, if you please, for I've a plaguy deal to attend to, and must be very busy."

Chattermohun raised his hand, enveloped in its snowy, muslin drapery, slowly to his forehead, and made me a profound salaam, but stirred not—there was evidently something in the background. At last, out it plumped.

"Will master please to *ishpik* in my favour?"

"To whom? for what? what the d— —l do I know of you, Chattermohun?"

"Captain Belfil, I learn by proper intelligence, have need of 'spectable writer. I won't go back old army bis'ness, Calcutta—bis'ness not make too much pecuniary profit—therefore, master please to give me recommendation, I shall, *plis* God, get that place."

"Oh, oh!" said I, "Mr. Chattermohun; and this is the object of your visit to me, eh!—of your everlasting gratitude, and my newly-dubbed paternity?"

"No, sair, 'pon my honour, not for that only, but master I think have great benevolence to do me favour."

I liked Chattermohun; those who cannot carry it by storm, must try it by sap; so I promised to certify on paper all that I knew in his favour, and a little more.

To my surprise, it produced the desired effect. Chattermohun got the *writership*, joined the fleet, and became our *comapagnon de voyage*.

They say there is no word for *gratitude* in the native language, and consequently that the quality is unknown; certainly, Chattermohun was grateful to me, poor fellow, for the service rendered him, as far as was in his power to be so. Gratitude is certainly more easily professed than felt amongst black and white; but to deny that it can exist, is to libel human nature.

Capt. Belfield and his sister gave me a most kind and friendly reception; as an agreeable earnest of the pleasure of the voyage, breakfast was on the table when I entered the budgerow, Miss Belfield presiding over its arrangements with English neatness and propriety, just as she had been accustomed to do, no doubt, for many a happy year, at Long Somerton.

The windows or venetians were up on both sides, affording an agreeable view of the river and its banks; under one, there was a grand scene of bathing, praying, and filling of water-pots. Many a dark eye of a Hindoo girl stole furtive glances at the strange meal and paraphernalia of the terrific European, while the sharp aspirations from the lungs of numerous *dhobees*, or washermen, banging their clothes, sounded along the shore.

The *dandies*, or boatmen, now drew on board the *seree*, or plank connecting us with the shore, threw water over the figure-head, touched their foreheads, shouted *"Gunga gee ke jy!"*—"Success, or victory to the holy Ganges"—leaped on board, and our whole fleet was soon under weigh: beginning act the third of my griffinage.

This mode of travelling in India though extremely tedious or perhaps rather, I should say, occupying a vast deal of time, and, when the river is swollen by the periodical rains and the melting of the snow, attended with considerable danger, is, nevertheless, in some respects, exceedingly pleasant and convenient.

The sitting-room in a good-sized budgerow is as large as a small parlour, seven or eight feet in height, and, when fitted up with table, chairs, couch, book-shelves, &c., is as comfortable as an apartment on shore. The venetians open inwards, and may be raised and hooked to the ceiling along both sides of the rooms or cabins, of which there are usually two, one a dormitory, affording, as you glide along, a pleasant view of bathers, boats, temples, ghauts, and the other various picturesque objects which generally adorn the banks of Indian rivers.

The *dandies*, or boatmen (not quite such dressy fellows as their namesakes at home, a rag or waistcloth constituting their working suit), tow the boats at the rate of fourteen or sixteen miles a day; each man has a stout piece of bamboo, with a string attached; the latter he attaches to the towing line, placing the former over his shoulder.

In ascending, the oars are seldom made use of, excepting in crossing the river, or in passing long lines of moored boats, when they are sometimes deemed preferable to passing the towing line over each separate masthead, which is a troublesome operation, and productive of infinite squabbling and abuse between the crews.

The term *budgerow* is a corruption of the word *barge*, and the idea of those in common use in India has evidently been taken from the state barges, once more used by colonial governors than at present, as a state appendage, and which once also in London, in the olden time, served the purposes of transit amongst the great which coaches do at present. Specimens of them still survive in the Lord Mayor's barge and those of public companies.

We soon left Barrackpore behind us, and the pretty Danish settlement of Serampore opposite—the Bengal city of refuge for the fugitives of John Doe and Richard Roe—and in a little time passed the French possession of Chandernagore, and the Dutch factory of Chinsurah.

In the evening we reached Bandel, an ancient Portuguese settlement, celebrated for its cream cheeses, which are rather so-so, and a pretty Roman Catholic chapel and convent, coeval, I imagine, with the earliest settlement of the Portuguese in Bengal.

The shades of evening were gathering around as we slowly brought to and moored our boats for the night. Lights from many a nook and ghaut on the river began to shed their trembling rays across its surface. The crescent moon, in silver sheen, like a fairy of light, was just rising above the tops of the cocoa-nut trees; and the clash of gongs and cymbals resounded from the neighbouring bazaars, telling it was the hour of joy and relaxation.

Captain Belfield proposed a saunter before tea, to which his sister and myself gladly assented; and it was agreed that we should explore the little paraclete before us, which, in its pure and modest whiteness, seemed, as it were, tranquilly reposing in the mingled moon and twilight.

The captain took his stick, a stout shillelagh of some Javanese wood, on the merits of which he afterwards often expatiated; Miss Belfield, bonneted and scarfed; I tendered my arm, like an attentive young man, and followed by a chaprassee and the captain's black terrier, *Thug*, we commenced our first evening's ramble.

"How delightfully tranquil is your evening hour in India!" said Miss Belfield. "As far as my experience goes, I should almost say it compensates for the fiery sun of the day."

"It is a relief, certainly," said the captain. "Old Phœbus' disappearance below the horizon in this country, and the effect produced by it on man and beast, remind me of that which usually followed the exit of my old preceptor from the school-room—a general uproar and rejoicing."

CHAPTER XX

The little church of Bandel is a pleasing, modest structure—its white tower, cross, cloisters, and adjoining priest's house and garden, creating a pleasing illusion; transporting the spectator in imagination (forgetting he is in India) to the orange groves of Portugal or Madeira.

The vesper bell had ceased to sound as we slowly entered the building. The interior was invested with a deepening gloom, but partially broken by the waning light of evening, which, streaming in at the windows, chequered the worn pavement, pencilling, as it were, with its sad and sober ray, the touching but evanescent record of another departing day.

Within, all was silence and repose, save when slightly broken by the closing of a door, or the echo of a distant footfall.

The altars, with their splendid adornments of the Romish ritual, tapers, crucifixes, &c., sparkled through the "dim, religious light" of the place, whilst here and there a few solitary native Portuguese women, on their knees, met our eyes, absorbed in silent prayer.

The scene was solemn and impressive; my light thoughts fled, and a deep sense of the holiness and loveliness of devotion fell upon me. We moved through the body of the church and the adjoining courts and cloisters, pleased with the tranquillity of the spot, before we bent our steps towards the budgerow, whose whereabouts was now plainly indicated by the numerous fires of our servants and boatmen, cooking their evening meal on the banks.

"Well, Ann!" said the captain to his sister, as we sauntered along, "what do you think of the old chapel of Bandel?"

"I have been greatly pleased with it," answered Miss Belfield; "with me, you know,

'Even the faintest relics of a shrine

Of any worship wake some thought divine.'

But truly there is something *par excellence* in these old Catholic ecclesiastical buildings, which always, good Protestant as I am, takes a powerful hold on my feelings and imagination; hallowed by their association with the events of the misty past, they awaken the most solemn reflections.

To have trodden, too, as we have just done, those very aisles where the adventurous Portuguese of the olden time of India (now some centuries past) have put up their orisons, is well worth our evenings ramble. Yes," she added, with some enthusiasm, "whatever be the defects of its tenets and doctrines, Romanism unquestionably contains the very poetry of religion."

"Ann! my dear Ann!" exclaimed the captain, "what would your old friend Parson Martext, of Long Somerton, say, were he to hear you talking thus? Fie! fie! The 'misty past,' as you poetically term it," continued Captain Belfield (who, I began to discover, was a matter-of-fact-man, who had curbed and double-bitted his fancy, and was not perhaps quite so orthodox as he should have been), "is too often a region of delusion, in which flying the dull realities of the present, the feelings and imagination love to revel—a sort of moral *mirage* rests upon it. With too many, as they approach it, judgment abandons the reins of the understanding, whilst enthusiasm seizes them, and drives away Heaven knows whither. In the distant mountain fading— in aerial tints of gold and purple, infancy paints a heaven, whilst experience tells of rocks and caverns, cataracts and precipices. I am myself, I confess, disposed to entertain many of your feelings in such situations, but reading and reflection have taught me to moderate them—to distinguish, I hope, between feelings and rational convictions—romance and reality—in more senses than one; be assured the 'heart of man is deceitful above all things.' But, my dear Ann," he added, "we are becoming a vast deal too solemn and didactic. I'm sure our young friend here will think so. These subjects are caviare to those just entering on the spring of life, to which we, you know, are beginning to turn our backs. Here we are at the budgerow, love! Tea, too, on table! Now, then, take care how you walk over the plank; a dip in the Hoogly would be a chilling *finale* to your evening's ramble. Mr. Gernon, give my sister your hand, if you please. Here we are, once more, on board our first-rate."

I was not long in discerning that Captain Belfield was a learned Theban—a great Oriental scholar; a prodigious number of books he had, too, lying about the cabin, in worm-eaten Indian covers, and in all sorts of crambo characters—Persian, Nagree, Pali, and I know not what besides; with dictionaries, many of formidable bulk.

He maintained—for Captain Belfield, like most men, had his hobby, and was, moreover, at that time writing a book to prove it—that we have received almost all our *raw* notions of things in general from the East, to which we are, in fact, more indebted than it suits the policy of the world to acknowledge; and that now, after a score or two of centuries, we are merely rendering them back their own in a *manufactured* or modified form.

Our feudal system, our juries, our best jokes, our cleverest tales, our wisest aphorisms, and much more besides, were, according to him, all filched from the Hindoos. The captain was not a man to be led away by strained analogies and forced etymologies; so I put great faith in his *dicta* — a faith which has not been shaken by my post-griffinish researches.

He had better grounds to go upon than the old Irish colonel, who took up the converse of the proposition, and proved, or endeavoured to prove, that the Hindoos sprung from the Irish, that Sanscrit was a corruption of their vernacular, their veneration for the cow nothing more than a natural transition from their well-known partiality for *bulls*; and that the mildness, temperance, and placability of the race all smacked strongly of Tipperary.

On the evening to which I am referring, Captain Belfield soon became absorbed in his books, whilst Miss Belfield and I sat down to chess. We had two well-contested games; I won them both, and though I bore my victory meekly enough, I perceived, or thought I perceived, that it would not do to repeat my triumphs too often.

Chess is a fine, intellectual game, no doubt, but, somehow or other, a sad tryer of the temper; and, whether beaten or victorious, unless possessed of more than ordinary tact and self-command, you may chance to quarrel with, and possibly alienate, your friend.

Thus, then, with some little variety, reading, or conversation, passed we the evenings of our sojourn together — the pleasantest by far of my griffinage.

The voyage to Burhampore, the first large military station on the river, occupied ten or twelve days. I shall briefly touch on a few more of its incidents.

In spite of General Capsicum's friendly advice to indulge moderately in field sports, like ninety nine out of every hundred griffins, I commenced my popping operations almost from the day of starting, keeping up a sort of running fire, with little intermission, till I reached my destination.

My knowledge of Indian ornithology being extremely limited, I declared war against all of the feathered race that presented themselves — particularly the paddy-birds and snippets. The first, a sort of small crane, abounding in the rice-fields, and which it is considered by sportsmen the *acmé* of Johnny-rawism to shoot, under the impression that they are game; the second, a sort of sand-lark, which runs ducking along the banks of the river, and are so tame, being accustomed to boats, that it is difficult to make them take wing. These, in my simplicity, I took for Bengal snipes, and sometimes, poor little devils, opened a point-blank battery on them from my bolio window, knocking them, of course, to "immortal smash."

I had, it is true, gained an inkling from Tom and Marpeet touching the nature of such proceedings, with some warnings to avoid them, though it was reserved for Captain Belfield, a few days after we left Hoogly, to renew the admonition, with better effect. This arose out of the following occurrence.

I returned one evening to his budgerow, laden—*i.e.*, Ramdial, bearer, and Nuncoo, matar, were charged with the porterage of the following miscellaneous bag of game, to wit: a cock-vulture, with fine red wattles (which I shot, thinking he was a wild turkey), four snippets, five paddy-birds, three doves, a gillarie, or striped squirrel, a braminy kite, and a jackal.

The boats were just coming to, the poor dandies, after a hard day's pull, winding up their tow-lines, and old Phœbus himself just sinking to rest, spreading his glorious hues over the broad bosom of the Bagheriti, as,

> Spent with extreme toil,
>
> Weary and faint,

I made my appearance, after a long exploration among mango groves, paddy fields, and sugar-cane kates,[33] in search of game.

The captain was seated on the roof of the budgerow as I hove in sight; his amiable sister, parasol in hand, beside him, talking of Long Somerton, in all probability, and enjoying the beauties of the scene and the coolness and tranquillity of the hour.

"Well, Gernon," said the former, who had now dropped the "Mr." in addressing me, "what sport? what have you killed?—too well employed to think of dinner, of course!"

"Oh! capital, sir," said I; "all in that bag, and more besides."

"Quantity, certainly; but what are they?" added he, "for that, after all, is the main point."

"Pray bring them on board," said Miss Belfield; "I am curious to see some of the Indian game, to ascertain in what respect they differ from ours at home."

"With the greatest pleasure," returned I, glad of an opportunity to exhibit the contents of my bag; "you shall see them immediately."

So saying, I went on board, and joined my friends on the roof, Ramdial following with the bag, and Nuncoo dragging up the jackal by the tail. Ye

Gods! how the captain, albeit a grave man on ordinary occasions, did laugh, as Ramdial tumbled out the contents of my cornucopia!

"Ha! ha! ha! why, you have made a day's sport of it, indeed," he exclaimed; "but you don't intend, I hope, that we should eat them all?"

"The snipes and the doves," said I, modestly, "and those things, something like woodcocks, might not, I thought, be bad eating."

"Snipes!" echoed the captain, "I see no snipes."

"No, sir! why, what are these?" I asked, holding up one of my snippets by the bill; "aren't these Bengal snipes?"

"Bengal snipes! no! nor snipes at all; miserable snippets; but with you, I presume, all long bills are snipes?"

"No, not exactly," said I; "but allowing for difference of latitude and longitude, I thought these might very well be snipes."

"Ah! I see," said the captain, "I must put you in the way of managing matters. I have long relinquished the gun, for I found I was getting too fond of it, and, after a few years, the sun tells; but I must resume it for a day or two, in order to initiate you a little into the proper nature of Indian sporting, and to show you where real snipes and game are to be found. All this is mere waste of powder and shot (which you will find a very expensive article, by the way, in India), and will get you, if you continue it, dubbed an egregious griffin or greenhorn. A jackal, too! what made you shoot him?"

"He bolted from a bush, and I thought he was a wolf and floored him beautifully; as I rolled him over 'twas fine fun to see the courage with which Teazer and the bull attacked him when in his last agonies. However, I should not have spared him, had I at first been aware of what he was, for I owe the whole race a grudge for their infernal yellings. I was kept awake for some hours last night by a troop of the fiends close under my bolio window."

"Ah!" said Belfield, "you have destroyed a useful scavenger; never kill without an adequate purpose; if we have a right to slay, it is not in mere wantonness; 'shoot only what you can eat' is a good maxim."

"Mr. Gernon," said Miss Belfield, "though my brother undervalues your sport, it may be some consolation to you to know that I do not; I want to sketch all the curious birds and animals I see, for a very dear friend of mine at Long Somerton, who exacted a promise from me, at parting, that I would do so. Will you, therefore, bring them all on board to-morrow, the poor jackal included, and you shall group whilst I sketch them?"

"Capital!" said I; "with the greatest pleasure; and we'll have Nuncoo as the Indian huntsman in the foreground: we shall," I added rather wickedly, "in this little dedication to the fine arts, be working out the captain's utilitarian principle, as applied to sporting."

Captain Belfield was as good as his word; he put his double-barrelled Manton together, after a long repose apparently, in its case, where, in dust certainly, if not in *ashes*, it had mourned its state of inaction, mustered several of his servants, and out we sallied in the afternoon of the following day.

Captain Belfield, from his perfect knowledge of the language and the people—whom, I observed, he always treated with great kindness—was soon able to ascertain the spot in the neighbourhood of the river where the game was to be found (there is but little, comparatively, in this part of Bengal), and which I should probably have been long in discovering; to them we accordingly went, and found hares, black partridges, and abundance of real snipes, which I perceived did not differ in the smallest degree from English ones; and I had the supreme felicity of bagging something more respectable than paddy-birds and snippets, which I afterwards treated with proper contempt.

The captain, although he had been so long on the retired list as a sportsman, fired a capital good stick nevertheless, and knocked the black partridges about, right and left, in great style; indeed, he once or twice, to borrow a not very delicate sporting phrase, "wiped my nose" in a very off-hand manner, proofs of his powers as a marksman with which I could have readily dispensed; as next probably, to a smack in the face, there are few things more disagreeable than having your "nose wiped."

The black partridge of India, I must inform the reader, is a beautiful bird; its breast (*i.e.*, the male's), glossy shining black, spangled with round and clearly defined white spots; its haunts are the long grass on the borders of jheels and marshes, from whence it creeps, in the mornings and evenings, into the neighbouring cultivation.

When flushed, up he goes, as straight as a line, to a certain elevation, and then off with him, at a right angle, like a dart. He is by no means an easy shot, though, from his mode of rising, it would appear otherwise.

It will be long ere I forget the thrill of pleasure I experienced when I dropped my first black partridge on this occasion, and how pompously, after ascertaining his specific gravity, I consigned him to my bag, taking him out about every five minutes, to indulge in another examination. It is difficult to express the contempt with which I then viewed my quondam friends, the snippets and paddy-birds.

The prodigious quantity of water-fowl to be seen on some of the shallow lakes or jheels of India, is well calculated to astonish the European beholder. I have seen clouds of them rise from such sheets of water, particularly in the upper part of the Dooab, with a sound sometimes not unlike the roar of a distant park of artillery; geese of two or three sorts; ducks, teal, coots, saruses, and flamingoes; the latter, however, should perhaps be excepted from the concluding part of the remark, for a string of these beautiful scarlet and flame-coloured creatures, floating silently in the air, or skimming, on lazy pinions, over an expanse of water, seem like a chain of fairies, or bright spirits of some Eastern tale, descending gently to earth; nor do I think this is an exaggerated description, as all will allow who have seen the flame-coloured cordon on the wing.

Having now been put in the way of doing things according to rule, I no longer, as I have before hinted, molested such ignoble birds and beasts as, in my state of innocence, I was wont to destroy. No more did I nail the unhappy snippets to the bank from my bolio window nor disturb the 'lorn cooings of the turtle-dove in her bower of mango shade, by a rattling irruption of No. 6; but in a steady, sportsmanlike form, accompanied by Ramdial (who, by the way, had no sinecure of it), laden with *chattah* (umbrella), game-bag, and brandy-pawney bottle in leathern case, and Nuncoo, the dog-keeper, with Teazer and the bull-dog, I was almost daily in the jheels and swamps, mud-larking after the ducks and snipes.

The reader will think, probably, and I am not disposed to question the correctness of his opinion, that bull-dogs are not the best of the species that can be selected for snipe-shooting.

Granted, I say again; but he will be pleased to remember that there are such disagreeable things as tigers and wild boars (and great *bores* they are too) to be met with in India. It therefore struck me that, in case of an unexpected rencontre with one or other of these creatures, the bull-dog might do good service, by making a diversion in my favour, and in concert with Teazer, attacking the enemy in flank and rear, keeping him in check, whilst I fell back on the fleet, as many a valiant and experienced general had done before me.

Hector, however, though reserved for such important purposes, took no pleasure in the sport; his heart was with the flesh pots of Whitechapel, and Nuncoo had sometimes hard work to get him through the swamps; Teazer behaved better, and, indeed, for a dog of such very low extraction, displayed a better nose than I expected.

Griffin Mudlarking in the Jheels.

Happy! happy days of my griffinage! first full swing of the gun! none before or since have been like unto ye! Had I then set up for a second Mahomed, and described a paradise, snipe-shooting in a jheel would have infallibly been included amongst its most prominent enjoyments!

The country in this part of Bengal is a dead flat, composed of a rich alluvial soil, in a high state of cultivation. Rice, sugar-cane, Palma Christi, and fifty other tropical productions, flourish luxuriantly, and charm the sight by their novelty.

The face of the country is covered with groves of mango, tamarind, and plantain trees, &c.; and numerous towns and villages are scattered here and there, but which, however, have little that is striking or interesting in their appearance, mud or matting being the predominant materials with which they are constructed.

Still the vastness of the population, the number and variety of the boats on the river, transporting up and down the rich and varied produce of India, and the diversity of the objects to be seen on the banks as you slowly glide along, are extremely pleasing. Miss Belfield, being a finished sketcher, was daily in raptures with all she saw. Full often would she summon me to the budgerow window, to look at something exceedingly picturesque—some glimpse, effect, or "pretty bit," as she was wont to term it, and which had awakened all her admiration.

Some old and magnificent banyan-tree, exhibiting a forest of shade, and whose tortuous roots, like sprawling boa-constrictors, overhung the stream; village maidens filling their water-pots beneath it, or fading like phantasmagoric figures in the deepening gloom of the receding woodland-path; or some Brahmin standing mid-leg in the water, with eye abased, and holding his sacred thread; cattle sipping, or the huge elephant, like a mountain of Indian-rubber, half-immersed, and patiently undergoing his diurnal scrubbing and ablution.

I caught all her enthusiasm, and great was the sketching and dabbling in water-colours which followed thereon.

Captain Belfield possessed a far more extensive library than my friend Tom Rattleton, comprising many standard works on Indian history, geography, antiquities, &c.; to these, for he was no monopolist in any shape, he kindly gave me free access, and when not occupied by blazing at the snipes, or in aiding Miss Belfield in her graphic operations, I found in his library stores an ample fund of amusement.

I pored over the *seer ul Mutakhereen*, and formed an extensive acquaintance amongst the twelve million gods of the Hindoo Pantheon.

How genuine, how refreshing, by the way, is the *bonhomie* of the Mahomedan author of the *seer ul Mutakhereen!* with what grave simplicity and *naïveté* does he relate the sayings and doings of our valiant countrymen in the early times of Anglo-Indian history!

His comparison of the red Feringhie[34] soldiers, firing in battle, to a long brick wall, belching forth fire and smoke, is admirable. And how excellent the story of Beebee Law, and the stem reproof administered to the fawning Asiatic parasite, the young noble at Patna, by the sturdy English commander, when the former tried to ingratiate himself by insulting his fallen enemy, the gallant Frenchman!

How striking, too, when recording these acts, the energy and astonishment with which, as if irresistibly impelled thereto, he apostrophizes the virtues of the English—their high-souled contempt of death—their fortitude under reverses, and moderation in success—likening them to the Rustums and Noushervans of old, Asiatic types of valour and justice; showing that there is a moral sense, an eternal standard of nobleness, which no adverse circumstances of habit, climate, and education can wholly obliterate or destroy—that virtue is not wholly conventional!

And oh! admirable Orme! thou minute chronicler of still minuter events, ungrateful, indeed, should I deem myself, did I not here acknowledge my obligations to thee; did I not record the many pleasant hours I have spent in poring over thy pages, whilst tracing the career of thy now antiquated worthies, from Clive to Catabominaigue!

As we approached the classic ground of Plassey, both poetry and patriotism began to stir within me. I studied Orme's account of the battle attentively, and determined, as doubtless many had done before me, to attempt to identify the existing local features with those incidentally mentioned in the narrative of that important event, the first act of the greatest work of modern days, — the conquest, government, and civilization, by a handful of remote islanders, of one hundred millions of men; a work, be it observed, though still progressing, which if left to liberal and practical minds, can hardly fail to be effected (though yearly increasing in difficulty), if fanaticism on the one hand, and ultra liberalism on the other, be not allowed prematurely to mar it.

Miss Belfield expressed great veneration for the memory of the Indian hero, and begged to be allowed to accompany us to the scene of his crowning exploit.

"The more the merrier, my dear," said her brother, and out we all sallied to visit—thrilling name—"The field of Plassey."

A very pleasant stroll we had, too; but all our endeavours to harmonize the then aspect of the country (and doubtless it is much the same now) with Orme's description of it were utterly nugatory; hunting lodge, mango tope, and every other memorial and mark of the fight mentioned by that accurate historian, having been swept away by the river, which, since 1757, has entirely changed its course.

If any future Clive should fight a battle in Bengal, decisive of the fate of India, and feel at all desirous that the field of his fame should remain intact, I would respectfully advise him not to come to blows within twenty good miles of the Ganges, if he can possibly avoid it, for that headlong flood, in the course of its erratic movements, will sooner or later be sure to sweep it away.

An example of the tortuosity of the course of the Bagheriti, and of the way in which both it and the great Ganges abandon their beds and form new ones, leaving miles of their former channels unoccupied, or formed into stagnant lakes, was afforded at Augurdeep, a few miles from Plassey.

After a long day's journey (some fifteen or sixteen miles), we observed, to our great surprise, that we had halted within a few hundred yards of the spot from whence we had set out in the morning, the masts of boats moored there being visible across a narrow neck of land, or isthmus, connecting with the main land the peninsula we had been all day circumnavigating.

This isthmus, in after years, was cut through, the river beating in full force against it, leaving, of course, a great extent of channel dry. If Clive's victory, therefore, had left no more lasting memorial than the field on which it was gained, we should know but little about it.

We were disappointed at our ill success, at least Miss Belfield and I; for the captain had anticipated that matters would be as we found them. I, however, consoled myself with a determination I had formed, to raise a monument of the victory a little more durable than the one which had just disappeared. I made up my mind to compose a poem, an epic, on the conquest of Bengal; Clive, of course, the hero, and Plassey the scene; on which, like the combatants, I proposed to put forth all my strength.

I had for some days felt the stirring of the divine *afflatus* within me, a sort of boiling and rioting of vast ideas; too vast, alas! I afterwards found, for utterance or delivery, for I stuck fast at "Immortal Clive."

Two or three days more brought us to the station of Burhampore. The day before we arrived, Captain Belfield received a letter from an old acquaintance at the station, one Colonel Heliogabalus Bluff, begging him to breakfast and dine with him on the morrow, and pass a day or two *en route*. The letter thus concluded:

"I hear you have your sister with you; shall, of course, be glad to see the Beebee Sahib too; send herewith a *dolee*, which pray present to her, with my *bhote bhote salaam*.

"A *dolly*, sir," said I, in astonishment, on Captain Belfield's reading this passage; "that's rather an odd thing to send: he supposes, I presume, that Miss Belfield is a child."

Captain Belfield was attacked with a most violent fit of laughter on my making this remark, and I saw that I had been once more unwittingly griffinizing.

When he had a little recovered his composure, "Gernon," said he, "it will, add, perhaps, to your astonishment when I tell you, that we intend to eat the said *dolly* for dinner, and shall expect you to partake of it."

Saying this, he ordered the article to be brought in, when, instead of a toy, I found the dolee was a basket of fruit, flowers, and vegetables.

"Who is the gentleman?" said Miss Belfield, as we sat at tea in the evening, "from whom you had the letter this morning, and to whom we are indebted for all this fine fruit?"

"Why, Colonel Bluff," said her brother, "an old fellow-campaigner of mine, a very rough subject; 'and though he is my friend,' as Mr. Dangle, in 'The Critic,' says, I must acknowledge, a very eccentric and far from agreeable character."

"Oh! pray describe him fully," said his sister: "I like much to have an eccentric character delineated, for, in this age of refinement, men have become so very much like one another, that a person marked by any peculiarity is as enlivening as a rock, or other bold feature, to the sight, after having been long wearied by the monotony of a low and level landscape: do, pray, give us a sketch of him."

"Well, then, the colonel is a stout, sturdy John Bull, underbred and overfed, combining with the knock-me-down bluntness of that character, as it once existed more strongly than at present, and a double allowance of all his ordinary prejudices, the *gourmanderie* and frivolity which an idle life in India is too apt to engender in the very best of us.

"He reverses the rule, that we ought to eat to live, for he lives to eat, and much of his time is occupied in devising dishes, or superintending his farm-yard, educating his fat China pigs, and looking after his tealery, and quailery and sheep.

"He has a constant supply always pouring in for him from Calcutta, of exotic and expensive luxuries—beer, champagne, pine cheeses, Yorkshire hams, Perigord pies, pigs' cheeks, and the like—of which he is certainly liberal enough; for no prince can be prouder than he is when at the head of his table, making his gastronomical displays; in short, he greatly prides himself on the surpassing excellence of his breakfasts and dinners, though those who partake of them must often, as their price, submit quietly to all his coarseness and brutality of manner. Folks in India do not generally trouble themselves much about English politics; at least, not so far as to identify themselves strongly with the sects and parties which are everlastingly worrying each other at home, and who remind me of vultures and jackals here over a carcase.

"Colonel Bluff is, however, an exception to the rule, and has always set himself up for a great church-and-king man, and a violent high Tory, delighting in talking of such subjects. He is a terribly violent fellow, and when excited by a few glasses of wine, pounds the table, and makes the glasses dance again, as he denounces all Whiggery and Radicalism.

"With all his faults, however, and he has more than an ordinary share, he possesses a good deal of Miss Hannah More's standing dish, 'good-nature' (provided he has everything his own way); and, indeed, but for this redeeming trait, he would be utterly unbearable."

Miss Belfield said she was curious to see this singular compound of *bon vivant* and politician, a feeling in which I expressed my hearty participation.

"You must be on your guard how you comport yourself before him, Gernon," said the captain, "for I assure you he shows no mercy to griffins, cutting them up right and left, when once he commences, with most unmercifully rough raillery."

"He had better leave me alone," said I, with rather a formidable shake of the head; "I'm not under his command, you know, sir, and may give him a Rowland for his Oliver."

"You'd better not attempt it, my dear fellow," replied the captain; "he has demolished many a stouter griffin than you are."

The next morning we reached the station of Burhampore, and a little before we brought to, I observed, approaching the banks, a very stout, burly officer, followed by an orderly sepoy, whilst a bearer held a chattah, or umbrella, over his head. It was impossible to be mistaken—this must be Colonel Bluff.

"*Kisha budjra hyr?*" (whose boat is that?)

"*Bilfil Sahib ka*" (Captain Belfield's), replied a servant.

"Ship ahoy! Belfield, get up, you lazy dog," shouted the "stout gentleman," with the voice of a Stentor.

The captain ran out in his dressing-gown, and my suspicions were at once confirmed; it was, indeed, the colonel; and a lively greeting now passed between them.

"Well, then, so you've deserted Java—cut the Dutchmen, eh?—and come back to the Qui-Hye's?—they seem to have used you well, though; you aint half such a lantern-jaw'd, herring-gutted looking fellow as you used to be—haw! haw! You were, I recollect, when you joined us first, 'as thin as a ha'porth o' soap after a hard day's washing.' as my father's old north country gardener used to say—haw! haw!"

"Complimentary and refined, as usual, I see, colonel; I can't congratulate you on any material alteration in that respect."

"Why, man, you don't expect me to compliment an old friend like you, do you? 'with compliments crammed,' you know the rest—haw! haw! But, come, stir your stumps, man! stir your stumps! breakfast's all ready up yonder, and as capital a ham for you as you ever stuck your teeth in. I wait breakfast for no man, woman, or child living; you know me of old. Talking of women, where's the Beebee? where's sister? she'll come, won't she? My compts—Colonel Bluff's compts—glad to see her; always proud to do the honours to the ladies. But who have you got in that boat astern, Belfield?"

"Oh, it's a young friend of mine, Ensign Gernon, going to join his regiment, under our convoy and protection."

"O! a griff, eh! a greenhorn: hungry as a hunter, I'll be sworn; bring him along with you, bring him along, and we'll fill him out. Rare fellows, your griffs, to play a knife and fork—rare trencher-men. I'd sooner keep some of them a week than a fortnight—haw! haw!"

"But colonel, had you not better take your breakfast with us? it's ready, and then we'll walk up and spend the rest of the day with you."

"Breakfast with you! No, hang me if I do: d'ye mean to insult me, sir? What! a man, after a voyage, with hardly a shot in his locker, ask a gentleman on shore, with a Yorkshire ham on his table, to breakfast with him! never heard such a proposal in all my life! No, come, come along, or I must march you all up under a file of Jacks."

All this, which I overheard very distinctly, and which was uttered at the top of an iron pair of lungs, was intended for heartiness and jocularity. No doubt there was kindness in it, and with mortals as rough as himself, it might doubtless have answered very well; but the captain, I could see, evidently winced under the infliction, though bent apparently on enduring it for a season, with proper resignation.

After finishing our toilets, and a few other little arrangements, we joined the colonel, who would take no refusal, on the bund or esplanade.

Captain Belfield introduced his sister and me. The colonel, on being presented to the former, raised his hat, and made as much of a bend as the sphericity of his form would allow; at the same time thrusting forth a leg far better adapted (to borrow the corn-law phraseology) for a "fixed duty" than the "sliding scale," with the air of a finished man of gallantry.

There was something so irresistibly comic in the momentarily assumed suavity of this huge *Ursa Major* (or *Ursa Colonel*, as Paddy would say), this attempt at the easy movement of the lady's man, that I was constrained to turn aside my head, in order to conceal a laugh.

The colonel gave us a superb breakfast and it was plainly observable that his reputation as a *gastronome* had not been overrated. Ham, fish, jellies, butter, creams, cakes—all the profusion of an Indian breakfast—

were severally the very best of their kinds; moreover, Colonel Bluff gave the history of every article, telling us to lay on, and spare not, as we should not meet with any like them between that and Mr. Havell's, the provisioner's, at Dinapore.

The dinner was equally remarkable for its goodness and profusion; Chittagong fowls, as big as turkeys, were there, and a saddle of mutton cased with two inches of fat, on which the colonel gazed with as much pride as some tender parent would look on a favourite child.

He had invited some eight or ten of the ladies and gentlemen of the station to meet us, and it was soon abundantly clear that the captain had drawn a most accurate sketch of his friend's character.

After the former had retired, he began to let out a little more of it. Seated at the head of his table—his burly King Hal person filling his capacious arm-chair—figure a little obliqued, a napkin over his knee, and the bottles in array before him, the jolly colonel looked the very personification of absolutism and animalism.

"Gentlemen, fill your glasses! Church and King! and after that what you will. Pass the bottle, Belfield; fill up a bumper; come, a brimmer; no daylight, sir; none of your Whiggery here; I thought you had left all that off?"

"I'll drink anything you please, colonel; but I fear our politics are wider apart than ever."

"You're not becoming a follower of that rascal Tom Paine, are you? I know you used to dabble in all sorts of books, and were but a few degrees off it—a republican, irreligious scoundrel—gone to the d——l, I hope, as he deserves—a fellow that had no respect for royalty, and would have upset, if he could, our holy religion, an infernal villain!"

"Why, you are warm, colonel," observed a middle-aged officer; "may I ask when you took so keenly to politics?"

"Yes, you may ask," said Bluff; "but it depends upon me whether I answer you—haw! haw! Come, fill your glass and pass the bottle, and don't ask questions—haw! haw! haw!"

Never did I see so rough a specimen of humanity. How he talked, laughed, thumped the table, and laid down the law, in the exercise of his unenviable immunity!

An incident occurred after dinner, which displayed in a strong light the violence of Bluff's character, especially towards the natives, and his perfect disregard of the feelings of his company.

As the bottles were placed before him by the apdar, or butler, a very respectable-looking bearded Mahomedan, something in their arrangement displeased our host, who, pointing with his forefinger to one of them, exclaimed, "*Yee kea ky?*" (what is this?)

The unfortunate domestic bent forward his head, though evidently in fear, to scrutinize the damage, when he received a back-handed blow in the mouth from the colonel, which rung through the room, and sent him staggering backwards, *minus* his turban, which had fallen from the shock.

The man—I shall never forget it—stooped and picked up his turban; replaced it on his noble-looking head—his face was livid from a sense of the insult; he put his hand to his mouth, and looked at it, there was blood upon it.

The company appeared and were disgusted; even Bluff, I thought, seemed ashamed of himself. Well it is that these things are becoming rare!

But enough of the colonel, of whom this sketch may give as good an idea as a more elaborate description. Of such characters there were a few, and but a few, in the Indian army, and it is to be hoped their number is fast diminishing.

CHAPTER XXI

We remained the following day, and accompanied the colonel, and one or two of his officers, to a grand entertainment, given by the Nawaub of Bengal, at his palace of Moorshedabad, in honour of the festival of the *Baira*. The whole station had, I believe, received invitations, through the Governor-General's agent at the court of his highness, and a grand spectacle was expected.

We left Burhampore, in a landau, in the afternoon, and after an agreeable drive through a level and wooded country, partly on the margin of a considerable lake, called the Motee Jheel, reached the city of Moorshedabad, and entering a lofty gateway, found ourselves in the enclosure or domain in which the nawaub's palace is situated.

This building is a lofty structure, in the European style, on the banks of the river, and bears the name of the *Aina Mahl*, which, if I am not in error, means the "Palace of Mirrors."

The whole scene was animated and striking, and particularly so to me, being the first thing of the kind I had seen in India.

Groups of richly-dressed Mahomedans, exhibiting a grand display of shawls, turbans and jewels; retainers and connections of the nawaub, or dignified inhabitants of the city; armed men, attired in the picturesque costume of the native soldiery of India, with shields, swords, and matchlocks; Abyssinian slaves, and Bengalese in their flowing muslin robes, constituted the native portion of the assembly. Amongst these were a numerous body of English officers, in their scarlet uniforms, and ladies elegantly dressed.

On the terrace of the noble house, overlooking the Baghiriti, stood the nawaub and his little court, their jewels and muslins contrasting with the plain blue coat and simple garb of the Governor-General's agent and other civilians about him.

Tables were laid out in the palace, profusely covered with wines and refreshments, in the European style; old hands and griffins, fair sex and civilians, seemed all determined to enjoy themselves, and to give his nabobship a benefit; to sweat his claret, as a slight off-set to the sweating his ancestors had given to ours in the Black Hole of Calcutta.

In the courts or pavilions below, Pulwahns, or athletæ, exhibited feats of strength; jugglers displayed their tricks, and two or three mimics enacted the sale of a horse to an Indian Johnny Raw, a sort of Brentford tailor, as far as I was able to judge from their action, expression, and the applause they elicited from the bystanders, with great humour and effect.

As night drew on, the whole place was illuminated, exhibiting a blaze of light; the party, native and European, were congregated on the terrace to look at the sports. A grand pyrotechnic display followed; the rockets whizzed in the air, and the blue lights shed their spectral glare around.

I was delighted: this is worth seeing, methought.

Anon, the river was covered with countless lamps in motion on its surface, and, soon after, a fairy palace, or structure forming one mass of gorgeous light, came gliding down the current, passing beneath the terrace.

The whole effect was beautiful and striking. I have hardly ever before or since seen anything of the kind which pleased me more.

The costumes and buildings of the East, and possibly of all semi-barbarous countries, harmonize well with pageantry and spectacle; all is in keeping, and nought appears to wound the sense of fitness and congruity. Not so, it strikes me, in our own country, where the pomp and glitter of the Middle Ages form strange patchwork with spinning-jennies and the homely toggery of our utilitarian and go-ahead times. Fancy going to a tournament by a railroad, or seeing a mailed champion riding cheek by jowl with a Kennington "'bus," or one of Barclay and Perkins's drays. If we must have splendour, let it be in unison with the age.

The next day, having replenished our stores with several additions from the colonel's garden and farm-yard, for it would be ungrateful not to acknowledge this liberality—a truly Indian virtue—we once more resumed our voyage.

Burhampore, like most of the great military stations of India, is intended to operate as a check on a large and important city; not that from Moorshedabad—once the capital of Bengal, a place long since sunk into comparative insignificance—much danger is now to be apprehended. It is the head-quarters of a brigade, partly composed of European troops.

The barracks and officers' quarters are superb, and form a vast square, of which the former constitute the face farthest from the river; that nearest to it is a continuous range of handsome houses and gardens, with colonnades and verandahs, occupied by civilians and superior military officers.

There are also other ranges of buildings running perpendicular to the river, partly barracks and in part officers' quarters. The whole is separated from the Baghiriti by a broad bund, or esplanade. The sepoy lines are about a mile inland, but the officers reside in the quarters, or in the fine bungalows scattered about.

The scene here in the evening was very lively; soldiers exercising in the square; officers riding on horseback, or driving in gigs; the band playing on the esplanade; groups promenading; in short, I was pleased with the place, and should have had no objection to have terminated my voyage there.

The morning of our departure, we were besieged by the vendors of silk piece-goods and handkerchiefs, as also of ivory toys and chessmen, for both of which this place and its neighbour, Cossim Bazar, have acquired a great reputation.

Some of the chessmen shown us were large beyond anything of the kind I had ever seen before; so much so, that to play with an irascible man with such ponderous and massive pieces might be unsafe.

The natives of India, it appears to me, though possessed of infinite perseverance and ingenuity, have no natural taste (at least, if they have any, it greatly wants cultivation); as respects progress in the fine arts, they appear on a par with our Anglo-Saxon ancestors at the time of the Conquest, and their sculpture, carving, and painting (and probably their music), in their leading and more marked peculiarities and defects, bear a considerable resemblance to those of such remains as we have of the olden time of England. It is, however, probable that the rude dawnings of knowledge are everywhere pretty much alike, though marked with more or less of native vigour and genius.

Of perspective, proportion, &c., they know little or nothing, and of this we had amusing examples, both in the carving and some pictures which were here offered us for sale, and which latter, in the richness of their colours and gilding, brought strongly to mind the illuminations of old missals, except that, in the false perspective and utter disregard of proportion, they beat them completely, outdoing Hogarth's illustration of that ludicrous confusion into which an ignorance of these things is wont to lead the graphic tyro: full views at once of three sides of a square building, flat roof inclusive, visible from below; chiefs, in gorgeous apparel, seated on carpets as large as the adjoining garden, and holding "posies to their noses;" antelopes scampering over hills somewhat smaller than themselves; groups of figures taller than the buildings, with dislocated limbs, and legs like wooden stocking stretchers; water reversing the laws of hydrostatics, and running up-hill, and objects increasing with the distance.

Miss Belfield's critical eye was shocked by these performances, though otherwise amused; and for my part, I do not think I enjoyed a heartier laugh since I was a griffin.

So completely vitiated is the native eye, by being accustomed to these deformities, that the majority of Indians can often make little or nothing of a European drawing; and I have often, in my post-griffinish days, seen one of them take a pencil sketch in his hand, turn it round about this way and that, and finally settle to its examination when upside downwards.

The Hindus, in these respects, seem more deficient than the Mahomedans, though, like the ancient Egyptians, in their ghauts, temples, and other works, they exhibit the vast and minute in perfection, showing what numbers and perseverance can effect without the aid of taste.

The Baghiriti, at Burhampore, narrows at the commencement of the cold season to a moderately broad stream, and was now fast falling, so that we were led to suppose some difficulty in getting into the great Ganges at the point of junction, some days' journey higher up. Sometimes this part becomes absolutely impracticable for large boats, which are then obliged to effect the passage by another branch.

As we approached the great river, our journey became rather one by land than by water. The river had fallen to the depth of a few inches in some parts, we were pushed by main force, by our indefatigable dandies, over sandy shallows, of miles in extent.

This was a labour, however, to which they had evidently been accustomed, and most philosophically did they set about it: planting their backs against the broad Dutch-built stem of the budgerow, they worked us along by almost imperceptible degrees, with insufferable yelling, groaning, and grunting, varied occasionally by the monotony of "*Tan a Tooney hy yah!*"

After a *dos-à-dos*ing it in this style for some days, we had at length the satisfaction to find ourselves fairly hacked out of the scrape, and riding in the Ganges.

The Ganges! Strange were my emotions as I gazed on the broad expanse of that famed and once mysterious river, with whose name were associated so many of my early ideas of Brahmins, Gentoos, burning widows, and strange idolatries! Alas! the romance of the world is fast departing. Steam, commerce, and conquest, are making all things common, and soon they will leave no solitary spot on this globe of ours where the imagination may revel undisturbed amidst dim uncertainties and barbaric originalities. There wants but a gin-shop on Mount Ararat, or a spinning-jenny on Olympus, to complete the work of desecration.

A day or two more brought us in sight of the blue mountains, or hills of Rajmahal, a great relief to the eye, after having been so long accustomed to the unvarying level of Bengal.

The low lands at the foot of these hills are well stocked with game, the neighbouring jungles affording them secure shelter. Everything is here to be found, from the rhinoceros to the quail. Here I shot my first chikor, a splendid bird, of the partridge kind, but twice the size of ours.

Accompanied by the trusty Ramdial and Nuncoo, with a few dandies whom I had pressed into my service as beaters, I sallied out one morning with the determination to make a day of it.

After walking some distance inland, and to within a few miles of the hills, I found myself in an extensive, flat, marshy tract, which had evidently a short time before been covered by the periodical inundations, to the depth of eight or ten feet.

This tract was covered with long coarse grass, a sort of reeds, which, having lost the support of the water, were prostrated like lain corn. Through these I was making my way, my beaters actively employed on both sides of me, when, suddenly, a noble bird rose, with a rare clatter, from under my feet; before I could cock my gun and close an eye, he was at a good distance from me; nevertheless, being a fair mark, I fired, and dropped him.

I was delighted, on picking up my sport, to find it a fine massive bird, of the partridge kind, bigger than a red grouse; in short, as I afterwards learned from the captain, the chikor[35] above described. I reloaded and advanced; and in a few moments flushed another, which I was equally fortunate in killing.

Immediately after the discharge of my barrel, and whilst standing on the prostrate reeds, I heard a rustling, and felt a movement close to me. I thought it was another bird, and cocked my remaining barrel, to be ready for him; instead, however, of a chikor, an enormous boar, caked with dried mud, and whom doubtless I had roused from a luxurious snooze, burst forth almost from under my feet, to my very great astonishment.

His boarship's ear was most invitingly towards me; I had no time to reflect on the danger of provoking such an enemy, in such a place—no rock, stump, or "coign of vantage," behind which I could have evaded his charge, had he made one—but instantly poured the contents of my barrel into his acoustic organ, at the distance of two or three yards. But the fellow was almost as tough as the alligator, whose end I formerly described: the shot produced apparently not the slightest effect beyond a shake of the head and a quickening of his pace.

Away he went over the country, floundering through the mud and pools in great style, Teazer, for some distance, hard on his heels, but with no serious intention, I imagine, of catching such a Tartar.

Had the brute resented the earwigging I gave him, as he might easily have done, a pretty little white cenotaph, on the nearest eminence, "*Hic jacet Frank Gernon*," and an invitation to the humane traveller to drop a tear in passing, would have been the probable result.

After bagging one or two more chikors, I proceeded to the foot of the hills, or rather of a spur proceeding from them, and soon found myself on the skirts of a most tigerish-looking jungle: tall yellow grass, sombre pools, with reedy margins, interspersed with irregular patches of bush and tree jungle, ramifying from the densely-wooded hills above. I would not have insured a cow there, for a couple of hours, for ninety nine and a half per cent. of her value.

I paused ere I ventured to plunge into these dreary coverts; but my hesitation was but momentary. It is an established fact that, in love, war, or the chase, wherever danger presents itself,

> *Griffins* rush in,
>
> Where *old hands* fear to tread.

Besides, there were Teazer and the bull, and half a dozen black fellows, *ready picked*, constituting long odds in my favour, even should a hungry tiger appear.

In short, I entered, and was soon forcing my way, gun in hand, through this most perilous locality, my heart in my mouth, and in a feverish sort of tip-toe expectation that, in a second, I might find myself hurried off, *à la Munro*, by the waistband of my breeches.

Things stood thus, my party a little scattered, and all advancing through the reedy margin of a winding piece of water (well stocked with alligators, I had not the slightest doubt), when a shout, a yelp from Teazer, a violent rush, a glimpse of some animal, an instinctive discharge of my gun, and a huge hog-deer rolled head-over-heels at my feet; all the work of an instant, into which was compressed as much alarm (for verily I thought it was one of the royals) as would have served (diluted into anxiety) for seasoning six months' ordinary existence.

Truly proud was I of my exploit, as the hog-deer, doubled-up, lay kicking at my feet, in the agonies of death. By a fortunate chance, I had lodged the whole charge of shot under his shoulder.

Never was griffin more elated. "What will the captain now say?" thought I; "no more jeers or undervaluing of my sporting qualifications after this!"

My first care now, after slinging the deer, was to get out of the jungle— for this successful feat had given a new relish to existence, and I felt indisposed to run more risks. His legs were soon tied; a young tree was cut, and thrust through them; and, supported by four men, I proceeded in triumph to my budgerow.

"Well, Mr. Gernon, you have indeed been fortunate this time," said Miss Belfield.

The kind captain also congratulated me on my success, but warned me against venturing on foot in such places again, as, in fact, I had really incurred considerable risk. In return, I favoured them with a detailed account of my whole day's operations.

The hog-deer, being a very bulky animal, served to feast the whole crew and domestics, his throat having been cut when he fell, without which operation no Mahomedan would have touched him. We also had some collops of the flesh, which were tolerably good, though not to be compared to an English haunch of venison.

I am not writing a book of travels, so shall touch but lightly on the scenes and occurrences which presented themselves on our subsequent route to Dinapore, where my friends and I parted—they remaining there, I, after a time, continuing my onward course to the capital of the Moguls.

Hitherto, our route had lain through Bengal, a country of mud huts and inundations; but we were now approaching a higher level, and one inhabited by a finer race, living in a superior climate, and where the Mahomedan spirit, which approaches nearer to our own, has imparted its more enduring traces in the shape of substantial towns, and more lasting, though still decaying monuments and edifices. Captain Belfield had excited our curiosity by his account of the ruins of Rajmahal, the some time transient capital of Bengal, during the reign of the Emperor Aurungzebe, and we consequently indulged in pleasing anticipations of the rambling and sketching we were to enjoy there.

It was evening when we approached that place; the sun was setting gloriously on the Ganges as we moored our boats in a little bay near the ruins, on one horn of which stood an old grey mosque, partially hidden by tangled shrubs and jungle, and the tapering and feathery bamboo—one, perhaps, of the greatest and most striking ornaments of Indian scenery.

"William," said Miss Belfield, "you must positively remain here to-morrow, for I can never consent to leave all these fine old ruins unsketched behind me."

Her brother willingly consented to her wish, and a delightful day of it we had, rambling, pencil in hand, amongst decaying mosques and dilapidated palaces, where the voice of the imaun, or the sounds of revelry, had long given place to the hootings of that mocker of human vanity, the owl.

There are not, in the whole round of the feelings and sensations, any to me so exquisitely, yet sadly pleasing, as those that arise in the mind when we wander amidst the deserted courts of kings, and the monuments of departed power and glory: how strongly do they link us with the past, and how powerfully does the imagination, with such a footing, "body forth" the things that were, but are not!

Captain Belfield, who, like his sister, as I afterwards discovered, was somewhat of a poet, though in most things a matter-of-fact man, amused himself, while we were sketching, in composing the following lines:—

Lines on the Ruins of Rajmahal and the Palace of the Sungy Dulaun, some time the Capital of Bengal.

> Ye mould'ring corridors and halls,
> Which o'er the steep your shadows cast;
> Ye ruins drear, which sad recall
> The faded glories of the past:
> Where the lone trav'ller pensive sighs,
> And light winds pipe at evening hour,
> Low blending with the lapwing's cries,
> The requiems of departed power:

> How changed your aspect, since of old
> Gay orient pageants filled your bound,
> And trumpet and Nagara[36] told
> Of regal state that reign'd around.
> Here Sujah,[37] in his happier hour,
> Poor victim of a brother's hate!

Enjoy'd the transient sweets of power,
Bright contrast to his darker fate.

Here Heav'n display'd its vengeful ire,
And Meerun[38] felt the fatal blow;
Here fell the retributive fire,
That laid the foul assassin low.
Where once the minstrel's voice was heard,
Now nightly sounds the jackal's yell;
There hoots the melancholy bird,
Grim cynic of the darksome cell.

Within the Harem's latticed screen,
Where beauty once its radiance shed,
No bright eyes, save the owl's are seen—
The rank green jungle rears its head.
A carcanet of gems—the snake
Lies coil'd where jewell'd beauty prest,
Unwinding, seeks the tangled brake,
Or fierce erects his horrid crest.

Column and arch, with sculpture traced,
Crush'd by the peepul's[39] circling folds,
Like writhing Laocoon embraced,
Art dies—and nature empire holds.
Hail, sombre fabric! type of life
Once gay and smiling, now forlorn;
Wreck of thyself, with ruin rife,
Of all thy first attractions shorn.

Like some volcano—dead its fires—
Here now no more the passions rage;
Ambition, hate, or fierce desires
Long past—no longer conflicts wage.
Sadly thou breath'st the moral old,
Earth's vanities—man's chequer'd lot,
By seers and sages often told,
In life's fierce tumults soon forgot.

As o'er the mould'ring wrecks of time
With silent step we pensive steal,
In every land, in every clime,
Oh! say, whence spring those thoughts we feel?
Why hush'd the passions? touch'd the heart?
What prompts us all our state to scan?

What animates each better part?
Why breathe we love and peace to man?

'Tis that awhile withdrawn from cares—
Earth's cares, with strife and sorrow fraught,—
Sweet contemplation lowly bears
Her treasures to the mint of thought.
In such a frame—in stilly tone
Waked fancy hears these words exprest,
"Oh, pilgrim! this is not your home,—
Look upwards for thy place of rest."

A tear trembled in Miss Belfield's eye as she read her brother's verses; they had touched some tender chord, and the feelings they expressed were evidently in unison with her own; she arose and retired to her cabin, her head slightly averted, to conceal her emotion. As she passed, the captain fondly stretched out his hand towards her; she seized and pressed it—it was all the commentary she made.

The ruins of Rajmahal are not very extensive, nor are the buildings of any extraordinary magnitude or beauty; nevertheless, some mosques, and two or three old gateways, in the Moorish style of architecture, which seems everywhere to have preserved its original character—from Delhi to Morocco—are highly picturesque.

Captain Belfield, who was well acquainted with the place and its history, acted as our Cicerone, pointing out the most remarkable buildings; amongst these, by far the most considerable was the palace erected by that crafty and most consummate villain Aurungzebe, of which there are some very considerable remains, halls, baths, courts, &c., also the tomb of Meerun, the assassin of Surajah Dowlah.

Rajmahal was the residence and capital of the unfortunate Sultan Sujah, one of the brothers of Aurungzebe. The tragic end of this prince, amongst the wilds of Arracan, is touchingly related by the accurate historian Bernier, whose history of this family is a perfect romance. The relator has traversed the wild forests in Arracan towards Myamootie, where the hapless Mogul prince is supposed to have met his fate.

There are Mahomedans naturalized in Arracan, who differ in many respects from the aborigines, though they wear a similar garb. They are supposed to be descendants of those followers of Sultan Sujah, who escaped the massacre described by Bernier, and were retained in slavery by the Mughs.

When the city of Arracan was captured by the British, the head of the Mahomedan inhabitants, singularly enough, bore the name of Sujah. The writer remembers him well, and a wily fellow he was, playing, on the approach of the army, a well-managed double game, with British and Burmese, which was to benefit himself, whichever party succeeded.

Poor Sultan Sujah! the howling forests of Arracan must have presented a melancholy contrast to the marble halls of the palace of Aurungzebe! Like Sebastian of Portugal (to whose fate his own bore some resemblance), he was long believed to be alive, and fondly looked for by his adherents in India, and several impostors appeared to personate him.

Rajmahal has long fallen from its palmy state, and what remains of the town is ruinous, and thinly inhabited. Leaving this place, we continued our route, having the woody ranges of hills on our left, at various distances from the bank of the river.

At Sicrigully, a low spur of the hills touches the Ganges, crowned at its eminence with an old mosque or tomb; beneath is a small bungalow, for travellers, and hard by, a straggling village.

Here I was gratified by the sight of a brother sportsman, in the person of an Indian hunter, or shekarri. He was a little, spare, black creature, a native of the hills (a race perfectly distinct from the people of the plains), armed with a matchlock, whilst sundry bags and pouches adorned his person. He brought a fawn and a brace of jungle fowls, which he offered for a rupee, and some English powder and shot.

The jungle fowl are the domestic cock and hen in a wild state, of which there are many varieties in the East, though they are not often found in the jungles far beyond the tropics. The plumage of the cock bird is rich, varied, and beautiful, far more so than that of the civilized chanticleer; the hens, however, are generally of a uniform dun or slate colour, having callow bluish wattles, and spots of the same colour around the aural orifices. These were the first I had ever seen, though I had heard them in the Sunderbunds, and was not a little surprised to learn from the captain that they were not only game, but capital shooting also, and what to many may be considered a still further recommendation, very good eating to boot—of this, indeed, we had next day satisfactory proof.

So completely, however, are the cock and hen associated with scenes of civilized life, so perfectly are the highly respectable couple identified with man and his comforts—the stack and barn-yard—that it is almost impossible to fancy them wild, or still more to "make game" of them.

I recollect well, in after-times, the extraordinary feeling I experienced on contemplating the first jungle cock I ever shot. I had heard him sound his bugle-horn just before—a plain, matter-of-fact, English *cock-a-doodle-doo*; and there he was, with his comb, bright red wattles, and fine, curved, drooping tail, lying dead at my feet.

It required the full consideration that I was in a wild forest in India, to convince me that I had not done one of those "devilish deeds" perpetrated now and then at 'Igate and 'Ampstead, by adventurous gunners from the vicinity of Bow Church.

These hills of Rajmahal, with their various attractions of scenery, wild inhabitants, and peculiar productions, constitute a very pleasant break to what many may deem the monotony of a voyage up the Ganges in a budgerow; for many days they presented to me successive novelties.

One evening, our boats moored at a place called Peer Pointee—a holy saint, or *peer*, is interred on a neighbouring eminence—and in the evening, after sundown, the captain, his sister, and myself, took a stroll, in order to pay our respects to the shrine or tomb of his holiness.

To gain this, we had to ascend a low and rugged hill, on one side of which, about half-way up, is an old mosque, with an arcade in front, a pendant, doubtless, to the neighbouring durgah. The path was difficult, but we soon found ourselves on the spot where the holy man's ashes are enshrined.

The tomb occupied the centre of a terrace, surrounded by a low wall. Lamps burnt around it, if I rightly remember, and the attendant fakeer told the captain, who communicated it to us, the legend of Peer Pointee, and the cause which obtained him his present celebrity. The particulars of the legend I have forgotten.

The fakeer assured the captain, that not only was the memory of the saint venerated by man, but that it was also held in great respect by the wild beasts of the adjoining jungles, particularly by the tigers, one of whom came regularly every Friday night, and swept up the floor of the durgah with his tail.

It happened that the day of our visit was the very one on which the tiger was wont to perform this office; Captain Belfield told the fakeer that he had a great desire to witness it, and had some intention of sitting up for the purpose. The fakeer assured him, however, that it would be utterly useless, for the animal had such an insuperable aversion for all but true believers, that, if any other were near, he would certainly not make his appearance. [40]

The next day we passed Puttergatta, a woody prominence, where there are some caves, and a pretty white Hindoo temple. I went on shore to examine them, and found Chattermohun Ghose paying his respects to a many-armed god, with goggle eyes, and a vermilion mouth, seated far back in the dim recess of a temple.

I have already hinted, that I had a regard for Chattermohun, so I thought this a favourable opportunity for converting him to Christianity, which I forthwith set myself about to achieve, breaking ground by a few pungent sneers at his idol. I found Chattermohun, however, a doughty polemic, and did not make the impression I expected.

"Master will believe what master's father and mother have teach him for true; Hindoo man do same thing. S'pose I make change, then will lose caste—no one ispek to me; this very had thing; too much for family man."

There was no making anything of him; he was obstinate, so I gave him up. I must not, however, omit one little incident, which my proselytizing efforts elicited.

"Master tell Hindoo religion got too many god—too much veneration for image. Master's Europe religion have plenty god too."

"What do you mean, you foolish fellow?" said I. "You don't know what you are talking about."

"Yes, sare, I know very well. I one Europe book got tell all about that."

To cut the matter short, Chattermohun afterwards showed me his book, which was the Roman Pantheon, with cuts representing the deities of Olympus!

Passing the two picturesque rocks of Colgong, which stand out in the river, boldly breasting its current, we in due time reached the headland of Sultangunge, opposite to which is the romantic islet of Junghera, with its white temple and curious sculptures.

Here our budgerow was boarded by two sturdy beggars, who levy contributions from all passers-by; one of whom was the Hindoo fakeer from the rock, the other his Mahomedan *vis-à-vis*, of the main land, ministers of rival creeds, but agreed on that point on which we everywhere find an astonishing unanimity, the *auri sacra fames*.

The Mahomedan fakeer was a very venerable old man, with a long beard. He was seated on a decked portion of the boat, a tiger skin spread beneath him; a disciple in very good case, rowing the boat.

"Mr. Gernon," said Miss Belfield to me, the next morning, "the scene of yesterday has induced me to try my poetic powers. Here," said she, handing me a manuscript; "I have courted the Muse with somewhat more success than you did at Plassey. Pray read this, and give me your opinion."

EVENING ON THE GANGES.

'Tis eve! by Ganges palm-clad shore
Now lightly sounds the dipping oar,
As slow it breaks with sparkling gleam
The molten silver of the stream.
And list! a song, in fitful notes,
Soft o'er the tranquil current floats,
Mingling its cadence, as it dies,
With the lone hunza's[41] mournful cries;
(Sad cries, which, wafted on the gale,
Seem like some pensive spirit's wail;)
The mûllah's[42] song, ere, toil-oppress'd,
He seeks his nook and evening rest.
Afar Junghera's rocky isle,
Crown'd by the tapering temple's pile.
On rolls the sacred tide its course
Majestic from its mountain-source,
Afar in dim and mystic glades—
Which nought save pilgrim's foot invades,
'Midst ice-bound glens, where, cold and lone,
Himaleh rears his snowy throne,
High over realms chaotic hurled,
The monarch of the mountain-world;
Whilst, far away, a sheeted throng
Of spectral peaks his state prolong;
Cold, death-like, mutes on high they stand,
Eternal nature's pageant hand.

Receiving homage as it goes,
Onward the mighty current flows,
Dispensing, as with regal hand,
Its bounteous blessings o'er the land:
Type of that power whose mercies flow

O'er all this wildering scene below.
But ah! too oft its noble tide
By horrid sacrifices dyed,
Whilst bright self-immolating pyres
Shed o'er the stream their flickering fires.
Now from cool groves, whose mellow shades
No prying ray of light invades,
The low, fond cooings of the dove
Tell 'tis the hour of peace and love;
And light-winged zephyrs gently play
O'er the Mimosa's quivering spray.
The setting sun its parting gleam
Sheds over Gunga's sacred stream,
Which seems to blush as waning light
Consigns her to the arms of night;
And many a mosque and idol-fane
Reflect the crimson hue of shame,
Which slowly seems to ebb away
The vital tide of dying day.
By yon blue mountain's brow afar
Now twinkles bright the evening star;
Translucent ray! the brightest gem
That decks its glittering diadem.

Now deeper shades invest the shore,
The weary boatman rests his oar,
Glides slowly, that his eye may seek
The shelter of some friendly creek.
Abroad the night winds freely rove,
And countless fire-flies deck the grove.
Swift-winged brilliants! gems of light!
Bright jewels of the tropic night,
Than which the diamond of the mine
In richer lustre ne'er could shine!
Now sparkling forth from nook and bay,
Long-scattered fires succeed the day,
And round them gathering, to their meal,
The dusky forms of boatmen steal,
Like wizard, demons of the wold,
Who round a pile their orgies hold,
Framing, on Scandinavian fell,

Some direful charm or potent spell.
The simple meal despatched, the song
And merry drum the joy prolong;
Or some light jocund tale gives birth
To honest bursts of simple mirth.
At length, the song and story past,
Silence profound succeeds at last,
By every sound unbroken, save
The turtle's splash or rippling wave.
Thus by life's woes and cares opprest,
The weary spirit sinks to rest,
And ebon pall and marble tomb
Invest the closing scene with gloom.
But cease not thus—in sombre guise.
As o'er that darkling stream
Another sun shall haply rise,
To cheer it with its beam.
So, on the soul, its chast'ning o'er,
Shall burst eternal light—
The light that gilds that happy shore.
Whose day shall know no night.

A few days more brought us to Boglipore, a very beautiful station, surrounded by rich park-like scenery.

Having visited the boiling spring of Seetacoond, to which a plentiful crop of legends is attached by the credulous natives, filled a few bottles with the water, which is remarkable for its purity, and I believe medicinal virtues (though, as I was not much of a water-fancier at that time, I rather give this on report than from actual experience), we soon reached the ancient fortress of Monghyr, a place which cuts a considerable figure in Indian history, although more celebrated in modern times as the seat of an extensive manufactory of tea-kettles, turn-screws, toasting-forks, &c., as also of fire-arms, after European models.

These guns have occasionally winged a few griffs, and have consequently a bad name, though the vendors are willing to prove them in your presence. Nevertheless, though dirt-cheap, they are not often bought, except by the very green. There is no enjoyment in a suspected gun, any more than in a doubtful egg.

On bringing to at the ghaut, we perceived a regiment of chapmen, all eager to present their wares. One fellow carried a huge tea-kettle, another a double-barrelled gun, a third a chafing-dish and a handful of toasting-forks, a fourth a cage of beautiful green and blue birds from the hills, &c.

With these gentry I drove several bargains, assisted by Ramdial, who afterwards had to fight a few stout battles on his own account for *dustoorie*, or customary perquisites, claimed, though unwillingly allowed, on all disbursements in India.

A rare stock of valuables I had on leaving Monghyr, including three cages of birds, one of avidavats, all swept off, some time after, by a terrible epidemic, which found its way amongst them.

Here I observed, for the first time, a peculiar mode of capturing the river turtle; several natives paddled a light dingy or canoe along, one standing in the prow, with a light dart or harpoon in his hand; presently I saw a huge turtle raise his head above the water, and in an instant the harpooner flung his light weapon, having a cord attached, which reached its object with an unerring aim; all was now bustle, and in a few minutes I saw them haul in a turtle, which, as far as looks went, might have made an alderman's mouth water.

As I am on the subject of harpooning, I may here mention a somewhat similar mode in which the natives catch the mullets. These fish, the most delicious and highly prized of the Ganges, swim in shoals in the shallows, with their heads partly above the surface of the water: the shape of which, by the way, and position of the large eyes, give them much the appearance of serpents—indeed, the first I saw, I took for a brood of water-snakes.

The dandie, or fisherman, whoever the sportsman may be, follows them in a crouching attitude, having in his hand a long light bamboo, terminating in a number of unbarbed spikes, fastened on like the head of a painting brush; and when within striking distance, he launches this slantingly amongst the shoal, transfixing one or two fish, perhaps, whilst the rest dive or swim off, and soon re-appear with their heads as before, above the water, and slowly stemming the current. I used to watch this operation with great interest, but could never make anything of it myself, though I often essayed.

The fort of Monghyr is of vast extent, though the walls are now in a decayed and dilapidated state; within the wide area are tanks, bungalows, and some fine houses on rising grounds, commanding fine views of the ruins, and the distant woods and hills, which latter here present a rather bold and serrated outline.

A few days more, and we were gliding past the great Mahomedan city of Patna, and in a short time after we found ourselves moored off the military cantonment of Dinapore—a second edition of Burhampore—and the station of a brigade of troops, European and native.

Here are two fine squares of officers' quarters and barracks, with numerous bungalows to the rear of them, somewhat similar in their disposition and appearance to those at Burhampore.

Here, as I before mentioned, I was destined to part with my kind and amiable companions, who were engaged to visit a friend at Patna for a month before proceeding to their ultimate destination. Our leave-taking was marked by unequivocal proofs that we had become dear to one another; and both gave me little tokens of their remembrance.

CHAPTER XXII

On the evening of my arrival at Dinapore, I was sitting on the roof of my boat, observing the *dobees*, or washermen, thumping their clothes, natives cleaning their teeth with primitive tooth-brushes of stick, and other similar sights which diversify the animating scene of an Indian ghaut, when the distant and inspiring strains of a full military band broke upon my ear. "Egad!" thought I, "there's some fun going on; a promenade, no doubt, with all the beauty and fashion of Dinapore assembled; I'll go and see."

I ordered Ramdial to bring out the *jubba walla coortie* (the laced jacket), which had never yet graced my person in any public assembly. A splendid thing it was, with a huge silver epaulet, and "tastily turned up with a brimstone-coloured lapelle;" I thought there could hardly be its fellow in all Dinapore. A neat white waistcoat, crimson sash (tied in a *dégagé* knot under the fifth rib), coatee over all, hat a shade on one side, and flourishing a clean bandanna in my hand, with a sprinkling of lavender upon it, *me voilà*, an ensign of the first water.

I soon reached the scene of attraction in the principal square, and a lively scene it was. There were congregated groups of officers, chatting and laughing around belles seated in tonjons; others, three or four abreast, promenading backwards and forwards, hands behind them, and examining the structure of their legs; gigs and carriages drawn up, their occupants attentively listening; syces walking their masters' chargers up and down; chuprassies, silver-stick men, and other native servants, mingled with the throng of sepoy orderlies and European soldiers in undress.

I mingled with the crowd, and promenaded too; but, alas! I knew no one; and who so solitary as he who, amongst a crowd, experiences the sickening reflection that there is no one of the many assembled with whom he holds the slightest community of thought or feeling!

The shades of evening were deepening—the assembly thinning—the *finale*, "God save the King," was playing—busy memory had awakened thoughts of those who did regard me, far, far away—and I was waxing thoughtful and sad, when I suddenly heard the sound of a familiar voice.

I turned, and recognized in the speaker my shipmate and brother-cadet, honest Grundy. I sprang forward to address him.

God knows—for it is hard to answer for that fickle and selfish thing, the human heart, which has rarely the courage to brave the "world's dread laugh," and follow its own more generous dictates—whether I should always have done it with equal promptitude, for Grundy, in a mere fashionable sense, was not an acquaintance to be proud of; but now I stood in need of sympathy, and there are seasons when anything in the shape of a friend is acceptable—when we are not fastidious, and are overjoyed to exchange greetings with aught in the shape of humanity.

"Grundy, my boy," said I, facing him, "don't you know me?"

Grundy stared vacantly for a moment, for I was considerably metamorphosed by my new habiliments; but soon recognizing me, his features relaxed into an expression of good-humoured delight.

"Odds life, Gernon! is that you, man?" said he, grasping my hand; "why whaur the dickens are you from?"

I soon satisfied him, and he told me he was now doing duty with a regiment at Dinapore, and lived in a bungalow not very far off.

"Are you alone, Grundy?" said I.

"Alone!" replied my friend with a sigh; "oh, no; there are six of us in the bungalow—Griff Hall, as they call it—all young hands, none of us a year in the country, and a tearing life we lead; it does not suit me at all, though, and I mean to leave them as soon as I can get another place and a quiet man to chum with."

"Yes, I know your pacific habits, Grundy, and wonder how you got amongst such a set; who and what are they?"

"Why, there's first, Mr. McScreechum, an assistant surgeon; three infantry ensigns, besides myself, and a Lieut. Fireworker,[43] of artillery. I think they are all mad, particularly the doctor, for such a man for mischief I never met with in all my born days. But, Gernon, lad, I hope you will stay for a day or two, at least," said he, slapping me on the shoulder; "for it glads my heart to see you again, man."

I accepted Grundy's invitation, and we proceeded to Griff Hall.

We found the doctor, with two or three others, on the *chabootra*, or terrace, of the bungalow, all laughing and joking. The former, a huge fellow, six feet two, with a freckled face and a carroty poll, in the act of compounding a glass of brandy-and-water. Grundy presented me as his friend on the way to join my regiment.

"Glod to see ye, sir; glod to see ye," said the doctor, presenting me his shoulder-of-mutton hand; "we'll use you weel at Griff Hall, sir, and eeneetiate ye intoo oor Eleuseenian mesteries. What's for dinner, Larking?" said he, turning to a slender, pale youth, in a red camlet raggie; "what have ye got for a treat to-night? Nae mair of your d——d skeenny kid and tough goat mutton I hope. Ah! ye'r a braw chiel to cater for a gentleman's mess."

"I'll resign my post to you with pleasure, doctor, if not satisfied with my proceedings," replied the caterer; "but I think things will be better to-day, for I have given Rumjohn a good trouncing for palming that stuff upon us yesterday. I'll tell you what there is, doctor, by-the-bye, a capital rooee muchee,[44] for I secured it myself this morning."

"Weell," said the doctor, "a rooee muchee's nae bad thing, if it's frash."

At this moment, three more ensigns, inmates of Griff Hall, hove in sight, rattling up on tattooes, or galloways—tits combining some pleasant varieties of fiddle-head, goose-rump, swish-tail, &c.

In India, every one (*i.e.*, European officer) must keep a piece of horse-flesh of some sort or other, though it must be allowed that griffins, for obvious reasons, were never remarkable for possessing superior studs. As the new-comers approached, full canter and shuffle, the doctor put forth a screech, compounded of an Indian war-whoop and a view halloo, by way of welcome: the fun was evidently beginning.

One of the ensigns on the terrace jumped down into the road, took his hat off his head, whirled it round, and hooted loudly, to make his friends' horses bolt or shy. The doctor, too, seizing a sort of long besom which stood in an angle of the bungalow wall, darted forward with it to aid in putting the detachment to the rout.

"Doctor, what the deuce are you about, man?" shouted the immediate object of his attack; "don't be so infernally ridiculous."

"Stir him oop with the lang pole," roared the doctor, nothing daunted; "stir oop the bombardier's wonderful animal."

And so saying, he poked the besom under the tail of the tattoo, who resented this rear attack by launching out his heels, jerked off the Lieut. Fireworker's cap, and finally bolted, with his rider half-unseated, across the compound, amidst the shouts and laughter of his comrades, the doctor, with his wild red locks flying, and his feet in slippers, pursuing him with his besom at the *pas de charge.*

McScreechum soon returned, puffing and blowing, and flourishing his besom, and the Lieut. Fireworker shortly after joined the group, having disposed of his runaway Bucephalus, but with a countenance darkly portentous of mischief.

"Dr. McScreechum," said he, "I'll thank you, sir, not to take such liberties with me in future, for I will not put up with them."

"Stir him oop with the lang pole," said the doctor, still flourishing his besom.

"Others may submit to them, but I will not."

"Stir him oop with the lang pole," again replied McScreechum.

All joined the medico in rallying the indignant lieutenant out of his wrath. The good-humoured Scotchman brewed and presented him a glass of grog, to allay the fury of "the black dog," as he termed it.

"A soft answer turneth away wrath," saith the proverb, and on the same principle, even a practical joke, though ever to be avoided, may be so softened by a little tact as to allay the anger which, in nine cases out of ten, it is sure to excite.

All these wild doings at an end, and matters properly composed, we adjourned to the dining-room, being summoned by a rather dingy-looking butler, or khanseman, very much resembling the worthy who has been recorded in these pages as having so suddenly decamped with my plate-chest.

Six wall-shades with oil glasses, a long table occupying the centre of the room, and about as many chairs as guests, constituted the sum total of the furniture.

In accordance with the almost universal custom of the military circles in India, camp fashion was the order of the day—that is, each gentleman had his own plates, knives and forks, and glasses, with a brace of muffineers, containing pepper and salt, flanking the same; these last, of every variety of size and shape, of glass, silver, or pewter, with a corresponding variety of patterns in the cutlery and plates, constituted as motley a show as can well be imagined.

The servants, too, were of the Rum-Johnny order—a dissolute, dirty set of Mahomedans, whom I have before described—those usually picked up by young officers on account of their speaking the English language, a qualification which is pretty certain to insure their rejection by old Indians. The dingy attire and roguish looks of these fellows harmonized well with the style of the entertainment.

The doctor took the head of the table; the noble fraternity of Griff Hall and their guests were soon seated. The khanseman-jee appeared, staggering under a huge dish, which he deposited at the head of the table; having done so, he lifted up the cover with the air of a major-domo, and there smoked the rooee muchee already mentioned.

"Wha's for fesh?" asked the doctor, plying the fish-knife with the vigour of an Irish bricklayer when handling his trowel. "Wha's for fesh? Here's a bonnie fellow; 'a sight like this is gude for sair een,' as my old father, the provost, used to say."

The rooee muchee was in great request, and other viands followed, all very good of their kind, I thought, and proving the efficacy of the rattan in some cases. Great was the talking and laughing, and the dinner sped merrily. Never has it been my lot to encounter a more light-hearted, thoughtless, and jovial set of fellows than the inmates of Griff Hall.

The cloth removed, hookhas bubbled; the bottle passed freely, and the conversation became animated; among other things, the scenes and flirtations at the band that evening were passed in review.

"Who noticed Miss Simper, the new spin, talking to that old fellow, MacGlashum?" said Ensign O'Toole, a young Hibernian; "sure I hope she's not going to take that broken-winded old fellow."

"By my saul, I don't know," replied Ensign MacClaymore; "but I think if she gets a major, and a gude Scotchman to boot, she could na do better."

"Faith, I think she'd find an Irishman suit her better than an old or a young Scotchman aither: oh, an Irishman's heart for the ladies!"

"Meaning yourself, I suppose," retorted the Highlander, dryly; "you Paddies think there's nought like yeer'sels in the world."

"Faith, now, I don't think we've half the consait of your Scotchmen, at all," replied O'Toole, "though a grate dale more to be proud of. Where will you find janius like that which auld Ireland has produced—such poets, statesmen, and haroes?"

"Proud!" said the other contemptuously; "hooever may fall short in those respects, thank Gude, auld Scotland was never conquered,—never conquered, sir, as some other countries have been."

"I'll tell you the reason," said the other bitterly; "the poor beggarly country was never worth the trouble and expense of conquering."

"Eh! sir," said the young Caledonian, his eyes flashing fire, "what's that you say, sir? I'll no sit here and listen to that. What do you mean, sir?"

"Mean!" retorted the other, sternly, "just what I've said, Ensign MacClaymore, and so just make your most of it; if you've more to add, let it be outside."

Several attempts were made to check this angry dialogue, but in vain. All was now confusion; the angry patriots half arose, and darted fierce looks at each other across the table, their more peacefully disposed neighbours endeavouring to quiet and retain them in their seats. Things were fast verging towards "war, horrid war."

Dr. McScreechum now arose, like Satan in Pandemonium, thumped the table to engage attention, and with the voice of a Stentor, proclaimed silence, and called the belligerents to order.

"Gentlemen," said the doctor, "silence if you please, and listen to me. I am the moderator of this assembly, and by vairtue of the pooers confided to me, I proclaim *pax*. I'll have na quarrelling here; doun wi' your foolish naytionalities; aren't we all kintramen and brithers, as my gude old father, the provost, used to say? You, Donald MacClaymore, and you, Denis O'Toole, I'll fine you each a dozen of claret, and proclaim you baith ootlaws of Griff Hall, unless you shak hands, like sensible fellows; shak hands, ye fire-eating donnard deevils ye, and then I'll gee ye a sang. 'Auld lang syne, my dear, for a' lang syne.' Wha's for a sang?" This seasonable interruption, in the doctors peculiar way, turned the tide of war. A furious drumming on the table followed; glasses danced and jingled, and "Auld lang syne for ever!" resounded through the hall. MacClaymore and O'Toole caught the spirit of the movement, shook hands across the table, and the glorious Scottish air broke forth splendidly, like an elegy over buried animosities.

The doctor, half-seas-over, was now completely in his element; his huge red head rolled from side to side, and one eye, half shut, leered with Bacchanalian philanthropy around the table.

Thus he stood, his arms crossed, and holding the hand of each of his right and left neighbours, as he worked them up and down with a force and energy proportioned to the varying sentiments of that celebrated ditty, which has to answer for being the proximate cause of more boozing and maudlin sentimentality than any ever written; for oh, that potent collocation of words, "for auld lang syne," goes direct to the exile's heart, particularly when softened by the genial glass; touches its tenderest chords, and awakens, like the "Ranz de vaches," the sweetest and most soul-subduing reminiscences of youth, and all its never-to-be-forgotten associations.

After this bout, anchovy toasts and broiled bones were put in requisition, Ensign O'Toole insisted upon mulling a saucepanful of port, to keep the beer and claret warm. At length, some fell asleep in their chairs; others, including Grundy and myself, dropped off to bed, though abused by the peep-o'-day boys for our recreant qualities.

Away we went, heartily tired, leaving a few choice spirits to keep it up, the doctor talking in thick and almost inarticulate tone about "Sheshero's Epeestles to Hatticus."

"You may well be tired of such a life as this," said I, next morning; "it would kill me in a week; how do you stand it?"

"Why," replied Grundy, "I keep as clear of it as I can; besides, it is not very often that we have quite such a jollification as we had last night; however, the eternal racket we have does not suit me, and I shall cut it as soon as I can; it goes against my conscience, too, to witness some of the tricks they play upon one another. One day they hanged one of the lads for fun by the punkah rope till he was black in the face; and about a month ago sent a sub., a poor soft fellow, a voyage on the Ganges in an open boat; and as he did not return for a week, it was a mercy he was not starved or drowned."

"How was this, Grundy?" said I.

"Why, the doctor and the lads were always poking fun at him, and making him a *boot* (butt). One night, something such another as last, they made him believe he had been insoolted, and must fight. Sawney said he would rather take an apology, but they told him it was quite impossible that the affront could ever be washed out but with the blood of one of them. They said it must be settled immediately, and went out with lanterns to the back of the bungalow. The unfortunate lad was in a dreadful fright, but they made him fire; the pistols were loaded with powder only, but his antagonist fell; they said he had killed his man, and must fly immediately, or, if he fell into the hands of the civil power, he would inevitably be hanged. They hurried the poor young fellow off the ghaut, put him on board a fishing-canoe, telling him to row for his life till he came to some station, one hundred miles or so down the river, where he would have a better chance of a fair trial, and must give himself up. It was about a week before he was brought back to cantonments, burnt as black as a tinker. There was a terrible kick-up about it, and well there might be, for 'twas a cruel joke. The doctor and all the parties concerned were threatened with a court-martial; but, somehow or other, it all blew over."

Pranks such as these are now, I believe, happily rare in India, as everywhere else; but those who remember the country twenty or thirty years ago will doubtless be able to recall many such manifestations of boyish folly.

It is not desirable that youth should be converted prematurely into thoughtful philosophy; care, in the ordinary course of things, will come, soon enough, and need not be hastened; but I am an advocate for its buoyancies being restrained within moderate bounds, that with it fun should not be allowed to degenerate into mischief or cruelty, wit in vulgarity, and friendly intimacy into coarse familiarity and practical joking.

We breakfasted very late, and the tenants of Griff Hall dropped in one by one *en déshabille*, evincing painful symptoms of the previous night's debauch—red eyes, trembling hand, and glued lips. One took a dose of seidlitz, another five grains of calomel, and as for appetite, there was none.

These are a few of the early effects of intemperance; its ultimate consequences are not so briefly described.

I remained but one day more at Dinapore, which was partly devoted to reporting my arrival, *en route* to join—a measure enjoined on all military voyagers, but not always attended to. I also saw the troops, European and native, at brigade exercise, &c.; and in the evening witnessed a tattoo race—officers riding their own ponies. This was a very comical affair.

It was a little before sunset when Grundy, the Lieutenant Fireworker (who had entered his pony), and I, walked down to the course, which is situated a little behind the cantonment, being separated from it by a dry nullah,[45] over which there are one or two bridges.

We found a great number of the inhabitants of the cantonment—some in gigs, some on horseback, and others on foot—assembled to witness the sport.

There was a good show of ponies, some of them certainly "rum'uns" to look at, but, as was fully proved in the sequel, "devils to go." Long tails and swish tails, stumps, crops, and wall-eyes were there in perfection. The young officers who were to ride them, amongst whom I recognized more than one of the inmates of Griff Hall, marched about in their top boots and velvet hunting-caps, cracking their whips with countenances expressive of the full sense they entertained of the awful contest in which they were about to be engaged.

Some, too, tightened their ponies' girths; others passed their hands down their fore-legs, as if to rub out the knots and clean the back sinews; some put their arms lovingly round their animals' necks, or gratified their love of tormenting by pinching the flanks of their steeds, and enjoying their abortive attempts to bite.

Amongst this throng was a very remarkable character, well known at Dinapore, the clerk of the course, or whatever other name properly appertains to the master of the ceremonies on such occasions. He was a little, old, sun-dried, invalid sergeant, of a meagre form, but most determined spirit. I was greatly amused by the consequential air of the diminutive old fellow, as he stumped about in a rusty hunting-cap, cracking a tremendous whip, and clearing the environs of dogs, boys, and all other interlopers.

The time for the race having arrived, the young men mounted, some in red jackets, some in white, and others in full jockey attire. The clerk of the course ranged them all in proper order; eagerness was in every eye as they bent forward, impatient for the word. Ladies stood up in carriages, and many a neck was outstretched to catch a glimpse of the start: when at last a thundering "Ready," "Off," from the little mummified sergeant, and away flew the tattoos, "Punch," "Cocktail," and "Mat-o'-the-Mint," and many a nameless steed besides. Such digging, spurring, and straining; such crossing and jostling as was there! one pushing ahead for a space, and then another passing him, and so on!

When the whole troop had got about half-way round (it was a sweepstakes, round the course), the leading pony bolted, and was followed by all the rest, entering the gates leading to a bungalow, the first of a series there commencing; there they very deliberately drew up, where doubtless they had often drawn up before, when carrying their masters on their rounds of morning visits.

Intense were the roars of laughter which issued from the spectators assembled, occasioned by this little episode. Haul, dig, pound, and spur, and they were again placed, and off—but ah! the unlucky fates! the meridian of another bungalow entrance no sooner reached, than away with them again, follow my leader, like a flock of sheep through a gap, or a string of wild geese.

I thought verily I should have died outright, and as for honest Grundy, and many of my neighbours, they stamped and roared till the tears ran down their cheeks.

All this time we could see, though the distance was considerable, that the jockeys were hard at work, getting their tattoos once more under weigh through the opposite segment of road leading from the attractive bungalow, the other horn, as it might have been termed, of the dilemma.

The course regained, away they went once more: the struggle was becoming warm; they had turned the curve, and were in a line with the winning-post; bettors were now on the *qui vive*—"ten to one on Cocktail"— the little sergeant squatting bands on knees, taking a judgmatical observation, when lo! no sooner had they reached a certain bridge before mentioned, leading in a rectangular direction to cantonments, than away they sidled, and at last one and all made a fair bolt of it, right before the wind, for "home, sweet home."

"Zounds!" said the sergeant, "if they bea'nt all off agin, I'm a Dutchman."

And off sure enough they were, amidst renewed peals of laughter. I doubt if any race ever produced half the amusement. "They are gone, they are gone, and never will return."

This was literally the case with some; but several of the heavy sailers managed to tack, and came in amidst the half-mad shouts of unexpected winners, proving truly that "the race is not always to the swift," and that the best-founded expectations may be unexpectedly disappointed.

Two or three races on a smaller scale followed; but all was flat after the *unique* scamper I have attempted to describe; pleasure and excitement had expended themselves, and were not to be renewed immediately. Under these circumstances, Grundy and I bent our steps towards the band, accompanied by the young artillery officer, who, having proved the winner, was in high spirits.

Our dinner this evening passed off far more soberly than that of the preceding one. The doctor was evidently suffering from a reaction of the vital spirits, and on more than one occasion seemed disposed, like a certain old gentleman when he was sick, to be religious and sentimental. After a bottle or two of Hodgson, however, and a due proportion of claret, he rallied, and proposed a round game at loo, as a mode of passing the evening, which was joyfully assented to by the whole party.

The tables were consequently cleared, wine-glasses, &c., were placed on teapoys and side-tables, and to work we all proceeded, keeping it up till two in the morning, when I retired *minus* a very considerable pinch of General Capsicums "snuff," with a firm determination to cut cards from that time for evermore: a resolution which I religiously kept—till the next time temptation came in my way.

At the time to which my Memoirs refer—and I am not aware that any material change has since taken place—gambling was unfortunately too prevalent in India. I have known nearly the whole of a small station, ladies inclusive, keep it up for weeks, alternately at each other's houses, rarely missing a day.

The party would assemble after breakfast, and having distributed fish, and set pen and ink to write I O U's, would commence business in good earnest. Tiffin would constitute a break, and after being rather impatiently despatched, operations would be resumed, and continued till time for the evening's drive. After this, and dinner over, another round of this absorbing amusement would close the day.

What a world of bad feeling in men, of keenness and unfeminine cupidity in women, have I seen elicited on those occasions, and what studies for the curious in physiognomy; what expressions of various kinds have I observed in the faces of the party, when the hour drew near for inditing I O U's and settling the accounts of Dr. and Cr.; what earnest pleadings for another round on the part of the losers, and conscientiously-expressed determinations to retire to rest on the part of the winners!

Cards and dice are pests, the offspring of idleness, and the parents of vice and crime. They are the concomitants of semi-barbarism, and their gradual disappearance is one of the indices of advancing civilization and mental improvement. I began to think this one night after losing Rs. 1,100 at hazard and double-or-quits, and the impression has continued to gain strength ever since.

Next morning, after breakfast, I bade adieu to Griff Hall and honest Grundy; had my hand almost squeezed to a jelly by the good-natured son of the provost, and, repairing on board my bolio, was soon once more under weigh for the "far west."

Very different, however, were the feelings which now attended my onward progression. I had lost my kind and pleasant Mentor, Captain Belfield, and his amiable maiden sister. There were no more social rambles, no more agreeable disquisitions, no more tours in search of the picturesque, no more chess.

I felt how insufficient my own thoughts were to supply the *hiatus* caused by their absence, and mentally ejaculated, as I occupied my lonely cabin at night, with poor Alexander Selkirk,

> "Oh, solitude, where are the charms
> That sages have seen in thy face?"

I cannot quit the subject of my two friends without saying a few more words regarding them. I have already stated briefly that Captain Belfield and his sister afforded a fine example of that tender attachment—that perfect love and affection which should ever subsist between persons so nearly connected. They truly lived for each other, and the imparting of mutual pleasure seemed to constitute one of the highest gratifications of their lives. It was quite refreshing to observe the warmth and cordiality with which they met in the morning, as she, the picture of neatness and refined simplicity—the very beau ideal of the real English gentlewoman— stepped from the sleeping apartment of the budgerow, whilst he, closing his ponderous Sanscrit or Persian folio, and laying it on the breakfast-table, would rise with extended hand and a cheerful smile to greet her. Then at night, too, after the short but fervent prayer to the Father of all, which the captain himself would offer up extempore, how attentively would he light her taper, and then with a tender salute commend her to her chamber and repose.

If two or three can love in this way, I have since sometimes thought, why not all the world? but all the world, my good griffin, are not brothers and sisters. True, true; I had forgotten that. The more, alas! the pity.

Though, however, the hearts of the pair were thus united, there was not an equal accordance in all their sentiments and opinions. This, however, though productive of numerous discussions, never led to acrimonious disputes. They agreed to disagree. Nature had cast the brother and sister in the same mental mould, to borrow a phrenological term (which I do with respect); the organization was equal. The same fine sense and kindliness of disposition in both; but circumstances had favoured in different degrees the development of their respective qualities. Benevolence, veneration, and ideality must have been large in both, though the captain had evidently been at pains to curb the vagaries of the latter. He had left his home a mere boy, with his mind almost a blank sheet, on which anything might have been inscribed. Whilst others his contemporaries plunged into idleness and dissipation, he, by some chance, flew to the solace of books. In them he studied that mystery of mysteries—man, comparing, as life advanced, the living manifestations of his character with all that he found recorded of his acts; he perused the works of historians, theologians, and metaphysicians, on all sides of all questions; and arrived at one grand conclusion, which is, that truth is a very hard thing to get at, and, like the ideal good of Goldsmith's Traveller, "allures from far, and as we follow, flies." He certainly sought it ardently, though he could not felicitate himself, he said, exactly in having yet found the "true truth." A self-taught genius, who thought vigorously, and expressed himself strongly, he was, no doubt, somewhat of an Utopian; at least such I know Captain Marpeet thought him.

Miss Belfield had been reared in the elegant seclusion, but subject to the somewhat contracting influences of an English country life (nature, if I may so express it, seems to have intended nations as well as individuals to be gregarious), enjoying in her father's pretty vicarage her pets, her flowers, and the agreeable and polished society of the superior gentry of the vicinity. In the neighbouring village she dispensed her little charities, assuaged the sorrows of the poor and needy, and did all the good she could in her limited sphere; but of the sufferings of the world on a grand scale she knew not much, and as little understood, perhaps, their real causes and remedies.

High as were her qualities of heart and intellect—and admirably would she write and speak on all matters on which she allowed them free scope—she was not (and who is?) without a defect; hers was one frequently to be met with amongst the most amiable and estimable of our countrywomen, a gentle intolerance and quiet assumption of infallibility on those subjects on which a very little reading and reflection ought, perhaps, to convince us that we should hold our opinions with the most trembling diffidence—I mean religion, and other kindred subjects relating to the powers and duties of mind, and the great interests of society, but particularly the former. This would evince itself in the expression of extreme pity and commiseration for the obstinacy or delusion of those who conscientiously differed from her in such matters, she, by her manner, never seeming to entertain the smallest shade of suspicion that she herself might be in error. This spirit, partially veiled by the graces of her manner, the kindness of her heart, and the evident rectitude of her intentions, did not look so ill as the ugly monster intolerance generally does; still it was her dark side, and but ill accorded with the general good sense by which she was characterized; her reading on these points had been as exclusive as her brother's had been general.

Equally holding to certain fundamental points, they were both anxious to regenerate mankind, but were widely opposed in respect to the means to be employed for that purpose. The captain looked primarily to schools, lectures, locomotion, and the wide diffusion of commerce and intelligence, and thought if man fell by eating of the tree of knowledge, he figuratively was destined to rise by a repetition of the act. Miss Belfield principally relied on the multiplication of churches and Sunday-schools, the extension of missionary labours, the early conversion of the Jews, and the like. He thought that religion was the first subject to which an instructed mind would direct its attention. Miss Belfield, on the contrary, considered it the very last on which, if not forced upon him, he would seek to be informed. She considered man as radically vicious, that suffering was necessary to try him, and that it was perhaps better to preach resignation to evils, than to waste time in vain attempts to diminish them materially. Her brother differed, too, in this, and thought that happiness was quite as well calculated to fit us for heaven as misery; and that it was almost a libel on the Deity to suppose that the thanks and praises of a rejoicing heart would not be as acceptable as those emanating from one bowed down by sorrow and suffering. He thought that the evils inseparably annexed to our condition, such as death, sickness, and the loss of those tenderly beloved, were trials sufficient, without our unnecessarily increasing the load by fictitious ones—clearly the result of our follies, contentions, and prejudices.

He used to compare society, as at present constituted, to a body of undisciplined troops, composed of jarring detachments, under incompetent leaders, and amongst whom the finest military qualities and powers are neutralized or impaired by want of concert and organization.

"Educate your masses," he would say, "for without you do that no conceivable form of government will produce happiness to the governed. Construct the finest piece of mechanism you may, on the strictest principles of art, if the material is rotten and unsound, it must give at some point—the due antagonism of its springs will be destroyed, and it will not work."

This diversity of views, which I have endeavoured to describe, used to give rise, as I have already stated, to numerous animated discussions.

I used to listen to these collisions of intellect, during the evenings we passed together, with much interest; and when I could see my way through the *pros* and *cons*, was wont sometimes to venture an opinion, to which the captain and his sister always listened with eagerness, as if anxious to know how the matter would strike on my young and unsophisticated mind.

Some of these discussions, that is, the substance of them, I still remember, and had I space, and were this the place for them, I might here be tempted to record.

Lest my reader may be inclined to think otherwise, I must here state, in justice to the good captain, now no more, that he was no leveller; he considered perfect equality as impracticable as to construct a perfect column without a base and a capital, and that the fabric of society must ever fine away to a point, but that instead of being, as at present, founded, in great part, on misery, prejudice, indigence, and ignorance, it might be made to rest on the solid basis of virtue and happiness.

His grand axiom was—and he used frequently to repeat it to his sister— "If by reading, observation, and reflection, I have learnt anything respecting my fellow-creatures, it is this: that eight-tenths of their sufferings have been and are entirely of their own creation, and that it is within the powers of the human mind to diminish the amount of moral and physical evil to an incalculable extent. The upper classes appear to govern the world, but in reality it is the ignorance and prejudice of the 'tyrant majority' which rule it. In these, the more educated find what physically Archimedes sought—the fulcrum to move the world: the head is the governing part of the body, but we all know how a disordered stomach will affect it."

I had but little more intercourse with the good captain and his sister during my stay in India, though we met now and then, and maintained an occasional correspondence. He, poor fellow, was never destined to revisit his native land, for after saving a small competence, and just as he was preparing to return, death, by one of its most appalling agents—cholera—lodged a detainer against him, and instead of enjoying the easy evening of life he had fondly anticipated amongst the scenes of his boyhood, he was destined to fill a cold tenement, six feet by two, in St. John's churchyard, Calcutta.

'Tis not for me to describe Miss Belfield's feelings on this occasion; indeed, who can describe the anguish of heart, the utter desolation, which the loss of a brother or a sister, endeared by union of sentiment and every tender association of youth, necessarily occasions? I learnt that she almost sunk under the blow; and a few, very few lines, which she wrote me shortly after, told forcibly the extent of her sorrows, and indicated the gratifying fact that she considered I had a right to participate in them.

Well, years rolled away. I returned home, with a broken constitution, and a *lack* of rupees, in the English sense of the term;[46] and some time after that event received the following letter:—

"Swines-Norton, June 10th, 18—.

"My dear Captain Gernon,

"I have for some time been aware of your return to your native land, having heard of you from mutual friends. Pray, when your avocations will allow of your leaving London, endeavour to visit my retirement. I have a small room in my cottage at your service, and shall enjoy great pleasure, in some respects a sorrowful one, in meeting you again, and in reviving old recollections of those days when first we became acquainted. I will reserve all further communications till we meet; in the meantime am,

"My dear Captain Gernon,

"Yours most truly,

"A. Belfield."

"To Brev. Capt. Gernon,

"5, Peppercorn-buildings,

"Pimlico."

I was not long in finding out Miss Belfield's retreat. The Highflyer coach dropped me at the Bull, a foaming, rampant fellow, the only thing evincing any signs of life and animation in the small sleepy village of Swines-Norton, in ——shire. A few smock-frocked clowns, a bandy-legged ostler, and a recruiting-sergeant, who seemed wofully out of his element, loitered in front of the little inn as I descended.

"What luggage had you, sir?"

"Nothing but a small carpet-bag."

"Come, Bill, bear a hand, and get the gentleman's bag out of the hind boot."

The bandy-legged ostler soon disengaged my property; the spruce bluff coachman clutched his reins and cracked his whip, and made the over-frisky off-leader dance a saraband.

"Has Davy brought up that there black mare?" said the landlord, sauntering out with his pipe and tankard of half-and-half.

"Yes; he's down there along o' Tom at the Blackbird."

All right—crack—whisp—a nod to the pretty chambermaid at the window—ya-hip! and away bowled the Highflyer, leaving me "alone in my glory," saving and except the drowsy specimens of humanity afore-mentioned.

"Can you tell me where a lady named Miss Belfield resides?"

"Miss Bulfield—Miss Bulfield—be that she, Jem, as lives furder end o' Tinker-pot-lane?"

"The lady, I mean," said I, "returned from India some years ago, and resides in something cottage, but I have forgotten the name."

"All right, sir, that's she—now you mentions the Heast Hinjies. I knows she've a-got a parrotkeet—jist go on to the church, and then turn to your right hand, and keep straight on as ever you can go 'til you comes to a lane; when you be at the top o' that, get over the stile and go across the footpath till you comes to the furder end o' the field, and then anybody'll tell you where Myrtle Cottage is."

"Thank you, my man," said I.

And I forthwith set out on my voyage of discovery. It was a sweet summer's evening, glorious, tranquil, sad. I heard with delight the cuckoo's voice, the tinkle of the sheep-bell, and the cry of the jackdaws, as they sported about the burnished vane of the old weather-stained steeple. I was in no hurry, but loitered in the quiet village churchyard, where naught was moving save some two or three little ragged sheep; and oh! who could describe the sensations, the sadly pleasing, confused, but undefinable sensations, which crowded upon me during the little half-hour that I spent there?

Seated on an old grey tombstone, alone, and looking up at that rustic monitor, the village clock—whilst the soft summer air played on my face, and soothing rural sounds fell on my ear—the events of my past life, the images of friends departed—all I had done and left undone—passed like visions—dissolving views—before me. Brother Indians, try sometimes, after your period of toil is o'er, the effect of a summer's musing in a rural churchyard—'twill calm the perturbation of your spirits, place things in their true lights before you, and act as oil on troubled waters. But, to be brief, I found Miss Belfield's cottage—neat, modest, elegant, and retiring, just as I remembered herself. The parrot screamed in the little hall, and a very antiquated dowager of a spaniel, with an opaque eye, emitted a husky bark as I entered.

"Be pleased to take a seat, sir," said the tidiest and modestest of little maids, "and my mistress will be with you immediately."

I took a seat—my spirits were in a flutter, almost bordering on pain. The door opened, and the hand of Miss Belfield was locked in mine. We both started a little.

"Most truly glad to see you," said she, with deep emphasis, her eyes full of tears. I placed my other hand over the one of hers which I held in my grasp, and answered her by a soft and earnest pressure, which told how deeply I reciprocated the feeling.

"Well," said she, smiling, after a pause, "I suppose we must not compliment each other on looks, for I am almost afraid to think how long it is since we parted—but I hope our mutual regard has not suffered by the lapse of time."

I assured her that my respect and esteem for her were as fresh as ever. Years and ill-health had given me a slight curve in the shoulders. The freshness of my complexion had long been converted into a delicate yellow; my hair was grey beyond the power of Macassar oil to restore, and crows' feet had dug their ineffaceable marks at the angles and corners of my face.

Miss Belfield's eyes I once or twice caught resting on me, as if involuntarily—for she instantly averted them on their encountering mine. She was doubtless comparing me to my former self—and exclaiming inwardly, "Oh! what a falling off is here!"

If she was struck by my changed appearance, I was no less so with hers. Time and Care, rival ploughmen, had deeply furrowed her brow—her *embonpoint* was gone; and the iron-grey locks peeped here and there through the muslin of her cap. Still, as of old, the ease, the urbanity, the refinement, and, at the same time, the simplicity of the gentlewoman, shone in Miss Belfield as conspicuously as ever.

As we stood near the fire, and during the pause which followed the ardour of question and answer incident to a first meeting, Miss Belfield drew my attention to a portrait over the mantelpiece; it was that of an officer, in somewhat old-fashioned regimentals.

"Do you know that?" said she, in a subdued and choked tone, pointing to it with her finger.

I did indeed; 'twas my old friend, the good, the kind, and thoughtful captain. There he sat, serenely, with his book half-opened and resting on his knee, just as he was wont to look in days of yore, when I rattled into his budgerow, after one of my shooting excursions.

"Come," said Miss Belfield, gently withdrawing me from its contemplation, "lunch awaits us in the next room, and you must require refreshment."

I must reserve a more detailed account of Miss Belfield for some future part of my autobiography,—that devoted to England; let it here suffice to state, that after a week's visit to my amiable friend—one characterized by every thing that was pleasing—I returned to London, having first promised to repeat my visits from time to time, to draw and botanize, and talk of old times; and settle, over a cup of Howqua's mixture, the great questions now agitating the world. But to proceed.

I passed the old fort and station of Buxar, where a few invalids doze out the evening of their Indian existence, and saw some European veterans, almost as black as the natives, with large mushroom hats, bobbing for fish on the banks of the river, and in due time reached Ghazepore, the station of one of H.M. regiments.

Here I found my shipmate, Ensign O'Gorman. The ensign, on whom I called, received me as an Irishman and a British officer in the royal service might be supposed to do. Could a volume say more for its warmth and cordiality? I dined with him at his mess, at which urbanity, kindness, and good cheer combined their attractions to render this one of the pleasantest evenings I had spent in India. Oar ship adventures were discussed; our fellow-passengers were passed in review, and we were supremely happy.

"By the way," said I, rather carelessly, "have you heard what has become of Olivia Jenkins?"

"Oh, didn't you hear she is married?"

"Married!" I exclaimed, and a mouthful of pillaw stuck *in transitu* in my œsophagus, nearly producing a case of asphyxia.

"Good heavens! you don't say so?"

"Oh, it's a fact," said O'Gorman; "but what's the matter? you appear unwell."

"Oh, I am quite well," said I; "but let's take a glass of wine."

I tossed off a bumper, and felt relieved.

"And so—little—Olivia—Jenkins—is actually—married? Good heavens! only think of that!"

"Why, sure," said the ensign, smiling, "there's nothing very strange in a pretty girl getting married; but," added he, looking hard at me, and after a pause, "I suspect you were a little touched in that quarter yourself; am I not a true diviner?"

"I acknowledge it," said I; "I did like that girl. Good heavens! and so little Olivia Jenkins is actually married!"

The ensign pressed me to stay with him a week, but I was forced to decline his hospitality, and resumed my onward route the next morning.

In a few days I reached Benares—Kasi, the splendid—the Jerusalem or Mecca of the Hindoo world. What a treat to look upon a picture of human existence, just as it probably was when Alexander the Great was a little chap!

As I glided past the swarming ghauts, where the pure-caste damsels, the high-born Hindoo maidens, of this strange and antique land, displayed their lovely forms, and laved their raven tresses in the sacred stream; where the holy bramin and the learned pundit, seated cross-legged, marked with ashes and pigments, pattered their Veds and Purans, I felt this in all its force; whilst the blowing of the conch, or the tinkling of bells, announced the never-ending round of *Poojah* and devotion!

Here and there, the sacred Bull of Siva, and the *yoni* and *lingam*, festooned with wreaths of lotus or chumbalie, met the eye; whilst crowded boats, jingling bylies (ruths or native carriages), armed natives in the varied costumes of India (here assembling in the common centre of religious hopes and duties), with an elephant or two half-immersed, would serve to complete the foreground of this interesting picture.

Behind arose, somewhat after the manner of those congregated architectural masses in Martin's pictures, though of course inferior in the boldness of their proportions and general taste and magnificence of the outline, the closely-wedged masses of this most curious and old-world city; the continuity of buildings occasionally broken by masses of foliage, or a cuneiform temple, with its tapering bamboo and blood-red pennon.

High over all, in the centre of the city, on a natural eminence, towered the celebrated mosque of Aurungzebe, with its two lofty minarets, which command a magnificent prospect of the surrounding country. This mosque is erected, it is said, on the site of a Hindoo temple of great sanctity, which was previously desecrated by having the blood of a cow sprinkled over it.

When the Mahomedans and Hindoos have a serious flare-up, the cows and pigs are pretty sure to suffer for it. The one is held in the highest veneration by the Hindoo, the other in utter abomination by the Moslem; consequently, the killing of one in a mundil, and of the other in a mosque, in pursuance of the *lex talionis*, generally constitutes the crisis of a religious dispute.

Such is revenge, when passion and fanaticism are in the ascendant, and such the *gusto* with which, by contending religionists, the stab is given in the most tender and vital part.

Having nearly cleared the city, I landed, accompanied by Ramdial Sirdar, to take a peep at the interior of this strange place; and strange, indeed, I found it. Streets swarming with people, and some so narrow that one of our draymen could hardly work down them, unless edgeways. Here, in the crowded chowks, waddled the huge braminy bull, poking his nose into the bunyah's grain basket, in disdainful exercise of his sanctified impunity; whilst byraggies, fakeers, pundits, and bawling mendicants, and much more, that I cannot here describe, made up a scene as curious in itself, as striking and interesting to me from its novelty.

In the course of my ramble, Ramdial gave me to understand that, if I was desirous of an *hummaum*, or bath, after the Indian fashion, I could have one at Benares for a rupee or two, which would purify my outer man, besides being wonderfully agreeable. I had heard much of such baths in the "Arabian Nights," and in works of the like sort, and thought this a good occasion to compare facts with early impressions; in short, I determined to be parboiled, and having intimated the same to Ramdial, I departed with him and my kidmutgar, after an early dinner, to the *hummaum*, or Ghosul Kaneh.

This was a considerable distance from my boat, in a garden, in the outskirts of the city. We entered the building, and Ramdial having explained who I was and what I wanted, an attendant of the bath showed me a small apartment, in which I was requested to disrobe. Having *peeled*, a pair of curwah drawers, or *pajammas*, were given to me, which descend about half-way down the thigh, and are tied in front with a string.

All being ready, I, rather nervous, submitted myself to the guidance of an athletic native, similarly habited to myself.

We passed through a narrow dark passage, and I began to look out for adventures. The slave of the bath showed me into a little confined apartment, some ten feet by four, filled with steam, on one side of which were reservoirs of water of different temperatures, in separate compartments, about (as well as I can recollect) breast-high.

Here I found another attendant, who, after sluicing a bowl or two of water over my body, laid me out on a long board, occupying the centre of the narrow apartment, and, aided by his companion, commenced rubbing me with soap and pea-meal from head to foot.

This over, they proceeded to rub me down slowly with *keesahs*, or rough gloves, bringing off flakes and *rouleaus* of cuticle and epidermis astonishing to behold. Flayed alive, they proceeded to shampoo and knead me, producing the most pleasing and grateful sensations.

The strong man now bade me rise, and then and there began to play the castanets on my vertebral column, beginning at the topmost articulation; this he effected by placing his leg behind me, swinging my body gently backwards and forwards, and then by a sudden jerk, the very reverse of pleasant, producing the desired dislocation and its accompanying crack; having done with the spine, he rung the changes on my toes, knees, and fingers. To effect all this, he entwined his brawny limbs about me in a most gladiatorial style, which was far from agreeable.

At length, after a few more sluicings, I was given to understand that my purifications were at an end; something was then thrown over me, and I was led back to the place from whence I came. There I dressed, and never in my life experienced such a feeling of purity and buoyancy. I felt as if a new man, cleansed mentally and bodily, and ready to open a fresh account with the world.

My kitmudgar, Fyz Buccas, a worthy little fellow, had not been idle or inattentive to my comforts during my absence; for no sooner had I dressed, and was giving the last shake to a clean cambric handkerchief—the *finale* of the toilet in India—than he presented me with a cup of hot coffee, which he had prepared outside, and brought in afterwards my kalioun, which I had recently set up; taking this then in my hand, and putting the mouth-piece between my lips, I stretched out my legs, leaned my head back, and, half-closing my eyes, immediately departed for the seventh heaven, in a cloud of odoriferous incense.

The following day brought me to Sultanpore, the station of a regiment of native cavalry, about midway between Benares and Chunarghur. Here I stayed a few days with a cornet, to whom I was the bearer of a letter.

There are no native cavalry lower than this in the Bengal presidency; these, consequently, with the exception of the Governor-General's body-guard (who are differently attired), were the first I had seen of that arm.

On the whole, this body of black dragoons pleased me well; their dress was French grey, buckskin breeches, and long military boots, with high blue mitre-shaped caps, terminating at the apex with a sort of hemispherical silver knob; those of the native officers were covered with red cloth, with silver mountings.

The European officers wore helmets (since changed to shakos), but in other respects were dressed like their men. Some of the troopers were tight, well-made fellows, and the native officers large, portly gentlemen; but, if I may be allowed a pun, should say there were more *Musulmans* than *musclemen* amongst them.[47]

Europeans in general *peel* much better than natives, though the latter, being generally taller and more equally-sized, look better, I think, in a body; nevertheless, amongst the sepoys are frequently found men, models of symmetry and muscular vigour, with whom few Europeans would be able to cope. Their great degree of strength is, however, in general, artificially induced by the continued practice of gymnastics, the *magdas*, or clubs, and the use of the iron-stringed bow, &c.

I arrived at Sultanpore during the great Mahomedan festival of the *Mohurrum*, and the cantonment, neighbouring bazaars, and villages, were resounding with firing and shouting.

This festival, as is pretty well known to all in any degree acquainted with Oriental history, is held in honour of the martyrdom of Hussain and Hosein, the sons of Ali, who fell on the fatal field of Kerbela, a catastrophe beautifully told by Gibbon, and which even he, who attaches no belief to the pretensions of Mahomed, can hardly peruse without emotion.

If such are the feelings of the infidel, what must be those of the believer? The *Sunni* makes it a season of silent grief and humiliation, whilst the *Sheahs*, or followers of Ali, abandon themselves to the wildest and most passionate demonstrations of sorrow.

Tazeahs, or representations of the shrine of Kerbela, of all sizes and shapes, more or less richly adorned with gilding, &c., are borne daily in procession for a period of many days, followed by crowds of the faithful, shouting "Hussain! Hosein!" beating their breasts, and indulging the most violent semblance of grief.

My friend, the cornet, drove me out one evening to witness the *tumasha* (sport). As we approached the spot where the greatest concourse was assembled, my ears were saluted by alternate shouts of what I was subsequently informed were intended for the words "Hussain, Hosein," but uttered by the whole mass as sharply and compactly as a well-delivered platoon fire, or the fitful escapes of steam from an engine.

The English soldier, with the natural proneness of honest John Bull to effect a national assimilation whenever he can, calls these processions "Hobson, Jobson;" and it is but fair to allow, that "Hussain, Hosein," when shouted forth in the manner described, sound exceedingly like "Hobson, Jobson."

On reaching the dense crowd, in the centre of which the tazeah, like a ship on a heaving sea, rocked to and fro, a wild scene of excitement met our view. Here were numbers of Mahomedan troopers, in their undress, many of them carrying tulwars[48] under their arms, with fakeers, servants, and bazaar people, all lustily lamenting the fate of Hussain and Hosein.

The tazeah had a splendidly gilded dome, and in the front of it was the figure of a strange creature, with the body of a camel, and a long tapering neck, terminating with a female face shaded by jet black ringlets; round the neck of this creature, which I take it was intended to represent Borak, on which Mahomed made his nocturnal journey to heaven, were strings of gold coins.

All this magnificence was supplied at the expense, I was told, of a devout old begum, the left-handed wife of an invalid general at Chunar, with whom, as will appear, I became subsequently acquainted.

On the seventh night of the *Mohurrum*, it is usual to celebrate the marriage of Hussain's daughter (nothing being perfect in this world without a little love) with her cousin, a gallant partisan of the house of Ali; Dhull Dhull too, the faithful steed of Hussain, his housings stuck full of arrows, forms a part of the pageant, and serves to create a still more lively image of the touching event which it is intended to commemorate.

The Mahomedans, when worked up to a high state of religious excitement and frenzy, on these occasions, are dangerous subjects to deal with; very little would then induce them to try the temper of their blades on the carcases of any description of infidel, Hindoo or Christian.

The relator was once at Allahabad when the great Hindoo festival of the *Hoolee*, a sort of Saturnalia, and the Mahomedan *Mohurrum* unluckily fell together; and was present with the judge, Mr. Chalmers, when a deputation from each of the religions waited upon him in connection with the subject of the apprehended bloodshed and disturbance, in case the processions of the two should meet.

The requests and the reasonings of the parties were highly characteristic of the genius of their respective religions. The Hindoos urged, mildly, that as their ancestors had possessed the country from time immemorial, and long before the Mahomedans came into it, they did not see why they should postpone the celebration of their religious rites, because the former chose to take offence at them; they disclaimed the slightest wish to insult or offend the Faithful, but contended for their right to parade the city in procession, with music, &c., as of old.

The Mahomedan moollahs, on their part, urged that, as the Hindoos were kaffers and idolaters, it must be (and they put the case very feelingly to Mr. Chalmers) exceedingly galling to them if they were allowed to parade their music and processions near their mosques and tazeahs:

"Betwixt the wind and their nobility."

The judge endeavoured to impress upon these last reasoners that the poor Hindoos had virtually as good a right as they had to perform their religious rites in their common city; and as for their being unbelievers, they could with equal reason return the compliment.

All this, however, had no effect; they could neither perceive the reason or justice of it, and declared their dogged determination to shut up shop and suspend proceedings, unless the Hindoos were forced to postpone theirs, or remove to a distance; to this the judge refused his assent, declaring that both parties should have equal justice, and that he would avail himself of both the civil and military power to keep the peace between them.

Some time after the departure of these deputations, information was brought that bodies of armed Mahomedans were coming into the town and assembling at the barree, or residence of one of their principal men, a great landholder, who was considered the head of the Sunnis there. The judge immediately ordered his gig, begged me to step into it, and, accompanied by a couple of orderly horsemen, we drove to his residence, which was situated on the banks of the Jumna. It consisted of many buildings irregularly disposed through one or more courts, in which were also situated two or three small mosques.

On dismounting, and entering the first enclosure, we observed many Musulmans, with heads inclined as if in profound thought, slowly moving about, and habited in long black tunics, the mourning garb of the Sunnis, with real or well-simulated looks of dejection. There we were met by the

Mahomedan chief, who appeared to deem himself insulted by the suspicion which the unexpected visit implied.

"Follow me, Sahib," said he, "and examine all the arms my place contains; you will find they are few, and only loaded with powder, and could not have been bought for the purpose you imagine."

On saying this, or something to the same effect, he took us to where several rows of matchlocks, rusty and dingy pieces of ordnance, were piled. The judge said he had feared that it was their intention at night to commence an onslaught on the Hindoos, and that he was determined to preserve the peace. The chief disclaimed any such intention, but I well recollect his concluding observation.

"Our religious observance," said he, "is *gum* (grief), theirs is *shadee* (uproar, literally 'a wedding'), and they ought not surely to be allowed to pass within our hearing; pray consider this;" and so forth.

The result of all this was, that half a battalion and a couple of six-pounders were ordered down to the city in the evening, and occupied the chowk, or marketplace, during the night. This grievously offended both parties, and they kept quietly within their several bounds. But for this interference, there can be little doubt that blood would have been spilt.

CHAPTER XXIII

The cornet took me with him to breakfast and dine with his friend, the old invalid general commanding at Chunarghur. This was my first Christmas Day in India; the weather was as cold as an English October, and I enjoyed the trip.

The pretty invalid station of Chunarghur is a few miles from Sultanpore, on the opposite bank of the river; as you approach it, the fort, crowning a lofty table rock, and abutting on the Ganges, has, with its numerous Moorish buildings and lines of circumvallation, a very striking and picturesque effect; and its reddish hue and that of the rock contrast pleasingly with the verdant gardens and white residences of the European inhabitants.[49]

The general, a hoary old Indianized veteran, gave my friend, with whom he appeared to be on intimate terms, a very hearty reception. It being Christmas Day, he had mounted his red uniform coat, which, from the hue of the lace, and other unmistakable signs, it was very clear, had been laid up in ordinary for a considerable time; but though his upper works were European, all below indicated one who had imbibed, in the course of fifty or sixty years' service, a taste for the luxurious appliances of an Indian existence. His legs, like those of Colonel Lolsaug, were encased in voluminous *pajammas*, which finished off with a pair of Indian gilt slippers.

We had a capital breakfast, at which an abundance of solid cheer, interspersed with glasses of amber jelly, and garnished with evergreens and flowers, "jasmin and marigolds," produced a truly Old English effect.

The old general leaned back in his easy chair, stretched his legs on a morah, smoked his magnificent hookha, and prepared to receive a host of people waiting outside to pay their respects.

In India, Christmas Day is called by the natives our "*Burra Din*," or great day. Our native soldiers and dependants attend in their best attire, to pay their respects, and present, according to their means, little *nuzzurs* or gifts, as tokens of good-will and fidelity. Your Kansaman brings a basket of sweetmeats; the shepherd, a kid from the flock; the gardener, a basket of his choicest fruit, flowers, and vegetables; the bearers deck the bungalow with evergreens, or plant a young tree in front of the door, and so forth.

It is a pleasing homage to master and his faith; and altogether, with the temperature of the weather and the solidity of the fare, tends strongly to awaken bygone recollections of youth, and all the charities and endearments of our island home at that delightful and merry season.

The *chick*, or blind, being now rolled up, a *posse* of venerable veteran native officers entered, exhibiting on their persons the various obsolete costumes of the Indian army of half a century back, gradually approximating from the uncouth attire of the sepoy of the olden time, with its short vandyked *jangheeas*, half-way down the thigh, cut-away coat, and ludicrous triangular-fronted cap, to the more perfect Europeanized dress at present worn.

Each bore on his extended palm a folded-up handkerchief, on which lay a certain number of gold mohurs or rupees, which the old general, contrary to the usual custom in such cases, groped off, and laid beside him in a heap, having previously touched his forehead, by way of acknowledging the compliment.

Besides the pecuniary offering, many of the veterans held their swords to the general and my friend, who touched them, and then their foreheads. This pretty custom is universal amongst the military of India and Persia, and is finely expressive of a soldier's fidelity and devotion. He offers you his sword; what can he more?

After the military had entered, various civil functionaries, connected with the bazaar and garrison, and the general's domestic servants, all arrayed in their holiday attire, were ushered in, and made their salaams and gifts. The latter were set aside in the room, and formed a goodly display of oranges, pomegranates, sweetmeats, sugar-candy, &c., enough wherewith to set up the store of a general dealer in a small way.

Last of all, several trays were brought in, each covered with an embroidered roomal or handkerchief; the bearers, having arranged these on the floor, withdrew the coverings with a grand air, as much as to say, "There! what do you think of that?" and a magnificent display of good things appeared. The Kansaman whispered the old general; the old general smiled, and my friend laughed. It was a Christmas gift from Begum Sahib, his pious left-handed Moosulmanee wife, and whose funds had supplied, as I before mentioned, the magnificent *tazeea* at Sultanpore, Benares.

Whilst its examination was going on, I thought I perceived a few curious eyes peeping from behind the curtain, which concealed the *sanctum sanctorum* of the *zenan khaneh*, or female apartments.

After the whole party had retired, and the general and my friend had resumed their chat and their hookhas, I observed the aforesaid curtain once more on the move, and, immediately after, the figure of an old withered Indian lady, covered with a profusion of rings and jewels, with a pair of garnet-coloured trousers of formidable dimensions, and a milk-white *doputta*, or scarf, over her head, issued therefrom.

She stood for a moment, placed her finger archly on her lips, as a signal for my friend to be silent, and then gliding slowly towards the veteran, whose back was turned towards her, she placed her long dark slender hands, sparkling with rings, over his eyes.

"Halloa!" said the old gentleman, "who have we here? what rogue is this?" smiling pleasantly, and knowing all the while who it was.

The old lady laughed, withdrew her hands, and stood before him.

"General Sahib," said she, in Hindustanee, "I am come to make my salaam to you on your *Burra Din*."

She now took a chair; my friend the cornet, who evidently knew her well, made her a respectful salaam, and they held a very animated conversation together, of which, from their eyes being directed towards me ever and anon, I guessed myself to be the subject. I was a modest youth in those days, and felt a little embarrassed at the idea of being overhauled and discussed in an "unknown tongue."

The cornet said: "The Begum has been asking about you; she says you look very young; quite a *chokra* (boy), and have a very *gureeb* (quiet) look, though, she dares to say, you are a bit of a *nut cut* (roguish fellow) for all that."

"Pray tell her," said I, "that she does me too much honour, and that I really want language to express the extent of my obligation. As for the first fault, time doubtless will correct it; with respect to the other, you may say it is an hereditary complaint in our family."

The cornet explained, or tried to explain; the old lady laughed, nodded her head, and said it was "*burra taiz bhat*" (a very smart reply). She now retired to her apartment, after a fresh round of salaaming between her and the cornet.

"I thought," said I, when she had gone, "that it was not usual for native ladies to exhibit themselves in that way."

"Nor is it," said he, "generally; but age and other circumstances lead to exceptions in this as well as in everything else. Besides," added he, "though the old lady is both rich and devout, she does not, of course, hold a foremost place in native estimation."

The general, who had left us for a few moments, now returned, and after some little conversation, of which she was the subject, being spoken of in a laudatory strain, "Well, now," said he, as if he had been revolving the matter deeply, "I don't know, but I consider that old woman as much my wife as if we had had a page of Hamilton Moore read over to us. My faithful companion for forty years, and the mother of my children!"

"But," said the cornet, "your friend the Padre, you recollect, when he was passing, took dire offence at her making her appearance one day when he was here; do you recollect that, general? You had quite a scene."

The general here emitted a panegyrical effusion touching the whole clerical body, and the scrupulous Padre in particular, which, however, I will not repeat.

After tiffin, the general, the cornet, and myself, went out to visit the fort and the neighbourhood, which I had a desire to see; the former, being old and infirm, rode in his *tonjon* (a sort of chair-palankeen); my friend and I were on horseback.

The fort of Chunarghur, to which we ascended from the town side by a somewhat steep road, occupies the summit of a table rock, some hundred feet above the surrounding country, and terminating abruptly on the river side. A strong wall, defended by numerous towers, runs round the edge, and the interior contains modern ranges of barracks, magazines, &c., and some fine masses of old buildings, in the Moorish style of architecture, characterized by the cupolas, horseshoe arch, &c.

The views on all sides are extensive and interesting: on the one, you look down upon the roofs of the closely-built native town, its temples and intermingled foliage, and tall bamboo pigeon-stands, with the white houses and luxuriant gardens of the adjacent station, the broad Ganges skirting the verdant slopes in front, and stretching away through many a sandy reach towards Benares; on the opposite side, above the fort, a rich and cultivated country, waving with crops, adorned with mango groves, and dotted here and there with old mosques or tombs, extends far in the distance, traversed by bold sweeps of the river, which, sprinkled with many a white sail, or strings of heavy boats, advancing with snail-like pace against the current, glistens brightly below.

The general pointed out to me the particular part of the wall where we made our unsuccessful assault in the year 1764, with some other lions of the place; after which we left the fort by another gateway, and a somewhat zigzag descent, on the opposite side to that on which we had entered.

In passing a guard of invalids, however, before emerging, I was highly entertained to see the old veterans, who were rather taken by surprise, hobbling out from their pipes and repose in a mighty pother, to present arms to the general, which they managed to effect before he had left them far behind, with a most picturesque irregularity.

Chunar, some thirty or forty years before the period to which I am adverting, had been, I believe, one of our principal frontier stations, and the head-quarters of a division, though then, as now, scarcely occupying a central point in the immense line of the British dominions on this side of India. The cantonments of this large force were situated on the plain last noticed, above the fort, and present small station, though almost every trace of it has long disappeared, at least of the abodes of the living, for the mansions of the dead still remain nearly *in statu quo* to tell their pensive tale.

We paid a visit to this now remote and forgotten burying ground (or rather to one of them, for there are two) a mile or two beyond the fort; and I confess, albeit a juvenile, that I was touched at the sight of these lonely mementoes of the fact, that a bustling military cantonment, of which hardly a vestige remains, once occupied the immediate vicinity.

How changed is now the scene from what it was in the *qui hye* days of our fathers! The clang of the trumpet, the roll of the drum, and the gleaming ranks, have long given place to more peaceful sounds and sights; the creak of the well-wheel, and the song of the ryot, as he irrigates his fields, supply the place of the former. Grain now waves where troops once manœuvred, whilst the light airs of the Ganges pipe, amidst the white mausoleums, the dirges of those who "sleep well" beneath, many of the once gay inhabitants of the scene:—

"Ah! sweetly they slumber, nor hope, love, nor fear;

Peace, peace is the watchword—the only one here."

There are few things which address themselves more strongly to the feelings than the sight of the tombs of our countrymen in a far distant land. In the cemetery to which I am referring, now rarely visited, it being out of the track of travellers, where grass and jungle are fast encroaching, and time and the elements are pursuing their silent dilapidations, many a Briton— many a long forgotten Johnson and Thompson—quietly repose, far from the hearths of their fathers.

I have since more than once visited this and similar places, which may be compared to wrecks which the onward flow of our advancing power leaves behind it, and as I have stood and mused amongst them, have pleased myself by indulging in dreamy speculations touching the histories of the surrounding sleepers (for all have their little histories), of all their hopes, fears, and cares, here for ever laid at rest.

We extended our excursion to some distance beyond the cemetery, and visited the mausoleum of a Mahomedan prince or saint, the history of which I have forgotten. I have now only a faint remembrance of its mosaic and lattice-work—its inlaid scrolls from the *Koran*—the sarcophagus covered with an embroidered carpet, the lamps around, and the ostrich eggs suspended from the vaulted roof.

On returning home to the old general's house, rather late, we found two or three of his friends, invalid officers of the garrison, assembled to do justice to his roast beef and other Christmas fare. A very social party we had; the general "shouldered his crutch," and the invalid guests gave us plenty of Indian legendary lore; all hearts expanded under the influence of good cheer, and a couple of bottles of "Simkin Shrob" (Champagne), which the general produced as if it had been so much liquid gold, reserved for high days and holidays.

A glass or two of champagne is your grand specific for giving the blue devils their *quietus*, and liberating those light and joyous spirits which wave their sparkling wings over the early wine-cup and the genial board; but, like other ephemeræ, soon pass away, drowned, perhaps, like flies, in the liquid from whence they spring, leaving but a pleasing remembrance of their having once existed.

The next morning, after breakfast, the cornet and I rode back to Sultanpore, and in a few days I bade him adieu, and in a short time found myself sound in wind and limb, but quite out of *rootie mackun* ("bread and butter"), and other river stores, in sight of the far-famed fortress of Allahabad, at the confluence of the Jumna and Ganges.

The view of this fortress, with its lofty walls and numerous towers, is, as you approach it, very striking; one sees few such imposing masses in England; and as for our feudal castles, few of them are much bigger than the gateways of such places as I am describing.

The fort which occupies the point where these two famous rivers meet, though perfectly Oriental in its general character, has been "pointed," and strengthened in accordance with the principles of European fortification, particularly on the land side. It is impregnable to a native force, and one of the principal depôts of the Upper Provinces. This, as is well known, is one of the *Prayagas*, or places of Hindoo pilgrimage.

During the great *Melah*, or fair, which subsequently it was often my lot to witness, the concourse of people who assemble here from all parts of the Hindoo world, from the Straits of Manaar to the mountains of Thibet, is prodigious. The sands below the fort exhibit, on that occasion, a sea of heads, intersected by lines of booths, and here and there an elephant or a camel towering above the congregated mass.

The point where the all-important regenerating dip is effected, is covered by the many-coloured standards of the Brahmins and Fakeers, looking at a distance like a dahlia show, or a gaudy-coloured bed of tulips.

In crossing over to the fort, in my bolio, I was forcibly struck by the very different appearance in the water of the two streams. The one, the Jumna, deep, blue, and pure; the other, the Ganges, yellow and turbid. It was curious to observe them blending in many a whirlpool and eddy—the flaky wreaths of the dirty old "Gunga-Jee" infusing themselves into the transparent element of the sister river.

Here I laid in a store of eggs, bread, poultry, mutton, and the like—of the latter I purchased a magnificent hind-quarter from a bazaar kussai, or butcher, who came staggering on board with it, patting and attitudinizing it, and after pointing out its incomparable beauties, its masses of fat, and the fine colour of the lean, &c., let me have it for four rupees, just three rupees eight annas more than it was worth.

A few days brought me to Currah Munickpoor, where I found a sub, on solitary outpost duty, who looked upon my arrival as an agreeable break to the monotony of his life—a perfect Godsend—and treated me with uncommon hospitality. I found him a very pleasant fellow, and his manner of life—smoking, eating, shooting, &c.—so much to my taste, that it did not require any very urgent solicitation on his part to induce me to spend two or three days with him.

I dined with him at his bungalow, some short distance inland, on the first day, when he showed me the objects worthy of notice in the neighbourhood, and thinking this a good opportunity to dress my hind-quarter of mutton, I invited him to partake of it next day, on board my bolio.

My acquaintance was a "mighty hunter," as most young Indian officers are. He shot, fished, and kept a pack of mongrels, and a greyhound or two, with which he hunted the hare, fox, and jackal; he was also a great adept in the use of the pellet-bow, in the mode of discharging which he obligingly gave me some lessons.

I am not aware whether this sort of bow is known in Europe or not. If it were as generally made use of amongst boys in England as by young men in India, we should certainly have a fearful number of blind and one-eyed gentry amongst the population.

This bow is generally made of a split bamboo, which, being highly elastic, renders it peculiarly adapted to the purpose; it has two strings of catgut, which, at about a foot from one extremity, are kept separate by a small piece of stick, about an inch and a half in length, the ends ingeniously secured between the strands of the string; immediately opposite to that part of the bow grasped by the hand, and which is well padded, there is a small piece of leather, about two square inches in size, sewn to the two strings, and presenting its flat surface to the handle; in this a pellet of hard, dried clay is placed, and being seized by the thumb and forefinger of the right hand, is then discharged at the object.

The great danger of the tyro is that of striking the thumb of the left hand, within an inch or two of which the ball must always pass, though by the practised bowman a collision is always avoided by giving the wrist a peculiar turn or twist. The force with which the ball goes, when thus propelled, is surprising; and uncommon accuracy in striking an object may be in time acquired by a due regulation of the hands and eye. I have brought down with the pellet-bow pigeons and kites, when on the wing, from a great height, and cut off the heads of doves and sparrows sometimes as completely as if it had been done with a knife.

As my friend and I strolled in the tamarind grove, near to which my boat was moored, he exhibited his skill upon the squirrels and paroquets, much to my astonishment.

"Will you let me have a shot?" said I, eagerly.

"Certainly; but have you ever attempted it before?"

"Never," I replied; "but there appears to be no difficulty in it whatever."

"'Tis far more difficult than you imagine," he replied; "it was months before I got into the way of it; here," he continued, "if you are determined, you must. Now, twist your wrist thus, or you will infallibly hit your thumb: there, so!"

"Oh! I see," said I; and immediately seized the bow.

A dove sat invitingly on a neighbouring bough; I gave a long pull and a strong pull, and, och! hit my thumb a whack that bared it to the bone. Away I tossed the pellet-bow to the distance of about twenty yards, thrust the mutilated member into my mouth, and immediately fell to dancing something very like Jim Crow. In a little time the agony subsided; I had swathed the ex-member in fine linen, when Fyz Buccas came to summon us to dinner.

"Come along, sir," said I; "I hope you can dine off a hind-quarter of mutton and a Bombay pudding."

"Nothing can be better," said he; "but where did you get your meat?"

"I bought it of a bazaar fellow at Allahabad, and a splendid joint it is."

My companion, more experienced in the tricks of India than myself, smiled incredulously, and then looked a little grave.

"I hope they have not given you a made-up article."

"Made-up!" said I; "I don't understand you."

"Why," he replied, "these bazaar rascals stuff and blow up their meat, and use half a dozen other different ways of taking in the unwary passenger."

"'Pon my life," said I, "you frighten me; if this my best bower fails, we shall go plump on the rocks of short commons, that's certain."

"Oh, never mind," said he; "at the worst, my place is not far off, and there is abundance of prog there; besides, I can eat bazaar mutton, or goat, or anything else at a pinch, particularly if there is a good glass of Hodgson to wash it down."

This dialogue was cut short by the entry of the mutton; it certainly did not look as respectable mutton should look. I seized the carver, eager to know the worst, and gave a cut; the murder was out, and so was the wind; the unhappy mutton falling into a state of collapse.

"Ha! ha! ha!" roared the sub: "I thought as much; now try that mass of fat containing the kidney, and you will have farther evidence of the skill with which an Indian butcher can manufacture a fat joint of mutton."

I made a transverse incision into the membraneous sac, and there lay a beautiful and compact stratification of suet, skin, and other extraneous matters, which I extracted *seriatim* at the point of my fork. I confess I was thunderstruck at this profligacy of the heathen, which is, however, common enough.

Currah is an interesting spot, abounding in picturesque ruins; and good sporting is to be had there, the neighbourhood abounding in hares, wild pea-fowl, grey partridges, and quail; the best cover in which to find the latter is, my friend told me, the soft feathery undergrowth of grass to be found in the indigo fields. In some of the islands of the Ganges, black partridge, florikin, and hog-deer are to be met with, and there are also plenty of wolves and hyænas amongst the ruins, for those who are fond of such sport.

The town of Currah, about fifty miles above Allahabad, is situated on the Ganges, close to its banks, and presents to the view a confused mass of mud buildings, buried in the foliage of numerous neem, peepul, and tamarind trees; interspersed with these are several temples, musjids, or mosques, as also some houses of stone or brick, displaying a considerable appearance of comfort and convenience for this part of India.

The vicinity is much cut up by deep ravines, formed by the annual rains in their descent, through the loose soil, to the river. A little below the town are the remains of a considerable fort, which from the Ganges has rather a picturesque appearance; its gateway, and some lofty circular bastions, are in a very tolerable state of preservation.

Lower down still, on the spot where I moored, are some pretty Hindoo mundils or temples, from which ghauts or flights of steps lead to the river; these are overhung by noble trees, principally the tamarind, shedding a cool and refreshing shade over the spot.

Here I planted my chair on one or two evenings, with my friend the sub, beneath the shade of these trees, and, soothed into a state of tranquillity by the cooing of numerous doves, which fill the groves, I gazed on the boats as they glided down the stream, and yielded up my mind to the influence of tranquil and pleasing emotions. I thought of home—my mother—the widow—when I should be a captain—and other things equally remote and agreeable.

The tamarind, to my taste, is the most beautiful tree of the East— not even excepting the banyan—the foliage, which is of a delicate green, droops in rich and luxuriant masses, like clusters of ostrich plumes— overhanging a piece of water, or half-enveloping some old mosque, durgah, or caravanserai—with the traveller's horse picketed in its shade, or the group of camels ruminating in repose beneath it—nothing can be more picturesque.

This tree, beneath which no plant will grow, seems to be a great favourite with the natives, but particularly with the Mahomedans; it is almost invariably to be found near their mosques and mausoleums; and amongst them, I suspect, holds the place the yew, or rather the cypress, does with us—an almost inseparable adjunct of the tomb:

"Fond tree, still sad when others' griefs are fled.

The only constant mourner o'er the dead."

A nest of Brahmins is comfortably established in and about the ghaut and temple above mentioned, the duties of which latter they perform; these, with bathing, eating, sleeping, and fleecing European passers-by, constitute the daily tenor of their *harmless* lives. They regularly levy contributions from European travellers who pass this way, and make, I suspect, rather a good thing of it.

Their course of proceeding is as follows: one of the fraternity, with all the humility of aspect which characterized Sterne's monk, waits upon the traveller with a little present of milk, fruit, or a pot of tamarind preserve—the last, by the way, uncommonly good there—this, in a subdued tone, and with a low salaam, he tenders for acceptance, and at the same time produces for inspection a well-thumbed volume—of which it might truly be said, in the language of the Latin grammar, "*Qui color albus erat, nunc est contrarius albo*"—partly filled with names, doggrels, and generally abortive attempts at the facetious. In this the traveller is requested to record his name, the date of his visit, with the addition of as much epigram as he can conveniently squeeze out, or of any *extempore* verses he may chance to have by him ready cut and dry for such occasions.

Having made his literary contribution, and returned the valuable miscellany to its owner, in whose favour the traveller's romantic feelings are perhaps warmly excited, particularly if, like me, a "*tazu wulait*" (literally, a fresh-imported European), with some St. Pierre-ish notions of the virtuous simplicity of Brahmins and Gentoos, he begins to discover, from the lingering, fidgety, expectant manner of his sacerdotal friend, that something remains to be done—in fact, that a more important contribution is required—and that the "*amor nummi*" is quite as rife in a grove on the banks of the Ganges as anywhere else in this lucre-loving world. On making this discovery, he disburses his rupee in a fume, and all his romantic ideas of hospitable Brahmins, primitive simplicity, children of nature, &c. &c., vanish into thin air.

My friend the sub lent me a pony, and, accompanied by dogs, servants, and guns, we traversed a good deal of the surrounding country in search of game and the picturesque.

The country, for miles around Currah, is thickly covered with the ruins of Mahomedan tombs, some of great size, and combining, with much diversity of form, considerable elegance and architectural beauty. Two or three of these, more striking than the rest, are erected over the remains of peers or saints; one of these latter is, I was told, Sheik Kummul ud Deen, a very holy man, who, doubtless, in his day rendered good service to the cause of Islam, by dint, probably, of that very cutting and convincing argument the *shumshere*.[50] The adjacent village of Kummulpore derives its name from him.

Kurruck Shah, I learnt from my young friend, who was a bit of an antiquary, was the name of another peer of remarkable sanctity, who lies buried near the town of Currah; his durgah or shrine, which we visited, is situated in the midst of an extensive paved court, nearly encompassed by shabby whitewashed buildings, shaded by two or three gigantic trees, some of the arms of which were leaning for support on the buildings they had so long shaded, like parents claiming in age the support of their children— their natural props. It has, we were told, an establishment of peerzadas, or attendant priests, and land attached for their support, the supply of oil for the lamps, &c.

I could never learn clearly or positively the cause of so vast a congregation of tombs as this neighbourhood exhibits, many square miles being covered with them; but my companion was told by villagers whom he questioned on the subject, that they covered the remains of the slain who fell in a great battle. As, however, the dates on the tombs are of various periods, this must have been the hardest fought battle on record—or the process of interment singularly slow.

Joking apart, to trust to the *on dits* and traditions of untutored peasants in any country is far more likely to lead to error than to enlighten, in nine cases out of ten.

Having much enjoyed my three days' halt at Currah, I once more pursued my onward course, my hospitable host sending down to my boat a profusion of butter, fresh bread, and vegetables, for my voyage, with a piece of mutton, on the integrity of which he told me I might confidently rely: this was, at all events, *puffing* it in a proper manner.

I found the country between Currah and Cawnpore to contain nothing particularly remarkable; groves, ghauts, mud-built towns, ravines, and sand-banks constituted its leading features. On one of the latter, one fine cold evening, I performed the funeral obsequies of the one-eyed bull-dog, who had been long in a declining state; the climate evidently did not agree with his constitution, and he slowly sunk under its effects. The interment was conducted by Nuncoo Matar, and Teazer, now constituting the sum total of my kennel, stood by whilst his companion Sully was receiving those last attentions at our hands.

At Cawnpore I put up with the major, who, the reader may remember, was one of our passengers in the *Rottenbeam Castle*. He was a most worthy, gentlemanly fellow, as great a griffin as myself, though likely to continue so to the end of the chapter, for two very good reasons: one, because he had passed that age after which, as I have before stated, in an early part of these memoirs, the process of accommodation to Indian habits becomes an exceedingly difficult one; and secondly, because he had the honour to belong to one of H.M.'s regiments, in which it must be sufficiently obvious, without my troubling the reader or myself with an elaborate explanation, that a knowledge of Indian manners, language, and customs is not so likely to be acquired as in a sepoy corps, where a European is brought into constant contact with the natives.

The major, who was accustomed to the best society of England, had a considerable admixture of the exquisite in his composition; but it sat so easily upon him he did not know it, and being natural, was consequently agreeable.

I would not have it inferred, exactly, that I think all things which are genuine must necessarily please, but that nature is always a redeeming feature, and when associated with what is in itself excellent, it constitutes the master-charm.

The major gave me a room in his bungalow, to which I soon had all my valuables transferred from the bolio. The same day the manjee came up to make his salaam, and demand the balance of what was due to him for his boat. He was accompanied by his sable crew, jolly fellows, who had carried me on their shoulders over many a nullah, and plunged many a time and oft in the Ganges for me, to pick up a bird.

There they were, "four-and-twenty blackbirds all in a row," in the major's verandah, squatted on their hams, and dressed in their best attire. Every face had become familiar to me; I knew most of their names, their peculiar *fortes*, from the purloiner *en passant* of *kuddoos* [51] and cucumbers, the thief in ordinary to the mess, to the instructor of the paroquets, and the cook to the crew, and associated one or more of their names with almost every sporting adventure or exploit in which I had been engaged on my way up—a long four months' trip.

It is true I subjected them occasionally to the rigorous discipline of the Marpeetian code; in other words, thrashed them soundly when they hesitated to plunge into an alligatorish-looking pool after a wounded dabchick, or capsized my griffinship, as happened once or twice, when staggering with me Scotch-cradle fashion, gun and all, through the shallows, to my bolio; but the good-natured, placable creatures soon forgot it, and we were on the whole very good friends. I believe they knew I was a griffin, and, cognizant of the infirmities of that singular animal, made allowances for me, particularly as I gave them sometimes, by way of compensation, a rupee or a feed of *metais* (sweetmeats).

Oh paying the manjee, he tied up the rupees carefully in the corner of his turban, and made me a low salaam; his crew also bowed themselves to the earth. So much for business. He then put up his hands, and with an agreeable smile, and in an insinuating tone, said something which I desired Ramdial to explain, though I partly guessed its purport.

"What does he *muncta* (want), Ramdial?"

"He *bola* (says) if *Sahib Kooshee* will please give him *buckshish*."

"Yes, yes; we'll give him some boxes—*paunch rupee bus?*" (Rs. 5 enough, eh?)

"*Han Sahib* (yes, sir) *bus* (enough)."

Having, in my usual piebald *lingua franca*, thus consulted my keeper of the privy purse, I ordered him to disburse a gratuity of Rs. 5 amongst the crew, which they gratefully received, with many salaams. Thus we parted, never more to meet, and thus wound up my aquatic journey from the presidency to Cawnpore.

The curtain is now about to rise on act the last of my griffinage, and it may be some consolation to those who have sat thus long to witness the performance, that they are approaching the *dénouement*, the grand flourish of trumpets and *exeunt omnes*.

Cawnpore is the head-quarters of a division, and the station of several thousand troops of all arms—with some slight addition, indeed, of native troops, a force can be despatched almost immediately from this station with which hardly any Indian army of the present day could successfully contend in the open field.

At the period embraced by these memoirs, a regiment of dragoons, two of native cavalry, one of European, and three of native infantry, horse and foot, artillery, pioneers, engineers, &c., &c., constituted the amount of the military force at Cawnpore. The station itself has a bad name amongst Indian stations, and richly does it deserve it. Dust, ravines, and mangy black pigs are the most striking features of the cantonment; and the neighbouring country is flat, arid, and peculiarly uninteresting.

The society is large, and time is killed here pretty much in the same way as in other large stations—private and mess parties, masquerades and fancy dress-balls, and private theatricals.

I passed a week with the hospitable major, which was principally devoted to making the necessary preparations for my march. I had nearly emptied the general's snuff-box; had no pay due; and was consequently obliged to consider economy in my purchases, and to relinquish all ideas, if I ever had them, of travelling *en seigneur* or *à la nawaub*.

The first thing was to purchase a nag, and the major in this undertook to assist me—and thereby hangs a tale. He intimated to one of his regimental functionaries that a young gentleman wanted a pony; and straightway a rare assortment of Rosinantes in miniature made their appearance in the compound. I never beheld the phrase of "raw head and bloody bones" so completely reduced to matter-of-fact before as in some of these *biting* satires on the equine race, most of them grass-cutters' tatoos—the quintessence of vice and deformity—a breed peculiar to India, and the very pariar of horses. [52]

"Try this fellow, Gernon," said the major, laughing; "I think he'll do for you."

The major little thought how near he was to the mark. On his so saying, I mounted, or rather threw my leg over a very angular backbone, and seizing a primitive bridle of string or cord, solicited an onward movement with a "gee-up."

Now, whether it was that I touched a "tender point," or being of greater specific gravity than a bundle of grass, I know not; but certainly I was no sooner in a "fix," as the Yankees say, than the little devil emitted an appalling scream, clapped back his ears, and commenced a rapid retrograde movement, backing me into the midst of "seven devils" worse than himself.

In a moment, I had double that number of heels in full play around me, spite of the tatoo owners' attempts to drive off their animals. A thundering broadside in the ribs of my Bucephalus, which damaged my leg considerably, and other notes of battle sounding around, convinced me speedily that the sooner my friend and I parted company the better. I consequently rolled off, and scrambled out of the *mêlée*, receiving, in retreating, an accelerator in the shape of another kick on or about the region of the *os coccygis*. As for the major, he was almost in convulsions.

"Confound it, major, that's too bad of you," said I, "to get me on the back of that imp, and now to laugh at my misfortunes."

"Oh! then, by dad, you must forgive me," said he, his eyes still streaming; "but if it was my father himself I could not resist;" and again he laughed till he gave up through exhaustion.

This over, I proceeded to a more cautious selection, and finally bought a tolerably decent-looking animal for Rs. 25, and who, bating that his fore-feet were in the first position, was worth the money. A small tent, in India termed a routee, rather the worse for wear, I bought for Rs. 60, and this, with a Cawnpore-made saddle and bridle, a hackery, two bullock-trunks, and a pair of bangy baskets, constituted my turn-out for the march.

My friend the major kindly took me with him to messes and wherever he was invited.

These mess parties I then thought very pleasant, though I confess I should now derive very little pleasure from the scenes in which I was then wont to delight, particularly on what were considered public nights—toasting, speechifying, drinking, singing songs (many of the grossest description), roaring and screeching, with the *finale* of devilled biscuits, daybreak, pale faces, perhaps a quarrel or two, and half a dozen under the table, in a few words describe them.

Since those days, and twenty-five years are now equal to a century of the olden time as respects progress, things have improved; we have begun to learn in what true sociality really consists—even and tranquil interchange of thought, with a sprinkling of decent mirth, the genuine "feast of reason and the flow of soul"—to which eating and drinking, the mere gastronomic pleasures of the table, are considered as secondary rather than as principal sources of enjoyment.

The change, however, is yet but beginning; aldermen, it is true, have ceased to be inseparably associated (as twin ideas) with huge paunches and red noses—your seven-bottle men have enjoyed the last of their fame, which reposes with the celebrity of a Beau Brummel; but too much of the old Saxon leaven—the wine and wassail-loving and gormandizing spirit, with an excess of animalism in other respects—still characterizes us; and, little as it may be thought, is a serious hindrance to social and intellectual advancement.

The more exalted pleasures of the heart and intellect, let it be observed in passing, can only be enjoyed, individually and nationally, by those who can restrain their grosser appetites within moderate bounds. This great truth the Easterns of old perceived, though (like all truth when first discerned) it was pushed to a vicious extreme in this case—that of excessive mortification.

This inordinate love of that which administers gratification to the senses (allowable in a moderate degree) is, it appears to my humble apprehension, our prime national defect; it engenders a fearful selfishness and profusion— militates against that moderation and simplicity of character from which great things spring—marks a state of pseudo-civilization, and causes to be left fallow or but partially cultivated the field of the benevolent affections—the true source of the purest enjoyments.

When man shall be sought and prized for his qualities and virtues, and not for his mere adjuncts of wealth and station; when happy human hearts and smiling human faces shall have more real charms for the great and refined than the *pirouettes* of a Taglioni or the strains of a Rubini; when the glow of self-approval shall be able to battle with the fashionable sneer and the "world's dread laugh," and the duties of kindred and country shall take precedence of "missions to the blacks," and the like; then, indeed, shall we be opening a new field for the mighty energies of our race, and entering on a happy millennium.

What a power to effect good, by leading the young and awakening spirit of the age into paths of peace, do the aristocracy of this country possess, if they would but use it! Standing on the vantage ground of fashion, wealth and station, they might infuse fresh moral and intellectual vigour into the nation, and stem, by all that is liberal, ennobling, and refining, the somewhat sordid and mediocre influences of mere commercial wealth. "Truth," from them, would prevail with "double sway;" whilst philanthropists in "seedy coats" may plead in vain with the fervour of a Paul and the eloquence of a Demosthenes. "What's in a name?" says Shakespeare—"a rose by any other name would smell as sweet." There the immortal bard utterly belied his usual accuracy.

CHAPTER XXIV

A military execution must be, under all circumstances and to all persons, an awful and striking exhibition; but seen for the first time, it makes on the young mind a peculiarly deep and painful impression. An European soldier of one of the regiments at the station had, in a fit of passion and disappointment, attempted the life of his officer, and, agreeably to the necessarily stern provisions of military law, was sentenced to be shot. I witnessed the execution;[53] a solemn scene it was, and one which will never be effaced from my memory.

The troops of various arms, European and native, were drawn up when I reached the parade, and formed in three sides of an immense square, facing inwards. The arms were "ordered," and a portentous silence prevailed, broken only occasionally by the clank of a mounted officer's sword, and the tramp of his horses hoofs as he rode slowly down the ranks. The morning mists were beginning to disperse, and the bright sun was darting his long and almost level rays across the parade ground, and gleaming brightly on a forest of steel and dazzling accoutrements—the last sunrise the unhappy criminal was ever destined to behold.

The roll of the dram now announced his arrival, and soon the procession, in which he occupied a conspicuous position, rounded the flank of one of the sides of the square.

First marched, at a slow pace, a party bearing the coffin of the condemned, followed by the execution-party; then the band, playing the *Dead March* in Saul: it was a frightful scene, and sent a damp to my heart—what must have been its effects on the unhappy man himself?

Last in the melancholy procession came a litter (doolie), borne on the shoulders of men; and in it, with a white cap on his head, and a face calm and resigned, but deadly pale, sat the unfortunate soldier, for whom, I confess, I felt most deeply. By his side, arrayed in full canonicals, walked the chaplain, his book open in his hand, reading those prayers and promises—speaking of pardon and hope—which are calculated to cheer the parting hour, and to soften the bitterness of death.

The procession having passed slowly along the front of each regiment, which, from the great extent of the square, occupied a considerable time, now drew off to the centre of what, if complete, would have constituted the fourth side of the parallelogram: there it halted.

The coffin-bearers placed their burden on the ground and retired; the execution-party drew up at some distance from it. The prisoner left his doolie, and, accompanied by the clergyman, walked slowly and with a firm step towards the coffin; on this they both knelt, with their faces towards the troops, and prayed with uplifted hands.

Profound was the silence. A soul was preparing for eternity! Being a spectator at large, I selected my position, and being close to the spot, saw all distinctly.

After some time had been occupied in prayer, the chaplain retired, when the judge advocate, on horseback, came forward, and, drawing forth the warrant for the prisoner's execution, read it with a firm and audible voice; at the conclusion, the chaplain once more advanced, and, kneeling on the coffin, again, with uplifted hands, and deep and impressive fervour, imparted the last spiritual consolations to the condemned.

What feelings must have torn the bosom of that unhappy being at that moment! Set up as a spectacle before thousands—an ignominious death before him—and perhaps the thoughts of those he loved, of kindred and of home, never more to be seen, adding another drop to his cup of bitterness! But yet he quailed not—no muscle trembled—and a stern determination to die like a man was stamped upon his care-worn and marbly countenance.

The tragedy was now drawing to a close. The chaplain, with apparent reluctance, rose and retired, and at the same moment the sergeant of the execution-party advanced and bound a handkerchief over the prisoner's eyes, also pinioning his arms. Still not a muscle moved; there were no signs of weakness, though the situation might well have excused them, and the chest was thrown out and squared to receive the leaden messengers of death.

The "make ready!" and the crack of the muskets as they were brought to the "recover," were startling notes of preparation, and fell with sickening effect on my ear. I could scarcely believe it possible I was looking on a scene of reality—a fellow-creature about to be shot down, however deservedly, in cold blood, like a very dog.

"Present!"—"fire!" and all was over. A mass of halls, close together, pierced his heart—over he went like a puppet—fell on his back, and never moved a limb. Life seemed borne away on the balls that went through him, and to have vanished with the speed of an electric spark.

There he lay, like fallen Hassan, "his back to earth, his face to heaven," his mouth open, as if to put forth a cry which had died unborn with the passing pang; one blood-red spot on his cheek, where a bullet had entered, lending its frightful contrast to the marbly hue of his features; the heel of one foot rested on the coffin, the other on the ground; his hands open and on their backs.

A short pause now ensued, which was soon followed by a stir of mounted officers galloping to and fro, and the loud command to "wheel back into open column," and "march!"

In this order the whole force advanced, the bands of the several regiments playing in succession, as they marched past the corpse, the deep and solemn strains of the *Adeste Fideles,* or Portuguese Hymn, a dirge-like air, admirably adapted for such occasions, and which breathes the very soul of melancholy.

As the flanks of each company passed, almost touching the dead man, it was curious to observe the various expressions in the countenances of the soldiers, European and sepoy, as they stole their almost scared and sidelong glances at it.

The non-military reader will be a little surprised, as I am sure I was, when I tell him that each regiment, after having passed the body a few hundred yards, changed the slow to quick march, and diverged to their several lines, playing "The girl I left behind me," or some similar lively air, with a view, I presume, to dissipate the recent impression.

The wisdom of such a proceeding is by no means self-evident; it seems indecent, to say the least of it: to be consistent, we should always ring a merry peal after a funeral, or a gallopade home from church.

Bidding adieu to my friend the major, and duly equipped for the march, I left Cawnpore for Futtyghur, and the following was the composition of my rather patriarchal turn-out—hating the red coats and muskets of my escort: a naick and six sepoys of Nizamut, or militia; we might have passed pretty well for the section of a nomade tribe on the move in search of clearer streams and greener pastures.

A two-bullock hackery or country cart, a very primitive lumbering locomotive, whose wheels, utter strangers to grease, emitted the most excruciating music, conveyed my tent, trunks, and hen-coops, with the dobie's lady and family perched a-top of all.

Then there was a bangy-burdah, with two green petaras, containing my breakfast and dinner apparatus, whilst Ramdial, my sirdar, trudged on, bearing the bundle containing my change of linen, and dragging my milch-goat (for Nanny did not approve of marching) after him, *nolens volens*.

Nunco led my dogs in a leash; to wit, Teazer, and a nondescript substitute for the bull, with a few evanescent shades of the greyhound, which I had purchased at Cawnpore. I named this animal, rather ironically, "Fly," which Nunco manufactured into "Pillai."

Fyz Buccas, kidmutgar, trudged along, driving before him a knock-kneed shambling tatoo, which I verily thought he would have made a spread eagle of, laden with his wife, two children, and sundry bags, pots, pans, &c. Whether Mrs. Fyz Buccas was a beauty or not I cannot positively say, though, if I might judge from the sample of one coal-black eye, of which, through the folds of her hood I occasionally had a glimpse, I should decidedly say she was.

I generally rode ahead of the procession, armed *cap-à-pie*, and shone the very *beau idéal* of griffinish chivalry. My syce always carried my gun, to be ready for a shot at a passing wolf or jackal, and with one or two other servants, viz., a classee, or tent-pitcher, bhistee, &c., with my guard, we constituted a rather numerous party.

In the above order I left Cawnpore, for a small village on the road to Furruckabad, where, in an extensive mango grove, I for the first time in my life slept under canvas.

It is the almost invariable custom in India to march in the early part of the morning, so as to reach the halting-ground before the sun has attained much power; but I was either ignorant, of the practice, or thought it would be preferable to reverse the system; certain it is, that for some time I always marched in the evenings, arriving at my ground sometimes after dark; by that means I was enabled to rise at my own hour comfortably the next morning, and had the whole day till about sunset for my amusement.

About that time I would seat myself on a chair under a tree, with my kulian in my hand, and superintend the striking and loading my tent, &c. About half an hour after they were fairly off, I would rise like a giant refreshed, mount my steed, whilst my syce obsequiously held my stirrup, and, fairly seated, would follow the baggage.

I love to recall in imagination those days, the opening ones of my independent existence. How vividly can I recall the scene which this march so often presented! the waning sunlight of the cold winter evenings, a few bright streaks just tinging the horizon, my hackery slowly wending its way over the plain, and my scattered servants crawling behind it, in a cloud of dust; the mango groves—villages—mud huts, and all the accompaniments of a country life in Upper India!

I must not here omit to mention that, prior to my leaving Cawnpore, I received a letter from my friend and patron Captain Marpeet, with whom I occasionally corresponded; it was couched in his usual frank and half-bantering style, and informed me that his regiment was on the eve of marching to Delhi, and that he anticipated great pleasure in meeting me there. Thus it concluded:—

"Recollect, my dear boy, I shall have a room at your service, and that you put up with me on your arrival; you are not fit to take care of yourself yet, and require a little more of my drilling and paternal care. Give me a few lines from Futtyghur, and mention when I may expect you. A friend of mine, Judge Sympkin, is now out in the district through which you will pass, on some Mofussil business. I enclose you a few lines of introduction, and have written to tell him he may expect you. He is a princely fellow, a first-rate sportsman, and lives like a fighting-cock, as a Bengal civilian should do. Hoping soon to shake you by the hand,

"I am, worthy Griff,

"Yours, &c:.,

"J. Marpeet."

A few days brought me to Futtyghur, of which I have nothing particular to record, excepting that the adjoining town of Furruckabad is celebrated for the manufacture of tent cloth and camp equipage, and as the scene of the defeat of Holkar's cavalry by our dragoons in Lord Lake's war.

By the way, an officer who was in that action told the relator, that the Brummagem swords of the troopers would make little or no impression on the quilted jackets and vests of the Mahrattas, and that he saw many of them dismount and take the well-tempered blades of the natives they had pistoled, and use them instead of their own. The keen razor-like swords of the East give those who wield them a fearful advantage over men armed with our mealy affairs. The former will split a man down from the "nave to the chine," or slice off his head with infinite ease (*sauf karna*, "to shave him clean," is the Indian phrase), whilst ours require immense physical force to produce such a result.

The author once met some troopers of the 4th Regiment of Native Cavalry, some squadrons of which were dismissed for turning tail when ordered to charge the ex-rajah of Kotah's body-guard, and asked them how they came to disgrace themselves. The answer of one of them was,—

"Why, what chance, sir, have we with men in chain armour, and wielding swords of such a temper that they will cut down horse and man at a single blow?"

I mention this as hearing on recent acts and discussions, not in justification of the men, but as affording a probable clue to the backwardness of our cavalry on some occasions. I think we are prone to rely too much on the power of disciplined troops acting *en masse*, to the neglect of those matters calculated to increase individual prowess. Good arms are a first-rate consideration, not only for the superior execution they do, but on account of the confidence with which they inspire the soldier.

At Futtyghur my tent was besieged by the venders of cloth, &c., and one man brought a number of tulwars (swords) made at Rampore, in Rohilcund, a place celebrated for them, for sale. After some higgling, I purchased one, a keen and well-poised blade, for the small sum of Rs. 4. I longed to try it upon some neck or other, and, as luck would have it, soon had the desired opportunity, on a felonious pariar dog, which had made free with a portion of my dinner.

I had advanced some four or five marches beyond Furruckabad, each day diversified by some novelty in the scenery—some fresh object, in the shape of travellers, pilgrims, buildings, and the like—but still beginning to feel the want of a companion whose language was the same as my own, when one morning, as I was strolling, with my pellet-bow in my hand (for I had resumed it, in spite of the crack on the thumb), I observed at a distance a horseman slowly approaching.

As he came nearer, I observed he was mounted on a tall Rosinante-looking steed, with a flowing tail and mane; his head-stall was of a sort of red bell-rope-looking cord; a bunch of red cloth, something like a handkerchief, dangled under his horse's chin, from whence a standing martingale passed between his legs. Amulets and chains were round his animal's neck, and the saddle (or cushion, rather) was covered with a square broad cloth of red and yellow chequers.

The cavalier himself, a dark-bearded Mahomedan, was a fine specimen of the Hindoostanee irregular horseman. His *chupkun*, or vest, of yellow broad cloth, reached to his knee, and his legs were encased in long wrinkled boots, something like Jack Sheppard's, and which would not have been the worse for a touch of Day and Martin.

On his head he wore a cylindrical Cossack-looking cap of black felt or lambskin. A long matchlock was poised on his shoulder; a tulwar, or scimitar, was stuck in his cummerbund or girdle, and a circular black shield, of buffalo's hide, swung on his shoulders.

Altogether, though I was brought up in the orthodox belief that one Englishman is equal to three Frenchmen, and of course, to an indefinite number of blacks, I cannot say I should have liked to encounter him upon my tatoo. However, his was a mission of peace, as I soon discovered.

On seeing me, he dug his heels into his horse's flanks, and was soon beside me. Throwing himself off, he saluted me with an off-handed *salaam*, in which *hauteur* and civility were oddly blended, and then, taking off his cap, he extracted therefrom a letter, somewhat pinguinized and sudorificated, which he respectfully placed in my hands. It was addressed to "Ensign Francis Gernon, on his march to Delhi," and ran thus:—

"My dear Sir,

"Our mutual friend Marpeet has apprized me of your approach; I write, therefore, to say that, as a friend of his, it will give me great pleasure if you can spare me a day or two, if not pressed to join. Your Colonel Bobbery I know well, and will undertake to mollify him if necessary. The sowar, the bearer of this, will conduct you at once to my encampment, and you can instruct your people to follow in the morning. I have a spare tent and cot at your service.

"Hoping soon to see you,

"I am yours truly,

"Augustus Sympkin."

"That will do," I inwardly ejaculated, as, after examining the seal and superscription, I conveyed the letter to my pocket. I instantly ordered my pony, and girding on my spit, wherewith to destroy any chance giants or dragons I might encounter on the way, I gave the signal, and the sowar and I were soon in a long canter for the judge's tents.

After a ride of about eight miles, the turn of the road exhibited to my view the judge's encampment, in which were tents and people enough for nearly a regiment of five hundred men.

Under a spreading banyan-tree were a couple of elephants, eating branches of trees for their tea, as we do water-cresses, and sundry camels bubbling[54] and roaring, and uprearing their lofty necks by the well-side, where, from the force of association, I almost looked for Jacob and the fair Rebecca, as represented in those Scripture prints which in infancy we love to dwell upon, and whence probably originates that exquisite charm, that, through our future life, is ever interwoven with Eastern scenes and customs.

Under a couple of tamarind trees, four or five beautiful horses were picketed; amongst them a milk-white Arab, with a flowing tail. This was the judge's favourite steed. "Pretty well all this," thought I, "for one man, and he, too, perhaps, the son of some small gentleman."

My arrival caused a considerable stir at the large tent. Two or three chuprassies, or silver-badge men, darted in to announce me; the hearer caught up the huge red umbrella or chattah, to be prepared for the great man's *exit*, and to guard his honoured cranium from the rays of the now declining sun. One or two others held aside the purdahs, or chicks, and Mr. Sympkin, a well-compacted, hearty, jolly, but withal gentlemanly man, of forty-five or fifty, or thereabouts, stood forth to view; he was followed by a fat squabby man, of the colour of yellow soap or saffron, who, though attired in something like the European garb, did not, nevertheless, in other respects, seem to belong to our quarter of the globe.

The judge shook me heartily by the hand, and was at once so smiling and cordial, that I began to fancy I must certainly have known him somewhere before, and that this could never be the first of our acquaintance. It was true downright goodness of heart, bursting through the cobwebs of ceremony, and going slap-bang to its purpose.

"Well, Mr. Gernon, I'm happy to see you here sound and safe. I hope my sowar piloted you well; how far off have you left your tents?"

Having replied to these queries, he again resumed.

"When did you hear last from our friend Marpeet? not since I did, I dare say. Come, give your pony to that man, and he'll take care of him for you."

I resigned my tatoo, who was led off.

The judge's servants smiled, and exchanged significant glances, as my little jaded rat, with accoutrements calculated for a horse of sixteen hands high, was marched away. I confess, for the first time, I felt perfectly ashamed of him.

"Come in," said the judge, "we will dine somewhat earlier on your account; but, in the meantime, as you must be fatigued, a glass of wine will refresh you. *Qui hye? sherry-shrob lou.* By-the-bye," said he, recollecting himself, as we turned to enter the tent, "I had nearly forgotten to introduce you to a fellow-traveller. Ensign Gernon, the Rev. Mr. Arratoon Bagram Sarkies; Mr. Sarkies, Mr. Gernon."

The little fat man smiled benignantly, as with a look betokening that my youth and deportment had made a pleasing impression upon him, he, in a manner half-Asiatic, tendered me his hand, as if he felt himself bound in duty to back the judge's cordiality.

I was sorely puzzled to divine who this amiable little personage could be, and to what portion of the church universal his reverence belonged. Mr. Sympkin seemed, I thought, to enjoy my gaping looks of astonishment, but took an opportunity of informing me, very shortly afterwards, that Mr. Sarkies was an Armenian missionary, proceeding to Guzerat with a camel load of tracts, in divers Eastern languages, for the purpose of converting the natives.

At the same time that he gave me this information, he proposed, if agreeable to me, that we should keep each other company for the few marches during which our route would lie together. To this proposal I joyfully assented, for though the good missionary was not exactly the sort of companion I should have selected, had a choice been given me, nevertheless, an associate of any kind who could speak my own language was, under present circumstances, a great acquisition.

Dinner soon made its appearance in the tent, which was fitted up with carpets, glass shades, attached by clasps to the poles, and, in short, everything that could render it comfortable and luxurious, and make us forget that we were in the wilds of Hindostan.

The viands, which in excellence could not be surpassed by anything procurable, of their several kinds, at the most fashionable hotel or club-house at the west end of the town, were served in burnished silver. The wines and ales, of the most delicious kinds, were cooled *à merveille*, and we were waited upon by fine, proud-looking domestics, in rich liveries, who seemed fully sensible of the lustre they borrowed from their master's importance; in short, I found myself all at once revelling in luxury, and was made to feel, though in the pleasantest possible way, the vastness of the gap which separates a griffin going to join from the judge of a zillah court.

Mr. Sarkies, too, though his occupation referred more immediately to the other world, seemed, like myself, by no means insensible to the comforts of this mundane state of existence, paying very marked attention to the mock-turtle, the roast saddle of mutton, maccaroni, and other "tiny kickshaws" that followed in abundance.

In spite, however, of this little trait of the "old man Adam," the missionary appeared a most kind-hearted and benevolent creature; there was a childlike simplicity about him, evincing a total absence of all guile, which at once inspired a feeling of affection and regard, adding a proof, were it wanting, of the power of truthfulness and virtue, in whatever form it may appear. It was obvious, at a glance, that the Padre's heart was overflowing with benevolence and love of his kind, and that no one harsh or unamiable feeling harboured there.

The judge, though evidently of a jovial and bantering turn, and not at all likely to turn missionary himself, seemed clearly to entertain a mingled feeling of respect and esteem for his single-hearted, but somewhat eccentric guest, who, I found, owed his introduction to him to a somewhat similar chance to that to which I was indebted for mine—a feeling that, in a great degree, restrained the inclination which, in a good-natured way, would every now and then peep out, to crack a joke at his expense.

After a very pleasant evening, I retired to a comfortable cot, which my host ordered to be prepared for me; and next morning Mr. Sympkin, who was engaged on some special business in the district, left us after breakfast to attend to his duties and proceed to his cuchery tent, around which were assembled horses and ponies gaily caparisoned, and a concourse of native zumeendars, with their attendants, hosts of villagers, witnesses, and the various native functionaries in the judge's suite, who in India bear the collective appellation of the "omlah."

At tiffin he joined us, as full of spirits as a boy just let out of school, rubbing his hands in a gleeful way, and asked me if I was disposed for a day's shooting, for if so, he should be happy to show me some excellent sport, the neighbourhood abounding in game. I need hardly say that I was not backward in accepting his offer.

The day following was a most propitious one for sport, the air clear and bracing, and the sun, as is the case in this latitude and season, possessed of little power. Breakfast over, the judge ordered his gun to be laid on the table, and at the same time asked me how I was provided in that way. I told him I was possessed of a gun, but I dared say he would not deem it a first-rate piece of ordnance.

"Allow me to look at it," said he; "I'll send a man to your tent for it;" and with this he despatched a servant to my routee.

The judge clicked my locks, turned the piece about, took a peep at the muzzles, which were in rather fine order for cutting wadding, in the absence of the instrument usually employed for that purpose, shook his head, and returned it to me.

"Come," said he, "I think we can set you up with a better piece than that for the day; though," added he, archly, "it appears to have seen a little service too;" and so saying, he put together a splendid Joe Manton, the locks of which spoke eloquently as he played them off, and he placed it in my hands. "Have you ever shot off an elephant?"

"Never, sir," said I, "though I have ridden upon one more than once."

"Well, then, you must make your first essay to-day; it is no easy matter; you must allow for the rise and fall of the animal, and take care you don't bag any of the black fellows alongside of you."

I laughingly assured him I would endeavour to avoid that mistake.

"Come along, then," said he; "I think we are now ready."

The judge had two noble shekarrie, or hunting elephants, trained to face the tiger, and for sport in general, which stood ready caparisoned, with their flaming red *jhools*, or housings, in front of the tent. In the howdah of one of them I took my seat, whilst the judge occupied that of the other.

Duly seated, guns secured, brandy and lunch stowed away in the *khowas* or dicky, the stately brutes rose at the command of the drivers from their recumbent postures; the orderly Cossack-looking horsemen mounted; the troop of beaters shouldered their long laties or poles, and we were instantly bearing away in full swing for the sporting-ground. This lay at the distance of three or four miles from our encampment, and consisted of a long shallow jheel or lake, skirted by tracks of rank grass, terminating in cultivation, villages, and groves of trees.

The elephant moves both legs at one side simultaneously, consequently the body rises and falls, and his motion is that of a ship at sea, and I felt before I tried it that I should make nothing of my first attempt to shoot off one.

We now formed line, the judge's elephant at one extremity, or pretty nearly so, and mine at the other, and advanced.

"Keep a good look-out, Gernon," cried my host; "we shall have something up immediately."

He had scarcely uttered the words, when up flustered a huge bird from under the elephants feet, towering perpendicularly overhead; his burnished throat, golden hues, and long sweeping tail, proclaimed him at once a wild peacock. I endeavoured to cover him, but all in vain, my gun's muzzles, like the poet's eye, were alternately directed "from earth to heaven," through the up-and-down motion of the elephant. However, I blazed away both barrels, but without touching a feather. On attaining a certain elevation, he struck off horizontally, wings expanded, cleaving the air like a meteor; but, passing to the rear of my companion, he, with the greatest *sang-froid*, rose, turned round in his howdah, and dropped him as dead as a stone, amidst cries of *lugga lugga* ("hit")! *mara* ("killed")! and *wau, wau* ("bravo")!

It is not considered very sportsmanlike to shoot the full-grown peacock in India; the chicks are, however, capital eating, and are often bagged. In this instance, the judge had evidently brought down the peacock for my gratification; this I inferred from his immediately sending it to me by one of his horsemen, who hoisted it up into the howdah at the end of his spear.

As we advanced farther into the long grass, evidences of the deserved character of the spot began to thicken around us; black partridges rose every moment, and the judge tumbled them over right and left, but not a feather could I touch.

Our line now made a sweep, with a view to emerging from the grass, and immediately a beautiful sight presented itself; it was a whole herd of antelopes, roused by our beaters from their repose, and which went off before us, bounding with the grace of Taglioni. Two sharp cracks, and *lugga, lugga!* proclaimed that Mr. Sympkin had laid an embargo on one or more of them. This proved to be the case, and a fine black buck antelope, with spiral horns and a white streak down his side, and a fawn about half-grown, were soon seen dangling from the broad quarters of the elephant.

On approaching the very verge of the long grass, a cry of *sewer, sewer!* was followed by a wild hog's bolting. I fired at him, and put a few shots in the hindquarters of one of the judge's horses, who threat reared and plunged, jerked off his rider's cap, and had nearly dismounted the rider himself, whom I could hear muttering a few curses at my awkwardness. The judge also discharged a brace of barrels at him, but he got off, and we saw him for a great distance scouring across the plain.

Having issued from the grass, the judge drove his elephant alongside of mine.

"Well, how do you get on? I fear you found what I said correct, eh? You haven't hit much?"

"Much! I haven't hit anything, sir, except one of your sowars' horses, I am sorry to say: it is most tantalizing! I doubt if ever I should succeed in striking an object from an elephant."

"Oh, yes, you would," said my host, smiling; "a little practice makes perfect; but come, we'll try on foot, on your account, after we have taken some refreshment; we will confine ourselves to the skirts of the grass and bajrakates,[55] where we can see about us."

Having refreshed ourselves with a glass of ale and some cold ham and fowl, we proceeded to try our luck on foot, and I now had the satisfaction of killing my fair share of game.

"You have never, I presume, seen the mode in which the hog-deer is taken in this part of the world?"

I answered in the negative.

"Well, then," resumed Mr. Sympkin, "if disposed to vary your sport, we have yet time before dinner. My people have the nets, and I'll show you how it is done; this will be something to put in the next letter you write home to astonish them all."

Having mounted horses, which were in attendance, we proceeded at a smart amble to a pretty extensive tract of reeds lying at the distance of a mile; into this tract, which terminated rather abruptly at some distance, a line of men was placed, with here and there a horseman.

At the extremity of the tract of reeds, but in the open plain, two ranks of men, with intervals of forty or fifty paces between each man, were placed, in prolongation of the sides of the patch of reeds. These two lines converged, and were terminated at the apex of the cone by a row of nets, formed of stout tarred cords, slightly propped up by stakes.

The first-mentioned line now advanced with cries and shouts, and as it approached the confines of the bank of reeds, two fine hog-deer broke cover. The men composing the two lines above mentioned, whose termini appuyed on the nets, now squatted down close to the earth, and as the animals approached, they raised their heads successively; this alarming them, and preventing every attempt to quit the street in which they were confined.

In this clever way they forced the deer, edging them on at full speed into the nets, into which they tumbled headlong, rolling over and over, completely manacled in the toils. I never saw anything so cleverly managed; the fellows did everything with wonderful coolness and tact, and seemed perfectly masters of their craft.

Laden with game, after a most interesting day's sport, we returned to Mr. Sympkin's tent, where we found our smiling little friend, the Padre, with his ever-ready hand extended, and prepared to receive and to congratulate us.

After passing another day with our princely host, we took our leave and commenced our journey. Our tents had been sent overnight, and after an abundant breakfast, Ensign Gernon, the Griffin, and the Rev. Arratoon

Bagram Sarkies, soon found themselves jogging along, discussing things in general in as cosy dialogues as those recorded to have taken place between the renowned knight of La Mancha and his valorous squire. The good missionary, I was flattered to observe, took a warm and affectionate interest in me, which he manifested by a strong effort to impress upon me the deep importance of his religious views.

One afternoon, as the missionary and I were sitting outside our tents, my attention was attracted towards a group of sepahis engaged under a banyan-tree playing the game of back-sword. As the mode in which this exercise is conducted may be new to the reader, I shall describe it.

The first who entered the lists or circle of spectators were two handsome and well-formed Rajpoots, who would have served for models of Apollo, and who in this exercise display uncommon agility and suppleness of limb; they were naked to the loins, round which, the hips, and upper part of the thighs, was tightly wound the *dotee*, or waistcloth, which sustains and strengthens the back—the "girding of the loins," so often mentioned in Scripture, &c. Each of the men held in his left hand a diminutive leathern shield or target, less than a foot in diameter, whilst his right grasped a long wooden sword, covered also with leather, and padded and guarded about the handle.

Having exchanged salutes, one of them, holding his weapon at the recover, and planting himself in a firm attitude, bent a stern gaze on his adversary, which seemed to say, "Now do your worst."

The other now commenced those ludicrously grotesque antics which, amongst the Hindoostanee athletæ, are always the prelude to a *set-to*. He first, with the air of a *maître de ballet*, took two or three sweeping steps to the right, eyed his opponent for an instant, and then kicking up his foot behind, so as almost to touch the small of his back, he twirled round on his heel, and with his chest expanded and thrown proudly out, made another grave and prancing movement in the other direction; he now approached nearer, struck the ground with his sword, dared his adversary to the onset, and again retreated with two or three long back-steps to the utmost verge of the circle formed by the spectators. Like cautious enemies, however, neither seemed to like to commit himself until sure of a palpable hit.

At last, however, he who had been standing on the defensive, following with his hawk's eye the other's strutting gyrations, perceiving an advantage, levelled a blow at his adversary with the rapidity of lightning, which was caught on the target and returned as quick as thought. A rapid and animated exchange of strokes now took place, accompanied by the most agile bounds and movements; most of these blows rattled on the targets; head and shoulders, nevertheless, came in for an ample share of ugly hits.

The fight at length ceased, and the breathless and exhausted combatants rested from their gladiatorial exhibition, amidst many *"wau, waus"* and *"shabases"* ("bravos")! resigning their weapons to two others anxious to display their prowess.

Subsequent experience of them has convinced me that a finer body of men is hardly to be found than the sepoys of Hindostan, particularly in their own country; for, taken out of it into a climate where the food, water, &c., disagree with them, they lose much of their spirit and stamina.

Our countryman, the British soldier, possesses an unrivalled energy and bull-dog courage, which certainly, when the tug of war—the hour of real danger—comes, must, as it ever has done, bear everything before it; but justice demands the admission that, in many other respects, the sepoy contrasts most favourably with him—temperate, respectful, patient, subordinate, and faithful—one of his highest principles being "fidelity to his salt," he adds to no ordinary degree of courage every other requisite of a good soldier.

A judicious policy towards these men, based on a thorough knowledge of their peculiar characteristics, may bind them to us for ages yet to come, by the double link of affection and interest, and enable us, as an Indian power, to laugh alike at foreign foes and domestic enemies; whilst a contrary course, and leaving their feelings and customs to be trifled with by inexperienced innovators, may, ere long, produce an opposite effect, and cause them, if once alienated, to shake us off "like dew-drops from the lion's mane."

Serais, or places of entertainment for wayfarers—well known to all readers of Eastern tales as caravan-serais—I frequently met with at towns on my march, and sometimes encamped within or near the walls. The serais, like the generality of buildings in India, are almost always in a ruinous state, it being nobody's business to keep them in a state of repair.

These structures, some of them the fruits of the piety and munificence of former times, are a great public benefit; their construction is generally similar, and consists of four walls of brick, stone, or mud, sometimes battlemented, forming a parallelogram, having gateways at two opposite sides, through which the high road usually passes. Small cells or apartments, with arched entrances, run round the interior, in any one of which the weary traveller may spread his mat, smoke his pipe, and enjoy his repose as long as he pleases.

Each serai has its establishment of attendants, *bunyahs* (shopkeepers), *bhistees* and *mehturs* (water-carriers and sweepers), who ply their several occupations, and administer to the traveller's wants.

What a motley and picturesque assemblage do these serais sometimes exhibit! In one part saunters a group of fair and athletic Afghans from Cabul or Peshawur, proceeding with horses, greyhounds, dried fruits, and the like, to sell in the south; their fearless bearing and deep voices proclaim them natives of a more invigorating climate. In another, a drove of bunjarra bullocks repose amongst piled sacks of grain, and quietly munch the cud, whilst their nomade drivers smoke or snore around.

Under the shade of yon drooping tamarind-tree, on a branch of which his sword and shield are suspended, a Mahomedan traveller has spread his carpet, and with his face towards Mecca (his *kibla*), his head hanging on his breast, and his arms reverentially folded, he offers up his evening's devotions; near him, on the little clay terrace, is to be seen the high-caste bramin, his body marked with ochres and pigments, and, surrounded by his religious apparatus of conch, flowers, and little brazen gods, he blows his shell, tinkles his bell, and goes through all his little mummeries, with the full conviction that he is fulfilling the high behests of Heaven.

Groups of camels, tatoos, or the gaunt steed of some roaming cavalier—some Dugald Dalgetty of the East, seeking employment for his jaws and sword, or rather for his sword and jaws, for such is the order—serve to fill up the little picture I have been describing, and which in my griffinish days, and since, I have contemplated with pleasure.

In a day or two we reached Allyghur, where my good friend the missionary and I were destined to part, his route lying to the southward towards Agra, mine in a more northerly direction to Delhi. Here I received a few lines from Marpeet, saying that he was looking for my arrival with great pleasure. "You had better push on as fast as you can, my dear Gernon, for your commandant, who is a crusty old fellow, and a very tight hand, has been heard to express his surprise at your not having long since made your appearance."

This letter rather damped the buoyancy of my spirits. The following morning I took leave of my good friend the missionary; his eyes filled with tears as he clasped my hands in both of his, and whilst pressing them to his bosom, pronounced a prayer and a blessing over me.

If it indeed be true, and we have no reason to doubt it, that the prayer of the righteous man "availeth much," that prayer was deeply to be valued. Short as was the time of our acquaintance, I felt as if I had known him all my life, and was, consequently, much affected at parting. Half-choking as he rode off, I waved him a sorrowful, and what has proved a last, adieu.

CHAPTER XXV

A few days more brought me to my last day's march on the banks of the Jumna, and the mosques and minarets of the ancient capital of India broke on my delighted view.

I had scarcely dismounted from my pony at my tent door, which commanded a distant glimpse of the blue and "soft stealing" Jumna, when I perceived three Europeans on horseback approaching at a hard gallop. As they drew near, I recognized in one of the three my friend and Mentor, Captain Marpeet. He was soon up, and warm and cordial was our greeting.

"Well, my boy, long looked-for comes at last; glad to have you amongst us, Gernon," said he, presenting me to his companions, two laughing, beardless ensigns; "let me introduce you to my two boys, Wildfire and Skylark; two intractable dogs," added he, laughing; "have given me twice the trouble to break in that you did."

Wildfire and Skylark shook hands with me, and in ten minutes we were as intimate as if we had known each other for six months.

"Come, mount again, Gernon," said Marpeet; "you are but a few miles from Delhi, and it is useless for you to remain here all day. Come along; I have breakfast all ready for you at my shop; your things, you know, can follow to-morrow; you don't, though, appear to be overburthened with baggage, Frank, eh? Dogs, too—hah—regular terrier bunnow.[56] Great a griff as ever, I see—hah! hah!"

We pursued our course towards cantonments, Marpeet riding in the midst of his *protégés* as proudly as an old gander on a green at the head of three orphan goslings.

We crossed the river Jumna in a broad, square, flat-bottomed ferry-boat; and after riding through some rich cultivation on its banks, joined a road skirting part of the ruins of ancient Delhi, which from that point exhibited a confused assemblage of ruins—fort, mosque, tomb, and palace—stretching far away behind us in the distance, towards what I afterwards learned was the mausoleum of Humaioon.

I was particularly struck, as I rode on, by one large desolate building, which Captain Marpeet informed me was the ancient palace of Firoze Shah. A lofty pillar of stone, something like one of the round towers of Ireland, rose out of the centre of it, whilst the whole mass of building exhibited a touching picture of loneliness and desolation; long grass and the silvery roots of the peepul grew around the battered arches and casements, out of one of which a couple of fat and saucy jackals were peeping, to reconnoitre us as we rode beneath.

We entered the modern city near the mansion of the Nawaub Ahmed Buksh Khan,[57] through an embattled gateway occupied by a guard of Nujjeebs, a sort of highly picturesque militia, attired in the Hindoostanee garb, and armed and equipped with crooked-stocked matchlocks, mull-shaped powder-horns, and other paraphernalia of a very primitive and extraordinary description. These men, who were upon guard, were smoking, sleeping, and doing their best to kill old Time, that enemy who, in the long run, is pretty sure to kill us.

We were soon in that part of the town called Derriow Gunge, where a portion of the troops were cantoned,[58] and drawing up before an odd sort of building, of a very mixed style of architecture, my friend dismounted, and announced my arrival at Marpeet Hall, "to which, my boy," said he, with a squeeze, "you are heartily welcome, and where you may stick up your spoon, with my two babes in the wood there, as long as you please; don't blow me up, that's all, or set the house on fire, and you may do what else you like. So now for breakfast," said the captain, cracking his half-hunter (whip), as a hint, I presumed, to the *bawurchee* (cook) to be expeditious, and shouting "*hazree looe juldee*" ("breakfast quickly"), he motioned us to enter, and followed.

The captain's residence had been in the olden time a mosque or tomb, I cannot exactly say which; but with the addition of a terrace and verandah, and a few extra doors punched through walls six feet thick, it made a capital abode, combining the coolness in summer and the warmth in winter, which result from this solid mode of construction, with the superadded European conveniences.

My friend's house was but a type of that widespreading process of adaptation which is now going on throughout the East, and its inhabitants, and which, as long as it does not effect a too radical alteration of that which "nature and their stars" intended for a people so circumstanced, is much to be rejoiced at.

Breakfast was laid out in a vaulted chamber, as massive as a bomb-proof, the walls and roofs in compartments, with here and there a niche for a cheragh, or lamp. There were we, a jovial quartetto, eating red herrings and rashers of the "unclean beast," where the moollah had pronounced his "*Allah-il-Allah*," or possibly over the respectable dust of some mighty Mogul Omrah.

After breakfast, Marpeet took me to the adjutant of my new regiment—a tall, strapping, good-looking man, of about eight-and-twenty, who told me I must report myself immediately to Colonel Bobbery, the commandant of my regiment, as also of the station.

"You have been some time on your way up, haven't you?" said the adjutant, significantly; "we began to be half afraid that the Thugs had made away with you, or that you had gone on a pilgrimage to Hurdwar."

"I fear I have exceeded my proper time very considerably," I replied; "but I must ascribe it to the hospitality of friends whom I met with on the way."

"Well, you must settle all that," replied the adjutant, "with the colonel, who has often been inquiring for you, and to whose quarters we will now, if you please, proceed."

I began to feel confoundedly nervous, and to apprehend that I was now about to taste a few of the incipient sweets of military subjection. The adjutant buckled on his accoutrements, I did the like with mine, which, at Marpeet's suggestion, I had brought with me, and off we walked to the colonel's.

"Rather a harsh man, the colonel, isn't he?" said I, as we went along, hoping to elicit a little consolation in the shape of a negative.

"Why," said the adjutant, "he is certainly a great stickler for duty, and fond of working the young hands—what we call a 'tight hand.'"

I was "floored."

The colonel's bungalow was on the ramparts of the city, overlooking the Jumna, and the expanse of country through which it flows. Orderlies and a posse of silver-stick men, &c., were about the door; we entered, and the adjutant presented me to Colonel Bobbery, one of the most extraordinary-looking little mortals I ever beheld.

The colonel's height was about five feet four—perhaps less—and his body as nearly approaching to an oblate spheriod as any body I ever beheld. This orbicular mass was supported on two little legs, adorned with very crumpled tights, and a pair of Hessian boots, then much worn, and *minus* the usual appendage of tassels. His neck, which was remarkably long, was girt round with a very tight black stock, on the top of which, as may be supposed, was his head, the most extraordinary part of this very original specimen of "the human form divine;" his front face (profile he had none, which could be properly so called, bating an irregular curve with a large bulbous projection about the middle) was fat and rubicund; his nose Bardolphian, flanked by two goggle eyes, in which the several expressions of intellect, fun, and sensuality were singularly blended. A small Welsh wig completed the oddest *tout ensemble* I had yet seen in India.

"Oh! you are the young gentleman we have been expecting for the last five months?—better late than never—glad to see you at last, sir."

I mentioned something about friends—hospitality—and detention.

"Oh, yes, yes! I know all about that; the old story; yes, yes! but you must be quicker in your future movements—eh, Marchwell?" said he, turning to the adjutant; "*verbum sap.*, you know, *verbum sap.*"

After a rather prolonged conversation, during which I informed him I had done duty with the Zuburdust Bullumteers, and gave him some account of his friend, Mr. Sympkin, which he was pleased to receive, I rose to take my leave.

"Who are you with?" asked the colonel.

I told him with Captain Marpeet.

"Oh! my friend Marpeet, eh? Well, tell him to dine with me to-morrow, and bring you with him. I dine at six, and wait for nobody. Marchwell, Mr. Gernon will attend all drills, parades, and guard-mountings; we mustn't let you forget what Colonel Lolsaug has taught you."

I soon became comfortably domiciled with my friend Marpeet, who introduced me to my brother-officers, and put me generally in the way of doing all that was requisite in the new scene in which I found myself.

The more I saw of Marpeet, the more the extreme kindness and benevolence of his disposition became apparent. The tenderness of his nature, indeed, was frequently too much for his assumed rough and devil-me-care manner (which he thought manly), and would sometimes, if he was taken by surprise, show itself with almost a woman's weakness.

Marpeet, as I have before stated, from invincible shyness, or awkwardness with females, or dislike of the restraint it imposed, had renounced the character of a "ladies' man," and was evidently doomed to die an old bachelor. Still, we must all have something to love and be kind to, be it wife, child, friend, cat, dog, or parrot.

Affection, if it has not something external on which to rest, turns to gall, embittering the life which, under a happier state of things, it would have sweetened. Marpeet's benevolence displayed itself in his kindness to youth: rearing griffins, till fully fledged, constituting his extreme delight.

Never shall I forget the great satisfaction which his good-humoured physiognomy would express when surrounded by a bevy of young hands, all warm in their feelings towards him, and on perfect terms of familiarity, but at the same time exhibiting that profound deference to his dictum on deep and important points, such as the age of a horse, the manner of performing a manœuvre, or the way to make mulled port, and the like, which had the most bland and soothing influence on his feelings.

Skylark, Wildfire, and myself, were his immediate body-guard; we chummed with him, and though he allowed us to contribute to the house keeping expenses, the lion's share, if the phrase is here allowable, fell to him.

He and I never quarrelled; but I could generally infer the state of his feelings from the name or appellation by which he addressed me. "Gernon" and "Frankibus" were the zero and summer-heat of the scale, between which were "my lad," "young gentleman," "you confounded griff," "youngster," and so forth; all of which, by the invariableness of the circumstances which elicited them, indicated the state of his mind at the moment: as "Come, my lad, this noise won't do;" and "Young gentleman, I have to make out my report, and beg you won't interrupt me." "Well, old boy, how do you get on? are you disposed for a game at picquet?" and so forth; but, "Come, Gernon, I don't like that," told me his back was "hogged."

One blot and inconsistency there was in Marpeet's character: he was addicted to flogging his servants for what we here should deem trifling offences. On these occasions he always, however, put the offender through the form of a trial, in which, to save trouble, he acted in the quintuple capacity of plaintiff, judge, jury, witness, and counsel for the prosecution. After a dispassionate summing up, the guilty party was wont to be handed over to the kulassee, or tent-pitcher, to have administered a dozen or two of strokes with the rattan.

Marpeet would justify all this severity very logically, but I shall not trouble the reader with his reasons; certain it is, for all this, he paid his servants regularly, was in other respects kind, and on the whole very popular with them.

Not far from the Chandney Choke, the principal thoroughfare in Delhi, near which I was now located, is the Duriba, or Lombard Street, where the principal shroffs or bankers reside; here also many venders of sweetmeats have their shops; one of these, in my day, was a jolly fellow, who, out of compliment to his great Western prototype, was called Mr. Birch, to which name he always answered when summoned to produce some of his choicest imitations of English "sugar-plumery."

I think I now see the good-natured fellow, hurrying out through his ranges of baskets with a few samples for inspection. Many a time and oft have Marpeet, I, and two or three jolly subs, after dinner, and under the agreeable stimulus of an extra dose of the rosy beverage, visited Mr. Birch, in the Duriba, all clinging to the pad of an elephant, whilst the lights blazed in the bazaars around, fakeers shouted, women chattered, and crowds of the faithful, moving hither and thither, gave a most Arabian-Nightish character to the scene.

These scenes of the past come over me sometimes, when my heart is sorrowfully disposed, with a sadly-painful distinctness; the laughing faces of those who participated in them are vividly before me, but they, "my co-mates and brothers in exile," where are they? Alas! with a sigh I must answer the question—gone! gone! Others occupy their places; they will soon disappear to make way for more; "and thus wags the world."

Oh, life, life! sad are thy retrospects to the best of us, and great are the trials thou hast for even him whose lot is cast in the pleasantest places; in thy sweetest pleasures lurk the germs of thy greatest sufferings, and the more we cultivate and refine our natures, the more acutely do we feel thy sorrows!

Happy ignorance! fortunate credulity! blessed insensibility! ye all seem to have your soothing opiates; whilst he who girds up his loins to seek the talisman of truth from amidst its innumerable counterfeits—compensation for the past and something like certainty for the future—finds the farther he moves the less he knows, and, amazed and confounded at the profound and mighty mystery which surrounds him, at length sits down and weeps. Well may we exclaim,

"The ways of Heaven are dark and intricate,

Puzzled in mazes and perplex'd in error,

The understanding traces them in vain."

Virtue, immortal plant, ye will blossom, 'tis true, in heaven, but must ye here be ever rooted in sorrow and watered with tears? Oh! for some mighty intellect, some second Newton, to call order out of chaos, light out of darkness; to hush the Babel of discordant tongues, and give to religious and moral truth that clear, convincing, and commanding aspect which shall for ever abash the various forms of perplexity and error. The awakening mind of the world demands something like unity and certainty, and will have them if they are to be had. But to proceed.

One of the finest buildings in Delhi is the Jumma Musjid, the principal mosque of the place. It has three nobly-proportioned domes; also two lofty and magnificent minarets, which I have often ascended, and enjoyed from their summits a noble prospect of the city and surrounding country.

From this height you look down on the flat roofs of the houses, and on a fine evening may observe the inhabitants seated on them, and enjoying their favourite, though somewhat childish amusements, of flying paper kites and pigeons.

The pigeons, of which the Hindoostanees are great fanciers, and possess a vast variety, are trained to join other flocks in their aerial excursions, and then, by separating from them with great velocity, to carry off some of those with which they were commingled; these they bring back in triumph to their bamboo stands, at the call or whistle of their owners.

At one extremity of the city lies the British residency, always the scene of hospitable doings, but particularly so during the period to which I am referring. The Resident at that time was a gentleman who, with first-rate talents and solid virtues, combined those social qualities which at once command what it is often difficult to unite—the love and respect of all.

Nothing could be more agreeable than the residency parties, and on what were called "public days," invitations were extended to every one in the shape of an European; old Mahratta officers, Portuguese, French, and half-caste merchants, and others without the pale of the regular service, and not constituting an ordinary portion of the society, would swell the _levée_ on such occasions.

Punning, as a practice or habit, is the greatest of bores, and deserves almost all that Johnson and others have said against it; I say "almost," for I do not go the full length of that alliterative curmudgeon, when he says, "He who would make a pun would pick a pocket." Had this been true, many an accomplished Barrington would the residency of Delhi have turned out at this period, with their distinguished chief at their head.

How this itch for punning got into the residency I don't know, but certain it is it did get there, and proved remarkably infectious. A good pun was a first-rate recommendation, indeed, at the residency table, to him who made it. "_Aquila non captat muscas;_" which means, "Great wits don't condescend to make puns." Granted, as a rule; but every rule has its exception, and the Resident of that day was himself, "an the truth be spoken, but little better than one of the wicked," delighting to take the lead occasionally in this conversation-burking system, where a man lies in wait for his neighbour's words, pounces on one that suits his purpose, murders, mangles, and distorts it without remorse.

Occasional puns, if really good, give a poignancy to conversation—a tonquin-beanish sort of odour, which in moderation is very agreeable, but the excess of them is odious. I remember a few of the residency puns which I think may rank with some of the fairest on record.

The Resident himself was once asked where he acquired his taste for punning; he replied, that "he thought he must have picked it up when travelling through the *Punjaub*," through which country he had accompanied a mission. A fisherman, to whom he had paid handsome wages to supply him with fish, absconded. "I always considered him a very *selfish* man," said the Resident.

One of the gates of the palace is called the "Delhi Gate," and in my time a subaltern's guard was always stationed there. A young sub, on one occasion, at the residency table, I believe, asked a friend to take his turn of duty there. "Excuse me," said his friend, "I can't be your *delegate* (Delhi Gate) to-day."

One observed that grain in one part of the city sold for so much. "Yes," replied another, "but that is not the *aggregate* (Agra Gate) price."

These samples may suffice.

I soon began to discover the truth of the adjutant's remark, that Colonel Bobbery was fond of "working the young hands;" for, what with morning and evening drills, parades, and attending guard-mountings, &c., I had little rest or enjoyment. The plain fact was, that I was bent on pleasure and hated duty, and the colonel, by giving me "excess on't," *i.e.* of the latter, seemed injudiciously determined to increase my dislike.

The more I think on my early Indian career, and that of other youths, the more satisfied I am that the sudden transition from school to a state of independence is most injurious to the individual and his future happiness; detrimental to the interest of the state and that of the people we govern; and, in short, that school-boys are not fit to be masters of themselves or to command others.

Nationally, we possess vast science and almost illimitable powers of destruction; and nationally, too, we are respected; but not so much so, I think, individually.

I have met with a great amount of calm, quiet, unprejudiced good sense, much reasonableness and rationality, amongst the natives of India of a certain rank, and, when such are disposed to give you their confidence, nothing is more frequently the subject of remark with them than the amount of power we confide to inexperienced hands—to mere *chokras* ("boys"), as they term them, and at nothing do they express more surprise.

The natives of India are deeply susceptible of kindness, and possessed, on the whole, of fine and amiable temperaments. If Europeans on all occasions would regard their feelings and prejudices, which they certainly ought to do, considering how strong are their own, I verily believe that they might bind them firmly to us, that is, as far as aliens ever can be bound, and erect our power on the noblest of foundations—their hearts. Still they must never be allowed to think that our kindness springs from fear or weakness.

I am aware that the conduct of the English towards the inhabitants of India is much more conciliating than it was; still, John Bull is ever a rough subject, and too prone to employ the *fortiter in re*, rather than the *suaviter in modo*. His pride prevents him from being amiable and conciliating, and however much he may be feared and respected, he has not the good luck to be loved, from the Straits of Calais to the Great Wall of China.

I doubt if, in the present day, such freaks would be tolerated in a commandant as those in which our old buffer was continually wont to indulge, in order to gratify his odd and despotic feelings. Besides abusing the men in the most violent manner (he had a regular ascending scale—a sort of gamut of *Galle, i.e.* Hindoostanee Billingsgate—on which few could go higher than himself) till they trembled with rage and indignation, he would, when out of humour, carry them straight across the country, formed, in line, in a steeple-chase sort of style, over banks and ditches, through standing corn and ploughed fields, for three or four miles, as the crow flies, in a broiling sun, and then, galloping home, would leave the next in command, or adjutant, to bring them back, covered with dust and drenched with perspiration.

Once or twice he marched the corps in close column into the river Jumna; when they reached the banks—there shelving—they commenced marking time, which consists in moving the feet without advancing; but the old colonel, to their astonishment, roared "Forward!" and on we all went, till near waist-deep, when the column fell into a state of disorder; the adjutant, on one occasion, tumbled off his horse in the *mêlée*, and got a thorough soaking. The commander thought, I suppose, that, as good soldiers, we ought to be able to stand "water" as well as "fire."

After I had been about a month at the station, I was put in orders as the subaltern for duty on the Delhi gate of the palace, a vast structure, occupied by the king and his relations and dependants, which duty continued for a week. Having marched my company down to the gate, I found the sub I was to relieve, with his guard drawn up, all as stiff as ramrods, to receive me. After exchanging salutes, and receiving his instructions to take proper care of the "Asylum of the Universe,"[59] &c., he gave the word "quick march" to his men, sent them off under the subadar, or native captain, and then proceeded to introduce me to the quarters in which I was to pass my period of guard.

In passing the first archway, I found myself in an enclosure, formed by lofty walls, round the bottom of which ran a line of arcades or cloisters; at the other end of this enclosure was another noble arch, surmounted by a vast and lofty pile of buildings, with windows and galleries; these were the quarters of Major M., who filled the post of killadar, or commander of the fort and palace guards, a kind-hearted, hospitable, and brawny Caledonian, who, amongst other harmless eccentricities, entertained the most profound veneration for the "*Rowyal Hoose o' Teemoor*," as he was wont to call it.

My own quarters, to which the sub introduced me, consisted of a small turret, in an angle of the ramparts, covered with thatch, and having something the appearance of a bee-hive; it contained a table and a few chairs, considerably the worse for wear, and when my cot was placed in it, there was little room left for myself. Here, then, for seven long days, I read, shot paroquets with my pellet-bow on the ramparts, cursed the heat and the flies, and conjugated the verb *s'ennuyer* to perfection, through all its moods and tenses.

One interesting break occurred, and that was his Majesty Ackbar Shah's going out one day, in grand procession, to visit the tombs of his ancestors at the Kootub Minar.

On this occasion my guard was drawn up within the enclosure, to salute him as he passed, whilst another company of troops, and two six-pounders, were stationed without the second archway, on the plain between it and the city, for a similar purpose.

Little did I think, in my juvenile days, when I looked on the stern visage of the Great Mogul on the card covers, that I should ever have the honour of paying my respects to that fierce Saracen *in propriâ personâ*; but so it was. I had heard much of Eastern magnificence, but had never seen before, nor have I indeed since, anything that so completely realized my vague ideas of barbaric pomp, as this procession of the King of Delhi.

Though there was much in it that was imperfect, and which told of reduced means and insufficient resources, it was still a most striking pageant, and, as it issued tumultuously from those noble and resounding gateways, amidst the clang of wild instruments and echoing voices, I confess I was delighted and astonished, and was able to picture most forcibly what these things must have been when the Moguls were in the zenith of their power.

We had waited for some time, expecting his majesty to make his appearance; when at length confused sounds and a distant hubbub announced that he was on the move; presently, ever and anon, a cavalier, some omrah of the old noblesse, or inferior horseman, would come pricking forth from under the arch; then another and another; then steeds curveting and caracoling, and covered with rich housings and silver ornaments. After this came his majesty's regiment of Nujjeebs, hurrying forth, a wild-looking body of bearded Mahomedan soldiery, armed with matchlocks and shields, and attired in dark *chupkuns*, or vests, and red turbans; next came his camel corps, each man with a little pattereroe, or swivel gun, on the bow of his camel's saddle, ramming down and blazing away at a furious rate.

By the way, I was told that, on one of these occasions, a fellow, in his hurry, shot off his camel's head.

After these followed a confused assemblage of chiefs on horseback, a knightly train; their steeds, half-painted vermilion or saffron colour, adorned with silver chains, and housings almost touching the ground, some of them composed of the silvery chowries, or Tartarian cows' tails; mingled with these were litters, with dome-like canopies and gilded culesses, containing ladies of the harem, with numerous attendants.

The uproar now increased, and a numerous body of men followed on foot, bearing crescents, green standards, golden fish on poles, and other insignia of the royal dignity; all loudly shouting forth the now empty titles of the fallen monarch. These, his immediate avant-couriers, were followed by the king himself, seated on an enormous elephant, covered with a superb *jhool*, or housings, of crimson velvet; the huge tusks of the monster being adorned with silver rings, whilst his head was painted with crimson and yellow ochres, in bars and flourishes, like the face of a North American savage, when arrayed for battle.

The king, Ackbar Shah the Second, an aged and venerable man, adorned with jewels and aigrettes in his turban, sat immovable in a silver howdah, looking straight before him, neither to the right nor left, up nor down (for it is considered beneath the dignity of the "Son of the Sun and Moon" to notice sublunary matters), whilst his youngest and favourite son Mirza Selim, a youthful and handsome man, sat behind him, slowly waving over his head a chowry, or fan, formed of the tail of the peacock. His majesty's elephant was followed by many others, more or less superbly decorated, bearing his relations, and the various officers and dependants of the court.

The assemblage of these vast animals, the litters, horsemen, and multitudinous array, combined with the Moresque buildings around, so admirably in keeping, altogether constituted to my mind a perfect scene of romance, which it took me two sides of foolscap properly to describe for the gratification of my friends at home.

I pictured to myself, I remember, as I wrote that account, the delight it would cause when read by my mother to the fireside circle in the little green parlour, whilst old Thomas, our lame footman, lingered, with the kettle in his hand, to catch some of Master Frank's account of the "Great Mowgul in the Heast Hingies."

Well, time wore on; some months had elapsed, during which nothing very particular had occurred, excepting that I received a letter from the charming widow, announcing that my kind friend, the old general, had at last gone to his long home.

It was an admirable epistle, written with all that proper feeling which such an event would naturally call forth in the breast of an accomplished woman and affectionate daughter. It breathed a spirit of resignation, and contained many beautiful, though not very new, reflections touching the frail tenure of existence, and of that inevitable termination of it which is alike the lot of us all.

The general, she said, had not forgotten me in his parting moments, but sent me his blessing, with a hope that I would not forget his advice, and would strive to emulate my uncle, who seemed, indeed, to have been his model of a cavalier.

In conclusion, she stated that she was about to join some relations who were coming to the Upper Provinces, and hoped she might have an opportunity shortly of renewing my acquaintance, and of assuring me in person that she was "mine very truly."

Yes, mine very truly! I saw I was hooked for the widow, and began to put more faith than ever in the Chinese doctrine of invisible attraction. "Let me see," said I; "the widow is two-and-twenty, I eighteen; when I'm two-and-twenty, she will be six-and-twenty. Oh, 'twill do admirably! what matters a little disparity?" So I whistled *Lillabulero*, after the manner of my uncle Toby, concluding *affettuoso*—

And around the dear ruin each wish of my heart

Shall entwine itself verdantly still.

"Captain Marpeet," said I, one day, after breakfast, "I shall to-morrow have been just one year in the country, and according to the *Lex Griffiniensis* I shall be no longer a greenhorn."

"Have you, my boy? Why bless my life! so you have, I declare; then by the piper that played before Moses, I'll have a few friends to meet you, and we'll make a day of it. You've never seen a nautch, I believe; we'll have Chumbailie and Goolabie[60] and all that set—a devilled turkey, and a glorious blow-out."

Marpeet was as good as his word; he posted off *chits* (invitations) to a dozen choice spirits; ordered a fat sheep to be killed, which had been six months on gram; bought the best ham to be had in cantonments, and a turkey for its *vis-a-vis*; ordered half a chest of claret, and beer to be *tundakurred* (cooled); sent his bearer to bespeak a tip-top set of nautch-girls, and then, slapping me on the back, exclaimed,

"Now, Frank, my boy, we are all right and tight, and your griffinage shall close with a flourish of trumpets."

On the following day the guests assembled at dinner, and the old mosque resounded with the echoes of our revelry and mirth. Marpeet certainly boxed the kansamah[61] for omitting the pigeon-pie, and ordered the cook half a dozen rattans for underboiling the ham; but, on the whole, he was in splendid key.

Evening at length approached; more young officers came in; the wall shades were lighted, and chairs arranged in a semicircle; teapoys, port, mint, claret, were all *moojood* (present), when the curtain was rolled up, and a bevy of as pretty gazelle-eyed damsels, arrayed in robes of sky-blue, crimson and gold, bedecked with rings and chains, and redolent of oil of Chumbailie, as I ever saw, entered the apartment in stately guise, followed by sundry old duennas, and four or five rakish looking musicians, with embroidered skull-caps, long raven ringlets, and slender ungirdled waists, bearing some of the funniest looking musical instruments ever seen since the days of Orpheus.

After some excruciating tuning, thrumming, and twisting of keys, a couple of young sirens, fair Mogulanees, whose languishing eyes shone brightly through their antimonial borders, broke forth into a song, advancing with hands extended and slow movements of the feet, their anklet-bells jingling harmoniously the "*goongroo ka awaz*," by the way, a music on which the Indian poet loves to expatiate. As the song and the movement quickened, the heads of the fiddlers worked ecstatically, whilst they sawed away at their outlandish fiddles with surprising energy and vigour.

Marpeet was in raptures; he considered nautches superior to all the operas in the universe, and thought he could hardly ever have enough of them.

The "*Cahar ca nautch,*" or "dance of the bearer," a favourite in India, was now called for loudly, and the prettiest girl of the set, retiring a little on one side, and twisting a turban saucily round her head, after the fashion of that order of menial, and otherwise arranging her attire into a somewhat similar resemblance to the other parts of their dress, darted forward arms a-kimbo, *à la Vestris,* and danced an animated lilt, something of the nature of a Highland fling.

Rapturous were the "bravos" of the officers, and the "*wau! waus!*" of the natives. The girl's excitement increased with the applause; the fiddlers worked like heroes, whilst the *doog-doogie* man, or drummer, pegged away at his long drum, till, flushed and exhausted, she made her salaam, and retired within the circle amidst renewed plaudits.

This was followed by "*Mootrib-i koosh,*" "songster sweet," and other Persian and Hindostanee airs, not forgetting "*Sarrai teen pisa muchlee,*" *i.e.,* "three ha'porth of fish," by way of *finale,* till at length the dancing grew languid; the hookas bubbled faintly, and Marpeet, starting up, dismissed the dancers, and we all adjourned to do honour to the devilled turkey's legs and a saucepan of mulled port, of Marpeet's own brewing.

Enlivened by the change, the song and the toast went round, and Marpeet, who was half-seas-over, sung us,

> "Dear Tom, this brown jug, which now foams with mild ale,"

in his very best style; and, by particular request I warbled "The Woodpecker."

"Franco, your health and song, my boy," said my friend, rising on his legs; "and now, gentlemen (*hiccup*), I am about to propose the toast of the evening, and one which, I am sure, you'll all drink with as much pleasure (*hiccup*) as I have in giving it: gentlemen, off with your heel-taps; are you all charged? Wildfire, pass the bottle. Gentlemen, I am now about to propose the health of a young friend of mine, whom I consider in some respects a chick of my own rearing. We came out together, and I take credit for having made him the good fellow you all find him (*hiccup*). This is the last day of his griffinage, and to-morrow he is one of us old hands. Gentlemen, I give you, standing, with three times three, long life, health, and success to our friend, Frank Gernon, the griffin. Hip! hip! hurrah!"

1. The arms of the City of London supported by Griffins or Wyverns.

2. Milton speaks of the Gryphon as a "guardian of gold," but that can clearly have no connection with *our* animal, whose propensities in respect to the precious metals are quite of an opposite tendency.

3. Cant term for residents in the Bengal Presidency—"Qui Hye," "who wait," being constantly addressed to servants.

4. *Mulls*—cant term for Madrassees.

5. *Crannies*—Portuguese and country-born clerks in offices, and fillers of subordinate Government employments, &c.

6. *Ticca*, i.e. hired.

7. Honest Sancho Panza divides the world into two grand classes— the have-somethings and the have-nothings. Blacky, by an equally comprehensive arrangement, includes all mankind under the heads of Topee Wala and Puckree Bund, or *hat-men* and *turban-wearers*.

8. 6 bottles real Cognac, 1 pine cheese, 2 pot raspberry jam, 2 bag of shot.

9. Village-curs, appertaining to no one in particular.

10. A "made-up" terrier.

11. Liverpool, long considered a distinct empire from Great Britain by the natives, and as forming no part of Europe.

12. Sick *maun*, or sick man, one of the few phrases borrowed from the English, and applied to brutes, furniture, or anything damaged or out of order.

13. In this country of high-pressure morality, it may be right to explain that the same reluctance to mingle under one roof the children *legitimè procreati* with those less legally begotten does not exist in India, where unhappily, humanity and laxity flourish together, the reverse of what it should be, of course.

14. Broad-brimmed hat of pith or solah.

15. *Boosa*, chopped straw.

16. *Hilsa*, a fish slightly resembling the salmon.

17. *Soondur Bun*: i.e. the beautiful wood.

18. *Jhoul*, housings; *howdah*, seat.

19. The attack on the factory is an actual occurrence, and took place as described in all the essential particulars. The relator has been on the spot, and had the details from the principal actor in the scene.

20. *i.e.*, understand.

21. *Jow-jehanum*; a peremptory injunction to proceed to a place which it is not usual to mention to "ears polite."

22. Tales of a Parrot.

23. "Well."

24. "Very well."

25. A strong phrase for driving a lady out in a buggy; in India, looked upon as symptomatic of an approaching matrimonial crisis.

26. Oh! nurse, bring the Paun box.

27. Europeans—thus pronounced by English soldiers.

28. Seapie, sepoy.

29. In the native regiments there are two grenadier companies, in European corps only one.

30. Chick or sequin, four rupees.

31. Since this was written, medals have been ordered, I believe, for the officers who served in Affghanistan. Is it too late to give them to those who fought and suffered in Java, Arracan, Nepaul, &c.?

32. True—very well.

33. Plantations.

34. European.

35. The red-legged partridge of Kamaon is also called a chikor, but this is not the bird here meant.

36. Nagara: royal kettle-drum.

37. The Sultan Sujah, brother of Aurungzebe, fled to Arracan, where he was murdered.

38. Meerun, the assassin of Surajah Dowlah, killed by lightning.

39. Peepul (*Ficus religiosa*) entwines its silvery and tortuous roots around old buildings, and hastens their destruction.

40. A fact.

41. The hunza, or braminy duck. They fly in couples, have a plaintive cry, and are considered emblems of constancy by the natives. They are the Mujnoon and Leila of the stream. The hunza is the ensign of the Burman, as was the eagle of the Roman empire.

42. *Mûllah*—boatman.

43. Sub-lieuts. of artillery, a few years ago, were called Lieut. Fireworkers: the rank is now abolished.

44. *Rooee muchee*, a huge fish of the carp kind, one of the best in India.

45. Brook.

46. This was about two years before the worthy griffin, whose autobiography is here given to the public, died, as stated in the preface, of an old-standing liver complaint.

47. In both the descriptions and illustrations of these volumes, the military costume of Europeans and natives will be found slightly to differ from those at present worn. For example, Hessians now rank with Hauberks and other antiques; the shako has superseded the chimney-pot cap, and so on.

48. Scimitars.

49. Since this period, a church has been erected at Chunar, a square tower, with pinnacles; one of the most truly English structures I have seen abroad.

50. *Sword*, whence probably *scimitar*.

51. Gourd, vegetable marrow.

52. The English reader can have little idea of the viciousness of Indian horses and tatoos; they fight like tigers, particularly the last-named.

53. This is a faithful description of a real occurrence, though it did not take place at the supposed time.

54. When the camel blows out his water-bag from his mouth, the act is attended with a loud gurgling, or rather bubbling sound.

55. Fields of Bajra—*Holcus spicatus.*

56. *Terrier bunnow*—a village pariar dog, docked and cropped to make him pass for a terrier.

57. Whose son acquired since a dreadful celebrity as the murderer of Mr. Fraser.

58. Since this period, cantonments have been erected outside the walls of the city.

59. *"Jehan Punnah,"* one of the titles of the Mogul.

60. Jasmin and Rose-water; female names.

61. Butler.